GW01417341

Late Bronze Age Tell Atchana (Alalakh)

Stratigraphy, chronology, history

Amir Sumaka'i Fink

BAR International Series 2120
2010

Published by

Archaeopress
Publishers of British Archaeological Reports
Gordon House
276 Banbury Road
Oxford OX2 7ED
England
bar@archaeopress.com
www.archaeopress.com

BAR S2120

Late Bronze Age Tell Atchana (Alalakh): Stratigraphy, chronology, history

© Archaeopress and A S Fink 2010

ISBN 978 1 4073 0661 2

Printed in England by Blenheim Colour Ltd

All BAR titles are available from:

Hadrian Books Ltd
122 Banbury Road
Oxford
OX2 7BP
England
bar@hadrianbooks.co.uk

The current BAR catalogue with details of all titles in print, prices and means of payment is available
free from Hadrian Books or may be downloaded from www.archaeopress.com

To Joe and Jeanette Neubauer

Synopsis

The following work is a re-structuring of my doctoral thesis, which re-visits the Late Bronze Age stratigraphy, chronology and history of Tell Atchana as recorded by Sir Leonard Woolley in the 1930s and 1940s. I offer both a detailed analysis of the material culture of Late Bronze Age Alalakh and a political history of the region following the destruction of the Level IV^W palace.

My first step in this study was to understand the way in which the plans of Tell Atchana that Woolley published should be interpreted, and the implications thereof. The next was to establish the correct location, absolute and relative, of the Level I^W temples. Then followed an analysis of the stratigraphy of the Levels IV–0^W temples, which brought me to advance two major proposals:

1) that the Level IVA^F temple had an annexe and
2) that the walls and finds attributed to the annexe to the Level IB^W temple should be associated with the Paluwa Shrine, which postdates the Level I^W temples.

Based on the finds in each of the later temples, I corrected their dates and reassigned them to Tell Atchana levels, different from those to which they were originally assigned. This resulted, among other things, in a detailed study of the find-spot of the statue of Idrimi, now newly attributed to Level IVB^F, the first half of the fourteenth century B.C.E., probably not more than a few decades after the death of Idrimi, king of Alalakh.

The same stratigraphic analysis scheme that permitted me to rearrange and redate the temples was then projected on all the features and structures of Levels V–0^W, as summarized in Summary Tables 1 and 2 and in the plans of Levels VA–IB^F. Levels VA–IB^F include all the buildings and structures of Levels V–0^W, but most of them are dated differently. According to my new layout, many of these buildings are contemporaneous with different structures than they were before.

In short, my approach to Late Bronze Age Alalakh is significantly different than that of previous literature, and significantly revises Woolley's 1955 Final Report and Yener's 2005 summary. Detailed new phase plans for Levels VA-IB^F accompany this study. I conclude by presenting consequential material culture data that leads to a proposed absolute chronology of the relevant strata at Alalakh, accompanied by a discussion of the history of Alalakh in the Late Bronze Age.

Although this study is by no means conclusive, I hope that it paves the way for future investigation, and that its implications will be considered not only for Alalakh and Mukiš, but for the Late Bronze Age Levant as a whole.

Acknowledgements

This study is a rearrangement of my dissertation, which was written at Tel Aviv University under the supervision of Professors Israel Finkelstein and Nadav Na'aman. I thank them for their advice, thoughtfulness, encouragement and patience. It is owing to my dear friend, Professor Benjamin Sass, that I chose to write on Alalakh, and that I was able to complete my mission. He nourished this project from *alpha* to *omega*. The renewal of the excavation project at Tell Atchana by the Oriental Institute of the University of Chicago with the generous support of the Neubauer family was the trigger for this study. My senior role in the Tell Atchana project provided me with an intimate knowledge of the site, which is hopefully reflected in this book. I am grateful to the Director of the Oriental Institute of the University of Chicago, Professor Gil Stein, who supported the project in its better and harder times. Professor David Schloen of the University of Chicago, who was my advisor during my studies at the University of Chicago, is also my senior partner, both during our work at Tell Atchana and in our current project at Zincirli. Many of the ideas and thoughts articulated in my work were born out of, and developed during our endless discussions of the nature of the site, the stratigraphy, and the finds. I thank David for his counsel as well as his tolerance during this long process. I would also like to thank the following colleagues and team members for sharing their ideas and knowledge with me: Dr. Stephen Batiuk, Prof. Aaron Burke, Dr. Alexis Boutin, Prof. Jesse Casana, Dr. Dominique Collon, Prof. Asa Eger, Prof. Theo van den Hout, Prof. Jacob Lauinger, Susie Helft, Leann Pace, Virginia Rimmer Herrmann, Eudora Struble and Bike Yazıcıoğlu. I consulted with many of my colleagues, teachers and friends, and sought out their advice. Among them are Prof. Dorit Aharonov, Eran Arie, Dr. Celia Bergoffen, Dr. Yoram Cohen, Prof. Eva von Dassow, Shay Gordin, Dr. Robert Hawley, Prof. Gunnar Lehmann, Prof. Jared Miller, Dr. Marina Pucci, Dr. Carole Roche, Prof. Jeremy Rutter, Prof. Itamar Singer, Dr. Sebastiano Soldi and Boaz Stavi.

An early summary of some aspects of this research was presented at the *51ᵉ Rencontre Assyriologique Internationale*, which took place in July 2005 at the Oriental Institute of the University of Chicago, as well as at the 2005 annual meeting of *ASOR*, which took place in Philadelphia. An early version of parts of this work is already published (Fink 2008b)—I would like to thank Inbal Samet for her editorial work on this publication, and for her helpful remarks and suggestions. The editing and formatting of the current work were undertaken by Kathryn R. and E. Tucker Morgan, and I thank them both sincerely for their diligence and undue joy in its completion.

I would like to express my gratitude to the University College of London, Special Collections, for allowing me to study the archive of Sir Leonard Woolley and to the British Museum for facilitating the study of some objects and written records. I am especially thankful to Drs. Jonathan Tubb and Alexandra Fletcher, who went out of their way to help me. I gratefully acknowledge the financial support from the Dan David Scholarships, the *Bimat Hahoker* scholarship of Tel Aviv University and The State of Israel, The Ministry of Immigrant Absorption, which enabled me to complete this study. I achieved the greatest progress in research project during my six-month tenure at the Institute for Advanced Studies at the Hebrew University of Jerusalem (2008–2009), where I was a junior fellow in the group titled "Interconnections and Regional Narratives in Mediterranean Archaeology (ca. 1700–700 B.C.E.)." I am thankful to the IAS and indebted to the group of organizers, Profs. Aren Maeir, Assaf Yasur-Landau and Amihai Mazar, my mentor, who taught me how to dig.

It is it due to the generous support of Yad Hanadiv, who selected me as a Rothschild fellow for the academic year 2009/2010, that I was able to turn this study into a published manuscript during a year of post-doctoral research in France. These post-doctorial studies are also supported by a grant of the French Embassy in Israel in collaboration with the *Centre National des Oeuvres Universitaires et Scolaires* of France. I am thankful to my hosts at Lyon's *Archéorient*, in particulare to its director Prof. Pierre Lombard; to the *Orient et Méditerranée* CNRS team of Ivry-sur-Seine, directed by Prof. Christian Robin; and to Prof. André Lemaire.

My work was closely monitored by my late grandmother Irena Fischer (Anyu) and my parents Chava and Shalom Fink, as well as my aunt Annie Fischer, who were relieved once it was approved. My life partner and husband Yossi Maurey went on this odyssey to Ithaca with me. "Ithaca has given us this beautiful voyage. Without her we would have never set out on the road. Wise as we have become, with so much experience, we must already have understood what Ithacas mean."

Last but not least - Joe and Jeanette Neubauer have shown me unlimited generosity, and taught me the meaning of unconditional love. I dedicate this work to them.

Table of Contents

The New Stratigraphy of Tell Atchana	1
Introduction	14
Woolley's Method and Mapping Reexamined	16
2.1 The Discovery of the Idrimi Statue	16
2.2 Grid line labels and the mislabeling of squares	17
2.3 Grid deviations and magnetic declination	21
2.4 The find-spot of the statue of Idrimi	27
The LBA Temples of Alalakh (Levels IV–0^W): Archaeology and History	31
3.1 The relative and absolute locations of the Level I^W temples	31
3.2 The annexes to the Levels IV–0^W temples and the Paluwa Shrine	40
3.3 On the relative and absolute dating of the LBA temples at Alalakh (Levels IV-0^W)	49
3.4 The find-spot of the statue of Idrimi, uncovered	56
Alalakh Under the Mittani Empire (Levels VI^W–IVB^F): Stratigraphy, Material Culture and History	61
4.1 Introduction	61
4.2 Level VI^W	62
4.3 Levels V–IV^W (–1420/1400)	63
4.4 The Dating of Levels VI–IV^W	90
4.5 Level IVB^F (1420/1400–1353/1341)	93
Levels III–IB^F: Hittite Alalakh	120
5.1 Level III^F (1353/1341–1320/1313)	120
5.2 Level IIAB^F (1320/1313–1240)	138
5.3 Level IAB^F (1240–1190/1185)	141
Conclusions: Alalakh in the 15th–12th Centuries	143
References	145

Table of Illustrations

Tables and Adapted Tables

Summary Table 1	2
Summary Table 2	3
Table 1. The location of grid line labels in relation to squares bearing the same name	20
Table 2. Woolley's evolving records concerning the find-spot of the statue of Idrimi	28
Table 3. The sequence of excavations at Tell Atchana 1936–1949	30
Table 4. The square location of identical walls in different plans	32
Table 5. Level and date assignments of the later temples	50
Table 6. Opinions on the date of Level VI^W	64
Table 7. Opinions on the date of Level V^W	66
Table 8. Opinions on the date of Level IV^W	68
Table 9. Opinions on the dates of Levels III–0^W	93
Table 10. Atchana/Nuzi and Nuzi wares at Tell Atchana (after Herrmann 2005)	102
Casana Table 1. MBA–LBA Amuq sites according to different Amuq surveys (after Casana 2009: 15)	131
Haines Table 1. Amuq phases P–V (after Haines 1971: 1)	124
Haines Table 2. Amuq phases A–O (after Haines 1971: 2)	124
Meyer Table 2. The correlation between Amuq phases and trenches at Çatal Höyük (after Meyer 2008: 12)	126
Meyer Table 3. The correlation between Amuq phases and trenches at Tell el-Judaidah (after Meyer 2008: 14)	127
Pruss Table 1. Amuq phases and Alalakh: a comparative chart (after Pruss 2002: 162)	111
Swift Table 1. Excavated areas of Amuq phases K–O by site (after Swift 1958: 10)	112
Swift Table 2. The field campaigns relevant to Amuq phases K–O (after Swift 1958: 11)	122
Swift Table 5. Amuq phases K–O and Alalakh: a comparative chart (after Swift 1958: 58)	111
Swift Table 11. Chronology of Amuq phases N and O (after Swift 1958: 198)	122

Plans

Level VA^F	5
Level VB^F	6
Level IVA^F	7
Level IVB^F	8
Level III^F	9
Level IIA^F	10
Level IIB^F	11

Level IA[F]   12

Level IB[F]   13

Plan 1. Detailed plan of the Level V–II[W] temples (after Woolley 1955: 74, Fig. 31)   19

Plan 2. Level II[W] house 39/C (after Woolley 1948: 6, Fig. 2)   22

Plan 3. Detailed plan of the Level I[W] temples (after Woolley 1955: 83, Fig. 34a)   23

Plan 4. Level X[W] of Woolley's Level VII[W] palace sounding (after Woolley 1955: 27, Fig. 14)   23

Plan 5. Reconstructed plan of Level IA[W] temple (after Woolley 1955: 83, Fig. 34b)   24

Plan 6. Reconstructed plan of the Level IB[W] temple (after Woolley 1955: 83, Fig. 34c)   24

Plan 7. Level I[W] house 38/B (after Woolley 1955: 197, Fig. 69)   27

Plan 8. The Levels V–I[W] temples: superposition   33

Plan 9. The doorways of Levels II–I[W] temples. Detail of Plan 8   34

Plan 10. Level II[W] house 39/C (after Woolley 1955: 190, Fig. 66)   35

Plan 11. Plan of Level I[W] (after Yener 2005: 152, Fig. 4.33)   35

Plan 12. Section A–A of the Level VII[W] palace sounding (after Woolley 1955: 11, Fig. 2)   36

Plan 13. Levels V–I[W] buildings north and east of the temples (after Woolley 1955: 138, Fig. 53)   36

Plan 14. Reconstructed plan of the Level II[W] temple (after Woolley 1955: 79, Fig. 33)   37

Plan 15. Superposition of the Level IB[W] temple on the Level II[W] temple   37

Plan 16. Superposition of the Level IB[W] temple on the Level III[W] temple   38

Plan 17. Reconstructed plan of the Level III[W] temple (after Woolley 1955: 76, Fig. 32)   38

Plan 18. Superposition of the Level IB[W] temple on the Level IV[W] temple   39

Plan 19. Reconstructed plan of the Level IV[W] temple (after Woolley 1955: 72, Fig. 30)   39

Plan 20. Superposition of the Level IB[W] temple on the Level V[W] temple   41

Plan 21. Reconstructed plan of the Level V[W] temple (after Woolley 1955: 67, Fig. 29a)   41

Plan 22. A proposed plan for Level I[W] (revisiting Yener 2005: 152, Fig. 4.33)   42

Plan 23. Section A–A of the temple sounding (after Woolley 1955: 67, Fig. 29b)   42

Plan 24. Level VI[W] residences (after Woolley 1955: 173, Fig. 61)   43

Plan 25. The annexe to the Level IV[W] temple   43

Plan 26. The plan of Level IV[W] (after Yener 2005: 149, Fig. 4.30)   45

Plan 27. Sherd density map of fields surrounding Tell Atchana (after Casana & Gansell 2005: 165, Fig. 6.4)   63

Plan 28. Levels VI–V[W] buildings found in the sounding in the Level IV[W] palace
(after Woolley 1955: 107, Fig. 43a–b)   70

Plan 29. Plan of Level VI[W] (after Yener 2005: 139, Fig. 4.28)   71

Plan 30. Levels VII–I[W] fortresses and fortifications in the northeast (after Woolley 1955: 154, Fig. 58)   72

Plan 31. Level IV[W] fortress/Level VB[F] palace (after Woolley 1955: 152, Fig. 57)   73

Plan 32. Level IV[W] Niqmepa and Ilimilimma palace   74

Plan 33. Level IV[W]/IVA[F] palace (after Woolley 1955: 113, Fig. 44)   75

Plan 34. Level IV[W]/IVA[F] palace. Reconstruction (after Woolley 1955: 115, Fig. 45)   76

Plan 35. Levels III–II[W] fort/Level IVB[F] palace (after Woolley 1955: Fig. 59)   77

Plan 36. Level IV[W] houses 39/A–B and Level V[W] shrines (after Woolley 1955: 179, Fig. 63)   79

Plan 37. Plan of Level V[W] (after Yener 2005: 140, Fig. 4.29)   80

Plan 38. Superposition of Levels VII[W] and IV[W] palaces, the Level IV[W] fortress, the buildings around them
and a modern farmhouse   81

Plan 39. The Turkish government land registry of Tell Atchana, 1991.   82

Plan 40. Level IV[W] house 37 (after Woolley 1955: 176, Fig. 62)   83

Plan 41. Plan of Level IV[W] (after Woolley 1955: Pl. XXII)   84

Plan 42. Levels III–II[W] houses 37/A–D and 38/A (after Woolley 1955: 187, Fig. 65)   84

Plan 43. Level I[W] houses 37/A–B (after Woolley 1955: 194, Fig. 68)   85

Plan 44. Level IV^W house 39/C (after Woolley 1955: 181, Fig. 64)   87

Plan 45. Trench F (after Woolley 1955: 136, Fig. 52)   88

Plan 46. Plan of Level VII^W (after Woolley 1955: Pl. XIV)   90

Plan 47. Plan of Level III^W (after Yener 2005: 142, Fig. 4.31)   94

Plan 48. Plan of Level II^W (after Yener 2005: 143, Fig. 4.32)   95

Plan 49. Level I^W houses 38/A (after Woolley 1955: 192, Fig. 67)   116

Plan 50. Plan of Level I^W (after Yener 2005: 152, Fig. 4.33)   121

Plan 51. The Northern Levant in the 1930s (Amuq sites are marked) (after Haines 1971: Pl. 1)   128

Plan 52. The Amuq settlement pattern during phase M based on the University of Chicago 1930s survey (after Braidwood 1937: 50)   129

Plan 53. The Amuq settlement pattern during phase N based on the University of Chicago 1930s survey (after Braidwood 1937: 49)   129

Plan 54. The Amuq settlement pattern during MBA and LBA based on University of Chicago AVRP (after Casana 2009: 14)   132

Plan 55. Area vs. height plot of AVRP recorded tell sites in the Amuq (after Casana 2009: 17)   133

Plan 56. AVRP survey site size vs. number of households in the Level IV^W census data (after Casana 2009: 29)   133

Plan 57. The squares excavated by the University of Chicago expedition to Tell Atchana, 2003–2004   136

Plan 58. A proposed plan for Level 0^W (after Yener 2005: 144, Fig. 4.34)   141

Photographs

Photo 1. The Level III-II^W temples, Tell Atchana. The grid line markers are enlarged   18

Photo 2. The Levels II^W and I^W temples doorways in one view   34

Photo 3. The annexe to the Level III^W temple and the Levels III–II^W temples   46

Photo 4. The annexe to the Level III^W temple   46

Photo 5. The seal of Paluwa. AT/39/322   47

Photo 6. The Level IB^W temple (after Woolley 1939c: 867)   48

Photo 7. The Level IB^W temple   48

Photo 8. The orthostat of Tudḫaliya DUMU.LUGAL (after Woolley 1939c: 867)   54

Photo 9. The card of object AT/39/288, the throne of the statue of Idrimi   57

Photo 10. The find-spot of the statue of Idrimi (after Woolley 1939c: 869)   58

Photo 11. Some of the pits dug by Woolley at the Levels IV–0^W temple site   59

Photo 12. More of the pits dug by Woolley at the Levels IV–0^W temple site   59

Photo 13. Tell Atchana, Tell Ta'yinat and Küçük Ta'yinat in between in a CORONA 1970 satellite image (after Casana 2003)   89

Photo 14. Atchana/Nuzi ware ATP/37/2 (after Woolley 1955: Pl. CIIa)   104

Photo 15. Atchana/Nuzi ware ATP/37/240 (after Woolley 1955: Pl. CIIIa)   104

Photo 16. Atchana/Nuzi ware from Amuq phase O in Tell Ta'yinat   105

Photo 17. Nuzi ware from Tell Beydar (after Bretschneider 1997: Tf. II.2)   106

Photo 18. Nuzi ware from Tell al-Rimah (Postgate et al. 1997: Pl. 71)   106

Photo 19. Khabur ware excavated by the University of Chicago expedition at Tell Atchana   107

Photo 20. Nuzi beaker, excavated by the University of Chicago expedition at Tell Atchana. Area 2, Square 44.45, Locus 03-2077   108

Photo 21. Nuzi beaker, excavated by the University of Chicago expedition at Tell Atchana. Area 2, Square 44.45, Locus 03-2077   108

Photo 22. Nuzi ware excavated by the University of Chicago expedition at Tell Atchana, Area 2.   109

Photo 23. Nuzi ware excavated by the University of Chicago expedition at Tell Atchana, Area 2.   109

Photo 24. Nuzi ware beaker from phase M of Çatal Höyük (Amuq)   113

The New Stratigraphy of Tell Atchana

Summary Tables 1 & 2

Plans of Levels VA^F–IB^F

Summary Table 1

Summary of stratigraphy and chronology

Political status	Locality status	Level	Buildings/fortifications	Proposed Historical Attribution	Proposed Date
Kingdom	City (Tell: 21 ha.; lower city: ?? ha.) (Amuq M?)	VA^F	Level V^W temple begins? Level V^W shrines Level VAB^W fortress (Gates 1981) Level VAB^W site H	Mostly pre-Idrimi Seized by Idrimi	–1490/1465
		VB^F	Level V^W temple Level V^W shrines Level IV^W "fortress" (Gates 1981) Level V^W building fragments under Level IV^W palace Level V^W house 39/C & Level IV^W houses 39/A–C Level IV^W city wall & rampart Level IV^W site H	Idrimi	1490/1465–1465/1440
		IVA^F	Level IV^W temple Level IV^W "fortress" continued Level IV^W palace (Niqmepa & Ilimilimma wings) Level IV^W houses 39/A–C continued Level IV^W house 37 Level IV^W city wall & rampart continued Level IV^W site H continued	Niqmepa, Ilimilimma [Level IV^W archive]	1465/1440–1420/1400
		IVB^F	Level III^W temple Levels III–II^W "fort" Level III^W houses 37/A, C, 38/A, 39/C Level II^W houses 37/A–D, 38/A, 39/C Levels III–II^W city wall & rampart	Addu-Nīrārī? Itūr-Addu Conquered by Šuppiluliuma I [Idrimi statue, Atchana/ Nuzi ware]	1420/1400–1353/1341
Hittite territory	Stronghold (3 ha. at most) (Hiatus between Amuq M and N?)	III^F	Level II^W temple Levels III–II^W "fort" continued Level I^W houses 37/A–C, 38/A Levels III–II^W city wall with Level I^W revetment	Šuppiluliuma I– Arnuwanda II End of city: deportation by Muršili II? (year 9?) [LH IIIA:2 pottery]	1353/1341–1320/1313
		IIA^F	Level IA^W temple Levels III–II^W "fort" continued	Tudḫaliya DUMU.LUGAL	1320/1313–1280
		IIB^F	Level IB^W temple Levels III–II^W "fort" continued	Post-Tudḫaliya DUMU. LUGAL Šukur-Tešub. Paluwa?	1280–1240
		IA^F	Paluwa shrine Level I^W "house" 38/B	Paluwa?	1240–1210
		IB^F	Level 0^W temple Level I^W "house" 38/B continued	Ends no later than fall of Hatti & Ugarit	1210–1190/1185

Summary Table 2

Buildings, fortifications and their levels

Woolley's level	Level proposed herein	Woolley's date	Dating proposed herein
Level VI^W private houses	VIAB^W	1750–1595	
Level V^W northern shrine	VAB^F	1595–1447	?–1465/1440
Level V^W southern shrine	VAB^F	1595–1447	?–1465/1440
Level V^W temple	VAB^F	1595–1447	?–1465/1440
Level VAB^W fortress (Gates 1981)	VA^F	1595–1447	?–1490/1465
Level V^W house 39/C	VB^F	1595–1447	1490/1465–1465/1440
Level V^W building fragments under Level IV^W palace	VB^F	1595–1447	1490/1465–1465/1440
Level V^W site H	VA^F	1595–1447	?–1490/1465
Level IV^W site H	VB–IVA^F	1595–1447	1490/1465–1420/1400
Level IV^W temple	IVA^F	1447–1370	1465/1440–1420/1400
Level IV^W fortress	VB–IVA^F	1447–1370	1490/1465–1420/1400
Level IV^W palace (Niqmepa and Ilimilimma)	IVA^F	1447–1370	1465/1440–1420/1400
Level IV^W house 37	IVA^F	1447–1370	1465/1440–1420/1400
Level IV^W house 39/A	VB–IVA^F	1447–1370	1490/1465–1420/1400
Level IV^W house 39/B Northeast	VB–IVA^F	1447–1370	1490/1465–1420/1400
Level IV^W house 39/B Southwest	IVA^F	1447–1370	1465/1440–1420/1400
Level IV^W house 39/C	VB–IVA^F	1447–1370	1490/1465–1420/1400
Level IV^W city wall & rampart	VB–IVA^F	1447–1370	1490/1465–1420/1400
Level III^W temple	IVB^F	1370–1350	1420/1400–1353/1341
Levels III–II^W fort	IVB–IIB^F	1370–1273	1420/1400–1240
Levels III–II^W house 37/A	IVB^F	1370–1350	1420/1400–1353/1341
Levels III–II^W house 37/C	IVB^F	1370–1350	1420/1400–1353/1341
Levels III–II^W house 38/A	IVB^F	1370–1350	1420/1400–1353/1341
Levels III–II^W house 39/C	IVB^F	1370–1350	1420/1400–1353/1341
Levels III–II^W city wall(s), rampart	IVB–III^F	1370–1273	1420/1400–1320/1313
Level II^W house 37/B	IVB^F	1350–1273	1410/1390–1353/1341
Level II^W house 37/D	IVB^F	1350–1273	1410/1390–1353/1341
Level II^W temple	III^F	1350–1273	1353/1341–1320/1313
Level I^W house 37/A	III^F	1273–1194	1353/1341–1320/1313
Level I^W house 37/B	III^F	1273–1194	1353/1341–1330/1320
Level I^W house 37/C	III^F	1273–1194	1353/1341–1320/1313
Level I^W house 38/A	III^F	1273–1194	1353/1341–1320/1313
Level I^W city wall revetment	III^F	1273–1194	1353/1341–1320/1313
Level IA^W temple	IIA^F	1273–1194	1320/1313–1280
Level IB^W temple	IIB^F		1280–1240
Paluwa shrine	IA^F		1240–1210
Level I^W house 38/B	IAB^F	1273–1194	1240–1190/1185
Level 0^W temple	IB^F	1194–1140	1210–1190/1185

3

Level VA^F

Level VA^F

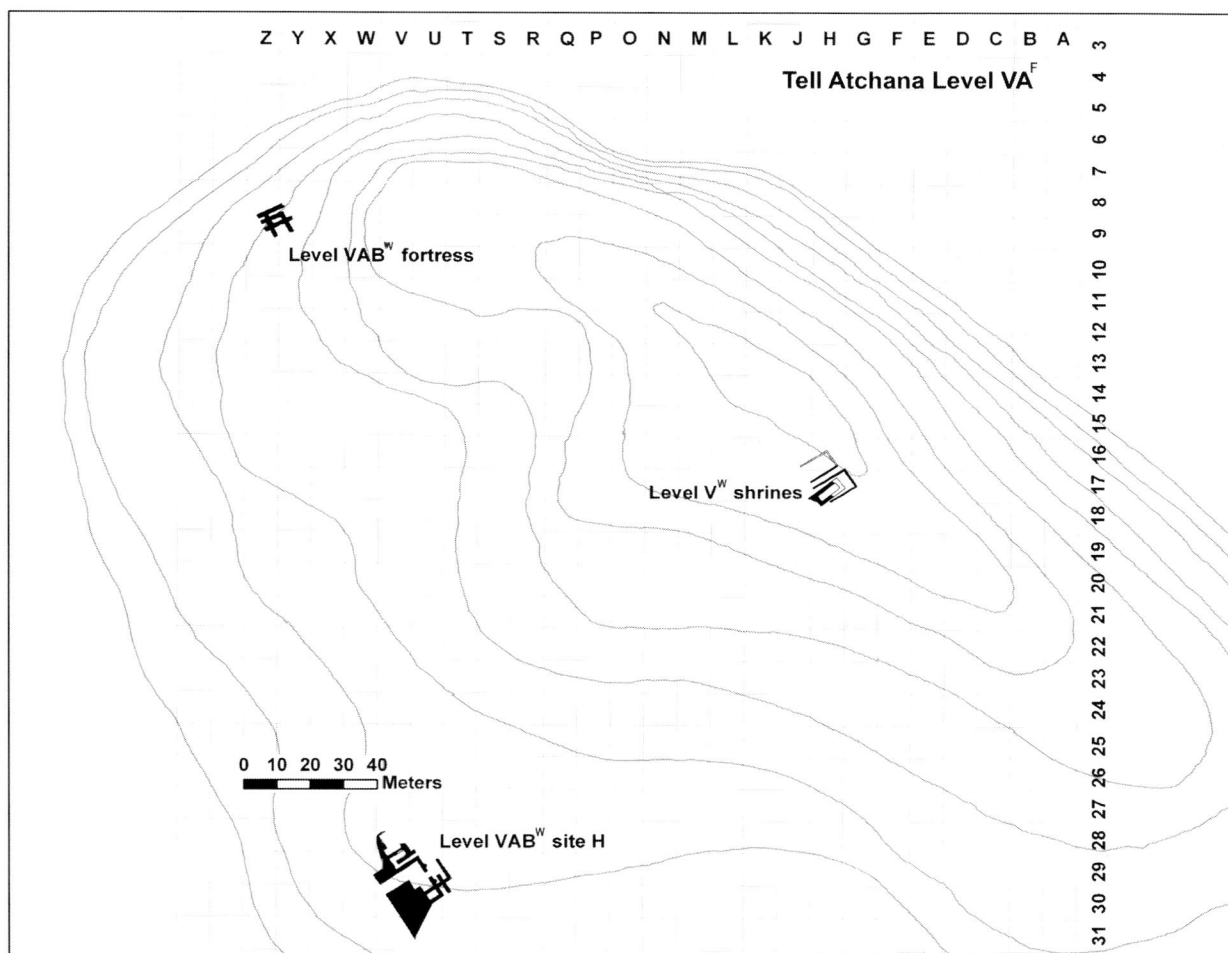

All Level Plans are by Eudora J. Struble

Level VB^F

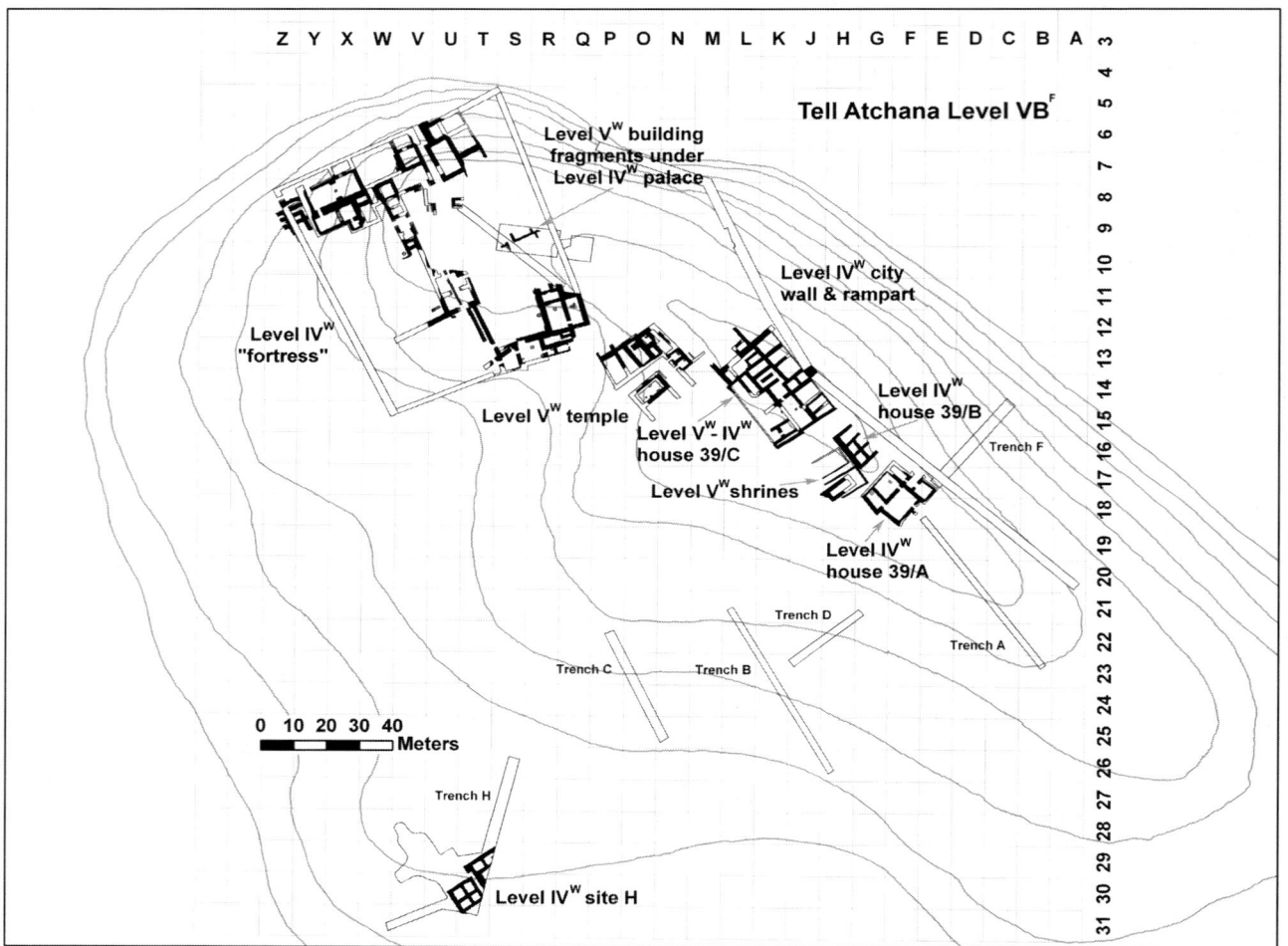

Tell Atchana Level VB^F

Level V^W building fragments under Level IV^W palace

Level IV^W city wall & rampart

Level IV^W "fortress"

Level V^W temple

Level IV^W house 39/B

Level V^W–IV^W house 39/C

Level V^W shrines

Level IV^W house 39/A

Trench F

Trench D

Trench A

Trench C

Trench B

0 10 20 30 40 Meters

Trench H

Level IV^W site H

Level IVA^F

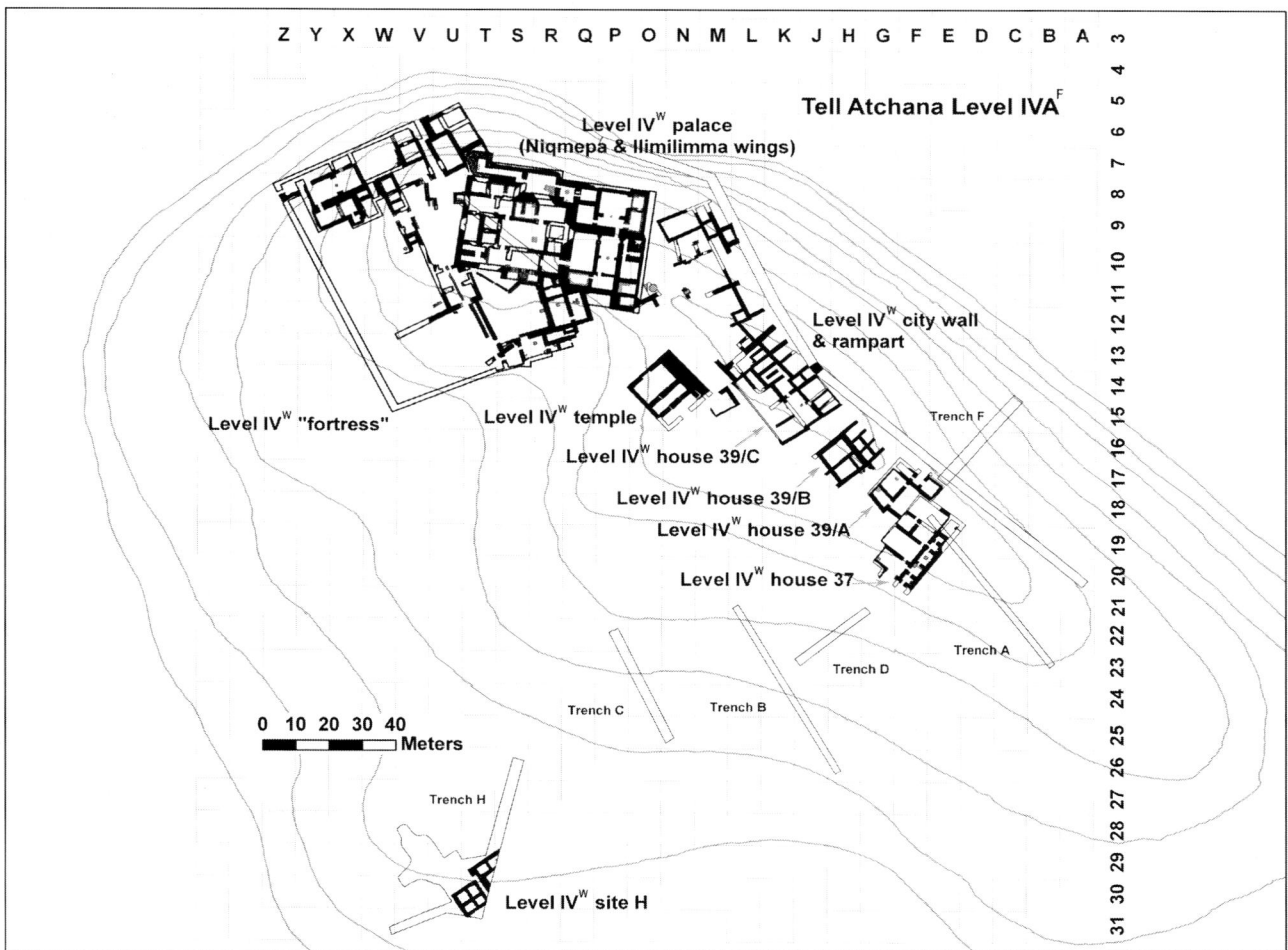

Tell Atchana Level IVA^F

Z Y X W V U T S R Q P O N M L K J H G F E D C B A

Level IV^W palace
(Niqmepa & Ilimilimma wings)

Level IV^W city wall
& rampart

Trench F

Level IV^W "fortress"

Level IV^W temple

Level IV^W house 39/C

Level IV^W house 39/B

Level IV^W house 39/A

Level IV^W house 37

Trench A

Trench D

Trench C

Trench B

0 10 20 30 40
Meters

Trench H

Level IV^W site H

Level IVB^F

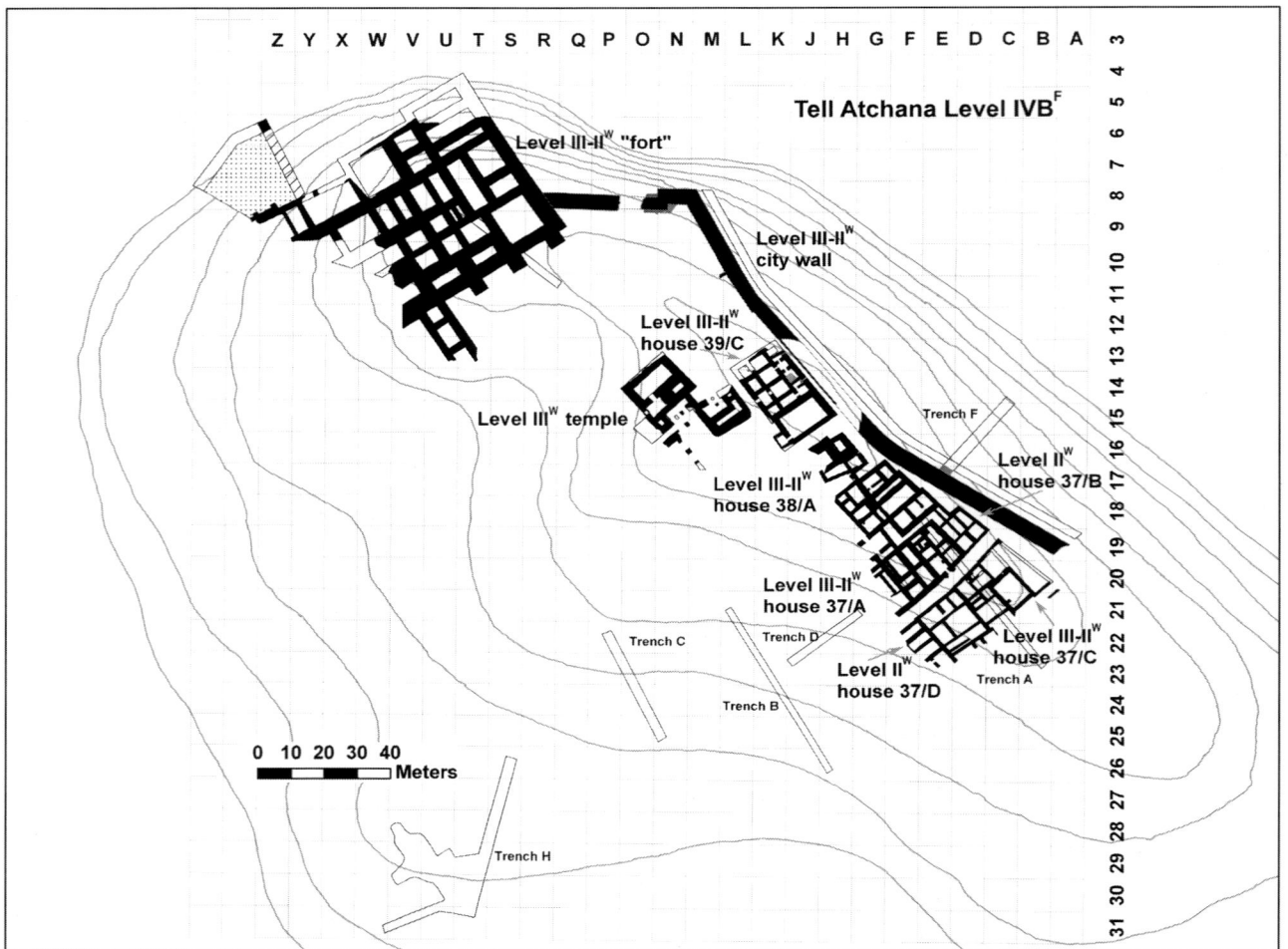

Tell Atchana Level IVB^F

Level III-II^W "fort"

Level III-II^W city wall

Level III-II^W house 39/C

Level III^W temple

Level III-II^W house 38/A

Level II^W house 37/B

Level III-II^W house 37/A

Level III-II^W house 37/C

Level II^W house 37/D

Trench F

Trench C

Trench D

Trench B

Trench A

Trench H

0 10 20 30 40 Meters

Level III^F

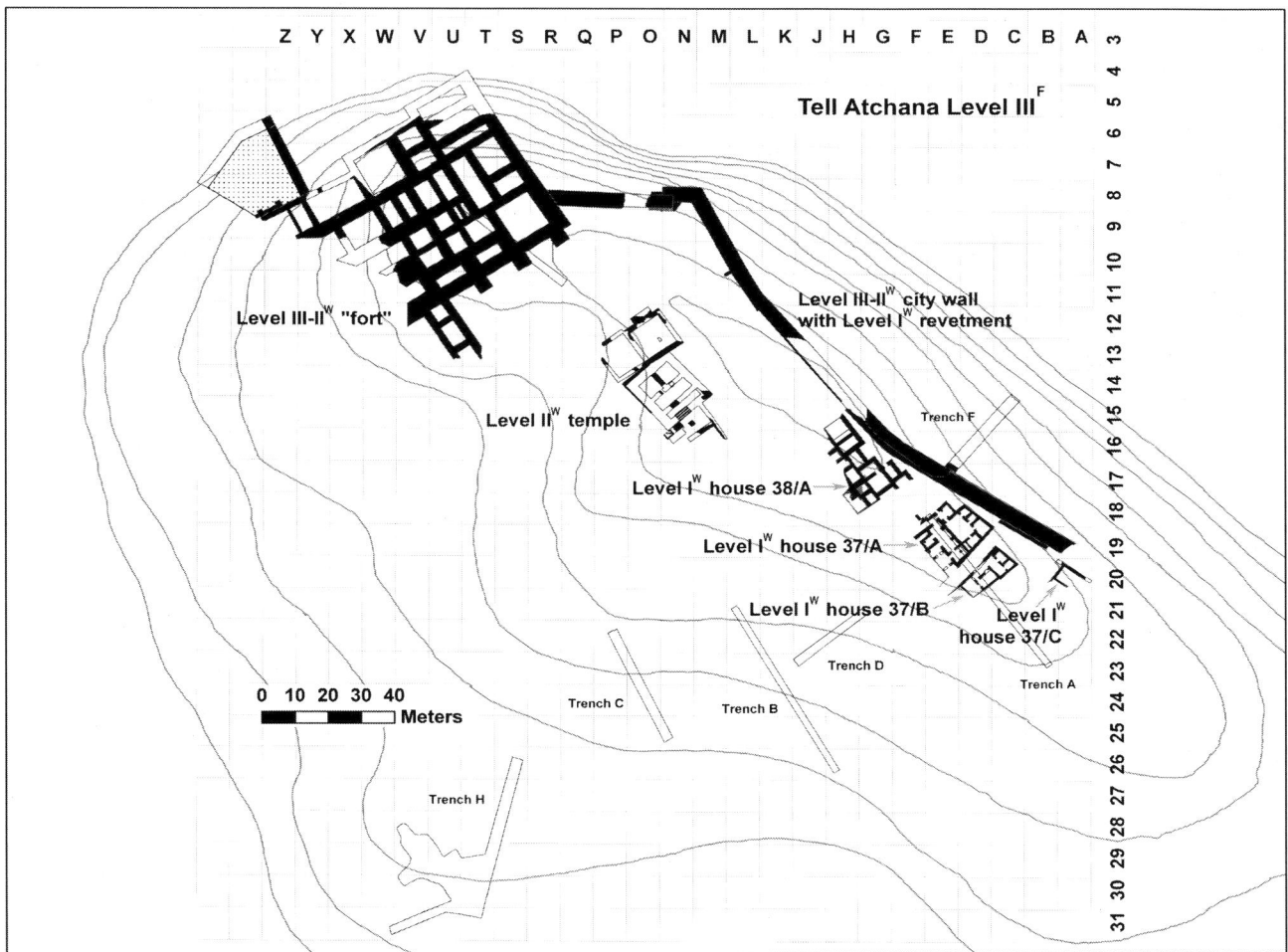

Z Y X W V U T S R Q P O N M L K J H G F E D C B A

Tell Atchana Level III^F

Level III-II^W "fort"

Level III-II^W city wall
with Level I^W revetment

Trench F

Level II^W temple

Level I^W house 38/A

Level I^W house 37/A

Level I^W house 37/B

Level I^W
house 37/C

Trench A

Trench D

0 10 20 30 40
Meters

Trench C

Trench B

Trench H

Level IIA^F

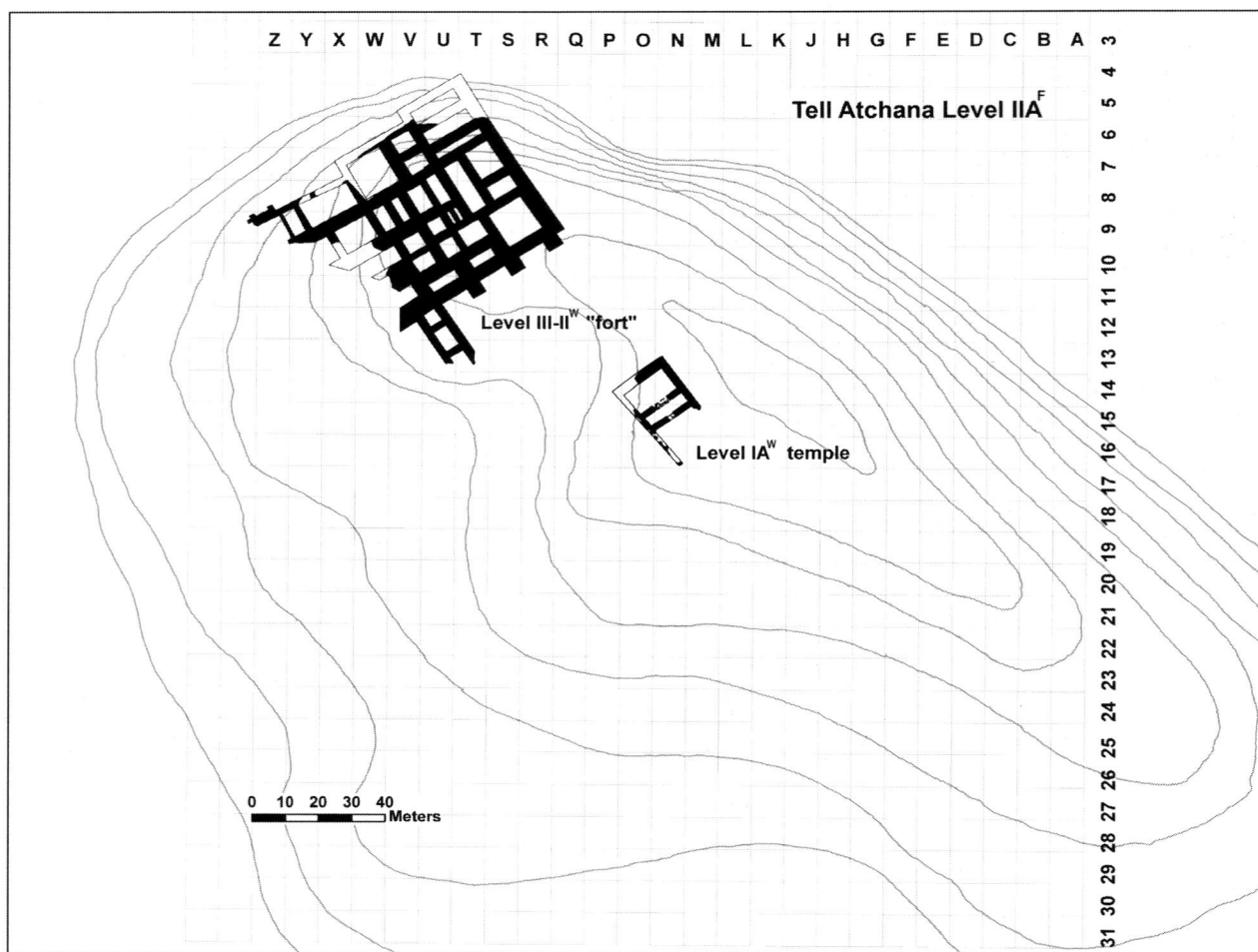

Level IIB^F

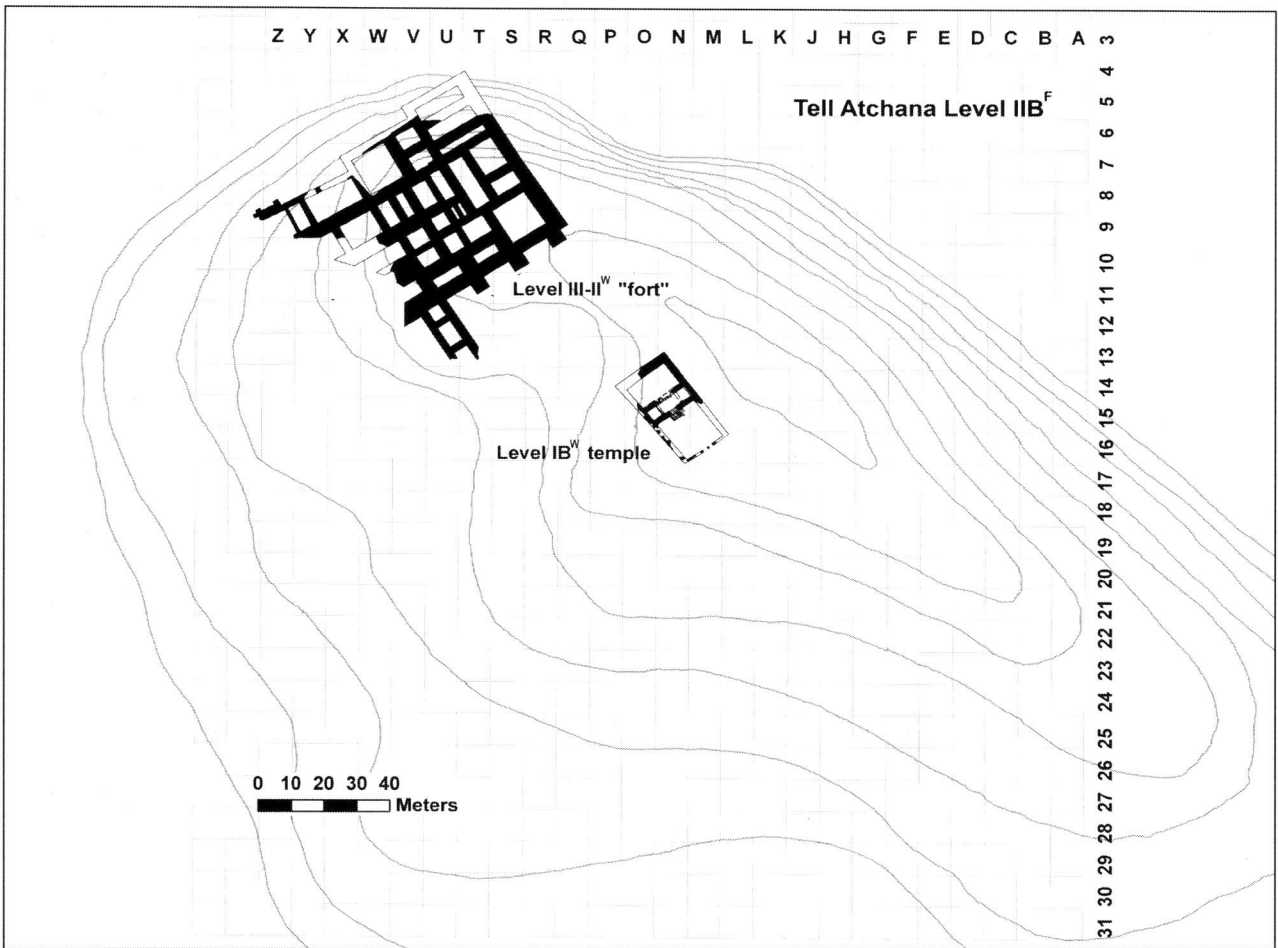

Tell Atchana Level IIB^F

Level III-II^W "fort"

Level IB^W temple

0 10 20 30 40 Meters

Level IA^F

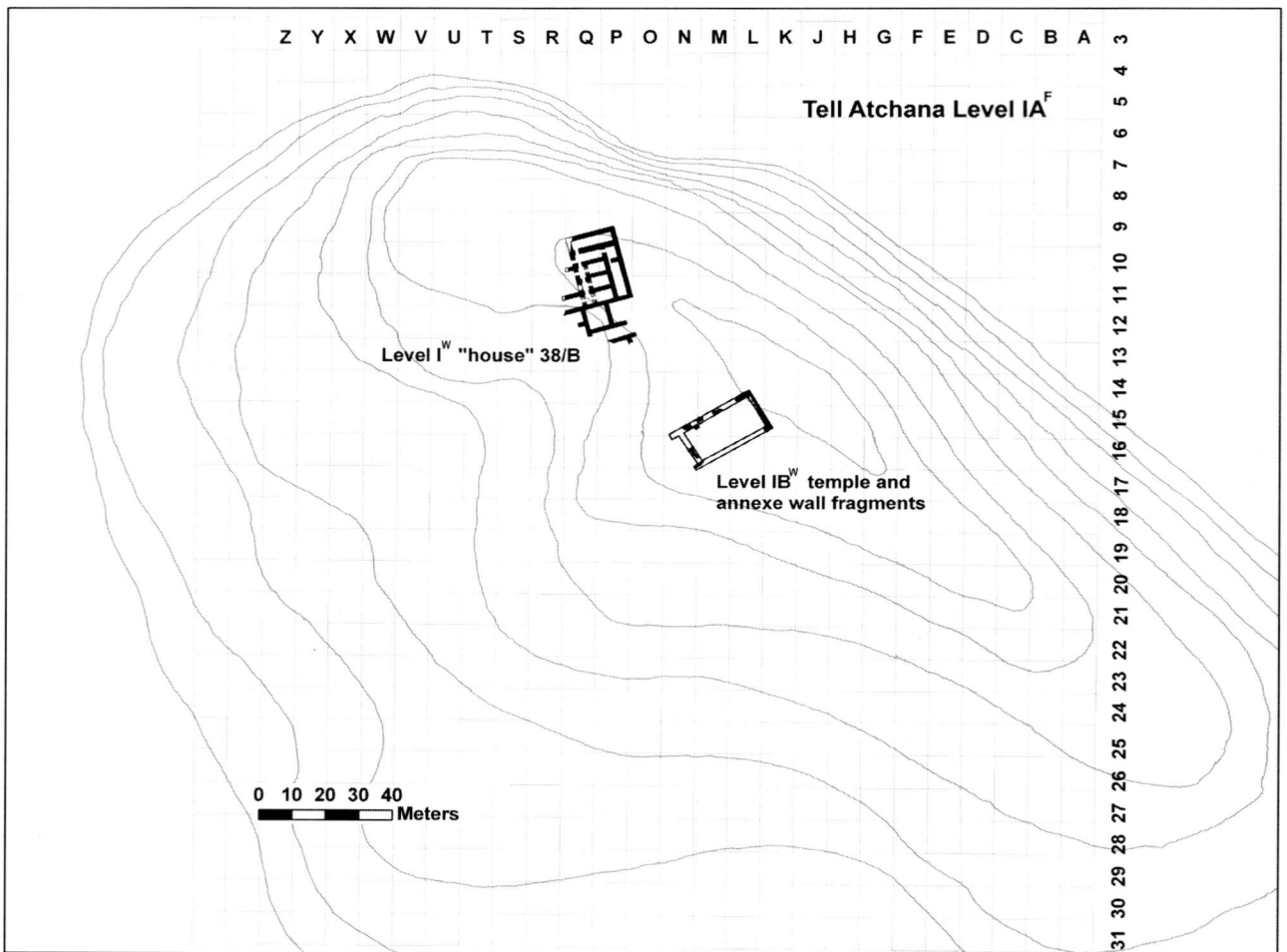

Tell Atchana Level IA^F

Level I^W "house" 38/B

Level IB^W temple and
annexe wall fragments

0 10 20 30 40
Meters

Z Y X W V U T S R Q P O N M L K J H G F E D C B A

3 4 5 6 7 8 9 10 11 12 13 14 15 16 17 18 19 20 21 22 23 24 25 26 27 28 29 30 31

Level IB^F

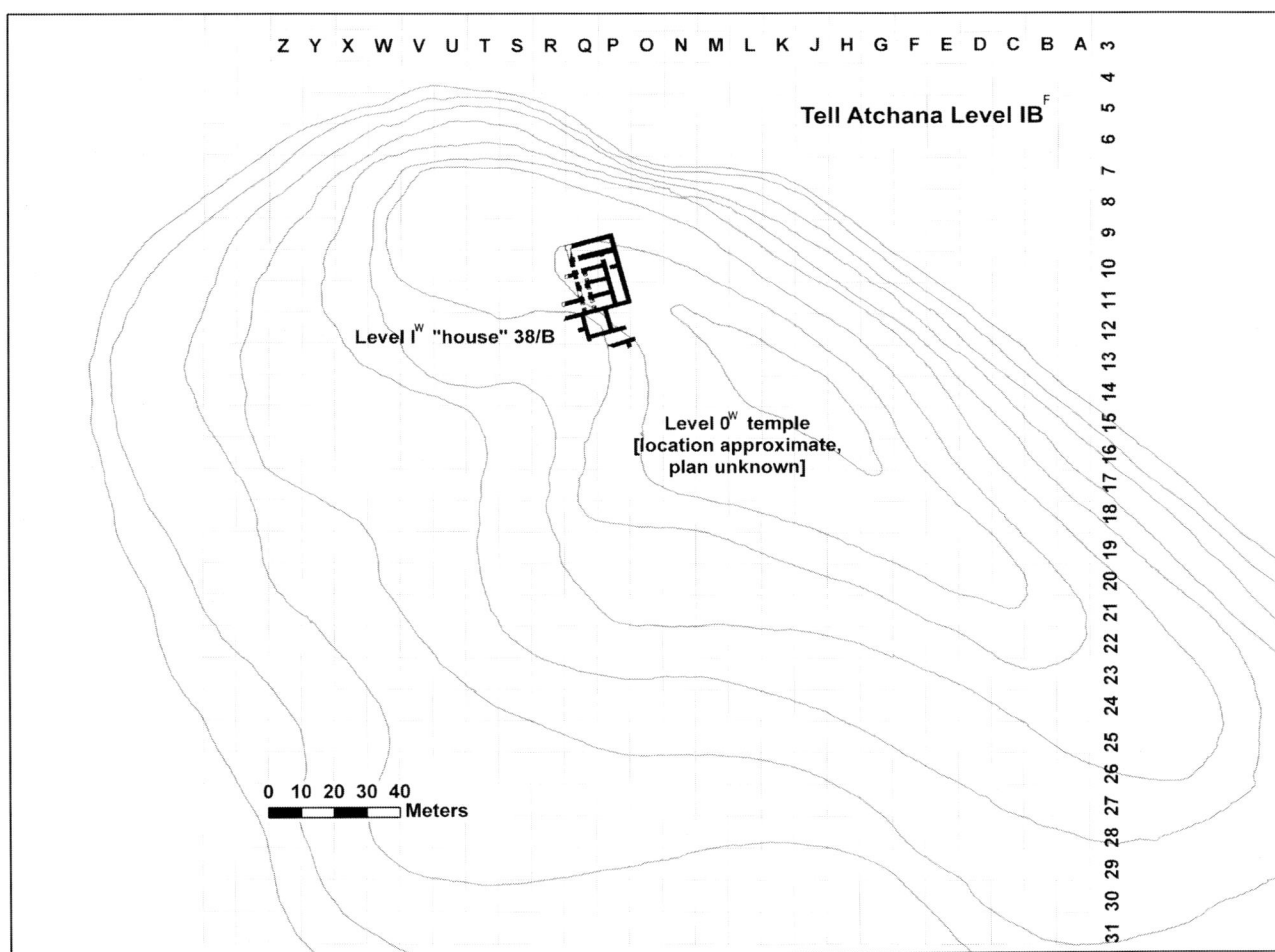

Z Y X W V U T S R Q P O N M L K J H G F E D C B A

Tell Atchana Level IB^F

Level I^W "house" 38/B

Level 0^W temple
[location approximate,
plan unknown]

0 10 20 30 40 Meters

13

Chapter One

Introduction

Tell Atchana, the site of ancient Alalakh, swells up above the eastern bank of the winding Orontes River (Asi Nahri). Atchana is the French transliteration of the Arabic ʿAṭšanah—Turkish Açcana Höyüğü. Twenty kilometers to the west is the bustling modern city of Antakya, ancient Antioch; the Syrian border is a short distance to the south. Tell Atchana's sister city, Tell Ta'yinat, is only a stone's throw to the northwest, both tucked in the sleepy southern edge of the Amuq valley, Turkey.

Yet for the research of the Ancient Near East of the second millennium B.C.E., it is hard to overestimate the importance of Tell Atchana. Since its initial excavation by Sir Leonard Woolley in the 1930s and 1940s, Tell Atchana has been a key site for the study of the Middle and the Late Bronze Age in the northern Levant. The site and its cuneiform tablet archives play an important role in discussing the political and social history of the second millennium, the Mesopotamian chronology, and the material culture and architecture of the Middle and Late Bronze Age.

Woolley excavated at Tell Atchana from 1936-1939 and 1946-1949. He worked mainly on the northwest summit of the site, helped by hundreds of workmen and only a few staff members. Woolley recorded eighteen strata (levels) in the city, which was the capitol of Mukiš. He unearthed temples and palaces, gates and fortifications, private houses and streets, as well as a plethora of small finds. His final report (Woolley 1955) was a milestone in the history of research of the ancient Eastern Mediterranean. Yet the crowning glory of Alalakh remains not its architecture but its treasure trove of texts: several hundred cuneiform tablets, written mostly in Akkadian, influenced by Hurrian and by the local Northwest Semitic dialect. There are additional tablets in Sumerian (lexical lists), and a few in Hittite. The lion's share of these was found in the archives of the Level VII^W and IV^W palaces. This corpus is considered the main historical source for the study of the northern Levant during the MBA and the LBA I, and has been since its earliest publication (Smith 1939; Wiseman 1953).

The Oriental Institute of the University of Chicago resumed work at the site in 2000, and held two excavation seasons there (in 2003-4). Since 2006 the site has been excavated by an expedition of the Mustafa Kemal University in Antakya.

While the earlier periods at Tell Atchana were studied by Heinz (1992) and Levels VI-V^W by Gates (1976), no comprehensive study of the material culture of LBA Alalakh, Levels IV-0^W, has yet been attempted. Furthermore, though the political history of Level IV^W has recently been thoroughly examined (by von Dassow, 2008), no such study is dedicated to the political history of Alalakh after the destruction of the Level IV^W palace. This work offers both: a detailed analysis of the material culture of LBA Alalakh and a political history of Alalakh following the destruction of the Level IV^W palace.

To this end, I begin in Chapter 2 with an analysis of Woolley's method and its associated difficulties. I examine the mapping, the grid system and its various orientations, the grid deviations and the problem of the magnetic declination.

Following this, Chapter 3 is dedicated to the Level IV–0^W temples at Tell Atchana (Alalakh). It includes a refinement of the recently published level plans of Tell Atchana (Yener 2005); a stratigraphic study of the temples and their annexes; and the re-association of each of the temples with a new, higher level and the consequent adjustment of their dates, paying close attention also to the finds. As a result, I am able to argue that the find-spot of the statue of Idrimi was not in Level IB^W, as reported by the excavator, but rather in the newly named Level IVB^F, dated to the first half of the fourteenth century B.C.E.

In Chapter 4 I describe in great detail the new stratigraphic paradigm of LBA Tell Atchana up to the Hittite conquest. In addition to the archaeological data I posit a reconstructed political history of each stratum. I conclude in Chapter 5 with a comprehensive summary of Hittite Alalakh.

With regards to terminology: In analyzing the stratigraphy of Tell Atchana, I could effectively have created a completely new numbering system for the site's phases as derived from my own study, but I chose not to do so. Woolley's level terminology has been common currency in hundreds, perhaps thousands of publications over the last sixty years. The Level VII^W and IV^W archives now have scholarly lives of their own; changing their number titles would have been both confusing and ineffectual. Analyses of Woolley's excavations in Alalakh should continue to use the level names of these archives as terminological anchors, while all other levels can be changed and reshaped as required by new study of the stratigraphy. Thus, for the purposes of this study, level numbers flagged with "W" refer to Woolley's chronology; those marked with "F" represent the levels as I understand them. I took some additional liberty in naming Level IV^W 'Level IVA^F'; but I did so only because Woolley himself divided Level IV^W into two parts, without naming them A and B as is his practice elsewhere. Woolley's use of A and B to describe sub-levels is in itself inconsistent: though the A sub-level is mostly earlier/higher than the B sub-level, he can use the two interchangeably (compare Woolley 1955: 144 and 399). Gates (1981: 6–8) fixed the use of A for early and B for late, and I follow her herein. Like Woolley, I did not come across any occupational gaps from Levels V^W to 0^W, and therefore this aspect, important to many such studies of stratigraphy, bears no weight in my discussion.

Chapter Two

Woolley's Method and Mapping Reexamined

2.1 The Discovery of the Idrimi Statue

Just one month before the Republic of Hatay was annexed to Turkey, Sir Leonard Woolley made an exciting discovery. On 21 May 1939 he sent the following from his dig-house in Tell Atchana, Hatay province: "A rubbish-pit at the temple gave us great surprise. From it there came a white stone statue just over a metre high of a Hittite king, a seated figure; the head and feet were broken off but except for part of the foot the statue is complete and in wonderfully good condition and even the nose is only just chipped. The figure is covered literally from head to foot with cuneiform inscription which begins on one cheek, runs across the front and one side of the body and ends at the bottom of the skirt, rather more than fifty lines of text.[1] Nothing like that has been found before" (Woolley 1939a).

Upon deciphering, the inscription revealed the statue to be that of Idrimi, ruler of Alalakh in the fifteenth century B.C.E. Idrimi was the probable offspring of the royal family of Aleppo (Márquez Rowe 1997: 183; van Soldt 2000: 109–111) and, according to the text itself, the author of one of the most fascinating autobiographies in the ancient world. Modern scholars might still agree: Woolley's assertion that "nothing like that has been found before" is a true one. The statue of Idrimi remains the single most important artifact found at Tell Atchana, and the royal autobiography of Idrimi testifies to a genre hitherto unknown in the region, an example of exciting innovation in the Levant (Greenstein 1995).[2] Woolley's reports on the archaeological context of the statue can be found in several different publications (1939b; 1939c; 1947: 60; 1949: 2; 1950: 12; 1953: 160; 1955: 89).[3] An *editio princeps* of its inscription was published by Sidney Smith only about a decade after its discovery; in the meantime the statue was stored in a war shelter (Smith 1949). A flurry of scholarship followed, in two waves: first came the reviews (Albright 1950; Dussaud

1950; 1951; Goetze 1950; Legrain 1951; Nougayrol 1951; Landsberger 1954; Aro 1954–1956; Oppenheim 1955), then, several decades later, a number of in-depth studies of the inscription (Na'aman and Kempinski 1973; Greenstein and Marcus 1976; Oller 1977; Dietrich and Loretz 1981; Sasson 1981).[4] Along with texts found in Tell Atchana's Level IV[W], the Idrimi inscription is today the cornerstone of many reconstructions of the history of the fifteenth century B.C.E. in the northern Levant.

Such excitement was clearly warranted; few such clear indications of Levantine chronology and kingship can otherwise be attested. Yet the statue and its context present as many questions as they do solutions. Several scholars have challenged the historical validity of the inscription. Klengel (1981: 272) and Liverani (2004: 85–96) emphasize the historical bias and literary formula typical to the genre, which may undermine the credibility of the inscription as an historical source. Sasson (1981), followed by Longman III (1991: 60–77), raises the possibility that this inscription is a "simulated" or "fictional" autobiography, composed by a certain Šarruwa, whom he believes was a scribe in thirteenth-century Alalakh. Oller (1989), Mayer (1995: 334–335), von Dassow (1997: 21–22) and Márquez Rowe (1997: 179–181) all rebut Sasson and Longman III on philological and historical grounds. Nevertheless, they do not fully address certain serious concerns raised by Sasson: namely, the thirteenth-century B.C.E. archaeological context in which the statue was found, and the unusual circumstances under which the scribe is mentioned in this royal inscription.

I, however, intend to do so. Where was the statue actually found? Woolley reports that the statue of Idrimi was found buried in a pit dug in an annexe to the Level IB[W] temple (Woolley 1949: 2), which he dated to the end of the thirteenth century B.C.E. (1955: 398–399).[5] Therefore, the statue

---

[1] The inscription comprises, in fact, 104 lines.
[2] Yet see Na'aman (1980: 110) for a discussion of the origin of this genre.
[3] Woolley (1948) chose not to include the statue of Idrimi and its find-spot in his preliminary report of the 1939 season.

[4] Detailed bibliographies on Idrimi, the historical context of his reign, and the statue itself can be found as addenda to the unpublished dissertations of Oller (1977: 250–266) and von Dassow (1997: 596–612), and published in von Dassow's recent book (2008).
[5] Woolley's dates for Level I[W] are 1273–1194 (1955: 399).

and its inscription represent, perhaps, a 200–300-year-old heirloom that survived the Hittite conquest of Alalakh and was still in use at the end of the thirteenth century (ibid.). Alternatively, the statue and the inscription—or possibly just the inscription—were fashioned late in the thirteenth century (Level IB[W]) (Sasson 1981: 323–324).[6] Even if we accept the philological and historical reasons for dating the statue and its inscription to the fifteenth/fourteenth century, there still remains the question of how a statue bearing a lengthy inscription praising the victory over Hatti could survive in a temple located merely a few meters from the fort of the Hittite governor of Alalakh.[7] It is highly unlikely that so prominent and monumental an inscription could have survived one hundred and fifty years of essentially Hittite rule in Alalakh—beginning with Šuppiluliuma I's first Syrian war—during which the city was essentially a Hittite fortress. Rather, I believe that the issue can be successfully reconciled with careful stratigraphic reorganization. Despite the limited archaeological data recorded by Woolley, I believe that it is possible to demonstrate that the statue of Idrimi was found in Woolley's Level III[W], not in Level IB[W]. For the purposes of this study, however, this is only the first step in a whole-scale stratigraphic reorganization of the site, and has profound implications for our understanding of the history and chronology of Tell Atchana and perhaps even the Late Bronze Age Northern Levant.

The conclusion of this study dates the statue of Idrimi to Level IVB[F], in my new chronology. Before I argue the validity of my reinterpretation, however, I must first expose the flaws in Woolley's inital methodology, coupled with an explanation of my own. This chapter consists of a meticulous review of Woolley's surviving plans, which, unfortunately for posterity, are largely fragmentary. The problems both of grid labeling and of grid orientation will be addressed in detail below.

2.2 Grid line labels and the mislabeling of squares

Perhaps the most significant issue with Woolley's record keeping is the lack of published level plans. Of the eighteen levels that Woolley excavated at Tell Atchana, he published level plans only of two: Levels VII[W] and IV[W] (Woolley 1955). All the rest of his many published plans are fragmentary—merely buildings or features within a stratum. Had Woolley published level plans more consistently, he would probably have avoided many of the inaccuracies of his final report.

Reevaluations of the architectural plans of the site as reported by Woolley were recently published (Yener 2005). These include the study of the inconsistencies in Woolley's plans, as well as Batiuk and Burke's mosaic work (2005) composing Woolley's many published plans into coherent level plans for VII–0[W]. This reevaluation of Woolley's architectural plans has brought to the surface a large number of crucial discrepancies in his publications, never before described in a systematic manner. In considering them, let us first review the work of Batiuk and Burke (ibid.: 145–146). In their study they identify the following major issues:

1) the orientation of Woolley's grid with respect to true north varies from plan to plan. This will be addressed in section 2.3;
2) his stylistic conventions are not uniform and errors were made even within the use of the different conventions;
3) there are critical flaws in the representation and location of fragments of architecture intended to serve as points of reference;
4) in some plans references to or indications of the grid are altogether missing;
5) the location of many of the sections is unspecified or unclear;
6) labels for features are frequently absent;
7) as noted in the Introduction to this work, inconsistent methodology is applied for describing sub-phasing within levels (sometimes phase A is later than B; at other times the opposite is true);
8) elevations are omitted on all but one plan;
9) on numerous occasions the squares in the excavation grid are mislabeled.

Of all these challenges, Batiuk and Burke rightly assert that the grid mislabeling is "perhaps the most significant observation next to false indications of north" (2005: 146). They optimistically suggest that "plans with incorrect grid references appear to be restricted to the period between April 1937 and 1938" (ibid.: 146 and repeated in 149); however, there are sufficient indications that this problem occurred well into the 1940s (see below in this chapter). I have determined that the grid mislabeling derives from a fundamental detail, which Batiuk and Burke do not suspect, nor does Woolley address: while in the field Woolley and his architects marked East–West *grid lines* with letters and North–South with numbers, Woolley later referred to the same letters and numbers as if they were assigned to the *squares*. Predictably, this produced (yet more) inconsistencies. In the first case, each square is described with two letters and two numbers, which correspond to the four grid lines surrounding it. In the second case, a square is represented by a combination of a letter and a number denoting its two sides. Furthermore, the post-excavation transformation from one system to the other was not consistent for both axes; relabeled plans were published side by side with mislabeled and preliminary field-labeled draft plans. In some cases plans were partly relabeled, which added much to the confusion.

---

[6] Sasson raises two additional archaeological arguments for the lower dating of the statue and inscription, well summarized by Oller (1989: 414–415): 1) The style of the sculpture and the throne base are late Late Bronze Age; 2) Woolley's perception was that the autochthones were actively and symbolically resisting the occupation and that this is archaeologically proven.

[7] The same governor was a high-ranking Hittite official, and at least in one case, a relative of the Hittite king (Niedorf 2002).

Photo 1. The Level III-II^W temples, Tell Atchana. The grid line markers are enlarged (unpublished photo at UCL Special Collections)

Woolley discloses no detail about this post-excavation transformation of the grid. Yet it was done annually from 1938 on, and records of partial, inconsistent or no transformation exist in each of the pertinent preliminary reports, as well as in the final report. This can be confirmed in published and unpublished photos taken at the site. Unlike the plans, the photos were neither reworked nor reinterpreted for publication, and they bear witness to the original grid system used by Woolley's architects.

The best example for this is an unpublished photo of the Level III^W temple (Photo 1). No baulks were left between squares during the excavation; nonetheless, grid lines and squares needed to be delineated in the field, so Woolley used benchmarks (small metal or wooden stakes) placed atop narrow, conical patches of earth that were deliberately left unexcavated. These can be observed in some of the photos. As work progressed the patches were taken down and the stakes driven further into the ground. In Photo 1 (see also Table 1) the markings on three of several observable signs are legible, reading "O-14," "O-15" and "N-15." Since the architecture in the photo is identifiable and Woolley published a detailed plan of this area (1955: 74, Fig. 31; Plan 1 herein), it is possible to compare the notation appearing on the signs with their locations on Plan 1. The sign showing "O-14" is located at O–N–13–14—the intersection point between North–South grid line O and East–West grid line 14 or the meeting point of four

squares in Woolley's square system: O13, N13, N14 and O14. Thus, it does not clearly mark any *one* square. The same applies for signs "O-15" and "N-15." Accordingly, grid line intersections were marked in the field by one letter and one number.[8]

Further evidence for the confusion regarding the designation of squares can be found in Woolley's reports and plans (see Tables 1 and 2). The first few preliminary reports from Atchana (Woolley 1936; 1937) make no reference to a grid or squares. In the first detailed plans of the Atchana excavations, published in the preliminary report of the 1937 season (Woolley 1938), Woolley makes no reference whatsoever to square designations. Four detailed plans of architecture were published there

---

[8] Other legible signs can be found in Woolley 1955: Pl. XXXIb. In this photo five of the square markers can be observed, and the notation on two of them is either partly of fully legible. One reads "W", but only part of the sign is included in the photo. The other one, I believe, reads "W-9." Based on the architecture that can be identified in the photo and on Fig. 57 (ibid.: 152) these points are W–V-9–10 and W–V-8–9, respectively. Therefore, W-9 stands for the intersection point between grid lines W and 9, and not for the name of a square. In Pl. XXVIa (ibid.) a sign clearly reads S-9. Point S–R–8–9 is located in room 9 of the Level IV^W palace, and once again the grid lines are marked and not the squares. Here, the point (S-9) is located at the upper right-hand side of the square with the same name—S-9. The Level IV^W palace and fort were excavated in 1938 and the Level III^W temple—in 1946. Therefore, the grid line-based labeling system seems to have been consistent throughout the years, but not its translation into the square-based system.

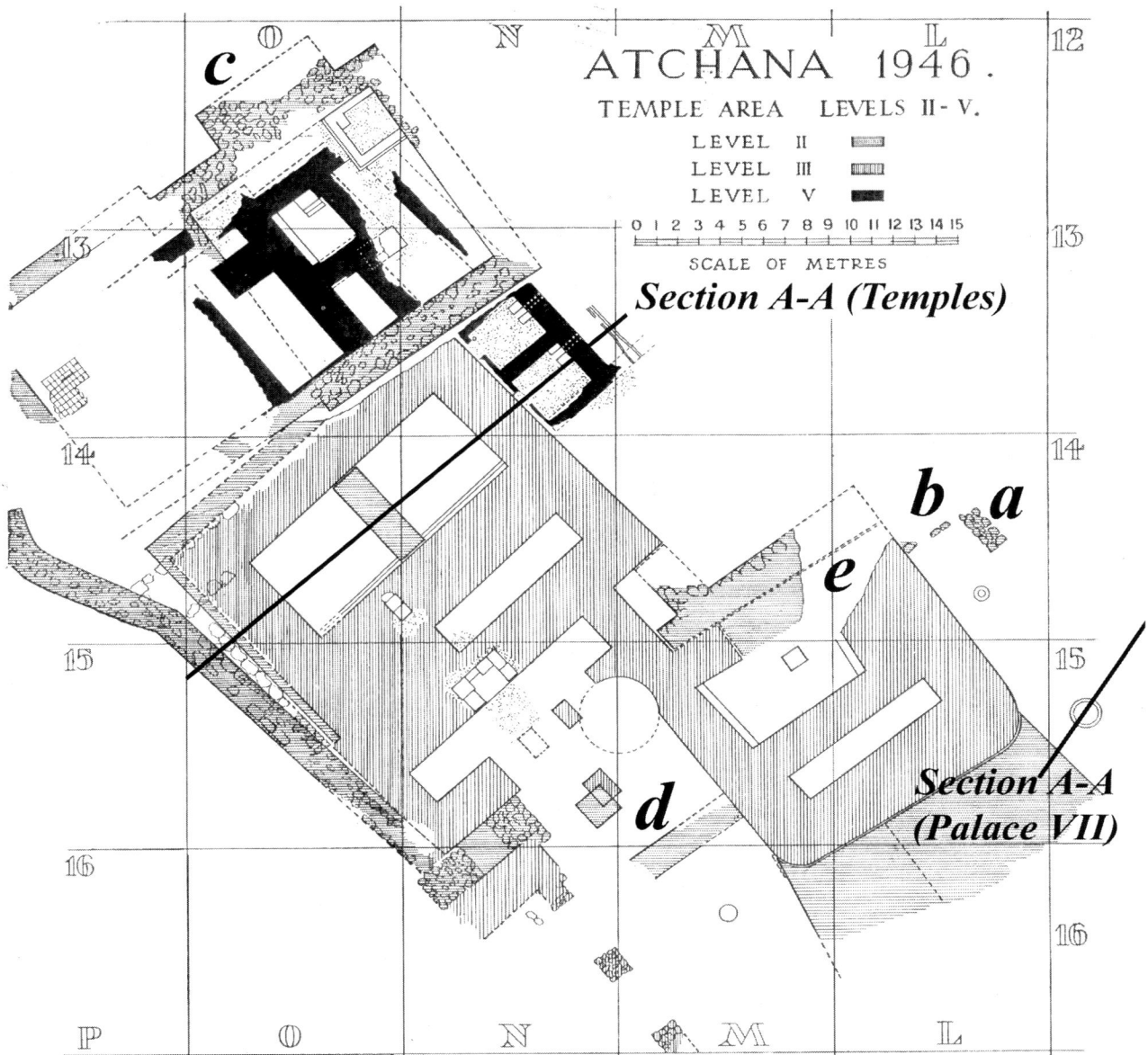

Plan 1. Detailed plan of the Level V–II^W temples (after Woolley 1955: 74, Fig. 31). All images adapted and edited by Eudora J. Struble

(Plans III, IV, V and XIII), all reproduced with some minor updates by Woolley in the final publication (1955: 170, 176, 187, 194) as Figs. 68, 65, 62 and 60, respectively. The grid line labels are located at the upper left side of the grid squares. Woolley did not convert the labeling system in the final publication as he did in other cases and, therefore, this is authentic evidence for his field recording system. When Batiuk and Burke (2005: 146, 148–149) examined these plans, they wrote the following regarding three of them: "Grid mislabeled: square designations are located on upper right corner", and "this mislabeling has resulted in the placement of certain structures, particularly the houses, 10 m. to the west of Woolley's plans."[9] However, the grid here is not mislabeled; it is simply not converted from the grid line-based labeling system to the square-

based labeling system. In the field, the architects assigned numbers and letters to grid line intersection points. In 1937 they were consistent in locating the letter-number label at the bottom right-hand corner of grid line intersection points. In the following years these labels were not located as consistently as they had been in 1937, but they always referred to the grid lines and not to the squares, as will be demonstrated shortly.

In 1938 Woolley (1939d) started assigning square designations in his report. In most of the plans the sides of the squares are marked, rather than the grid lines. Nevertheless, I believe that the methods of excavation and recording had not changed. My assumption is based on the photos from 1938, which were discussed above, and on Plan V, which was published in the same preliminary report (ibid.) and later reproduced in the final report (Woolley 1955: 146, Fig. 55). The architect Ralph Lavers

---

[9] A comparison between Figs. 60 and 59 (Woolley 1955) should have brought Batiuk and Burke to the conclusion that Fig. 60 is mislabeled, as Figs. 68, 65 and 62 are.

Table 1. The location of grid line labels in relation to squares bearing the same name

Medium	Marked as	Squares	Location of the square label relative to the square of the same name	
Photo	O-14	O–N-13–14	Upper right-hand side of the square	
Photo	N-15	N–M-14–15	Upper right-hand side of the square	
Photo	O-15	O–N-14–15	Upper right-hand side of the square	
Photo	W-9	W–V-8–9	Upper right-hand side of the square	
Photo	S-9	S–R-8–9	Upper right-hand side of the square	
Plans	vary	vary	Just right of the upper right-hand corner of the square	
Plan	vary	vary	Just right of the upper right-hand corner of the square	
Plan	M-14	M–L-13–14	The letter: just above the upper right-hand corner of the square; the number: next to the letter, diagonally from the upper right-hand corner of the square	
Plan	vary	vary	The letter: just above the upper right-hand corner of the square; the number: next to the letter, diagonally from the upper right-hand corner of the square	
Plan	L-14	L–K-13–14	The letter: just above the upper right-hand corner of the square; the number: next to the letter, diagonally from the upper right-hand corner of the square	
Plan	15, 16, 17	vary	The letter: just above the upper right-hand corner of the square; the number: next to the letter, diagonally from the upper right-hand corner of the square	
Plans	vary	vary	The letter: just above the upper right-hand corner of the square; the number: next to the letter, diagonally from the upper right-hand corner of the square	

follows in Plan V the same surveying method employed in 1937, marking grid line intersections.[10]

The excavation in 1939 is the core of this chapter. While the division of the grid into squares is not mentioned in the text of the preliminary report (Woolley 1948), all plans are reworked to include square designations. In the case of Fig. 2 (Woolley 1948: 7; Plan 2 herein) Woolley had not thoroughly completed the transformation from the grid line labeling system to the square-based one.[11] The marker M14 is placed out of position in the square system, but in the right position in the grid line system. The letter M is located at the bottom right-hand corner of square M13, and the number 14 is located at the bottom left-hand corner of square L13. Nevertheless, they comply with their location in the grid line system: the letter M just left of grid line M and the number 14 right above grid line 14.

Seven years passed before Woolley could renew the excavation, but when it was resumed in 1946 no significant change of field practices was introduced. Finds were recorded using the grid line labeling system and published mostly with reference to the square-based system, with some confusing remnants of the field records. This is confirmed by the 1946 unpublished photo of the Level III[W] temple (Photo 1), which was discussed above, and by plans published by Woolley in the preliminary (1950) and final (1955) reports. Fig. 9 in Woolley 1950: 20 (reproduced in Woolley 1955: 32 as Fig. 17) follows the same recording method that was employed in 1937 and partly in 1938 and 1939 in which grid line intersection points are labeled.[12] The plan of the Level I[W] temple site, excavated in 1939, and published as Fig. 4 in the 1946 season preliminary

---

[10] Here again, Batiuk and Burke (2005: 148) had the impression that the grid was mislabeled.

[11] The same plan is reproduced as Fig. 66 in Woolley 1955: 190.

[12] The location of the letter-number label relative to the square associated with it is as follows: The letter appears just above the upper right-hand corner of the designated square, and the number—next to the letter, diagonally from the right upper-hand corner of the designated square. In this case, too, Batiuk and Burke (2005: 146) had the impression that the grid was mislabeled.

Direction (location of the square in relation to the grid line intersection point)	Year of excavation	Source
Southwest	1946	Unpublished photo (Photo 1)
Southwest	1946	Unpublished photo (Photo 1)
Southwest	1946	Unpublished photo (Photo 1)
Southwest	1938	Woolley 1955: Pl. XXXIb
Southwest	1938	Woolley 1955: Pl. XXVIa
Southwest	1937	Woolley 1938: Plans III, IV, V and XIII; Woolley 1955: Figs. 68, 65, 62, 60
Southwest	1938	Woolley 1939d: Plan V; Woolley 1955: Fig. 55
Southwest	1939	Woolley 1948: Fig. 2; Woolley 1955: Fig. 66
Southwest	1946	Woolley 1950: Fig. 9; Woolley 1955: Fig. 17
Southwest	1946	Woolley 1950: Fig. 4; Woolley 1955: Fig. 34a
Southwest	1946	Woolley 1950: Fig. 4; Woolley 1955: Fig. 34a
Southwest	1947	Woolley 1955: Figs. 10, 12, 14

report (Woolley 1950: 9; reproduced as Fig. 34a in Woolley 1955: 83; Plan 3 herein) is a crux of this chapter and will be discussed in greater detail below. This plan suffers from partial transformation from the grid line labeling system to the square-based system.[13] One of the grid line intersection points is still marked as L14—a relic of the original system. All letters were removed and placed halfway between the grid lines, properly marking the squares sides, but the numbers, also removed from the grid line intersection points, were misplaced—located immediately above their grid lines rather than beneath them. This observation is strengthened by the comparison between this figure and Woolley's Figs. 1 and 2 (Woolley 1950: 3–4), later reproduced as Figs. 31 and 32 (Woolley 1955: 74, 76).

Perhaps the best example for the transition from a grid line labeling system to a square-based system made by Woolley (1955) is three figures, clearly drawn by the same

architect in the 1947 season (ibid.: 22, Fig. 10; 24, Fig. 12; 27, Fig. 14; the last is Plan 4 herein). Here, the letter-label indicating the North–South grid line is found left of the line, while the number-label indicating the East–West grid line is above it. Woolley's interpretation of square designations appears on the same figures. These plans are the deciphering key for the rest of the Atchana plans made by Woolley's architects. Here, for the first time, both methods are clearly manifested, enabling us to reexamine the earlier plans. The pattern is clear and, therefore, allows precise integration between the two recording methods. This leads me to the next issue: the orientation of these grid and squares.

2.3 Grid deviations and magnetic declination

Sir Leonard Woolley at Tell Atchana and the University of Chicago excavators of nearby Tell Ta'yinat both refer to French cadastral maps in their publications. While the Syrio-Hittite Expedition of the Oriental Institute bases its

---

[13] This discrepancy was not identified by Yener, who misplaced this temple in her Atchana Level I^W plan (Yener 2005: 144).

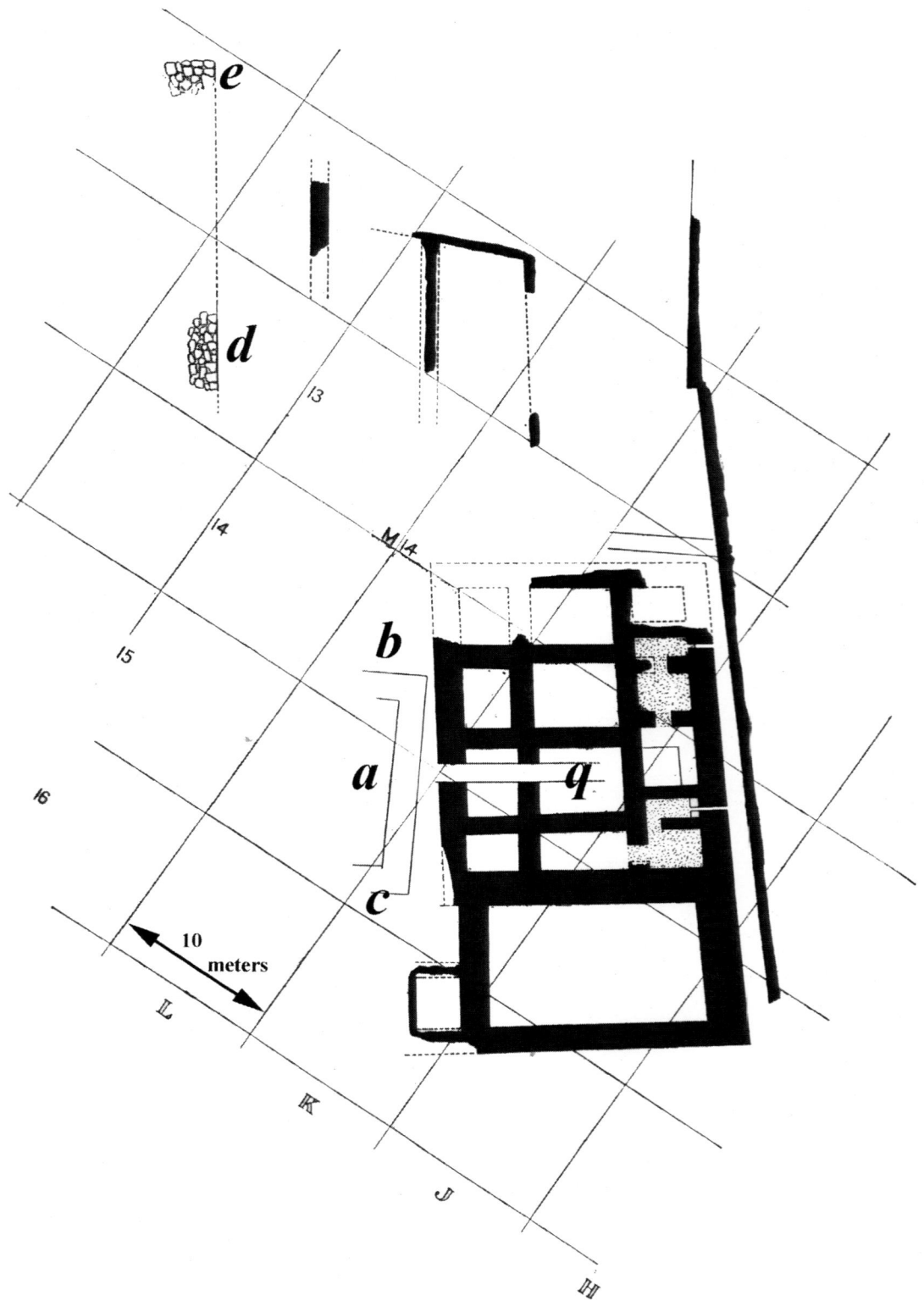

Plan 2. Level II^W house 39/C (after Woolley 1948: 6, Fig. 2)

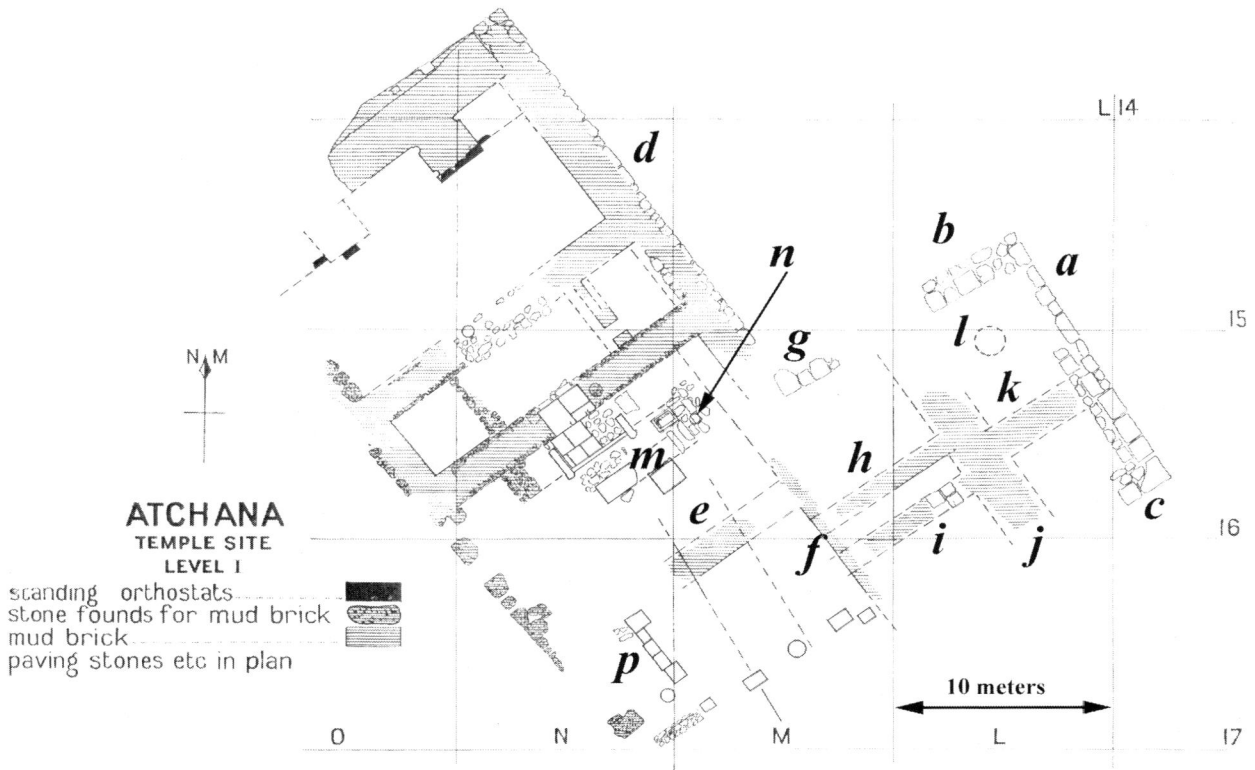

Above: **Plan 3. Detailed plan of the Level I^W temples (after Woolley 1955: 83, Fig. 34a)**

Below: **Plan 4. Level X^W of Woolley's Level VII^W palace sounding (after Woolley 1955: 27, Fig. 14)**

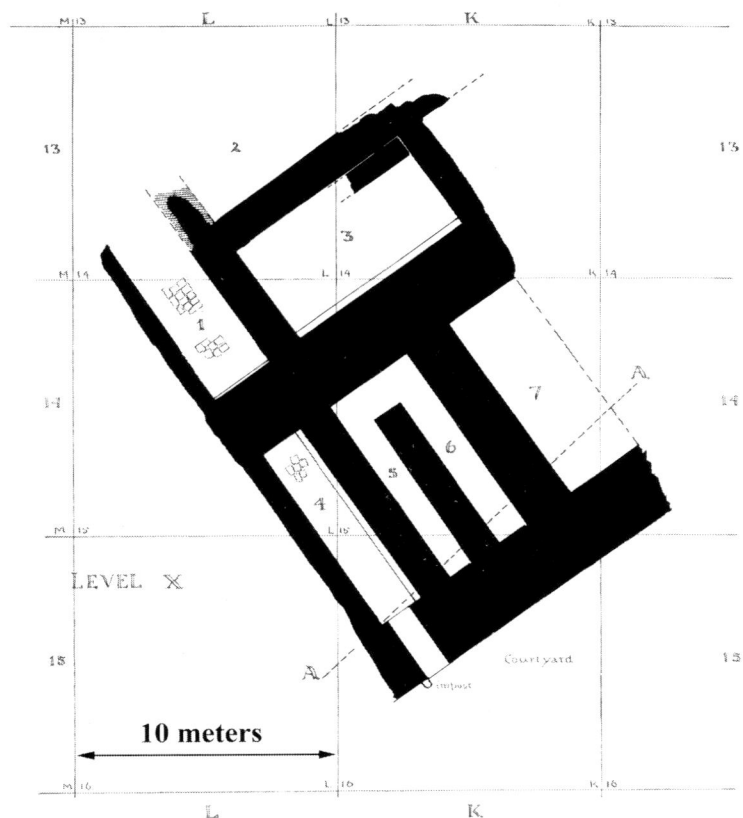

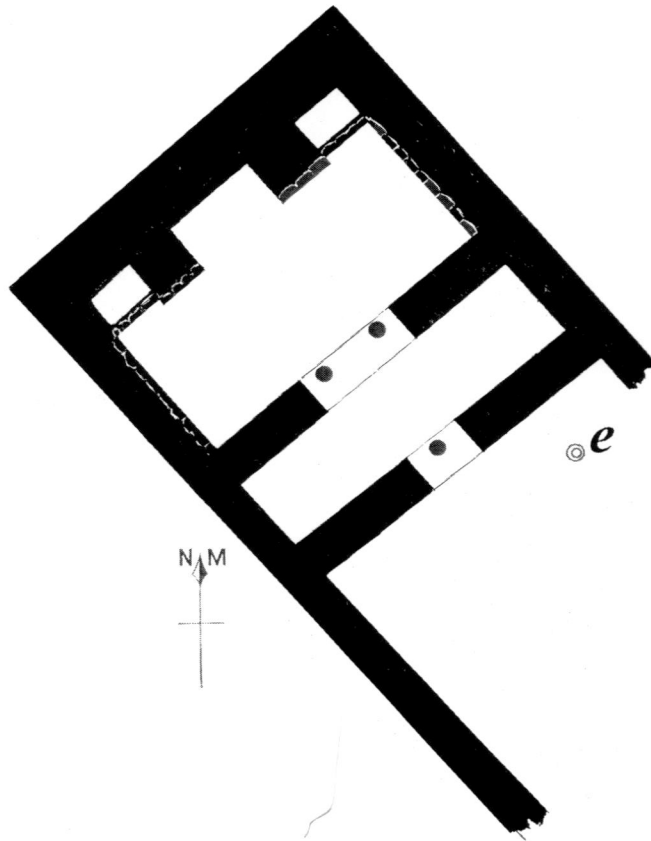

Above: **Plan 5. Reconstructed plan of Level IA^W temple (after Woolley 1955: 83, Fig. 34b)**

Below: **Plan 6. Reconstructed plan of the Level IB^W temple (after Woolley 1955: 83, Fig. 34c)**

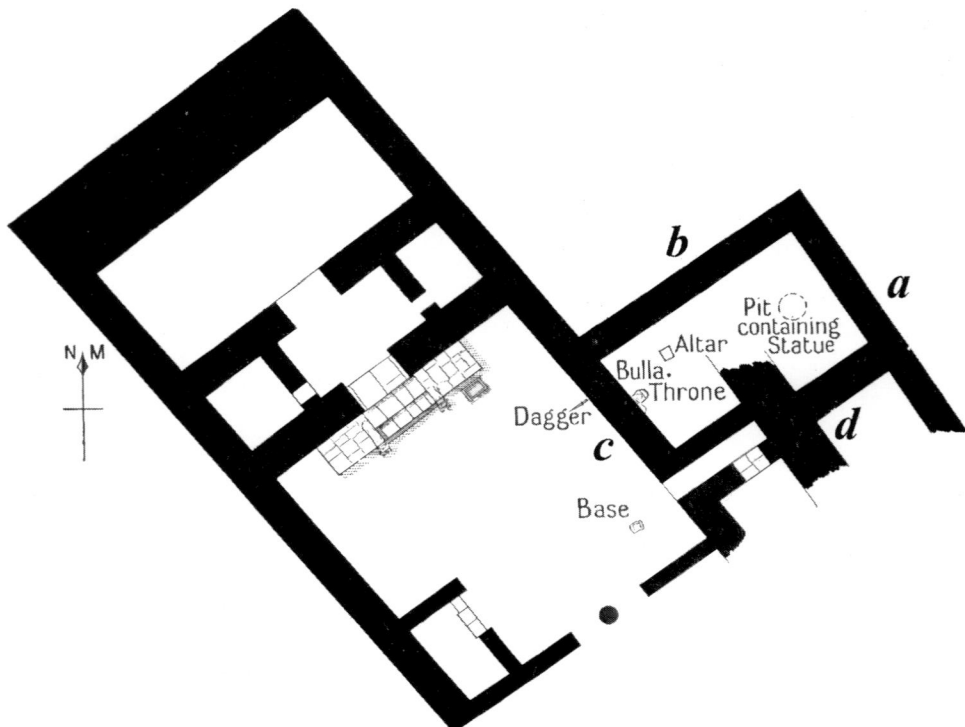

map on a 1925–1927 map (Haines 1971: 37),[14] Woolley relies loosely on the 1930 cadastral survey, but gives no precise reference to it (Woolley 1938: Pl. II). Moreover, a 5° deviation to the east of his grid from the French cadastral map clearly indicates that the two are not congruent.

On the plot plan of the Tell Ta'yinat excavations the magnetic declination, dated November 20, 1935, is marked as 2°2'0" E. This is a similar though not an identical magnetic declination to the one I calculated for Ta'yinat[15] for the same day at the American National Geophysical Data Center (NGDC) website: 2°10' E.[16]

Woolley made no reference to the magnetic declination on his plan (Woolley 1938: Pl. II). Nevertheless, he marked three of his plans from April 1937 as oriented to the magnetic north (Woolley 1955: 176, Fig. 62; 187, Fig. 65; 194, Fig. 68). The plans of the Level I[W] temple (Woolley 1955: 83, Fig. 34a–c; Plans 3, 5 and 6 respectively herein) are also marked as oriented to the magnetic north. They could have been drawn either in 1939 or in 1946.[17] According to the NGDC website, the magnetic declination for Tell Atchana[18] was 2°14' E in April 1937,[19] 2°20' E in summer 1939 and 2°36' E in summer 1946.[20]

Woolley's plans ostensibly show one grid, but, in fact, his findings are presented on three differently oriented grids with no indication given that they are not one and the same. In some publications the grids are oriented to true north (1955: 15, Fig. 5; 22, Fig. 10; Fig. 35; 113, Fig. 44; 115, Fig. 45; 140, Fig. 54a; 141, Fig. 54a–b; 146, Fig. 55; 152, Fig. 57; Fig. 59; 179, Fig. 63; 197, Fig. 69; Pl. XIV; Pl. XXII) and in others to magnetic north (see list above). Plans with no north arrow are probably oriented according to a third grid, published in 1938 (Woolley 1938: Pl. II).[21] A grid should be set

with unchanging X- and Y-axes. If indeed the Y-axis of Woolley's Atchana grid was oriented in two, three or four directions,[22] then Woolley had been utilizing a similar number of grids.[23] Nonetheless, I believe that the squares of these grids partly overlap: all grids must have shared a point on an intersection between an X-axis and a Y-axis; this point should be located within each of the four plans, which were oriented to magnetic north.[24] Therefore, when Woolley reports that a feature was found in a certain square it should be partly within or not more than a few meters away from the designated square for all grids.

The main problem remaining is the orientation of features and their precise location. This information is critical for an in-depth analysis of the different published and unpublished records. Moreover, neither square boundaries nor baulks are recorded in the entire corpus of published and unpublished field photos of Woolley's excavations. Noticeably, no section drawing of any of the baulks was reported or published, and all published sections are independent of Woolley's grid system, and are not even parallel to the X- or Y-axes (Yener 2005: 115, Fig. 4.2). The record keeping of the grid in the field was not lacking flaws, and one should not overrule the possibility that the grid was only poorly marked with a few unstable benchmarks, as described above.[25] Under these circumstances, it seems likely that the original grid was lost and a new grid was reestablished several times throughout the dig.[26]

---

[14] Haines's reference to the map is: Travaux du Cadastre et d'Amélioration Agricole des États de Syrie, du Liban, et des Alaouites, Sandjak Autonome d'Alexandrette, Plaine de l'Amouk (1925–27), Sheet 10, Scale 1:10000. I examined two maps of this survey (*Village de Arab-Khan* and *circonscription foncière de batraken tcherkess no. 54*), which are still in use in the *tapu* offices of the region. The first is on a scale of 1: 5000 (dated October 1929), and the other is on a scale of 1: 2000. Both are oriented to true north.

[15] assuming that Tell Ta'yinat is located at 36°15' N, 36°22' E.

[16] www.ngdc.noaa.gov/seg/geomag/jsp/struts/calcDeclination. I would like to thank Steve Batiuk for this reference.

[17] One of the plans was published before the others (Woolley 1949: 1). All three were published together a year later (Woolley 1950: 9–11), and they must have been drawn no earlier than 1939 and no later than 1946. The Level I[W] temples were excavated at the end of the 1939 season, and it is not clear that Woolley had the time to pencil them in that year. The next opportunity was in 1946. In that year the Levels II[W] and III[W] temples were excavated underneath the Level I[W] temples. Hence, the 1946 season was the latest in which the Level I[W] temples could have been measured. Batiuk and Burke (2005: 147) assume that these plans were created in 1946.

[18] with Tell Atchana located at 36°14' N, 36°24' E.

[19] Three plans drawn in April 1937 are oriented to magnetic north. See Woolley 1955: 176, Fig. 62; 187, Fig. 65; 194, Fig. 68.

[20] 1937 and 1939 or 1946 are the years in which Woolley published plans oriented to magnetic north (and not true north or grid north).

[21] Batiuk and Burke (2005: 145) believe that all references in Woolley's plans to true north are aimed to refer to grid north. Even if this were true, there still remained two different recorded orientations of the same grid.

[22] Magnetic north is not a stable orientation.

[23] Batiuk and Burke (2005: 148) draw our attention to an unexplained "deviation of about 6°" between two plans of the Level V[W] temple, both not marked with a north arrow. This deviation is very similar to the deviation between the grid north and the true north.

[24] What could have motivated Woolley's architects to orient their plans to magnetic north? In the case that all grid markers but one in a section of the excavation are lost it would be rather easy to create a grid based on this benchmark by orienting it to magnetic north. Traditionally archaeologists keep at least one benchmark that is more durable than the others. This benchmark would become the congruent point of the two grids.

[25] The legible benchmarks were described above. Other benchmarks (small metal or wooden signposts) can be observed in other published photos. Rarely would such a mark survive the winter. The one seen in Pl. IIb (Woolley 1955) is L–K–13–14. The one at the right-hand side of Pl. XVIIa marks the spot for N–M–8–9. In Pl. XXIVa two marks can be observed: R–Q–10–11 (right-hand side of the photo) and R–Q–9–10. R–Q–10–11 appears also in Pl. XXIVb. Marks appear also in Pls. XXIXa and XXIXb and in a few of the unpublished photos. In Pl. XXXIb five of the marks can be identified in addition to a long stick located on a similar narrow, conical, unexcavated patch of earth. This is probably Woolley's reference to elevation. While in some cases the grid is well marked, in others not a single mark can be observed. Clearly, Woolley had not removed these marks for the sake of photography, and I assume that if they are not in the photos, it is because they had fallen out in-between seasons.

[26] There are several possible explanations for the occurrence of inaccuracies in Woolley's work and reports:

1) The rapid pace at which the excavation was conducted, coupled with the fact that he had only a very small number of archaeologists supervising some 300 workmen (Woolley 1938: 1).

2) For most of his Atchana levels, Woolley did not prepare level plans, either during the field seasons or for the final report.

3) Seven years had elapsed (from 1939 to 1946) before Woolley could renew the excavation, unearthing the remains of the Level IB[W] temple and of its antecedents.

4) In some cases Woolley was required by law to backfill his trenches

In their study Batiuk and Burke claim that Woolley's grid "appears to have remained firmly in place throughout the excavations" (2005: 145). That is, despite the fact that the different plans of the grid are marked as if they were oriented in several different directions, they refer to them as if they all represent one grid that deviates from the French cadastral map by 5° to the east, as published by Woolley. Nonetheless, Batiuk and Burke refrain from orienting any of the maps they had prepared for Yener (2005) to the north, and recommend "[locating] prominent, surviving architectural features within the UTM coordinate system using GPS data."[27] Their suggestion would be workable only if they were correct in assuming that Woolley's grid remained unchanged between 1936 and 1949. By then Woolley had removed all architectural features recorded in the maps as oriented to magnetic north and it is, therefore, impossible to incorporate them into the UTM coordinate system.[28]

Batiuk and Burke observe the magnetic declination (2005: 145), and later disregard it. Buildings and walls that Woolley oriented to magnetic north appear in plans side by side with buildings and walls oriented to true or grid north, with no adjustment of the magnetic declination. One must remember, however, that doing so they followed Woolley, who uses both magnetic and true north grids interchangeably (compare grid in Plan 3, which is oriented to magnetic north, with Woolley 1955: 197, Fig. 69; Plan 7 herein, which is oriented to true or grid north).

Woolley published comprehensive plans only for Levels VII[W] (1955: Pl. XIV) and IV[W] (1955: Pl. XXII). Batiuk and Burke state that "these plans are drawn at so small a scale they are too schematic and therefore of limited use" (2005: 145). The orientation of the buildings in these plans is inconsistent with some of the building plans, including ones oriented to true north like the plans of Levels VII[W] and IV[W].[29] Therefore, the two level plans are inadequate for the study of the deviation of the orientation of the building plans and unreliable even in the case in which the orientation of the building plan is different from the orientation of the level plan.[30]

How can this be resolved? While it is possible that Woolley inadvertently marked a north arrow on some of the plans, despite their orientation with his published grid (Woolley 1938: Pl. II), it is less likely that he mistakenly marked magnetic north orientation. It seems highly unlikely that a plan be erroneously oriented to magnetic north, and more probable that this is a deliberate action. In order to harmonize the 1937 magnetic north plans with the grid we must first calculate the deviation of Woolley's grid from the magnetic north. Woolley's grid (ibid.) deviation of the French cadastral grid is 5° to the east; the magnetic declination for Tell Atchana in April 1937 was 2°14' E. Therefore, if accurate, the grid of the three plans (Woolley 1955: 176, Fig. 62; 187, Fig. 65; 194, Fig. 68) deviates by 2°46' west from Woolley's grid. The next step is to figure out the congruent point of the two grids. This is possible only if identical architectural features appear on both plans. A deviation of 2°46' between the grids can be considered minor only if the grids' congruent point is proximate to, or on the features, and if the features are relatively small.[31] The following discussion will be devoted to the magnetic deviation and the grid labeling of the plans of the Level I[W] temples.

---

in order to allow the cultivation of the site by the villagers (Woolley 1938: 2).

5) Woolley's architects and assistants were very often replaced (Winstone 1990: 203, 212, 248, 258), and not always given the chance to do their job. Sinclair Hood, who worked at Tell Atchana in 1948, told Winstone (1990: 256) that Woolley was determined "to work at the drawing board on his own plans and surveys, even when very capable architectural assistants were on hand. 'He was proud of his accuracy as a surveyor and planner,' Hood noted."

First were E. A. Lane, an assistant keeper at the Victoria and Albert Museum, A. E. F. Gott, Woolley's last architectural assistant in Ur, and Murray Thriepland. Ralph Lavers replaced Gott in 1938.

In 1939 "Colonel Burn of the India Army and the assistant Peter Olland took day-to-day charge while Woolley considered another task of topical importance" (Winstone 1990: 212). None of the pre-war assistants returned in 1946. After the war the assistants were William Brice, who later became an archaeology professor at Manchester University, Dr. Tahsin Özgüç of Ankara University and Dr. Bahadir Alkin of Istanbul University. A representative of the Turkish Office of Antiquities, Ahmet Donmez, was present at the dig, as required by the Turkish government. In 1948 Sinclair Hood replaced Brice as Woolley's main assistant, while Brice helped Woolley in preparing the Tell Atchana final report. All through these years Hamoudi and his sons, Yahia and Alawi, all from Jerablus, were the foremen and responsible for photography.

[27] Consequently, those plans published either by Yener or by Woolley that did not originally feature a north arrow, are reproduced in this monograph in similar fashion, that is, without a north arrow. I also omitted the north arrow in the new level plans, which were prepared for this book by Eudora Struble. Plans that are based on three different grids cannot be truly oriented to the north. The relative orientation of the different features in each of the new level plans is as accurate as possible, considering Wolley's modes of excavation.

[28] The Oriental Institute of the University of Chicago conducted full-scale excavations at Tell Atchana during 2003 and 2004. During the 2003 and 2004 seasons K. Aslihan Yener was the director of the Oriental Institute project, with the associate directorship of J. David Schloen and the senior field supervision of the author (Yener, Schloen and Fink 2004a, 2004b and 2005). The Oriental Institute has not conducted any fieldwork at Tell Atchana since the summer of 2004. The Oriental Institue activity at the site resulted with several published and unpublished studies, including works by Boutin (2008), Fink (2008a) and Lauinger (2008).

---

[29] Compare, for example, Woolley 1955: Fig. 35 and Pl. XIV.
[30] Nevertheless, the Level IV[W] house 37, which was published by Woolley (1955: 176, Fig. 62) with an orientation to the magnetic north, is a different case. When Woolley published the complete Level IV[W] plan, he corrected the plan of Level IV[W] house 37, tilting it several degrees to the east (ibid.: Pl. XXII). Yener, Batiuk and Burke published Woolley's Fig. 62 in their complete Level IV[W] plan (Yener 2005: 141, Fig. 4.30), ignoring his adjustment.
[31] The plans published in the preliminary report of 1937 (Woolley 1938), of which many were reproduced in the final publication (Woolley 1955), create a very confusing and incoherent group. Plan II sets the standard for conversion between true north and Woolley's grid (5° E). Surprisingly, Plans III, IV and V of the same report are neither oriented to grid north nor to true north, but rather to magnetic north. Was the grid in Plan II marked only when the season was over? Does this grid aim to represent magnetic north, and therefore agree with the plans of the same season, which are marked as oriented to magnetic north? The mystery is even more convoluted when we take into consideration the only additional plan of the 1937 season: Plan XIII. In this figure the north arrow deviates from the grid 2°15' to the east. This would have made some sense only if Woolley had referred to the grid as oriented to true north, and to the north arrow as oriented to magnetic north. In 1937 magnetic north at Atchana deviated from true north 2°14' to the east. Clearly, the 1937 plans require some further investigation.

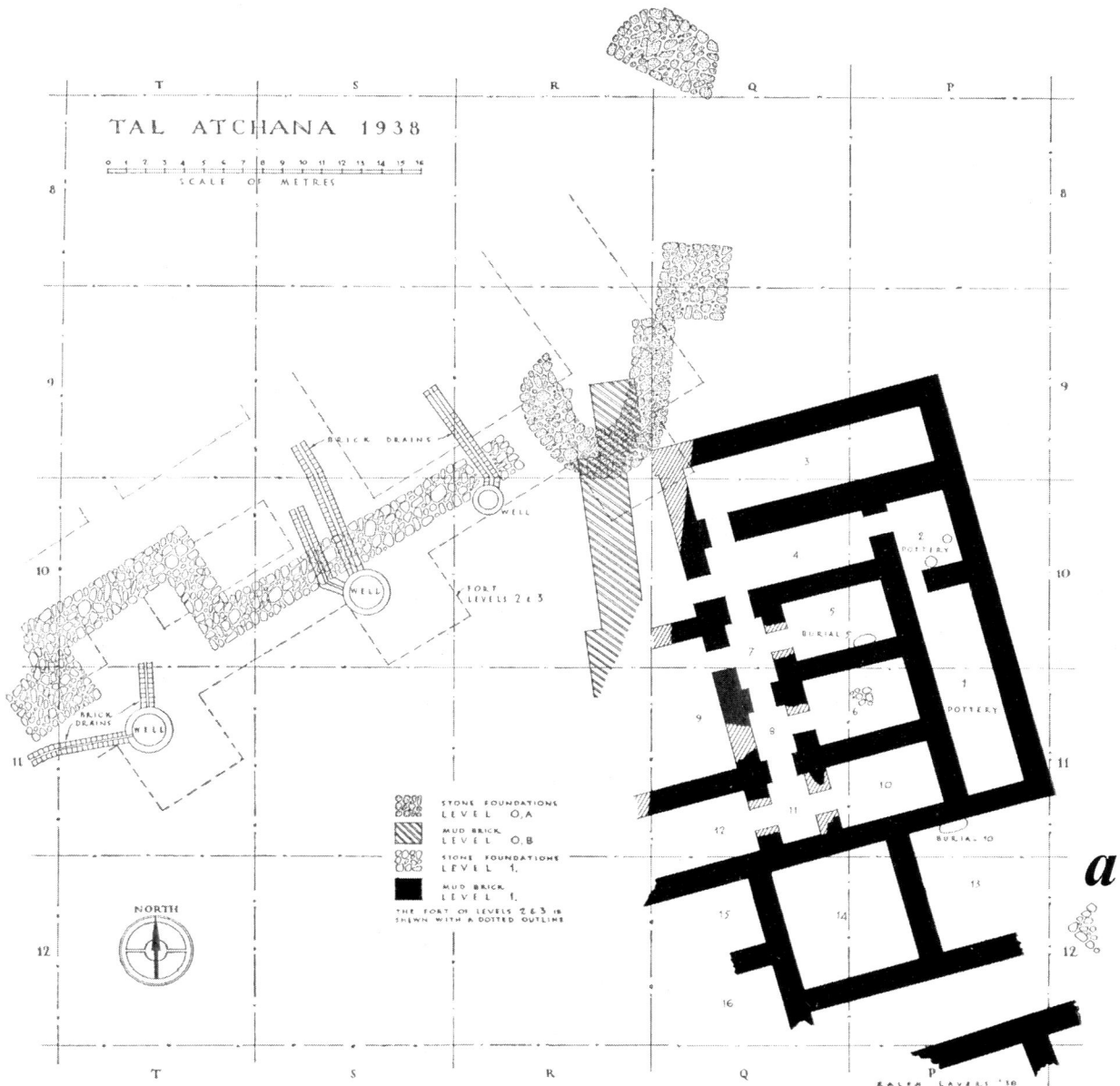

Plan 7. Level I^W house 38/B (after Woolley 1955: 197, Fig. 69)

In short, then, Woolley's recording system requires no small amount of unpacking in order to get at the substance of his reports. But what does this mean in practice for the modern scholar of Tell Atchana? Let us go back to Idrimi, whose discovery has for so long occasioned equal parts enthusiasm and consternation; he will serve as a concrete example of the issues at stake, before I attack my proposed solutions in Chapters 3, 4 and 5.

2.4 The find-spot of the statue of Idrimi

To the best of my knowledge, none of the previous evaluations of the later temples of Atchana (Levels IV–0^W) suggest that the statue of Idrimi was found elsewhere than the find-spot published by Woolley in his 1949 introduction to Smith's manuscript. Woolley's description of these temples and the correlation he offered between temple and phase were also well received.[32]

In his final note on the statue of Idrimi, Sir Leonard Woolley wrote the following about the statue's find-spot: "It was found in the ruins of the Level I temple and must have been preserved, and venerated, for over 200 years; this is remarkable, but it is an indisputable fact" (Woolley 1955: 393).[33]

---

[32] Naumann 1955: 400–404; Busink 1970: 509–510; Ussishkin 1970: 124–125; Wright 1971; Yadin 1972: 87–91; Matthiae 1975; Ottosson 1980: 34–36; Mayer-Opificius 1981: 285–287; Oesch 1996: 58–63; Bergoffen 2005: 14–16; Yener 2005: 114–118.

[33] It should be noted that Woolley, upon discovering the statue of Idrimi, even before reading the inscription, understood that it was not created in the time of the Level IB^W temple, although he originally thought that the statue was of a Hittite king (Woolley 1939a): "The discovery of this mass of Hittite sculpture was quite unexpected, if only for the reason that our latest level dates to about 1200 B.C., and few examples of Hittite stone carving have been assigned to so early date. But these are found reused in a temple of Level II, which must be of the thirteenth century,

Table 2. Woolley's evolving records concerning the find-spot of the statue of Idrimi

	Woolley 1939a	Woolley 1939b	Woolley 1939c	Woolley 1947: 60	
Where	The temple	Surface of grey mass stretching just inside stone wall of Level I^w temple	Inside the stone wall of the Level I^w temple	In the courtyard and in the eastern annexe of it	
Drawn plan	No	No	No	No	
The pit	A rubbish pit	A tilt in a hole	A pit sunk in the floor	Hole specially dug, as if for concealment	
Dug into		Surface of grey mass stretching just inside stone wall of Level I^w temple	Sunk in the floor		
In the pit		Crudely cut basalt column lying at a tilt. The column and a big building slab were removed only to expose another slab about 5 ft long … lifted in its turn…	Earth and large stones, all of them old building stones		
The statue of Idrimi AT/39/331	The head and feet were broken off but except for part of the foot the statue is complete… even the nose is only just chipped.	In the bottom of the hole was a statue of white limestone prone on its face, the head broken off and lying besides it.	At the bottom of the pit, lying on its face with the head broken off and lying by the body.	The inscribed limestone statue of a king, its head broken off but laid carefully by the side of the body.	
When		The end of the season	The end of the season		
Who		The workmen			
The throne AT/39/288	Found below the stairs of the temple	Found in the temple	Found in the long hall	Found in the courtyard and in the eastern annexe of it	

Woolley 1949: 2	Woolley 1950: 12	Woolley 1953: 160	Woolley 1955: 89
At the northeast end of the north room of the annexe to Level IB^W temple	Near the northeast wall of the annexe to Level IB^W temple	In one of the rooms of the Level IB^W temple	Inner (northern) room of the annexe to Level IB^W temple
Included	Included	Included	Included
A hole	A hole	A pit	A hole starting from Level IB^W
The floor of the room	The brick platform		The brick work of the platform from the floor-level of temple IB^W
It was filled earth and large stones (the largest weighed nearly a ton and a half).		The pit is sealed with great blocks of stone.	At the top disguised by bricks. Below the bricks were earth and stones, including two large orthostats and a basalt-footed column (1 by 0.43 m).
Underneath earth and large stones. The head was broken off and was set beside. The body, together with two smaller fragments, one of the beard, the other of a foot. Only part of one foot was missing.	Head and feet broken off but put into the hole with the body.	The fragments of the statue were found beneath the great blocks.	In the bottom of the pit. The fragments were carefully assembled.
Found close by in the north room of the annexe	Found in the eastern annexe	Found in the next room	Found in the small west room of the annexe

Table 3. The sequence of excavations at Tell Atchana 1936–1949

Year	Excavated features	Source
1936	Trenches A, E	Woolley 1938
1937	Trenches B, C, D and F Most of the residences of Levels I–IV^W Parts of the Levels III–II^W fort Parts of the Level IV^W palace	Woolley 1938
1938	Site H The rest of the Levels III–II^W fort The rest of the Level IV^W palace The Level IV^W fortress The Level VII^W gate	Woolley 1939d
1939	The Level VII^W palace Additional residences of Levels I–V^W The Level 0^W temple Parts of the Level I^W temples	Woolley 1948
1946	Parts of the Level I^W temples The Levels II–III^W temples The Levels V^W and VI^W residences Levels VIII–IX^W in the Level VII^W palace sounding	Woolley 1947; Woolley 1950; Stein 1997
1947	Levels X–XVI^W in the Level VII^W palace sounding Levels VIII–XVII^W in the temple sounding	Stein 1997
1948–9	Further explorations of the temple sounding and the fortifications of Levels I–VII^W	Stein 1997

This is the place to dispute the indisputable. Woolley includes details on the provenance of the statue of Idrimi in seven of his publications (1939b; 1939c; 1947: 60; 1949: 2; 1950: 12; 1953: 160; 1955: 89), as well as in his letter from the field (1939a). Table 2 is a summary of these written records—which also happens to illustrate the unreliable nature of Woolley's documentation.

Let us look more closely at Woolley's mode of excavation and narration in this case. The photos included in his excavation reports already suggest the rapid pace at which the excavation work was conducted, ignoring many of the basics of stratigraphic excavation. This is congruent with the working habits of many of Woolley's contemporary colleagues. The recording of objects and find-spots was partial, and the lion's share of the original records is now lost (Yener 2005: 103).

The temples of Levels 0^W and I^W of Alalakh were discovered in the spring of 1939, shortly before the season came to an abrupt end (Table 3). The spring harvest that year began earlier than expected (and was better than expected), forcing Woolley to cut the season short (Woolley 1939b), as labor force for his dig became scarce. He was in a rush to excavate as much as he could before the harvest began (ibid.). Tellingly, some of the important finds of the last days of this season were left unrecorded in 1939, and only much later on (probably in 1946) were they assigned AT/40–45 numbers (1950: 11). Woolley could not have known at the time (1939) that seven years would pass before he would be able to renew

the work at the temple site. By the time the excavation of the temples had resumed, a first mistake was clearly evident. A trench dug by Woolley penetrated the temples between walls *b* and *g* (Plan 3), cutting all the way down to the Level VII^W palace, just a few meters away from the reported find-spot of the statue of Idrimi (1955: 77, n. 2).[34]

Woolley describes the statue of Idrimi and its find-spot many times in writing; in this paper alone I have quoted eight of these descriptions (see Table 2). The fact that some of them are not in agreement with the others is probably the outcome of limited, missing or contradictory records. Only a detailed examination of the location, stratigraphy, architecture and date of the later temples, together with a close reading of Woolley's records, can lead to a well-founded re-evaluation of the find-spot of the statue. This demonstration requires several steps:

1) establishing the location of the Level IB^W temple in relation to other buildings at Tell Atchana, earlier, contemporary and later;
2) studying the architectural, stratigraphic and chronological data available on each of these buildings, and
3) determining the exact find-spot of the statue of Idrimi in view of the results of the first and second steps.

I devote the next chapter to the above.

---

and they have been taken from an earlier building of Level III or Level IV and might therefore go back even to the fifteenth century." (Woolley 1939b: 14).

[34] Woolley (1939a) writes the following: "Clearing from the surface for a probable extension of the palace we have lighted on a late temple…"

Chapter Three

The LBA Temples of Alalakh (Levels IV–0^W): Archaeology and History

3.1 The relative and absolute locations of the Level I^W temples

According to Woolley's published plan (Plan 3), the Level I^W temples (with sub-phases a, b and possibly c) were excavated in squares O14–16, N14–17, M15–17, L15–16 and J17. If this square designation is correct, then the temples of Level I^W in Alalakh were built ten meters south of the temples of Levels II^W, III^W and IV^W—built each atop the ruins of its predecessor (ibid.: 71–82). As demonstrated below, there are many indications that Woolley mislabelled the grid-line designations on the detailed plan of the Level I^W temples (Plan 3), and that the actual location of these temples should be shifted by a full square (ten meters) to the north.[1] Furthermore, the plan of the Level I^W temple is tilted to the west by several degrees—Plan 3 is one of the only plans in the report in which Woolley uses magnetic north instead of grid or true north. This inconsistent orientation of grids, discussed at length in Section 2.3, renders Woolley's grid system inaccurate.

There are several reasons for relocating the Level I^W temples a full square to the north of their location in Plan 3:

1) *Photo of temple thresholds* (Photo 2) In an unpublished photo from UCL Special Collections, looking southeast, two thresholds are seen: the threshold of the Level IB^W temple (marked here as A1–A3) and the threshold of the Level II^W temple (marked as B1–B4).[2] Compared with the detailed plan of the Level I^W temples (Plan 3) and that of the Levels V–II^W temples (Plan 1) it is evident that there is a discrepancy in the plans regarding the locations of these two thresholds, and that the stones of each of the thresholds in the photo are rotated 180°. This predicament is solved if we assume that the plan of the Level I^W temples

should, in fact, be shifted to the north by ten meters in reference to the grid. Superposing the shifted plan of the Level I^W temples over the plan of the Levels V–II^W temples (Plan 8), presents a picture that coincides with the photo. Plan 9 is a detail of Plan 8, presented right-side up in order to agree with the direction of the photo. The proximity of the thresholds, as one can clearly see in this photo, shows that the congruent point of the two grids of the Level I^W temples plan (oriented to magnetic north) and the Levels V–II^W temples plan (oriented either to grid north or to true north) is near or in the temples. The influence of the deviation of the north to our discussion is thus abated.

2) *The stumps* Woolley states that "by the time of the building of the Level I temple the ground all round the temple had risen considerably and the old podium had ceased to exist as such. The new construction was planned to be of the same size as the old, utilizing the stumps of the latter's walls as foundations" (ibid.: 82).[3] While the building does not follow the exact outlines of the previous podium (ibid.) it is obvious from Plan 3 that neither is it located ten meters to its south.

3) *Grid-lines vs. squares* In Plan 3 the same grid-line-based system was employed as was initially in Plan 4 (see Section 2.2). In the northeastern corner of the grids of Plan 3, Woolley did not relocate the grid-mark L14 and rather left it as it had originally been drawn by the architect. This grid-mark is one indication that this plan follows the grid-line labeling system and that Woolley misinterpreted it.

4) *Recurrences of the same walls in different plans I* Walls *a* and *b*[4] in square L15 on Plan 3 are most probably walls *a* and *b* in square L14 in Woolley 1955: 74, Fig. 31 (Plan 1);[5] walls *a*, *b* and *c* in squares L15–16, K16 in Plan 3 are most probably walls *a*, *b* and *c* in squares L14–15, K15 in Woolley 1955: 190, Fig. 66

---

[1] In Section 2.2, as well, I expressed my doubts concerning the accuracy of the location of the numbers on this plan.

[2] The original glass negative is at the archive of Sir Leonard Woolley, The Special Collections of University College London. I would like to thank the director of the UCL Institute of Archaeology for granting me the permission to publish this photo.

[3] Similar descriptions were published by Woolley elsewhere (1947: 60; 1950: 9; 1953: 158).

[4] Woolley did not number the walls; therefore, all wall letters are mine.

[5] For a summary of the recurrences of the same walls in different plans see Table 4.

Table 4. The square location of identical walls in different plans

Plan	Squares	Wall
1	L14	*a, b*
3	L15	*a, b*

Plan	Squares	Wall
2	L14–15, K15	*a, b, c*
3	L15–16, K16	*a, b, c*
10	L14–15, K15	*a, b, c*

Plan	Squares	Wall
2	L14	*a*
10	L14	*a*
12	Level I^W wall	

Plan	Squares	Wall
2	N13	*d*
3	N14	*d*
10	N13	*d*

Plan	Squares	Wall
1	M15–16	*d*
3	N17, M16–17	*e*
14	N16, M15–16	*a*

Plan	Squares	Wall
3	M16–17	*f*
14	M15–16	*b*

Plan	Squares	Wall
1	M14–15, L14	gap *e*
3	M15–16, L15	*b, g*

(Plan 10) and in Woolley 1948: 6, Fig. 2 (Plan 2).[6] Yener (2005: 144, Fig. 4.33; Plan 11 herein) shows walls *a*, *b* and *c* of Plan 3 side by side with walls *a*, *b* and *c* of Plan 10. Viewing this Plan, it is apparent that the walls, located ten meters away from one another on paper, are one wall in reality. If this were not the case they could not have functioned together in the same level. Moreover, the overwhelming resemblance in their level of preservation and in their orientation leaves little room for doubt that the walls on the two plans are, in fact, the same. Wall *a* in square L14 (Plans 2, 10 and I argue also in Plan 3) must be the Level I^W wall in square L15 represented in Woolley's Level VII^W deep sounding section (1955: 11, Fig. 2;

Plan 12 herein).

5) *Recurrences of the same walls in different plans II* Wall *d* in square N15 on Plan 3 is most probably wall *d* in square N13 on Plans 2 and 10, and wall *a* in Plan 13 (herein; ibid.: 138, Fig. 53). Plans 2 and 10 are in harmony with other plans in respect to the location of wall slab *e*, which, Woolley assumed, was connected with wall *d*. This wall *e* in square O12 in Plans 2 and 10 corresponds with wall *a* in Plan 7, wall *c* in Plan 1, and wall *b* in Plan 13.

6) *Recurrences of the same walls in different plans III* Wall *e* in squares M16–17 and N17 on Plan 3 is most probably wall *d* in squares M15–16 on Plan 1 and wall *a* in ibid.: 79, Fig. 33 (Plan 14 herein). Plan 14 is the reconstruction of the Level II^W temple, and it is to this level that Woolley chose

---

[6] Wall *q* in Plan 2 is not connected to wall *a*, while in Plan 10 they are connected.

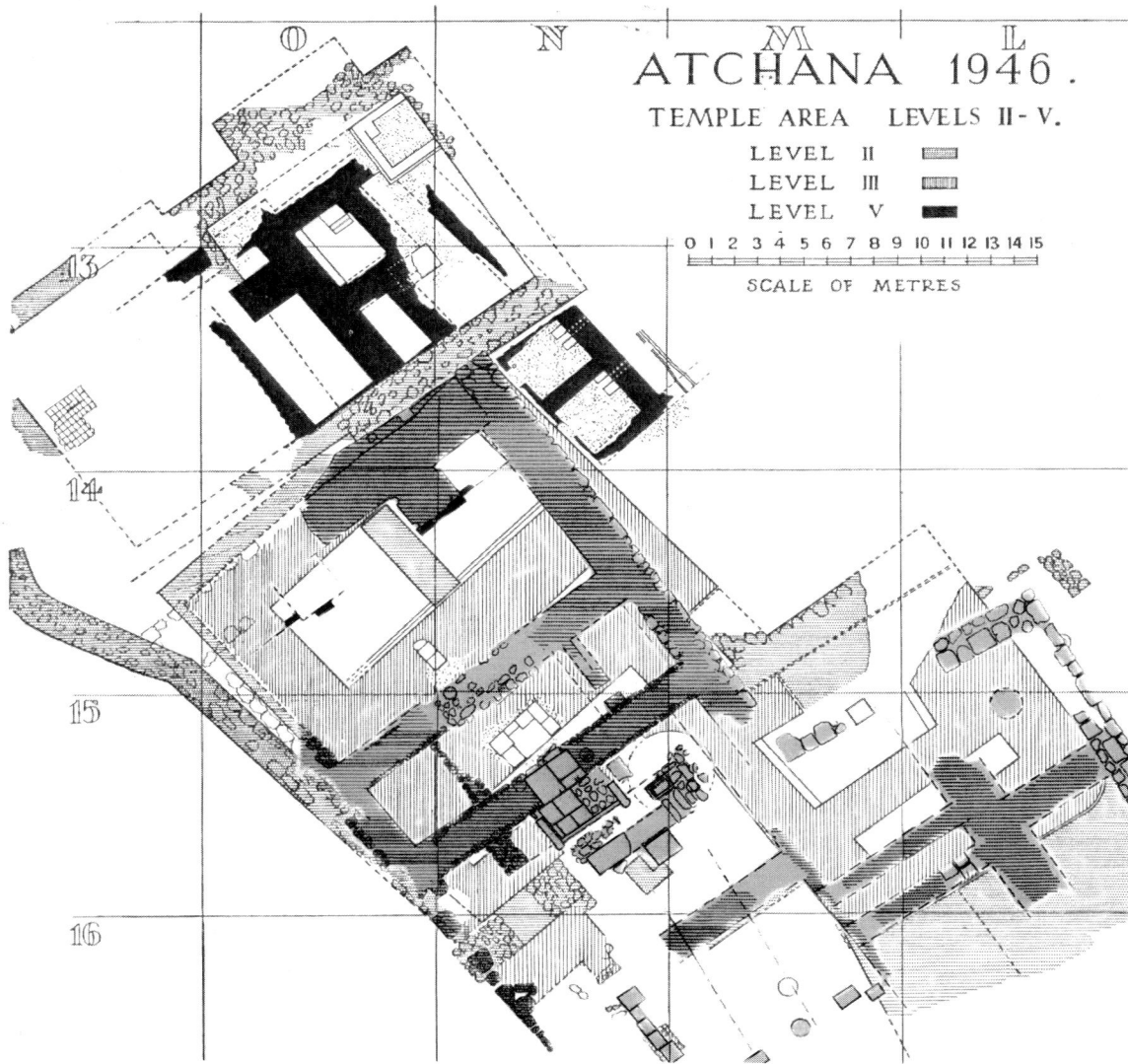

Plan 8. The Levels V–I[W] temples: superposition

to ascribe this wall and not to the reconstruction of the Level IB[W] temple (Plan 6) or to the reconstruction of the Level IA[W] temple (Plan 5). Wall *f* in squares M16–17 in Plan 3 is most probably wall *b* in squares M15–16 in Plan 14.

7) *Recurrences of the same gaps in different plans* The gap between walls *g* and *b* in squares M15–16 and L15 in Plan 3 is identical to *e*, the gap in squares M14–15 and L14 in Plan 1. Woolley himself confirmed that "the whole of the north corner of the building had been destroyed in part at least by us when following the wall of the Yarim-Lim palace before the discovery of the temple" (1955: 77, n. 2).

My proposal to place the Level I[W] temples ten meters to the north can be demonstrated in the following plans,[7] presenting superposed pairs of Woolley's plans:[8]

a) Plan 8 shows the location of the Level I[W] temples (Plan 3) with respect to the Levels V–II[W] temples (Plan 1). It demonstrates how the walls of the Level I[W] temples follow the general outlines of the walls of those of Levels IV–II[W].

b) The relative locations of the temples are clearer when viewed in pairs. Plan 15 shows the location of the Level I[W] temples (Plan 3) with respect to Woolley's reconstruction of the Level II[W] temple (Plan 14).

c) Plan 16 shows the location of the Level I[W] temples (Plan 3) with respect to Woolley's reconstruction of the Level III[W] temple (1955: 76, Fig. 32; Plan 17 herein).

d) Plan 18 shows the location of the Level I[W] temples (Plan 3) with respect to Woolley's reconstruction of the Level IV[W] temple (1955: 72, Fig. 30; Plan 19 herein).

e) Plan 20 shows the location of the Level I[W] temples (Plan 3) with respect to Woolley's reconstruction

---

[7] All plans were prepared by Eudora J. Struble.

[8] I ignore the magnetic declination on purpose. The congruent point of the two grids is unknown and, therefore, it is impossible to tell how significant the difference is. Nevertheless, Photo 2, which was discussed earlier, proves that this congruent point was either in the temples or in

proximity to them, and since the deviation is of less than 3° the squares should almost overlap. Additionally, I do not adjust the orientation of Level I[W] temples in Plans 8, 15, 16, 18, 20 and 22 to true north.

Above: **Photo 2. The Levels II^W and I^W temples doorways in one view (unpublished photo at UCL Special Collections)**

Below: **Plan 9. The doorways of Levels II–I^W temples. Detail of Plan 8**

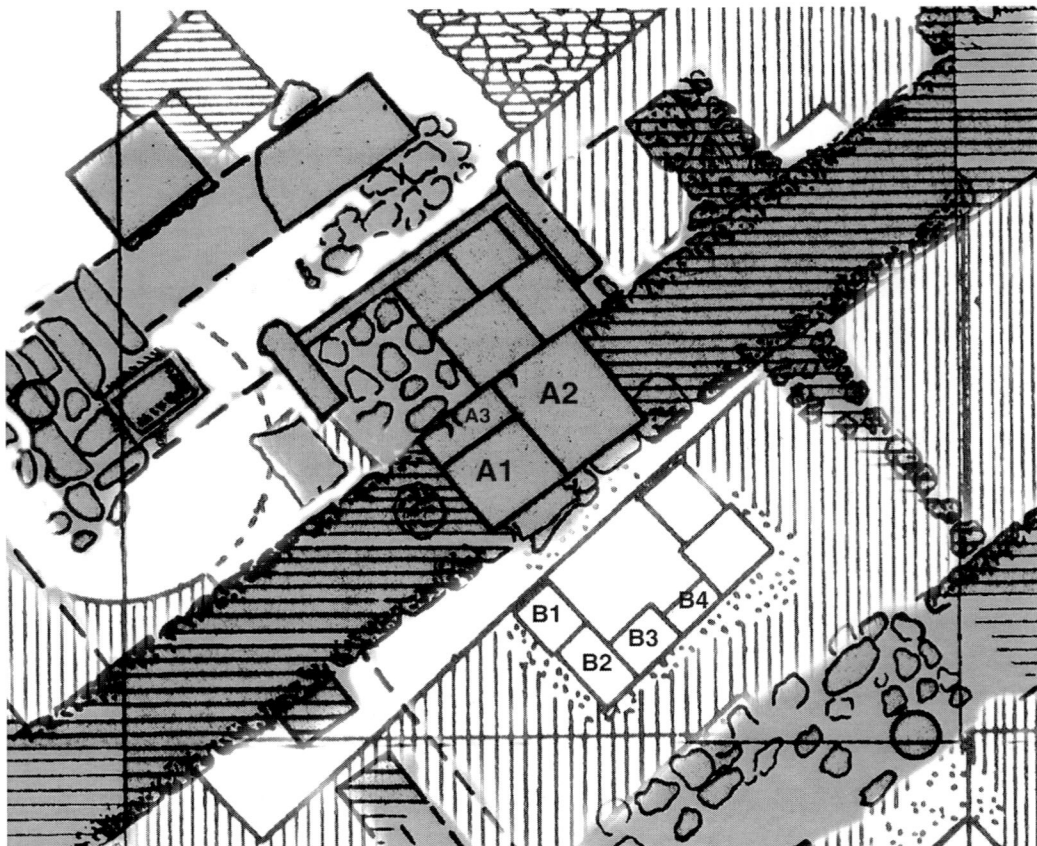

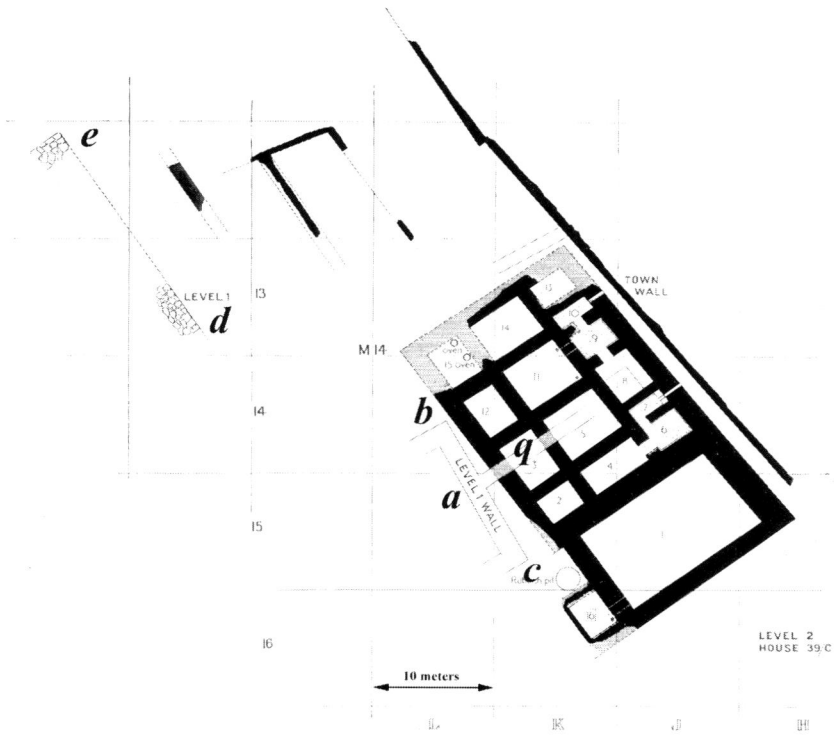

Above: **Plan 10. Level IIᵂ house 39/C (after Woolley 1955: 190, Fig. 66)**

Below: **Plan 11. Plan of Level Iᵂ (after Yener 2005: 152, Fig. 4.33)**

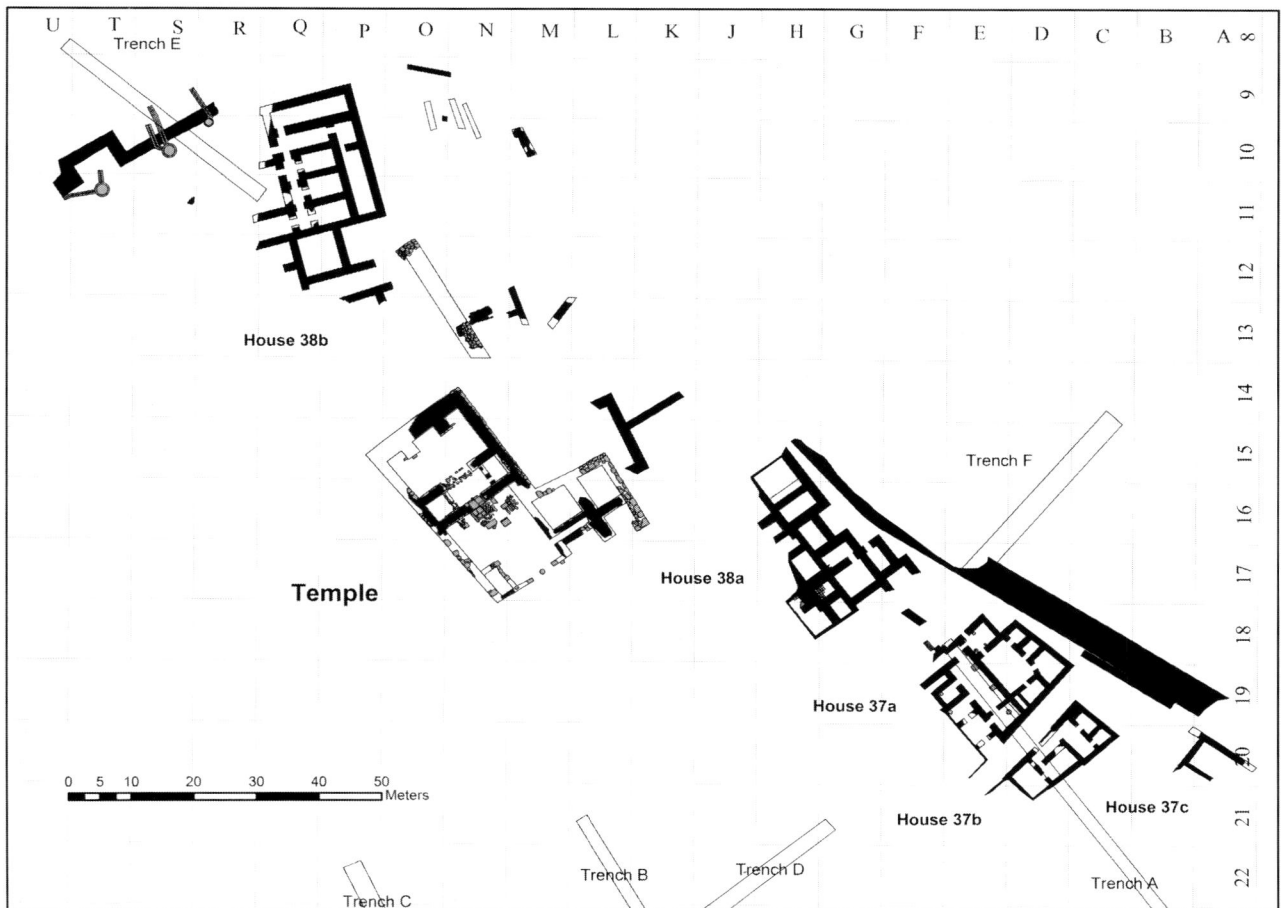

35

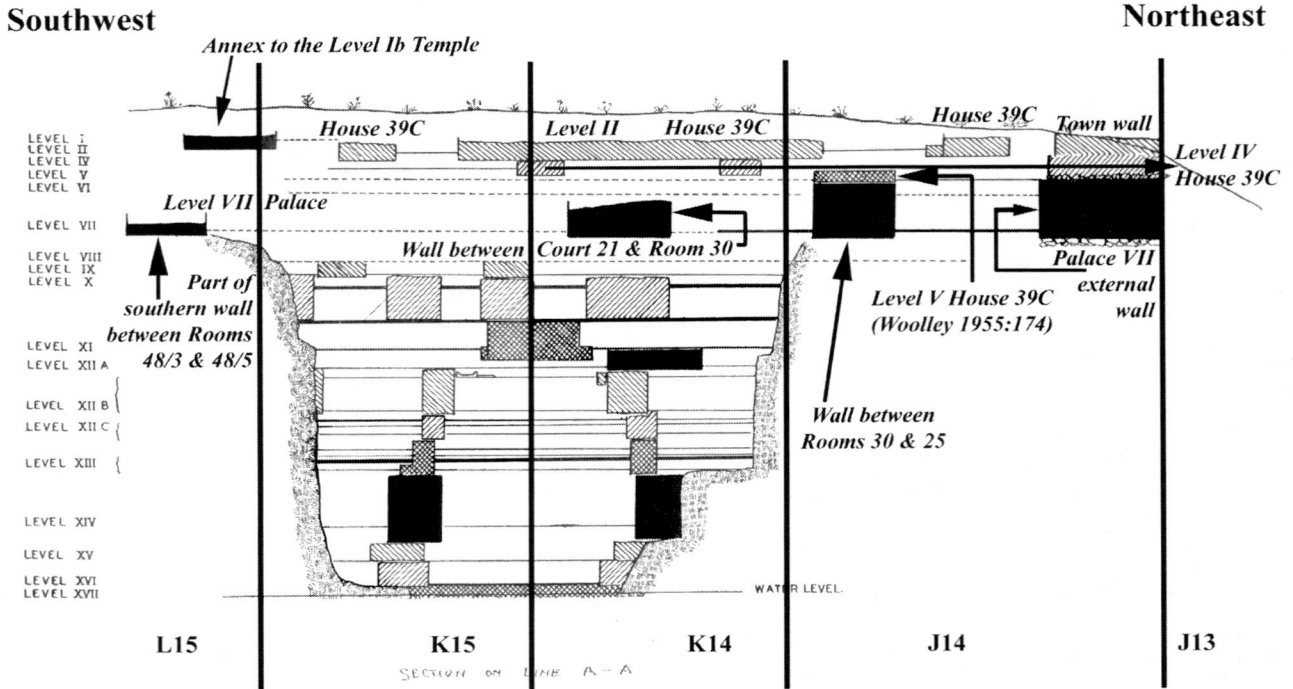

Above: **Plan 12. Section A–A of the Level VII^W palace sounding (after Woolley 1955: 11, Fig. 2)**

Below: **Plan 13. Levels V–I^W buildings north and east of the temples (after Woolley 1955: 138, Fig. 53)**

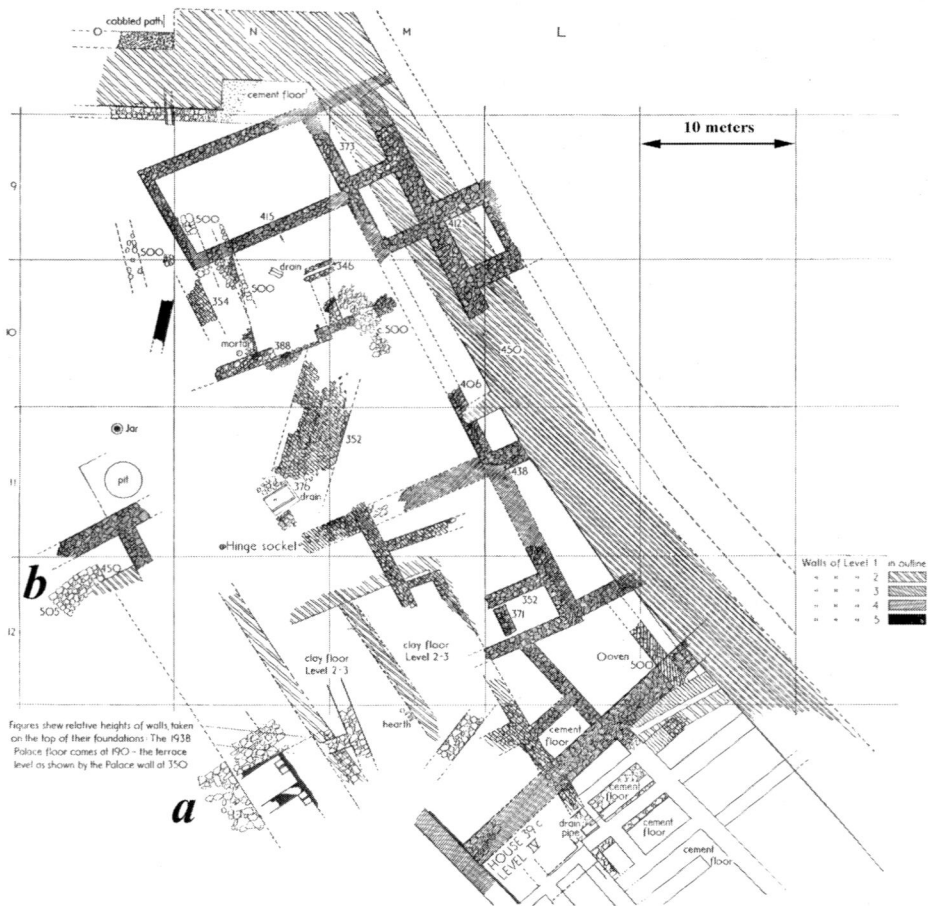

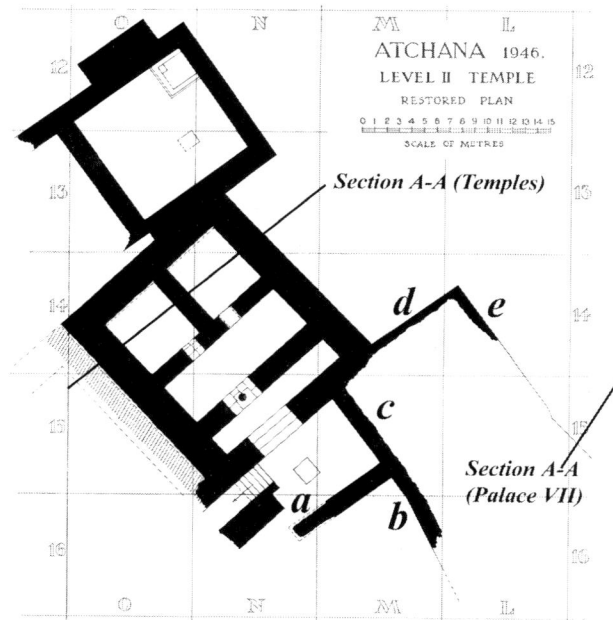

Above: **Plan 14. Reconstructed plan of the Level II^W temple (after Woolley 1955: 79, Fig. 33)**

Below: **Plan 15. Superposition of the Level IB^W temple on the Level II^W temple**

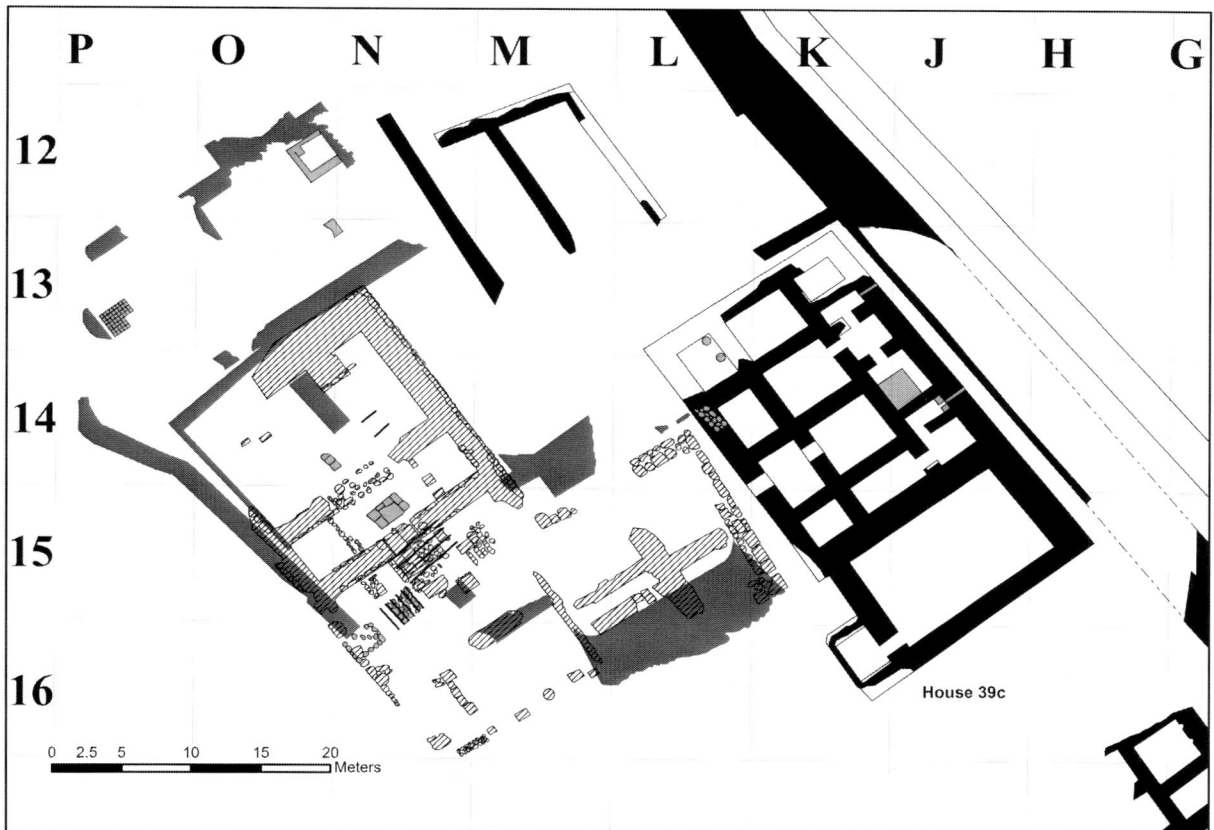

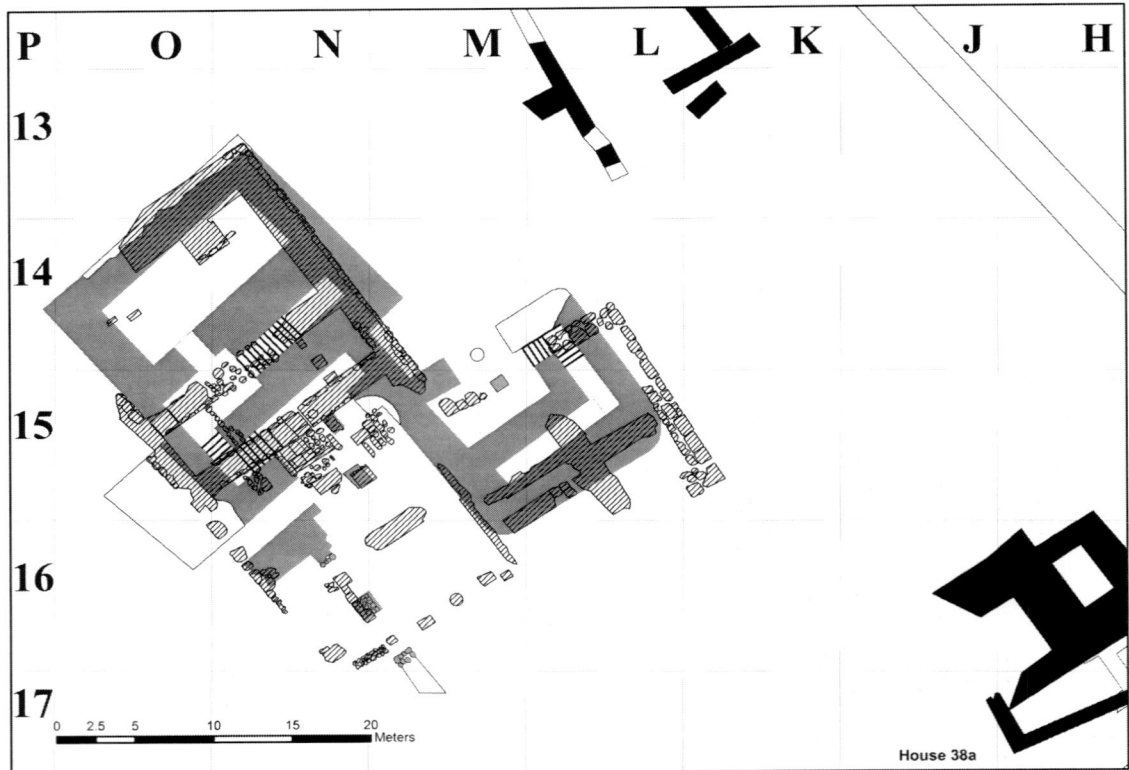

Level Ib temple

Level III temple

Other Level III buildings

Above: **Plan 16. Superposition of the Level IB[W] temple on the Level III[W] temple**

Below: **Plan 17. Reconstructed plan of the Level III[W] temple (after Woolley 1955: 76, Fig. 32)**

Level Ib temple

Level IV temple

Other Level IV buildings

Above: **Plan 18. Superposition of the Level IB[W] temple on the Level IV[W] temple**

Below: **Plan 19. Reconstructed plan of the Level IV[W] temple (after Woolley 1955: 72, Fig. 30)**

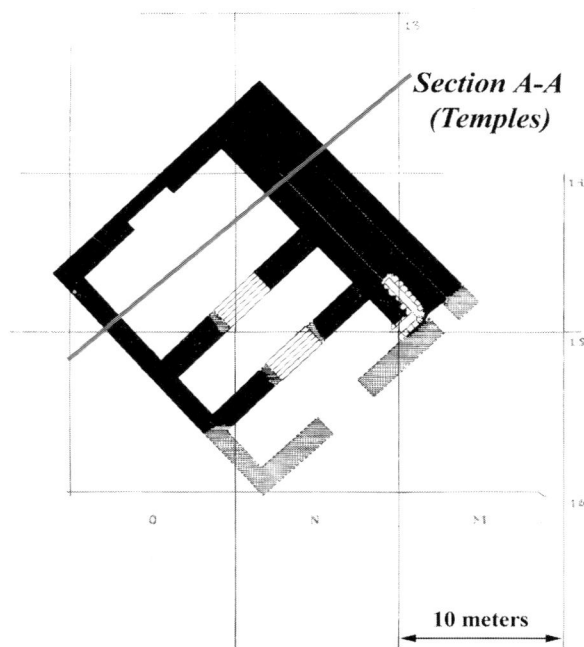

Section A-A
(Temples)

10 meters

of the Level V[W] temple (1955: 67, Fig. 29a; Plan 21 herein).

f) In Plan 22 a correction is suggested of the temple area in Plan 11, presenting the absolute location of the Level IB[W] temple.

Following these observations, there can be little doubt as to the relative location of the Level I[W] temples: they were erected on top of the Level II[W] temple, as Woolley stated in his text (ibid.: 88), but unlike his plan of the Level I[W] temples (Plan 3 herein). Consequently, their absolute location is also confirmed: they were located in squares P14, O13–16, N13–16, M14–16, L14–15 and K15.

3.2 The annexes to the Levels IV–0[W] temples and the Paluwa Shrine

The latest temples of Alalakh (Levels IV–0[W]) deserve an in-depth analysis. In what follows, I propose an alternative reading of some of Woolley's architectural plans and narratives describing these temples:

Deciphering the complex stratigraphy of the temple sounding at Tell Atchana remains one of the greatest challenges the site sets for its investigators. In this area, vestiges of temples and their podia were discovered, ranging from Level XVI[W] to Level 0[W]. Throughout the years the location of the temple podia gradually shifted southwest; thus, the distance between the early podia and the later ones is 20–30 m.[9] When the temple is located on a platform (as most of the LBA temples are), its seclusion from architectural surroundings increases the challenge of attributing it to the correct level, especially considering Woolley's sequence of excavation (Table 3). In 1936 Woolley opened Trenches A and E;[10] Trenches B, C, D and F were excavated in the following year, as were most of the residences of Levels IV–I[W] and parts of the Levels III–II[W] fort and the Level IV[W] palace (Woolley 1938). During the 1938 season work commenced at Site H and continued in the Levels III–II[W] fort, the Level IV[W] palace and fortress and the Level VII[W] gate (Woolley 1939d). The Level VII[W] palace, as well as additional residences of Levels V–I[W] and parts of the Level IB[W] temple, was excavated during the 1939 season (Woolley 1948). Work on the latter resumed only in 1946 (Woolley 1950). When Woolley began unearthing the temples in 1939, the excavated area around them was at least as deep as Level IV[W], and in some places even as deep as Level VII[W]. Hence, no physical evidence was available, upon which Woolley could base a stratigraphic attribution of the temples to the existing level numbers. I am unsure to what extent Woolley's record of elevation was critical in determining the precise correlation between temples and levels,[11] but even if we were to assume that

previously recorded elevations were available, the position of some of the temples on podia, and the construction of others as underground temples (Woolley 1955: 66) would have rendered absolute elevations useless for establishing correlation between temples and level numbers. Therefore, Woolley must have relied on the following parameters when assigning level numbers to the temples:

1) the position of the temple in the temple sequence;
2) the finds in each temple;
3) the different styles of architecture;
4) the reconstruction of historical events and the reflection of these events on the state of the temple.

Correlating between temples and levels becomes particularly complex when one wishes to study the southeastern annexes (sometimes referred to by Woolley as 'Shrine B') in Levels III–I[W] (ibid.: 73–89). These annexes were not built on the platform of the central shrines, and the elevations of their floors probably differed from that of the temple. Their state of preservation was different from that of the central shrines, and a physical connection to these shrines was fragmentary or nonexistent. Woolley's correlation between an annexe and a central shrine is sometimes as unsound as his correlation between temples and levels.

The annexe to the Level IV[W] temple

Woolley convincingly correlates the best-preserved annexe with the Level III[W] central shrine (Woolley 1955: 76–78). He considers this 'Shrine B' to be an innovation, which was introduced to Alalakh by the Hittites at the time of Šuppiluliuma I (Woolley 1953: 137). I propose that an annexe was already part of the Level IV[W] temple. The central shrine of the Level IV[W] temple was later used as the foundation of a podium, on which the Levels III[W], II[W], IA[W], IB[W] and possibly 0[W] temples were built, following nearly the same outline as the Level IV[W] temple.[12] Woolley misinterpreted the annexe to the Level IV[W] temple, excavating and publishing it as part of the residences of Level VI[W] (1955: 173, Fig. 61; Plan 24 herein). Merging the poorly preserved wall foundations *a*, *b*, *c* and *d* (Plan 24) with the Level IV[W] reconstruction (Plan 19), the outcome (Plan 25) would be a small, irregular annexe to the temple, probably not a part of its original blueprint.[13] Shifting walls from Level VI[W] to IV[W] is not a bold step in light of Plan 23, the section of the nearby temple podium. It shows that the foundations of Level IV[W] in the southwest are deeper than the remains of Level V[W], and as deep as the foundations of Level VI[W] in the northeast. In the northeast, a Level IV[W] wall is located directly on top of the Level VI[W] wall. Following the plan of the Level V[W] temple, where Woolley found toilets or bathrooms (1955: 69), he suggests that the Level IV[W] temple complex included rooms of the same function in square L16, even farther south of the

---

[9] This shift was accompanied by a faster, more dramatic shift of the palaces to the west. See Oren (1992: 106).

[10] See the summary plan published by Yener (2005: 115).

[11] Only on one of the figures did Woolley publish some relative elevations (Plan 13). Relative elevations can also be extracted from Woolley's (1955) Fig. 29b (Plan 23 herein). In the text Woolley often refers to the relative elevation of buildings.

[12] The preservation of the Level IV[W] temple was so poor that in one of the preliminary reports Woolley suggested that in the given location there was no temple in this level at all (1950: 2).

[13] Was this annexe built after the destruction of the Level IV[W] palace and before the remainder of Level IV[W] was ruined? I believe that the new dating of the Level III[W] temple (see below) rules out this possibility.

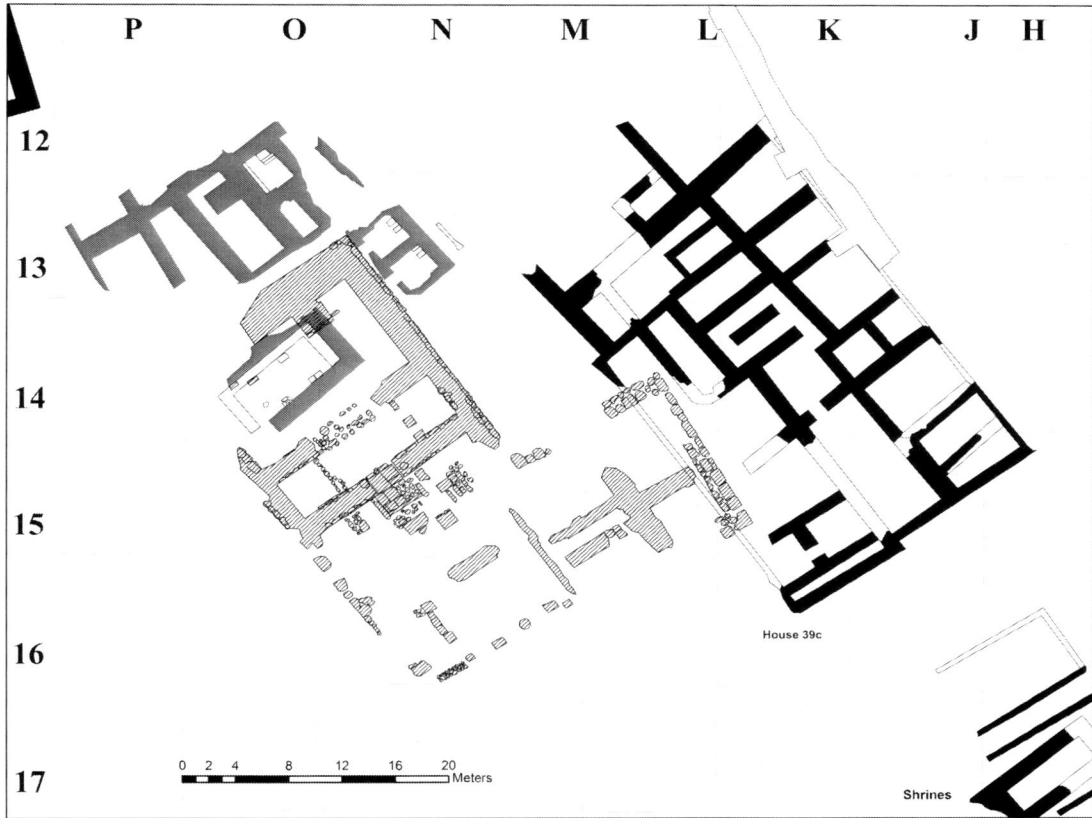

Level Ib temple

Level V temple

Other Level V buildings

Above: **Plan 20. Superposition of the Level IB^W temple on the Level V^W temple**

Below: **Plan 21. Reconstructed plan of the Level V^W temple (after Woolley 1955: 67, Fig. 29a)**

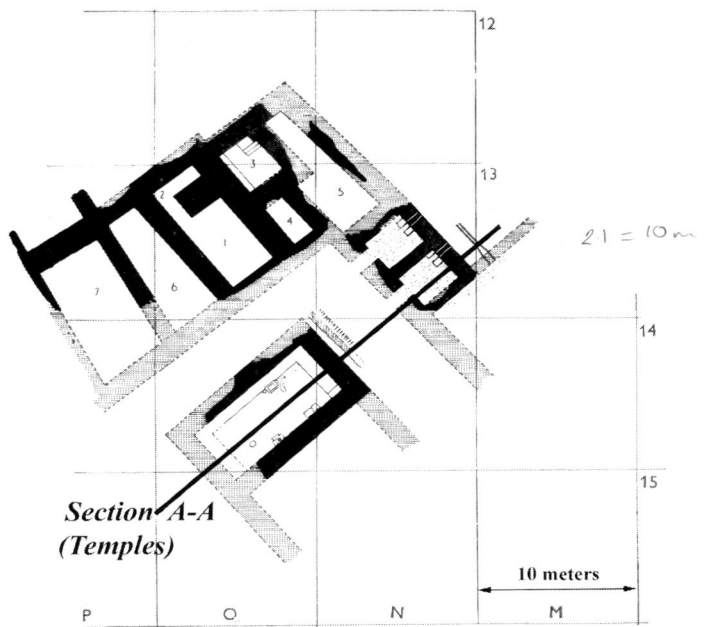

Section A-A
(Temples)

10 meters

41

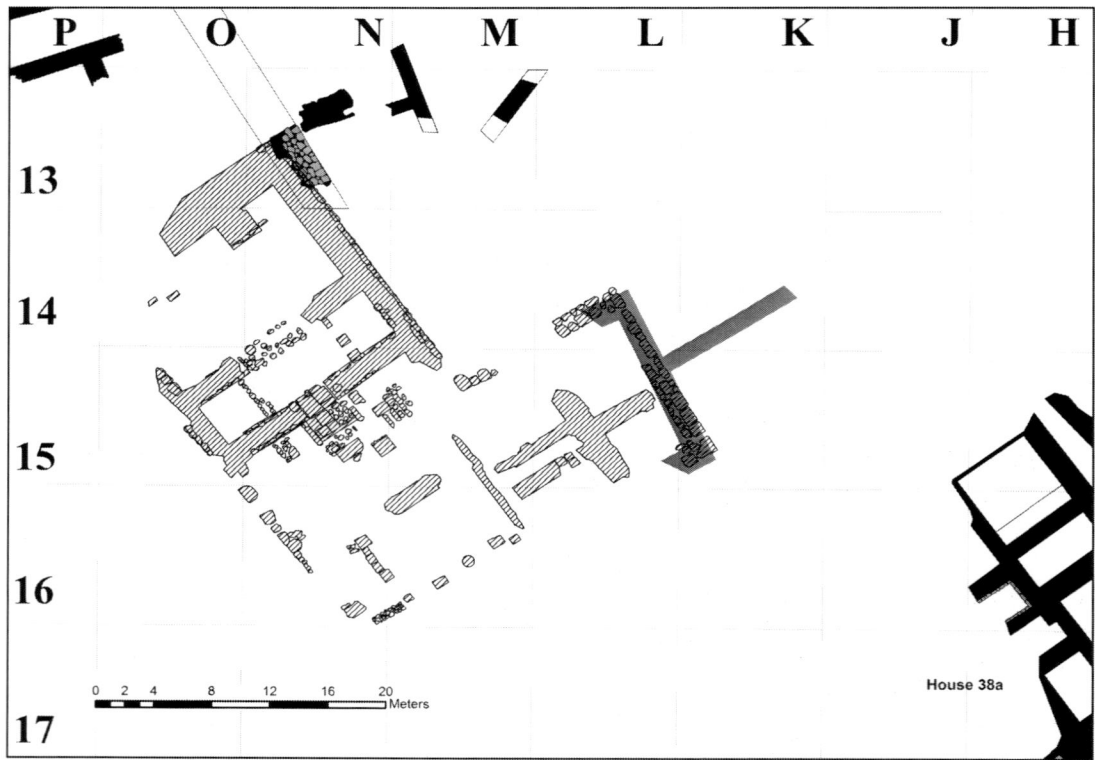

Level Ib temple from Plan 2

Level Ib temple from Plan 5

Other Level I walls

Above: **Plan 22. A proposed plan for Level I^W (revisiting Yener 2005: 152, Fig. 4.33)**

Below: **Plan 23. Section A–A of the temple sounding (after Woolley 1955: 67, Fig. 29b)**

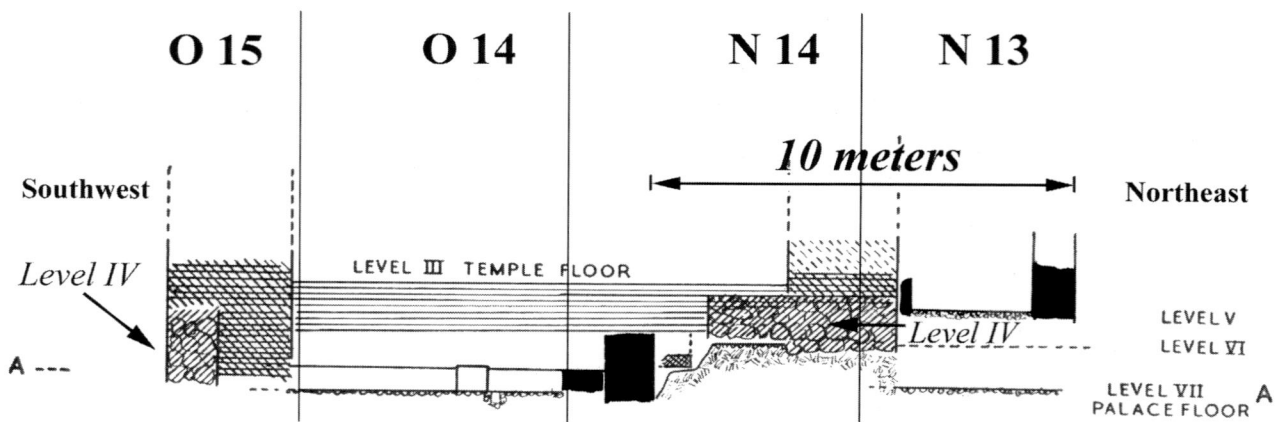

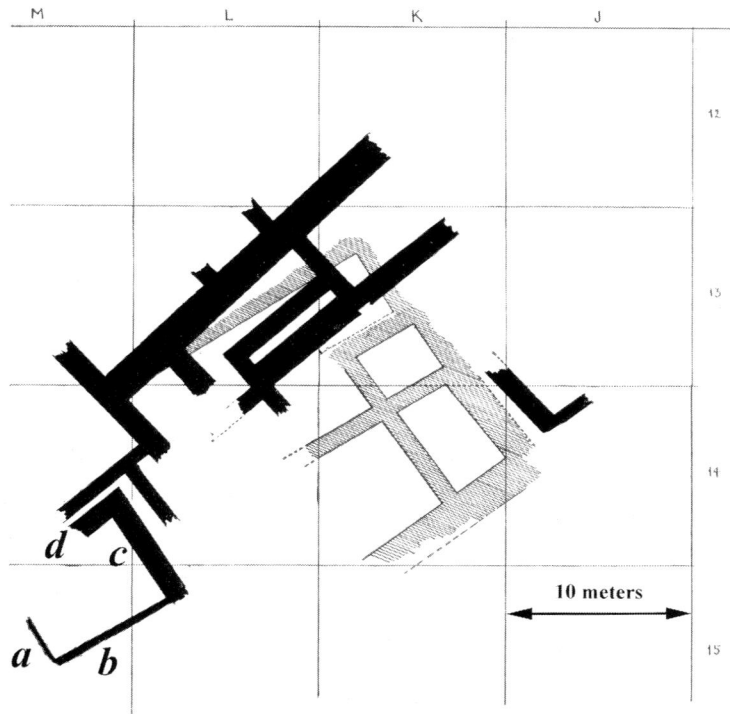

Above: **Plan 24. Level VIᵂ residences (after Woolley 1955: 173, Fig. 61)**

Below: **Plan 25. The annexe to the Level IVᵂ temple**

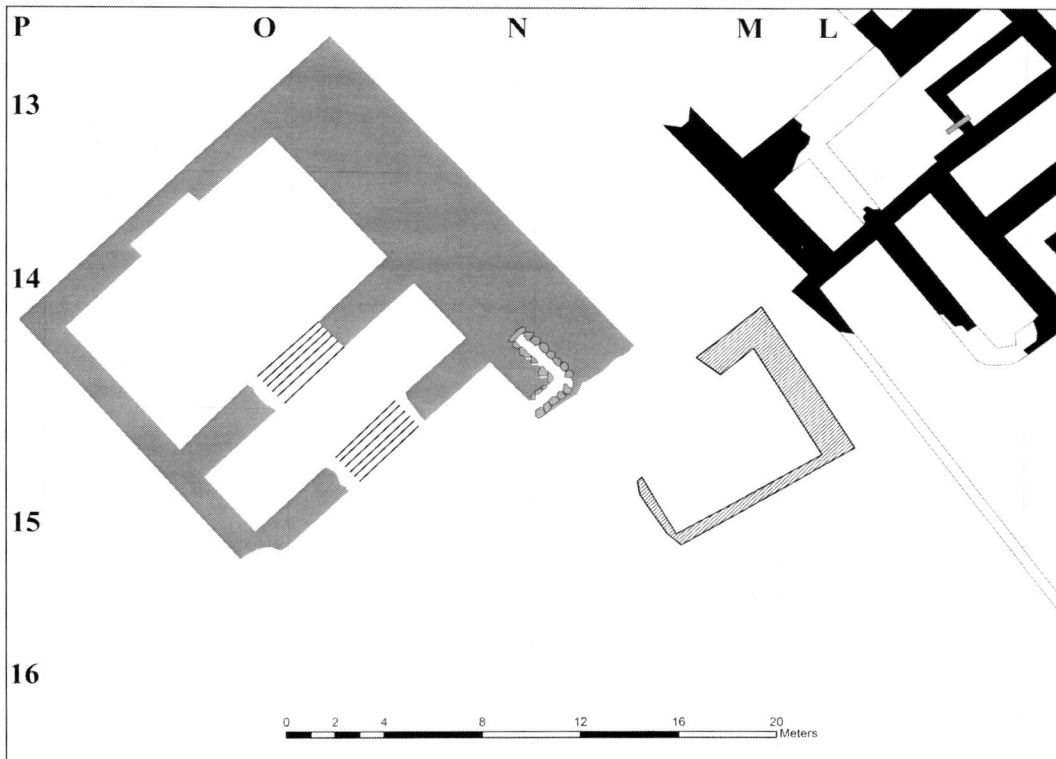

proposed annexe. Therefore, it had already been Woolley's perception that the Level IV[W] temple temenos comprised an entire complex of buildings extending far beyond the size of the central shrine. My proposal for Level IV[W] can be understood by comparing Plan 26 with the Level IVA[F] plan: Plan 26 is Yener's reconstruction of Level IV[W] (2005: 141), while the Level IVA[F] plan includes my proposal to add an annexe to the Level IV[W] temple.

The annexe to the Level III[W] temple

As mentioned above, the best-preserved annexe is the one correlated by Woolley to the Level III[W] central shrine (Plan 17). In accordance with his description of the architecture he unearthed, Woolley's reconstruction seems to be well founded. The walls of this building are relatively well preserved and a square hearth, made of burnt tiles, was discovered in the centre of the main chamber. Although the annexe was destroyed by fire, (rather than being abandoned), no significant finds were reported from it. No photo of this annexe was published, but I was able to locate at Woolley's archive at UCL Special Collections two views of the annexe and the Levels III–II[W] temples.[14] These give some indication of the conditions of excavation: Photo 3 was taken from the southern wall of the annexe looking northwest, and Photo 4 from the Levels III–II[W] temples looking southeast.

The annexe to the Level II[W] temple

Woolley's description of the southeast annexe to the Level II[W] temple raises some questions (1955: 80). Although he suggests that a new annexe was erected on top of the ruins of the Level III[W] annexe, which was levelled to a solid mud-brick platform, he found no real evidence of such a building ever having existed. The only remnants of this proposed building are walls *b-c*, *d* and *e* (Plan 14), which are heuristically and unconvincingly reconstructed— walls *d* and *e* in particular.[15] I would like to propose that considering the lack of evidence, there was no southeast annexe to the Level II[W] temple. As Woolley describes (ibid.: 81), during the lifetime of the Level II[W] temple a new annexe was built—the northwest annexe (Plans 1 and 14). This new building probably functioned in the same way that the annexe to the Level III[W] temple did, and replaced it. Some of the best examples of temple treasury goods in Alalakh were discovered in the Level II[W] annexe, including a unique lapis-lazuli figurine (AT/46/20) and other prestige objects.

The annexe to the Level I[W] temples and the Paluwa Shrine

It is widely accepted in the relevant literature that the statue of Idrimi was found in the annexe to the Level IB[W]

temple.[16] However, as Woolley clearly stated, the annexe to the Level IA[W] temple (the earliest sub-phase) and that of the Level IB[W] temple are one and the same (ibid.: 85), and all finds from this annexe are attributed to the last stage of usage, the end of Level IB[W]. Woolley characterizes his conclusions about the architecture of the Level I[W] temple southeast annexe as rife with uncertainty (ibid.: 77, 88). While the heavy stone foundations of the outer walls of the annexe (*a*, *b* and *c* in Plan 3) were easily observed, "inside them the whole area was an apparently uniform mass of mud brick" (ibid.: 88). Likewise, he describes the unearthing of walls *h*, *i*, *j* and *k* (Plan 3) as following: "By scraping the surface we were able to distinguish vague lines of slightly different colour, but only in one case and for distance of only about three m. was there anything so definite as a wall-face. In one of the lines, however, three flat stone slabs *in situ* gave us a threshold of a door and thereby proved that the discoloured line was indeed a wall, and assuming that this was always the case it was possible to restore the ground-plan" (ibid.: 88).

The idea that the Level I[W] annexe was an annex to the temple appears for the first time after the Levels III–II[W] annexes were excavated (Woolley 1947: 60), and is not mentioned in earlier publications (Woolley 1939a; 1939b; 1939c). Therefore, it is likely that Woolley's interpretation was a consequence of the discovery of the Levels III[W] and II[W] temples.[17] Nonetheless, most of the finds that Woolley attributes to the Level IB[W] annexe are reported in the early publications (Woolley 1939b; 1939c) as finds from a temple underneath the last temple of Alalakh (the Level 0[W] temple).

A close study of the plan and description of the annexe to the Level I[W] temple shows that this may not be an annexe after all, but a separate building that cancels the Level IB[W] temple stratigraphically and consequently postdates it. I name this separate building "The Paluwa Shrine", after Paluwa, perhaps the Hittite governor of Alalakh, whose seal (AT/39/322; Photo 5 and see below) was found in this building. My considerations are as follows:

1) Wall *f* (Plan 3) is represented in the reconstructed plan of the Level I[W] temples (Plan 6) as if it were a continuation of the temple's wall *d* (Plan 3). This is clearly not the case. Either wall *c* in the reconstructed plan is shifted several meters to the southwest (Plan 6), or, more likely, wall *f* (Plan 3) is actually wall *b* (Plan 14) of the Level II[W] temple or wall *a* of the Level III[W] temple. In any event, wall *f* (Plan 3), if it indeed belongs to Level I[W], precludes the existence of an entrance in wall *c* (Plan 6) as reconstructed by Woolley in his plan. In his narrative (1955: 87) he writes the

---

[14] I thank Prof. Stephen Shennan, director of the UCL Institute of Archaeology, for granting me the permission to publish these photos.

[15] Compare to Plan 1, especially in view of Woolley's explanation of the way he excavated this area (1955: 77, n. 2): "this… had been destroyed, in part at least by us when following the wall of the Yarim-Lim palace before the discovery of the temple."

[16] Woolley is inconsistent in his level numbering. When he occasionally refers to a Level IC[W] temple (1955: 398), for example, he is apparently referring either to the Level IB[W] or to the Level 0[W] temple.

[17] Woolley mentioned that already in 1939 he dug a small sounding into what most probably were Levels II[W] and III[W] temples (1939b; 1939c). At the time he thought that the four latest temples of Alalakh (Levels III–0[W]) dated to the time between the fifteenth and the twelfth centuries B.C.E. There is no record of the location of these small soundings.

Z Y X W V U T S R Q P O N M L K J H G F E D C B A

Gate

Castle

Temple

House 39c

House 39b

House 39a

House 37

Trench F

Trench A

Trench D

Trench C

Trench B

Trench H

0 10 20   40   60   80   100
Meters

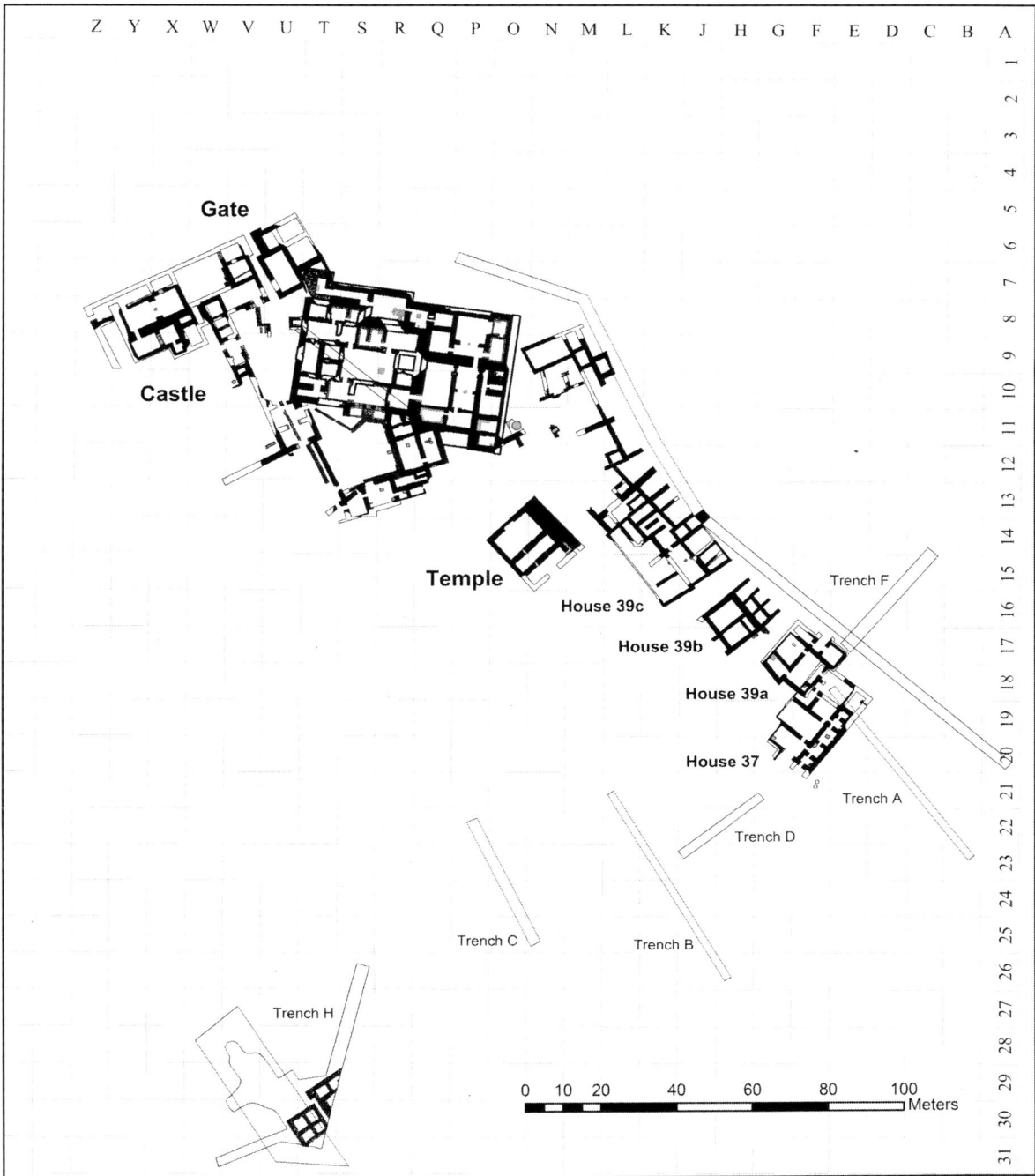

Plan 26. The plan of Level IVᵂ (after Yener 2005: 149, Fig. 4.30)

45

Above: **Photo 3. The annexe to the Level III^W temple and the Levels III–II^W temples (unpublished photo at UCL Special Collections)**

Below: **Photo 4. The annexe to the Level III^W temple (unpublished photo at UCL Special Collections)**

Photo 5. The seal of Paluwa. AT/39/322 (on display at the British Museum)

following of the Level IB[W] temple: "The raised mud-brick podium of the eastern annexe comes too far forward for the courtyard wall to have continued the line of the northeast wall of the temple." This description contradicts Plan 6, where wall *c* continues the line of the northeast wall of the temple as a courtyard wall. It also indicates that wall *f* (Plan 3) is the western edge of the Levels III–II[W] podium. Therefore, some aspects of Woolley's reconstruction of the Level IB[W] temple (Plan 6) are incorrect.

2) Wall *m* (Plan 3) is in line with walls *g* and *b* (Plan 3), and it is likely that they are part of the same wall.[18] Wall *m* is the only identifiable wall in any of the published photos of the Level I[W] temple (Woolley 1955: Pl. XIa; 1939c: 867; Photo 6 herein). Photo 6 is a reconstruction proposal made by Woolley, and not a record of where and how artefacts were found. In his early publication in the *Illustrated London News* Woolley discloses, at least in part, that Photo 6 was staged. The throne of Idrimi, marked with an *a* in the photo, was removed from its original find-spot (Plan 6) in the annexe to the Level IB[W] temple, and placed on the threshold of the Level IB[W] temple between the two lion orthostats visible at the back. The swan/duck altar (AT/39/287), marked with a *b* in the photo,

was also moved from the original find-spot (Plan 6). Studying the glass negatives in Woolley's archive at UCL Special Collections I discovered that Woolley took a series of staged photos of these two objects, of which he published two. Photo 7 is one of the photos in this series, and it is published here for the first time.[19]

3) Wall *m* (Plan 3) is built on top of a large and deep circular brick-lined well (Woolley 1955: 85) (marked with an *n* in Plan 3 and with an *e* in Plan 5—Woolley's reconstruction of the Level IA[W] temple). Woolley informs us that the well "was disused and filled in Level IB, [and that] it is a feature peculiar to the Level IA temple" (ibid.). But what was the well filled-up with during Level IB[W]? Among the stones that blocked the well, Woolley found the paws of one of the lions that stood at the entrance to the Level IB[W] temple, a "second pair of similar paws and a third lion, the head and forequarters complete" (1939b: 13; 1950: 11; 1955: 242–243; Mazzoni 2000: 1047). Thus, the paws of a Level IB[W] temple lion orthostat were found covered by wall *m* (Plan 3), which Woolley deemed as contemporaneous with the Level IB[W] temple (Plan 3).[20] The conclusion must be different: the filling of well *n*

---

[18] Admitting his methodological mistake Woolley assumes responsibility for the gap between walls *b* and *g* (1955: 77, n. 2; Plan 3 herein). He also believed that the two orthostats, which I mark as part of wall *m* (Plan 3), are the remains of a Level IB[W] temple installation (ibid.: 87)

[19] I thank Prof. Stephen Shennan, the director of the Institute of Archaeology at UCL, for his permission to publish this previously unpublished photo.
[20] Woolley ignores wall *m* (Plan 3) altogether in the reconstructed plan of the Level IB[W] temple (Plan 6).

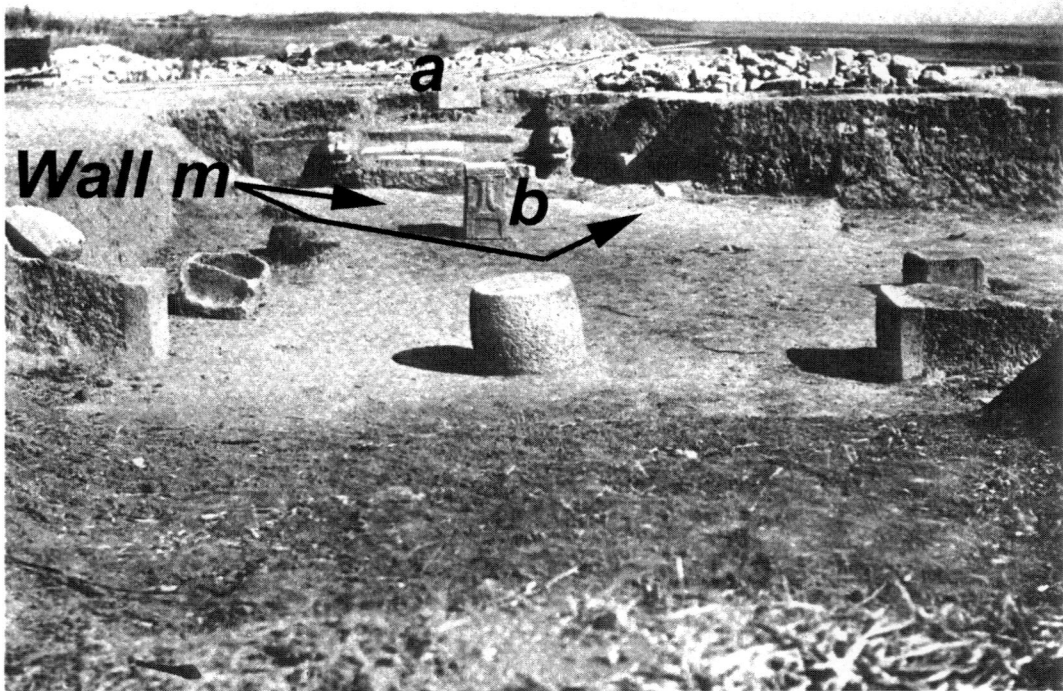

I. A GENERAL VIEW OF THE SECOND-LEVEL TEMPLE SHOWING (FOREGROUND) THE COLUMNED ENTRANCE, THE BASIN, AND "ALTAR" (RE-ERECTED IN THE CENTRE OF THE CHAMBER), AND THE SANCTUARY STEPS FLANKED BY LIONS, WHERE EXCAVATIONS WERE CARRIED BELOW FLOOR-LEVEL, TO DISCLOSE MORE OF THE SCULPTURED BODIES.

Above: **Photo 6. The Level IB^W temple (after Woolley 1939c: 867)**

Below: **Photo 7. The Level IB^W temple (unpublished photo at UCL Special Collections)**

(Plan 3), and consequently wall *m* (Plan 3), postdate the Level IB[W] temple, in which the lion orthostats were still in use and most probably intact.[21] If indeed wall *m* is the continuation of walls *b* and *g* (plan 3), then the so-called annexe to the Level IB[W] temple is part of the Paluwa Shrine, a rectangular building that postdates the Level IB[W] temple.[22]

4) Entrance *p* (Plan 3) could be the entrance to the Paluwa Shrine. Entrance *p* (Plan 3) and walls *m, g, b, a* and *c* (Plan 3) are arguably in harmony and could function together in the Paluwa Shrine. Walls *h, i, j* and *k* (Plan 3) could be part of the Paluwa Shrine, or, less likely, the walls of the annexe to the Level II[W] temple, if one existed. They are part of the same mudbrick podium of which Woolley identified no walls that could be attributed to Level II[W] (1955: 88).[23]

5) The orientation of the annexe to the Level IB[W] temple is not in harmony with the orientation of the temple itself. This fact does not prevent it from being an annexe, but it should be considered with the other observations.

6) No architectural connection between the annexe and the Level I[W] temples was found. In one instance, Woolley (1955: 85) names it "the disconnected remains at the southeast." While this fact does not prevent it from being an annexe, it should be considered with the other observations.

As Woolley put it: "The surroundings of the courtyard were terribly ruined and any reconstruction of the scanty remains is hazardous" (ibid.: 86). Under these circumstances the reconstruction of this area, which was accepted as an article of faith since the 1950s, must be reinvestigated, as will be done in the following sections.

The annexe to the Level 0[W] temple

Following the discussion of the annexe to the Level I[W] temples, it should be mentioned that Woolley reported the existence of a Level 0[W] temple and an annexe as well (ibid.: 89–90).[24] Although a plan of this temple was never published, a photo of it shows an impressive stone foundation (ibid.: Pl. XIIIb).[25] Woolley observed that the Level 0[W] temple "was planned to follow the lines of

the Level I[W] temple", and that "at the southeast end the foundations return southwest over the top of the Level I ruins, suggesting that the annexe of Level 0 enclosed a slightly smaller area" (ibid.: 89). The bottommost level of this foundation is one meter higher than the highest-preserved spot of the Level I[W] temple annexe. Although it is not as well preserved as the earlier temple, it was a significant building, possibly in use for several decades before its destruction or abandonment.

The new sequence of the LBA temples and their annexes

From Level IV[W] to Level 0[W] the only known temples at Alalakh were built consecutively in the same location, each reusing the stumps of the previous temple (see Table 5). The Level III[W] temple was built on the stumps of the Level IV[W] temple; the Level II[W] temple on the Level III[W] temple; Level IA[W] on Level II[W]; Level IB[W] on Level IA[W]; and Level 0[W] on Level IB[W]. I propose in this paper that the Level IV[W] temple had an annexe, which was probably added at a later sub-phase, and not included in the temple's original blueprint (see above). The Level III[W] temple and annexe were possibly built in unison. The Level II[W] temple was built on top of the Level III[W] temple, but its annexe was constructed northwest of the north corner of the temple. The Level IA[W] temple was built on top of the Level II[W] temple with no annexe. The Level IB[W] Temple is a rebuilding of the Level IA[W] temple. On top of the Level I[W] temples and partly on top of the ruins of the annexe to the Level III[W] temple a building was built with a new orientation: The Paluwa Shrine. It was later destroyed and covered by the last temple and annexe in Alalakh: the Level 0[W] temple.

3.3 On the relative and absolute dating of the LBA temples at Alalakh (Levels IV-0[W])

Once we have established the sequence of the later temples (Levels IV–0[W]) at Tell Atchana, it is necessary to examine briefly the time frame in which each of these buildings was in use. Woolley based his dating of the temples on his correlation between temple and level. Although he dated the levels in accordance with archaeological and historical principles, the time elapsed since the publication of his final report has witnessed some of his chronological conclusions disputed and challenged. The new chronology (Table 5; see also Summary Table 1) is based on the temple sequence, which I proposed above, and on the main chronological factors used by Woolley and his successors in dating the later temples of Alalakh. Applying other orthodox dating methods would probably prove ineffective here. Woolley's report on pottery found in the temples is limited to several vessels that cannot be reliably dated (Bergoffen 2005: 16), with very few exceptions.[26]

---

[21] As Woolley suggests, the lion orthostats were reused in the Level IB[W] temple (1955: 86). This is gleaned from the crude fashion in which they were positioned, partly covered by the steps. At the same time, the place where the broken paws were found—in the well, less than a meter away from the lion they originally belonged to—coincides only with my proposed reconstruction.

[22] According to Woolley (ibid.: 82, 85), the front courtyard of the Level IA[W] temple was raised only by 25 cm in the transition from Level IA[W] to the Level IB[W] temple. I believe that the courtyard was raised only in the transition from the Level IB[W] temple to the Paluwa Shrine. This is evident from the blocking of well *n* (Plan 3). See in particular ibid.: 86, n. 3.

[23] Woolley (ibid.) writes that "It was noted that the reddish colour of the bricks of the platform would agree with Level II; the wall bricks, also reddish but darker, might have belonged to Level I or to Level Ia; they are definitely not characteristic of Ib."

[24] More information about this temple, most of which is not found in the final report, was published by Woolley in the *London Times* (1939b).

[25] The photographer took the picture looking northwest. I believe it was taken from square L15 or K15.

[26] The exceptions are a whole LH IIIA:2 chariot-krater (Woolley 1955: 396, Pl. CXXVIIIa), which was found in the Level II[W] temple, and fragments of the same type, which were found in the Level III[W] temple (ibid.). The date of LH IIIA:2 (1390/1370 – 1320/1300 B.C.E.) is in-line with my new date of the temples. See the discussion on Mycenaean pottery in Alalakh in Section 5.1.

Table 5. Level and date assignments of the later temples

Temple level (Woolley)	Temple level (herein)	SE Annexe (Woolley)	SE Annexe (herein)	Dating (Woolley)	Dating (herein)	Chronological attribution (herein)
V^W	VB^F	–	–	1527–1447	1490/1465–1465/1440	Idrimi
IV^W	IVA^F	–	+	1447–1370	1465/1440–1420/1400	Niqmepa and Ilimilimma
III^W (and Levels III–II^W fortress)	IVB^F	+	+	1370–1350	1420/1400–1353/1341	Itūr-Addu and predecessor(s)
II^W	III^F	+	–	1350–1273	1353/1341–1320/1313	First temple under Hittite rule Šuppiluliuma I–Arnuwanda II
IA^W	IIA^F	+	–	1273–1194	1320/1313–1280	Tudḫaliya DUMU.LUGAL
IB^W	IIB^F	+	–	1273–1194	1280–1240	Post Tudḫaliya DUMU.LUGAL Paluwa? Šukur-Tešub?
	IA^F (Paluwa Shrine)		–		1240–1210	Paluwa?
0^W	IB^F	+	?	1194–1140	1210–1190/1185	Ends no later than the fall of Hatti/ Ugarit

Furthermore, ceramic assemblages—a highly efficient dating tool—were not attested. Other artefacts found in the temples, presumed to be heirlooms, have already been pointed out (Woolley 1950: 11; 1955: 82; Collon 1982: 67, 73–74). Dating according to architectural style is clearly unreliable, especially given Tell Atchana's geographical position as a meeting point of the Levantine, Hurrian and Hittite worlds.

The Level IV^W temple

Woolley's "Level IV temple" (Plans 18 and 19) yielded nearly no dateable finds, the exception being a cylinder seal found in the temple's foundation that "agrees with the 15th century date generally accepted for the other excavated examples" (Collon 1982: 83).

According to Woolley, the conflagration at Alalakh IV^W was confined to the palace and marked the end of its archives; other Alalakh IV^W edifices remained standing for some decades. The end of Level IV^W and the burning of the fortress are associated with the conquest of Alalakh by Šuppiluliuma I (Woolley 1955: 166, 395; see also von Dassow 1997: 42). Accordingly, Level IV^W should be divided into two sub-phases:

1) IVA^F: from Idrimi or Niqmepa to the destruction of the palace and the removal of Ilimilimma from the throne.[27]

2) IVB^F: from the destruction of the palace to the de-

thronement of Itūr-Addu by Šuppiluliuma I (Beckman 1999: 34–36; Altman 2002; 2004: 237–263; Devecchi 2007).

I believe that not only was the Level IV^W palace destroyed in that event, but that so too were the fortress (see below) and all the buildings attributed by Woolley to Level IV^W. Woolley knew that there was a time gap between the destruction of the Level IV^W palace and the conquest of Alalakh by Šuppiluliuma I, since the latter conquered Mukiš from a king named Itūr-Addu, while the last king who ruled from the Level IV^W palace was Ilimilimma. Woolley also had to bridge what he thought were solid historical identifications: that the Level IV^W palace was destroyed at the time of Ilimilimma, and that the Levels III–II^W fort was built by the Hittites. His archaeological solution for the above problem was to assume that only the Level IV^W palace was destroyed, and the rest of the Level IV^W buildings continued to exist during what I call

---

[27] Based on Cypriote and Mycenaean pottery excavated in the Level IV^W palace, Bergoffen (2005: 65) dates its destruction to 1380/75 B.C.E. This date is within the range of dates proposed by Stein (1989: 60). These views lower the date of the destruction by 25–50 years in comparison to the mainstream dates published earlier (Bergoffen 2005: 64–67). The date of the destruction is also tied to the Mittanian chronology since the reigns of both Idrimi and Niqmepa are respectively contemporaneous with the reigns of the Mittanian kings Parattarna and Sauštatar. There is no clear information about the duration of the reigns of Niqmepa and Ilimilimma, but even if they were rather long, dating the reigns of Parattarna and Sauštatar to a very early date requires a relatively higher date for the destruction of the Level IVA^F palace. Recently, Freu (2008: 8) proposed that Parattarna of the time of Idrimi is Parattarna I, whose reign he dates to 1500–1480, and Sauštatar of the time of Niqmepa is Sauštatar I, whose reign he dates to 1480–1460. This stands in contrast to another recent work, in which von Dassow (2008: 39–42, 46) assumes there was only one king named Sauštatar, who was the son of Parsatatar, the successor of Parattarna. Freu (2008: 8) agrees that Sauštatar II is the son of Parsatatar, but he believes Parsatatar is the successor of Sauštatar I, and not of Parattarna I. Freu dates Sauštatar II to 1440–1410. If he is correct, this date would align neatly with von Dassow's date of the destruction of the Level IVA^F palace circa 1400 (2008: 42), assuming that Sauštatar II was the contemporary of Niqmepa, king of Alalakh.

the Level IVB^F period. The division that Woolley makes between the Level IV^W palace (two integrated buildings by itself) and fortress is probably valid for the different dates of construction of these two integrated buildings. The Level IV^W palace was built in a different orientation (due to the given topography of the northwest end of the site) as two subsidiary sections into a probably earlier palace, the so-called fortress. From that point on the two buildings functioned as one palace, and therefore, the destruction of one was the destruction of both.

Once we assume that the Levels III–II^W fort and temple could date to Level IVB^F (see below), one can assume that Woolley's Level IV^W temple probably lasted for the same number of years as the Level IVA^F palace and fortress, and therefore should be called "the Level IVA^F temple."

The Level III^W temple and fort

As demonstrated above, Level IVB^F stretches from the destruction of the Level IVA^F palace to the conquest of Alalakh by the Hittites. There are no textual records that can be securely attributed to Level IVB^F with the exception of those found in Ugarit (Beckman 1999: 34–36; Altman 2002; 2004: 237–263; Devecchi 2007: 215–216).[28] Von Dassow (2005: 51–52) points out that Itūr-Addu is referred to as *šar ^matmukiš*, king of the land of Mukiš, in the treaty between Šuppiluliuma I and Niqmaddu II of Ugarit (Nougayrol 1956: 48), and not as the king of Alalakh. She suggests that "the [Level IV^W] archives were moved elsewhere during Ilimilimma's reign. That would account for the incomplete state in which identifiable archival groups were found, the apparent disorder, the absence of physically coherent royal or state archives and, above all, the total lack of documents or letters involving Ilimilimma himself as a party or addressee." Moreover, she proposes (2005: 51) that the location to which Ilimilimma and his archives could have been moved is the city of Mukiš (Niedorf 1998: 534–535; von Dassow 2002: 906), a site, which, to the best of my knowledge, has yet to be identified. It is certainly a possibility that some of the latest archives of Level IVA^F were removed from the palace before its destruction; of course, of the palace as I reconstruct it, a significant portion has yet to be excavated, so we should not rule out the possibility of illuminating future discoveries. Whatever the case, there is no reason to assume that Mukiš ceased to be ruled from Alalakh, either by Ilimilimma or by his successor; I believe in fact that it is archaeologically conceivable to trace this period (Level IVB^F) in the history of Alalakh.

Woolley (1955: 130–131, 166–167; Bergoffen 2005: 23) had no doubt that the fort, which was attributed by him

to Levels III^W and II^W, was built after Šuppiluliuma I conquered Alalakh. Nonetheless, it is my conclusion that von Dassow's textual analysis substantiates the argument that the destructions of both the Level IV^W fortress and palace were one event (1997: 99–101; 2005: 20–22, 49). None of the tablets found in the fortress have to be dated to later than early in the reign of Ilimilimma. The Level IV^W fortress archive ceased to exist at the same time that the palace archives did. Woolley admits that the stratigraphy of this area was very complicated, episodic and inconsistent (1955: 130–131). This fact together with his difficulty with the historical reconstruction (see above) drew him to the erroneous conclusion regarding the date of the destruction of the Level IV^W fortress, which should be named the Level IVA^F fortress, or even better, the Level VB–IVA^F palace. Thus, there are no archaeological, historical or philological reasons that stand in the way of dating the fort, which was attributed by Woolley to Levels III^W and II^W, to the beginning of Level IVB^F, shortly after the destruction of the Level IVA^F palace and fortress or the Level VB–IVA^F palace.[29] The building, named by Woolley "the Level III–II fort", could, in fact, be the stronger, larger and higher palace of Itūr-Addu, king of the land of Mukiš, or even of Ilimilimma, if he indeed survived the destruction of his palace. Moreover, this could have been the symbolic building that Šuppiluliuma I chose as the location for making the ceremony commemorating his treaty with Niqmaddu II of Ugarit, as the treaty itself states (CTH 46; Devecchi 2007: 215).[30] This building could have lasted for many years and served as the palace of the Hittite governor of Alalakh. The main motivation for Woolley (1955: 168) in dating the Levels III–II^W fort to the time of Hittite occupation at Tell Atchana is finding a "Boğazköy type" tablet (ATT/47/25 = AT447) under one of the few preserved floors in the fort. Yet the text is not Hittite, but rather a Sumerian lexical list (Lauinger 2005: 54). This subject is discussed in detail in the section on the Level IVB^F palace in Chapter 4.

Only scant remains of the Levels III–II^W fort superstructure were preserved, making it hard to track its building subphases. Nevertheless, at one point, at the northwestern edge of the site, Woolley notes two building phases of the foundations of this structure (1955: 155, Fig. 58d, 169–170). I attribute the earlier of these (Level III^W) to Level IVB^F, in the first half of the fourteenth century, and the later one (Level II^W) to the time when the fortress/palace functioned as the residence of the Hittite governor (see also Chapters 4 and 5).[31]

---

[28] But see my suggestion in reference to a group of tablets from Alalakh below. Devecchi (2007) considers the possibility that a treaty between a Hittite king and Mukiš, of which only a fragment, CTH 136, is preserved, is from the time of Tudḫaliya II or very early in Šuppiluliuma I's reign, even before the first Syrian war. Her tendency is to reject these two options, but if they were true this document would date to the days of Level IVB^F (see Section 4.5 on the Hittite treaty with Mukiš).

[29] The beginning date of Level IVB^F is sometime between 1425 and 1375 B.C.E., the range in which most scholars place their dates for the destruction of the Level IVA^F palace (van Soldt 2000; Bergoffen 2005: 65). In Table 5 I use the date 1420/1400 B.C.E., for grounds which are explained in Chapter 4.

[30] This is also the point when what is left of Mukiš is annexed to the Hittite empire. Still pending is the precise date in which the royal family of Mukiš was finally removed (Devecchi 2007: 216).

[31] The 2006 report on "Alalakh (Hatay)" in the under the 'Current Archaeology' tab in Turkey website http://cat.une.edu.au/page/alalakh claims that "in 2006 excavations in Area 1 uncovered casemate walling similar to that from Woolley's Hittite Fortress in Level III, although radiocarbon dates for the new wall suggest a date in the fifteenth or

The Level III^W temple, a significant building project in itself, was most likely built at the same time as the Levels III–II^F fortress; nonetheless, both building projects occurred during the Level IVB^F period, several decades before Šuppiluliuma I conquered Alalakh. Mellink (1957: 398) concludes that in all Levels IV–I^W temples "one seems to notice a persistence of a basically Syrian ground-plan, although the entrance-system may vary." Genz (2006: 503) sees no logic behind Woolley's assumption (1955: 78) that the Level III^W temple was built in a Hittite style. He argues that the Level III^W temple does not resemble any Hittite temple and in fact persuasively contends that no Hittite architecture is identifiable anywhere in the northern Levant.

It may be that the Level IVB^F palace was built in anticipation of a possible Hittite attack. We know that beginning in the reign of Tudḫaliya I (ca. 1400; absolute date unknown), the Hittites renewed their political and military interest in the northern Levant; it is also possible that Tudḫaliya I is responsible for the destruction of the Level IVA^F palace (Klengel 1992: 89). It is likely that Ilimilimma, king of Alalakh, or one of his successors (in the case that Ilimilimma did not survive the destruction of the Level IVA^F palace) had fortified the city, perhaps building a formidable new palace as a result. This would then have been the opportune moment to rebuild the Level IVA^F temple, since, as I had argued, it was most likely destroyed together with the Level IVA^F palace.

A tablet, ATT/46/3 (= AT 317), which was found in the Level II^W temple in square N14, 0.5 m. below the paving stones of the altar (von Dassow 2005: 19), may also contribute to this discussion. Woolley suggests that the tablet originated in Level III^W. Together with AT 309–318 these tablets form a unique group among the Akkadian texts of Alalakh (Goetze 1959: 64; Wiseman 1959: 58–59; von Dassow 1997: 460; 2005: 19, 30). Five tablets of this group were found together in square T8. In von Dassow's analysis of the archives of Alalakh IV^W (2005: 30) she suggests that "the stratigraphic level of the five tablets found in square T8 was misidentified at the time of excavation. Square T8 lay within the Level III^W fortress… and it seems likely that all 10 tablets' original place of deposition was in that building." My reassignment of the dates of the fort makes it possible that this group of ten tablets is actually the only known archive of Level IVB^F, dated to early/mid-fourteenth century, possibly to the time of Itūr-Addu, king of the land of Mukiš.[32] If not to Level

IVB^F, this group of tablets should date to Levels III–II^F, at which time the Level IVB^F palace functioned as the Hittite stronghold. The attestations in the texts of the Hittite name Tarḫuziti as well as of one "man of Hatti" may well support this idea (von Dassow 2008: 63).

The Level II^W temple

The dateable materials possibly associated with this temple are three fragments of a Hittite divination text (ATT/46/2a–c = AT 454). Woolley found the text in the foundations of the Level IA^W temple in square N14, and arbitrarily attributed the tablet to the Level III^W temple (Woolley 1955: 78, 84; Gurney 1953: 116–118).[33] It is unlikely that this Hittite text reached Alalakh, least of all its royal temple, before the Hittites took over the kingdom. Therefore, and given the attribution of the Level IA^W temple to the time of Tudḫaliya—possibly a governor or even a higher-ranking official, and a plausible contemporary of Muršili II (see below)—the Level II^W temple could have been founded when Šuppiluliuma I conquered Alalakh (in 1353/1341 B.C.E.). It could have gone out of use during the reign of Muršili II (Woolley 1955: 397).[34]

Three rare examples of ceramic vessels in Hittite style were found in the northwest annexe to the Level II^W temple (Genz 2006: 502; Woolley 1955: 80, Pl. CXI, 39). These are single-handled elongated jars, which Woolley maintains were locally made.[35] Genz (2006: 502) finds parallels to this vessel type in Emar. The first appearance in Alalakh of pottery made by a Hittite potter or in Hittite style is additional significant evidence supporting my assumption that the Level II^W temple was the first to be built under Hittite control.[36]

The Level I^W temples and the Paluwa Shrine

In the final excavation report Woolley concludes that

survived the destruction of the Level IVA^F palace—moved the active part of his archive to the new palace of the Idrimi dynasty, the Level IVB^F palace (the Levels III–II^W fort). This may explain why so few Ilimilimma documents were found at the Level IVA^F palace (Prof. Nadav Na'aman: personal communication).

[33] Woolley (ibid.: 78) explains the attribution of ATT/46/2 a–c to the Level III^W temple as follows: "It was in a pocket of burnt rubble used for leveling a depression in the Level I site." He believes that this burnt rubble could only have come from the burnt Level III^W temple, but no convincing reason is given for why it could not have originated from a later level.

[34] possibly in his ninth year (1320/1313). There is no direct evidence that the people of Mukiš took part in the northern Levantine uprising against the Hittites during the early years of Muršili II (Klengel 1992: 115–116). The residents of those Mukiš villages, annexed to Ugarit by Šuppiluliuma I, probably tried to take advantage of Ugarit's collaboration with the rebels in order to convince Muršili II to punish Ugarit by liberating them. However, Muršili II decided not to allow Mukiš any form of new independence and rejected any change in the border between Hatti and Ugarit (CTH 64, Beckman 1999: 173–175). See Section 5.1 on the deportation of the people of Mukiš.

[35] For the LH IIIA:2 pottery, which was found in this temple, see the section on Mycenaean pottery in Section 5.1.

[36] Mara Horowitz reported in her presentation at the ASOR annual meeting in New Orleans (November 19th 2009) that Hittite ritual assemblage was found in one of the later phases of the site by the Mustafa Kemal University expadation. No additional details are published.

fourteenth century." There is no doubt that from the mid-fourteenth century Alalakh was under Hittite suzerainty, and, therefore, these unpublished radiocarbon results do not seem to help here at all. Yener's 2007 web report (http://www.alalakh.org) describes the Level IVB^F palace as follows: "This administrative building had been constructed in the style of Hittite palace architecture. Especially striking were the use of casemate units in the construction of the walls." Yener's consistent desire to relate the architecture and finds from Alalakh to Hittite or earlier Anatolian Plateau material culture have already tainted her description of the architecture of Tell Atchana (Yener 2005).

[32] This is not a royal archive. However, many of the texts that were found in the Levels IVA^F and VII^W palaces are parts of private archives that were nonetheless kept in the palace. It is possible that Ilimilimma—if he

the relief found in the Level IBᵂ temple was an inscribed royal orthostat of Tudḫaliya "IV" (1955: 241),[37] and that, therefore, the public humiliation of the Hittite king in the temple had to do with the Hittites' expulsion from Alalakh (ibid.: 86, 398).[38] When, however, did this occur? Woolley had to consider the fact that the Tudḫaliya mentioned on the orthostat was referred to as DUMU.LUGAL, "the son of the king", not yet as the king himself; he therefore assumes that Alalakh became independent at the time of the father of Tudḫaliya "IV", Hattušili III (1267–1237). In the background of the Hittite withdrawal from Alalakh, then, was that king's treaty with Ramses II. Woolley dates this event to 1273, and correspondingly, the beginning of Level Iᵂ.[39]

Woolley's assumptions seem to be invalidated by the study of Niedorf (2002: 524; von Dassow 2008: 63–64), who suggests the names of three high-ranking Hittite officials in Alalakh as possible governors: Tudḫaliya, Šukur-Tešub and Paluwa. All three bear, among other designations, the title DUMU.LUGAL, "the king's son."[40] It is unlikely, however, that these were the only high-ranking Hittite officials serving in Mukiš during the 150–160 years spanning the conquest of Alalakh by Šuppiluliuma I (probably during his first Syrian war—1353/1341) and the city's final destruction (1190/1185) (Niedorf 2002: 523).[41] The best documented of the three is Tudḫaliya, who is known from four different records—or three, if we accept Miller's new analysis (2007a: 137 n. 40)—two of which were found at Tell Atchana: the Tudḫaliya orthostat and a large fragment of a letter. The first of the two from Tell Atchana is AT/40–45/2, the orthostat of Tudḫaliya from the Level IBᵂ temple. In it, Tudḫaliya is titled DUMU.LUGAL (REX.FILIUS) and possibly also GAL *KARTAPPU* (MAGNUS.AURIGA), "chief charioteer/groom"[42] (Photo 8 herein; see Woolley 1955: 86, 241–242; Laroche 1960: 33, no. 46/1, 113, no. 207/3, 150, no. 289; Meriggi 1975: 330, no. 305, drawing in Pl. XVII; Niedorf 2002: 521).[43]

Hawkins (2005: 304, no. 22) offers a different reading: MONS + *tu* MAGNUS(?) HATTI(?)REX.FILIUS, which stands for "Tudḫaliya, Great Prince of Hatti." Hawkins admits that "the sign(s) are too worn for any certainty." He assumes that "Great Prince of Hatti" is not a title as such, but a general honorary title. There are very few examples of monumental stone inscriptions bearing Hittite hieroglyphics from the Late Bronze Age Levant. The fact that Tudḫaliya was honoured by being inscribed on one of these few attests his importance and influence.

The second Tudḫaliya object found at Tell Atchana is the fragment of a letter, which Niedorf labels H4 or ATT 35 (2002: 517).[44] In it, the Hittite king, typically introduced as "the sun", addresses Tudḫaliya by name. Niedorf believes that Tudḫaliya was a high-ranking official in Alalakh during the time of Muršili II (1321–1295), and estimates that he served in his post for 20–25 years (2005: 522–523, n. 23). He bases this synchronism between Tudḫaliya and Muršili II on the third Tudḫaliya reference, Muršili II's dictate to Tuppi-Teşşub's antagonists: the king of Karkamiš, Tudḫaliya and Ḫalpaḫi (CTH 63.A). A new edition of this dictate was recently published by Miller, who rejects the correlation (of more than fifty years, since Güterbock 1954: 105, n. 15) between the two Tudḫaliyas, claiming that Tudḫaliya of the dictate is not the one from Alalakh (Miller 2007a: 131–132, 137). Based on the cuneiform syllabogram, Miller raises the possibility that Tudḫaliya of the dictate is a high-ranking Hittite official from Aštata or, less likely, Qatna.

Niedorf (2002: 522) identifies Tudḫaliya of Alalakh in a fourth record, KBo 9.83, a letter from one Tudḫaliya to the Hittite king. In it, the city of Gaduman is mentioned twice; it also appears on a fragmented list of cities on the border between Karkamiš and Mukiš, which is part of the earliest treaty between Karkamiš and Hatti— KUB 19.27 (CTH 50), between Šuppiluliuma I and his son Šarre-Kušuḫ (Singer 2001: 635). In KBo 9.83, Tudḫaliya repudiates a claim that he had not fulfilled a mission of either conquering or punishing Gaduman.[45] Hagenbuchner (1989: 48–49, no. 34) dates the letter, based on the form of one of the signs, to no earlier than the time of Muwatalli II, Muršili II's successor. However, this letter was sent to the king from the northern Levant, where new forms of signs were usually introduced earlier than in the Anatolian heartland (Niedorf 2002: 523, n. 24). It is therefore plausible that it dates somewhat earlier, to the time of Muršili II.

---

[37] ca. 1237–1228 B.C.E., according to Bryce (1998: xiii), but the exact years are unknown.

[38] Two smaller figures accompany the larger representation of Tudḫaliya on this orthostat, one visible on the same plane to his left, the second at a right angle to the first two, on the left side of the orthostat. Woolley assumed the figure immediately to the left of Tudḫaliya to be that of his wife (1955: 241–242); I believe now that both of those depicted are male, possibly officials. There is also a second hieroglyphic Luwian inscription, yet to be deciphered, between Tudḫaliya and the figure to his left. I thank Shay Gordin for pointing this out to me in personal correspondence.

[39] The Tudḫaliya orthostat was found in the Level IBᵂ temple, but it is more likely that it originated from the Level IAᵂ temple, as stated by Woolley (1955: 85–89, 398), and not from the Level IIᵂ temple. Therefore, Woolley, in accordance with his own argument, should have dated the beginning of Level IBᵂ, and not that of Level IAᵂ, to 1274.

[40] On the significance of this title, see Beckman 1995: 28; Singer 1997: 418–420; Hawkins 2005: 307.

[41] One of the dates that I cite for the first Syrian war of Šuppiluliuma I is in line with 1343/1344 B.C.E. as the king's year of accession (Wilhelm and Boese 1987: 105–109; Bryce 1998: 168; Wilhelm 2004: 72–74). Na'aman (1996) and Parker (2002) insist on an earlier date for his enthronement. Recently, Miller (2007b: 282–284), supported by Taracha (2008), dated the reign of Šuppiluliuma I to 1356–1330. Therefore, another possible date for the first Syrian war is 1353 B.C.E.; but see Simon 2009.

[42] For more attestations of DUMU.LUGAL together with *KARTAPPU* see Hawkins 2005: 302, n. 4 and 307, n. 37. On *KARTAPPU* and GAL *KARTAPPU* see Singer 1983: 9–11.

[43] Mora (1998: 196) notes that based on style and location (northern

Levant) the date of the inscription is no earlier than Šuppiluliuma I's conquest of the region, but it could be dated to any time between the mid-fourteen century and the end of the thirteen century.

[44] Niedorf reports that this tablet was excavated in Levels I/IIᵂ (2002: 517), but does not cite any dig-record in support of this information. I would like to thank Jacob Lauinger, who has been studying the Alalakh tablets at the Hatay museum, for the following information about the fragment of a letter, which is numbered by Niedorf H4 or ATT 35 (private communication): "This fragment is number 35 in drawer no. 4 in the museum's storeroom no. 1, and its museum registration number is AM 6277."

[45] I thank Shay Gordin for discussing this letter with me.

Photo 8. The orthostat of Tudḫaliya DUMU.LUGAL (after Woolley 1939c: 867)

Tudḫaliya was a popular name among the Hittite crowned heads, and it is possible that two or more different Tudḫaliyas served in the northern Levant, during the more than 150 years of Hittite hegemony in the region. On the other hand, Beckman has established that "in the pursuit of their duties, officials designated by the Sumerographic term DUMU.LUGAL, literally 'Son of the King,' traveled throughout Hittite Syria" (Beckman 2007: 165), and that "they do not seem to have been permanently posted to any single locality" (Beckman 1992: 47). The same official can be attested in more than one place, for example, in Ugarit and Emar (Beckman 2007: 116). I believe that we still need to consider the possibility that the two Tudḫaliyas (the one from the two documents from Alalakh and the one mentioned in CTH 63.A, who is possibly the one from KBo 9.83) are one person, recorded in different stages of his career.[46] The proximity of the dates given to all four documents and the fact that in all four Tudḫaliya is viewed as a major player in the northern Levantine arena, enjoying unmediated correspondence with the Hittite king, support this view.

Assuming that the orthostat of Tudḫaliya appeared in the original plan of the Level IA^W temple or was installed in it later, it is reasonable to date this temple to the end of the fourteenth or the beginning of the thirteenth centuries

B.C.E., that is, to approximately the time of Muršili II. This argument has ramifications not only for the Level IA^W temple: the main explanation Woolley offered for dating the beginning of Level I^W as a whole is no longer valid, since it was based on a misidentification of the Tudḫaliya of Alalakh as Tudḫaliya "IV" – rather than a Hittite official. The Level IA^W temple could not have been founded earlier than the reign of Muršili II, since Woolley found in its foundations the fragments of the Hittite divination text that almost certainly originated in the Level II^W temple, the first Hittite temple at Alalakh (see earlier in this section).

The Level IB^W temple must postdate Tudḫaliya's career and, therefore, any date around 1280 B.C.E. or later is a reliable beginning date for this temple. As a working hypothesis, I assign it to the DUMU.LUGAL Šukur-Tešub, in all probability a governor of Alalakh known from his introduction letter (Lackenbacher 2002: 95–96) to Ammiṭṭamru III, king of Ugarit (1260–1235; Arnaud 1999; Singer 1999).[47] Thus, a destruction date of circa 1240 B.C.E. is feasible.[48]

---

[46] Long and meaningful careers of officials are well recorded in the region in this period, such as those of Takuḫlinu and Ḫaya (Singer 1983).

[47] It is clear from the letter that when Šukur-Tešub was posted in Alalakh, Ammiṭṭamru III was already the king of Ugarit. Therefore, if indeed Ammiṭṭamru III ruled over Ugarit from 1260 on, Šukur-Tešub was not posted in Alalakh before 1260.

[48] Woolley (1955: 88, n. 1) points out the similarity between the bricks of the Levels III–II^W fort and those of the Level IB^W temple. Although brick quarrying sources may not be considered a reliable tool for dating, the resemblance between the two is worth mentioning.

The Paluwa Shrine is next in line, succeeding the Level IBᵂ temple, here attributed to Šukur-Tešub. Paluwa,[49] who left two stamp seals at Tell Atchana, inscribed in Hieroglyphic Luwian (AT/39/322; Photo 5 herein, found in the Paluwa Shrine, and AT/39/38(?), found in topsoil. Barnett 1955: 266–267), was a senior Hittite official and a member of the Hittite royal family (Klengel 1975: 63–64).[50] Paluwa's title is REX.FILIUS (DUMU.LUGAL) REGIO. DOMINUS (EN KUR): "The king's son, the overseer/ lord of the land." The second part of the title is equivalent to the Akkadian *ḫazannu* (Beal 1992: 437–442; Hawkins 1995: 75; Hawkins 2005: 306, no. 34), and it "may very well correspond to the cuneiform UGULA.KALAM.MA, 'Overseer of the Land,' one of the highest authorities in the Hittite administration of Syria",[51] whose "duties are strikingly similar to those of the *BĒL MADGALTI*, the 'district governor' in Anatolia" (Singer 2000: 70). Mora (2004) accepts Singer's hypothesis and brings to the fore more examples for this possible overlap of titles. Paluwa of Alalakh is most probably Palluwa[52] of a letter in Hittite from the Hittite king, found in Emar (Msk. 73.1097), in which he is named as a powerful, most influential official, who "dare[s] to benefit from the paternal property of the leading religious authority in Emar", Zu-Baʿla (Singer 2000: 70). The Hittite king orders that Palluwa and all other authorities give Zu-Baʿla back everything that was taken from him. The letter from the Hittite king is supplemented with a letter from the king of Karkamiš (BLMJ–C 37), delivering an abbreviated version of the same message (ibid.: 67). Singer (ibid.: 70) adds that if Palluwa "was indeed an Overseer of the land, this may explain why the king of Karkamiš tactfully avoided mentioning him in his accompanying letter. Very often the persons appointed to the highest offices in the imperial administration of Syria were close relatives or associates of the viceroy of Karkamiš. It would be quite embarrassing for him to admit that this blunt case of corruption was committed by one of his protégés." If indeed Paluwa of Alalakh is the Palluwa mentioned in the letter from Emar, then Paluwa is a contemporary of Zu-Baʿla, who is of the same generation as Muršili II (Yamada 1998: 324–325) or Muršili III/Urḫi-Tešub (Skaist 2005: 614; Cohen and d'Alfonso 2008: 12–14, 20, 25) and of both Šaḫurunuwa and Ini-Tešub, kings of Karkamiš (Yamada 1998: 332).[53]

Of the two, Ini-Tešub is a contemporary of Ammittamru III, king of Ugarit (1260–1235; Singer 1999) and of Tudḫaliya

"IV" (1237–1209; Skaist 2005: 610). We do not know securely which Hittite king composed Msk. 73.1097 and which king of Karkamiš supplemented it with BLMJ–C 37. Scholars suggest several identifications: based on Emar VI 201, Salvini and Trémouille (2003: 227–230) and Skaist (2005: 610–614) make the case for their being Muršili and Šaḫurunuwa respectively, but the question remains which of the Muršilis the Hittite king was.[54] Salvini and Trémouille propose that it was Muršili II, and date Msk. 73.1097 to 1312–1311, while Muršili II campaigned in the area (2003: 230).[55] Skaist (2005: 614) believes that if it was Muršili II, the letter was written late in his career, towards his death, circa 1290. Identifying the Hittite king as Muršili II requires that the reign of Ini-Tešub of Karkamiš lasted some 55 years. Skaist shows that it would make more sense to attribute the document to the reign of Muršili III/Urḫi-Tešub, dating Msk. 73.1097 to circa 1270. This lower date is supported by the stratigraphy of Tell Atchana, where at least one of the two seals of Paluwa, if indeed the same Palluwa as in Msk. 73.1097, was found in mid–late-thirteenth-century context. Another support for the lower date, although not as strong as the previous one, is that stylistically the seals of Paluwa seem to date to the thirteenth century (Buchanan 1969: 21, n. 16; Mora 1987: 288, 311, 346–351, XIIa, 2.21, XIIb, 1.40).[56] The Paluwa Shrine, either postdating Paluwa or built in his time, could be reasonably dated to 1240–1210 B.C.E.

While Tudḫaliya and Paluwa seem to have been very senior Hittite officials who visited Alalakh very often, used the site as their frontier base and possibly resided there part of the time, Šukur-Tešub was the actual commander or governor of the land of Mukiš. Following the archaeological data from Alalakh, Tudḫaliya is clearly the earliest of the three. Paluwa and Šukur-Tešub could have been coevals, especially if one follows Singer's assumption (2000) that Palluwa of Msk. 73.1097 is Paluwa of Alalakh, and Skaist's (2005: 614) later dating of this letter to circa 1270. At any rate, naming Paluwa's Shrine after this official is

---

[49] Other suggested spellings are Palluwa (Laroche 1966: 135, no. 922) and Pluwe (Niedorf 2002).

[50] According to the object card, (now at the Special Collections of the University College London library), AT/39/322 was found in square M15 in "Level 1–2" at the temple site. The object cards of AT/39/38A and AT39/38B describe bone objects, and not a seal or a seal impression. It is possible that the number AT/39/38, published by Barnet (1955: 267), is wrong or that the correct number is AT/39/38C or AT/39/338. Currently, the last numbered object cards of 1939 kept at the UCL Special Collections is AT/39/337.

[51] For discussions of this title see Beckman's studies (1992: 47–48; 1995: 28–29; 2007: 165).

[52] spelled pal-lu-ú-wa.

[53] Zu-Baʿla's son, ᵈIM-qarrād, was also a contemporary of Ini-Tešub (Yamada 1998: 332).

[54] Apparently, Skaist (2005: 612–614), unaware of Salvini and Trémouille's work (2003: 227–230), reached the same conclusion as they did, that Emar VI 201 is essential for dating and understanding Msk. 73.1097 and BLMJ-C 37.

[55] If one follows Miller (2007b) and Taracha (2008) the date is 1320–1319.

[56] Significantly, another seal of the same style, AT/46/12, was found in square N16, either in the courtyard of the Level Ibᵂ temple or in the Paluwa Shrine, as described in the object card (UCL Special Collections): "SW corner of courtyard behind basalt threshold. Square N16" (see also Barnett 1955: 267; Buchanan 1969: 21, n.16; Mora 1987: 330). Beran (1957: 46 = Bog III, 13), followed by Laroche (1966: 135, no. 922), suggests that Paluwa is most probably a Hittite nobleman whose name appears on a stamped bulla found in Boğazköy. Bog III, 13 reads: Pa-lu-wa-a₂ REX.FILIUS (DUMU.LUGAL) REGIO.DOMINUS (EN KUR). I thank Shay Gordin for this reading. As for the uniqueness of these three seals, Mora (2004: 482) adds: "If Singer's hypothesis were confirmed, Paluwa could be the only 'Overseer of the land' having the hieroglyphic title indicated on the seal. Perhaps it is no coincidence that the Paluwa's seals are circular, which is a typically Anatolian feature." Singer (2000: 70) points out that an exquisite silver seal of Paluwa, without titles, now in the Cabinet des Médailles of the Bibliothèque Nationale in Paris (BN 1972.1317.147), could have belonged to the same person. This double-faced seal is attached to a crescent-shape half ring by two pins. For a description, photos and a drawing of the object, acquired in 1972, see Masson 1975: 215–216, 231, Fig. 1, 234, Fig. 1.

due to the archaeological habit of naming a building after a name inscribed on an object, which was found in it, and not a historical observation.

The Level 0[W] temple

I share Woolley's assumption that a temple in the location under consideration was in existence in Alalakh up until the city's last days. Bienkowski (1982) and Kitchen (1982) establish that the main argument upon which Woolley depends for his late dating of the final destruction of Alalakh—1140—is invalid. Bienkowski (1982) emphasizes that cremation burials are known in Alalakh from Level V[W]; there is therefore no evidence to connect them specifically to the 'Sea Peoples', to whom Woolley attributes the destruction of Level I[W], and, consequently, some or all of the buildings of Level 0[W]. Kitchen (1982), on the other hand, analyzes a scarab found in one of the cremation burials (ATG/37/2), ascribed by Woolley to the time of Ramses VI, and concludes that it is from the time of Amenhotep III. This was, in fact, Woolley's only reason for dating Level 0[W] specifically to 1194–1140 (Woolley 1955: 202–203, 398–399). By re-dating this find from Alalakh, Bienkowski and Kitchen leave no reason to believe that Alalakh remained in existence after the fall of the Hittite empire and of Ugarit. I thus propose ca. 1190/1185 B.C.E. as the approximate date for the destruction of the Level 0[W] temple.

Explaining his secondary reason for dating the temple to 1194–1140 B.C.E., Woolley writes that "the finding of temple foundations overlying the Level I temple and laid some considerable time after its destruction forced me to go back to my first opinion [that it belongs to Level 0[W] and dated to post-1190/1185 B.C.E.—the author], since this could not be fitted into the time limits of Level I" (ibid.: 399). This assumption is based on Woolley's absolute date for Level I[W] and on his observation of a significant time gap between the destruction of the Level IB[W] temple and the construction of the Level 0[W] temple. Woolley's dating of the Level IB[W] temple has been rebutted (see above), and once Level I[W] is antedated, there is no need to date the Level 0[W] temple to post-1190/1185 B.C.E. Woolley's observation of the existence of a time gap between the Level IB[W] and the Level 0[W] temples originates in his belief that the statue of Idrimi was deliberately interred by someone who intended to unearth it, eventually, and failed to do so; but since it was not part of the Level 0[W] assemblage Woolley (1955: 90) suggests that the memory of the burial spot was lost. This assumption is hypothetical, to say the least, and is certainly not valid in view of the find-spot of the statue of Idrimi, which is discussed below.

Unlike Woolley, I ascribe the Level 0[W] temple to the last phase of Level I[W]/Level IB[F].[57] With the exception of the temple, Level 0[W] is a collection of scattered walls,

possibly from several periods, which does not represent any coherent urban settlement.[58]

3.4 The find-spot of the statue of Idrimi, uncovered

With this new understanding of the temple sequence at Tell Atchana, it is certainly possible, even necessary, to reevaluate the find-spot of so important a discovery as the Idrimi statue. Section 2.4 and Table 2 sum up the relevant information as Woolley recorded it. Let us first consider the rest of the available evidence, in light of my stratigraphic reanalysis, and then reevaluate the likely circumstances of its excavation.

The throne

The throne of the statue of Idrimi (AT/39/288) was found almost concurrently with the statue itself, but in a different place. Woolley says he unearthed it in the "west room" of the annexe (1955: 89), in the "north room of the annexe" (1949: 2) or in the "long hall" (1939c), on the floor that he attributed to the annexe to the Level IB[W] temple (see also Plan 6). I believe that this floor belongs either to the Paluwa Shrine (see above) or, more likely, to the annexe to the Level III[W] temple. The excavation reports are not explicit enough to be certain, but Woolley's object card (Photo 9) refers to the find-spot as "Temple Level 2." At any rate it was found in the area of the southeastern annexes; based on my reevaluation of the annexes, the Level II[W] annexe should actually be considered the annexe to the Level III[W]/ IVB[F] temple, which was destroyed by Šuppiluliuma I in 1353/1341 B.C.E. Although the throne was not buried together with the smashed statue, there is no doubt that the Idrimi statue was once positioned on it, and, therefore, Woolley reached a very reasonable conclusion: namely, that the statue was smashed, removed from the throne and buried by a devotee, and that the throne was left on the floor.[59] However, Woolley did not consider the possibility that after the mutilation of the statue and its burial, the throne was reused in the temple in subsequent years as well, like many other heirlooms found in the later temples of Alalakh.

---

[57] While Woolley believes inconsistently that there are three sub-phases of the Level I[W] residences, he refers most of the time to two phases of the Level I[W] temple (1955: 85–89, 398).

[58] These remains can be dated to any of the periods mentioned by Woolley in his long list of post-second-millennium-B.C.E finds at Tell Atchana (Woolley 1955: 399, n. 4). See also Casana and Gansell (2005: 157), as well as Mattingly (1939), although, most likely, this Byzantine hoard of coins was not found on the site. Since Woolley rewarded his workmen for finding exciting artefacts (1953: 24), some of the objects on this list could possibly have been "planted" after being collected in other Amuq sites.

[59] Judging by the manner in which the feet of the Idrimi statue are broken, Woolley's observation, that it was on its throne when smashed, is correct (1949: 2). More information regarding this throne was published by Mayer-Opificius (1983). Stein (1997: 58) writes that "it is unclear whether the statue was ever mounted on the basalt lion throne found nearby." I do not understand Stein's reason to disengage Idrimi's statue from the throne. Nonetheless, it should be noted that if Stein were right, attributing Idrimi's statue to levels earlier than IB[W] could be argued more easily, since currently the date of the destruction of the surface, on which the throne was found, makes the most plausible dating for the last usage of the statue.

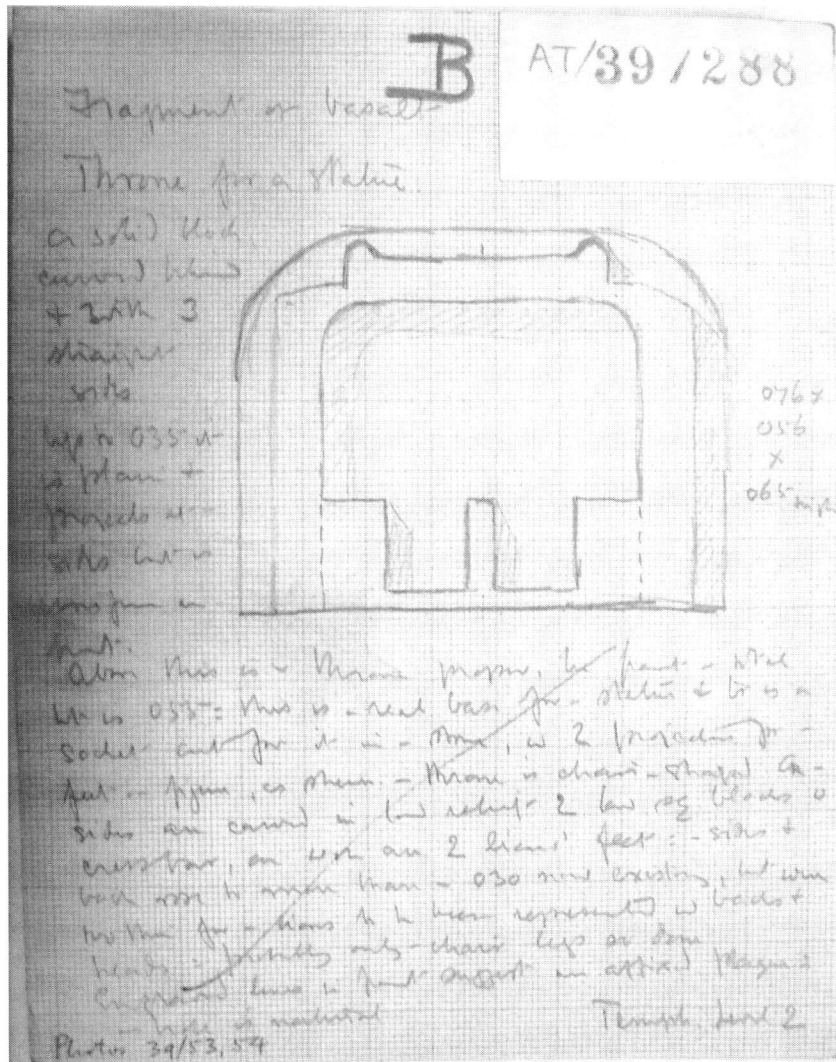

Photo 9. The card of object AT/39/288, the throne of the statue of Idrimi (from UCL Special Collections)

If the throne was not reused, one should follow Woolley's logic (1955: 89) "that the breaking of the statue was contemporary with the destruction of the Level IB temple was manifest not only from the observation that the pit in which it was hidden was dug from the floor level of that temple but even more clearly from the fact that the statue belonged to the lion throne found broken on the floor." If this floor was actually the floor of the annexe to the Level III^W temple, then, based on Woolley's argument, the statue of Idrimi was smashed and buried when the Level III^W temple ceased to exist. This happened when the Hittites conquered Alalakh during the first Syrian war of Šuppiluliuma I.

The building, the pit and the burial of the statue

The statue was uncovered in a pit, which appears on Plan 3 marked with the letter *l* and on Plan 6 with no letter designation. In Plan 3, the precise location of the find-spot is the centre of the grid-line between squares L15 and L16.[60] As previously established, the location that Woolley

intended to specify is, in fact, the centre of the grid-line between squares L14 and L15, ten meters away to the north. This correction now situates the find-spot of the statue at the heart of the annexes to the Level III^W temples, now re-dated to the time of Level IVB^F.

The fact that four different parts of the statue—the body, the head, the beard and one foot—were all found in the same spot (Woolley 1949: 2) indicates that the statue was indeed buried, or found in the spot where it was smashed.[61] The challenge is now to determine the surface from which the statue originated. The two buildings that are clearly represented in the stratigraphy at the find-spot are the Paluwa Shrine and the annexe to Level III^W. It would seem logical, therefore, to seek the statue's origin on the floor of either the shrine or the annexe.

---

[60] On the object card, (now at Woolley's archive at the Special Collections of the UCL library), this pit is designated "Pit No. (1)." There is no

additional reference to this name in Woolley's publications.

[61] In the photo published by Woolley (1939c: 869; Photo 10 herein), only the head and the body are shown. As they have both been turned over and removed from their exact find-spot they can no longer be considered *in situ*.

Photo 10. The find-spot of the statue of Idrimi (after Woolley 1939c: 869)

Unfortunately, Woolley's reports carry additional surprising details. The pit, described as being clearly observable in some publications, is said to have been "at the top...disguised by bricks" in another (1955: 89). This increases the probability that the pit was not excavated from the top of the brick mass, but from a lower point in the buildings' sequence.[62] Unpublished photos in Woolley's archive at UCL Special Collections may shed some light on the nature of these pits and on the fashion in which they were excavated (Photos 11 and 12).[63] The observable pits in these photos are extremely deep. In the bottommost pit seen in Photo 11 one can see a man standing, his head not even reaching the mouth of the pit. These pits were excavated in one instance, without first leveling the surface into which they were originally dug. While deep pits are not uncommon in Near Eastern archaeology, it is a rare phenomenon to find so many of them in one location. Moreover, most of these pits were not reported by Woolley.

This is supported and strengthened by the variety of descriptions concerning the content of the pit. The article published in the *Times* on August 3, 1939, shortly after the

end of the season in which the statue was unearthed, is most astounding in its description of what it took to find the statue: "...but in the meanwhile workmen...had come on a crudely cut basalt column lying at a tilt in a hole in the mud brick. The column and a big building slab were removed only to expose another slab about 5ft. long. This was lifted in its turn and below it in the bottom of the hole was a statue." Later publications present an equally complicated description of the find-spot that is different in content: "[The pit] was filled [with] earth and large stones (the largest weighed nearly a ton and a half)" (1949: 2), and "below the bricks were earth and stones, including two large orthostats and a basalt-footed column...a meter high and 0.43 m. in diameter..." (1955: 89). A five-foot-(1.5-m.-)long slab would be longer than the diameter of the mouth of the pit as marked by Woolley in his plans (Plans 3 and 6). The number of remarkably large and heavy building stones that Woolley removed on his way to the statue of Idrimi increases the likelihood that the buried statue originated from a lower surface, presumably the annexe to the Level III^W temple, now dated to Level IVB^F. This is the annexe in which this statue was originally placed, and it could have been smashed by Šuppiluliuma I when he conquered Alalakh in 1353/1341 B.C.E.

To sum up, the most likely scenario is that the smashed statue was buried in a pit dug from the floor of the annexe to the Level IVB^F temple (Level III^W), while the throne was found on that floor. Other scenarios, less likely in my opinion, may include the following variants:

[62] This suggestion is plausible only if Woolley's workmen were already on a lower surface when they excavated the pit, if the statue was found in one of the soundings dug deep into the annexe to the Level III^W temple, or if the pit was excavated from the side and not from top down. Clearly, these scenarios are not supported by Woolley's narratives. I would like to thank Prof. Glenn Schwartz for his comments on this subject (personal communication).

[63] I thank Prof. Stephen Shennan, the director of the Institute of Archaeology at UCL, for his permission to publish these previously unpublished photos.

Above: **Photo 11. Some of the pits dug by Woolley at the Levels IV–0^W temple site (unpublished photo at UCL Special Collections)**

Below: **Photo 12. More of the pits dug by Woolley at the Levels IV–0^W temple site (unpublished photo at UCL Special Collections)**

1) The throne was found on the floor of the Paluwa Shrine and the smashed statue of Idrimi was buried in a pit dug into that floor.

2) The throne was reused. It was found on the floor of the annexe to the Level IVB[F] temple or on the floor of the Paluwa Shrine. The statue of Idrimi was found in an unrelated earlier context, on which we know very little, due to the mode of excavation. One of the possibilities is that it was found underneath the bottom of a pit, which was dug into the floor on which the throne was found.

3) The statue and the throne were both found in the temple sounding, but due to the mode of excavation and the evolving records concerning the find-spot it is impossible to determine where exactly they were found.

The defiling, defacement or beheading of statues and their subsequent burial was a meaningful practice in the ancient Near East. It is uncertain whether the burial of the statue of Idrimi was part of a ritual or a salvage burial carried out by a devotee (Woolley 1949: 2; Ussishkin 1970: 124–125, 128; Mayer-Opificius 1981: 206; Oesch 1996: 62), or, contrarily, an act of humiliation carried out by the aggressor; the similarity between the position of the Tudḫaliya orthostat, facing down, and that of the Idrimi statue is clear. This issue is far from being resolved and deserves further examination.

Chapter Four

Alalakh Under the Mittani Empire (Levels VI^W–IVB^F): Stratigraphy, Material Culture and History

4.1 Introduction

Even before Leonard Woolley released the final report (1955) on the excavations at Tell Atchana, ancient Alalakh, Benno Landsberger published his own observations on the history of Mitanni, Aleppo and Alalakh (1954). Landsberger detected the disharmony between the historical reconstruction of Level IV^W, which was mostly based on documents from Alalakh itself, and Woolley's archaeological analysis of the same level (1954: 60–61)—a disharmony I have already begun to correct in Chapters 2 and 3. While the documents seem to indicate that the Level IV^W palace and fort were destroyed early in the reign of Ilimilimma, Woolley's Level IV^W ends when Šuppiluliuma I took over Alalakh from Itūr-Addu, several decades later. Landsberger briefly calls attention to this fact, writing that the time that elapsed from the defeat of Ilimilimma to the conquest of Alalakh by Šuppiluliuma I was a period of impressive, rather undocumented, economic prosperity (1954: 61).[1] Based on this historical analysis, and his intuition, he suggests that we consider Level III^W and the early stage of Level II^W to be remains from the second half (later sub-phase) of Level IV^W, the period between the overthrow of Ilimilimma to the downfall of Itūr-Addu. Landsberger's remark was overshadowed by the publication of Woolley's impressive volume (1955). It was left in disregard with the exception of a short and skeptical quote made by Machteld Mellink in the most important review of Woolley's magnum opus (1957: 398).

In Chapter 3 I divided Level IV^W into two sub-phases: Level IVA^F (early) and IVB^F (late). I also studied the Levels IV–0^W temples at Tell Atchana and concluded that the Level III^W temple and fort are in fact contemporary with Level IVB^F, a period that begins with the destruction of the Level IV^W, now IVA^F, palace and temple, and ends with the capture of Alalakh by Šuppiluliuma I. Consequently, the

Levels II–0^W temples were also given higher dates. This was the first stage in proving Landsberger's hypothesis. The second stage will be studying other remains from Levels VI–0^W, mostly palaces and residences, to see whether they were misattributed by Woolley to the wrong level. In this chapter I will treat the Mittani-period levels at Alalakh, up until the destruction of the city at the end of my level IVB^F. In doing so, I will try to decipher the encoding of Atchana's stratigraphy, as Woolley himself (1955: 133) stated that "our scheme of stratification at Atchana is based on the succession of houses in the residential area…" I believe that in fact, and contrary to his claim, Woolley shaped Levels VII–0^W at Tell Atchana around either a palace or a temple, or both.[2] In most cases, the level is dated to the lifetime of the palace or the temple, and its sub-phases/-levels correspond to the re-buildings of these features. There is no evidence in Alalakh for immense city destruction, although there are records of several conquests of the site, and clear archaeological evidence for violent demolitions of the Levels VII^W and IV^W palaces and of some of the private houses of Level II^W. Woolley never claimed that a level is equal to a city, which is built and destroyed as one event. He realized that buildings, and even units within buildings, could be built, destroyed and rebuilt during the lifespan of a level (1955: 172–173). He also thought that some of the residences lasted for longer than the duration of one level. Therefore, he did his best to match a feature (palace, temple, residence or fortification) to a level. This chapter aims to examine Woolley's considerations when making such a match, as well as its validity half a century later. I will especially take into account the textual and material culture data, often insufficiently explained by the excavators, that may help us in positing absolute dates for the myriad features present at the site. The results of this research are summarized and reduced to two tables and nine new level plans—Summary Tables 1 and 2 and the plans of Levels VA^F, VB^F, IVA^F, IVB^F, III^F, IIA^F, IIB^F, IA^F and IB^F, which should accompany the reader of this chapter and the next at all times.

---

[1] "Die leider schlecht dokumentierte Periode vom Ende des Ilim-limma bis zur Eroberung durch Šuppiluliuma, in die wir die Schichten III/II (zumindest des erste hälfte von II) verlegen, war eine Zeit beträchtlicher wirtschaftlicher Blüte" (Landsberger 1954: 61).

[2] with the exception of Level VI^W. This is defined as the level that was built on top of the Level VII^W palace and therefore postdates it.

This study of the stratigraphy may become essential in any discussion of the important Late Bronze Age ceramic sequence from Tell Atchana. In her Summary article on Late Bronze Age pottery production in the Northern Levant, Stefania Mazzoni (2002: 130) writes that "the lasting occupation of Tell 'Atchana VI–I does not have parallels in other sites of the region, but it is fully reflected in the main coastal sites, such as Ras Shamra."[3] This lasting occupation brings Mazzoni to use Tell Atchana as the reference-stratigraphy and typology and to date archaeological phases in the following sites: Tell Afis, Hama, Tell Hadidi, Tell Mardikh, Tell Rifa'at and others. Obviously, any change in the understanding of the stratigraphy of Tell Atchana will affect our understanding of the Late Bronze Age Northern Levant as a whole. Similar dependency on Levels VI–I[W] at Tell Atchana to describe the LBA I Northern Levant is presented by Akkermans and Schwartz (2003: 330–335) in their textbook on the archaeology of the Syrian Arab Republic.

I should not end this introduction without adding few words on the extraordinary size of the Tell Atchana residences. As shown by McClellan (1997; see also Bergoffen 2005: 30), the residences of Alalakh (called "private houses" in Woolley's reports) are on average almost twice as big as the average excavated domestic structure in any other Northern Levantine site. In size, structure, and nature of finds, many of Alalakh's residences resemble small palaces or patrician houses. This unique state of affairs can be explained, in part, by the following circumstances:

1) all the residences excavated by Woolley were located just southeast of the palace and temple compound—the second-best location in the city, at least from a geopolitical perspective;

2) the floor area of some of the residences is clearly oversized for a Late Bronze Age site of 21 ha., unless Alalakh was originally considerably bigger than we currently have reason to believe. In view of Tell Atchana's location in the midst of the alluvial plain of the Orontes River, which is subject to annual flooding, it is possible that a large lower town is buried under meters of sediments;[4]

3) since Woolley was not able to find many of the thresholds in these residences (see below for individual descriptions of each of the buildings), it is possible that some of them stand for more than one residential unit.

4.2 Level VI[W]

Table 6 summarizes the views on the date of Level VI[W].

Level VI[W] Residences

The earliest residences recorded by Woolley in Alalakh are those he attributes to Levels XVI–XII[W] (1955: 10–25; Heinz 1992: 23–36). Woolley found no residences in Levels XI–VII[W] (1955: 172). The earliest in effect widely exposed residences are those he attributed to Level VI[W] (ibid.: 173–174). These poorly preserved houses of incomplete building plans were found in squares J–M-12–15 (Plan 24, and in section in Plan 12), on top of the south-east rooms of the Level VII[W] palace; hence their stratigraphic *terminus post quem* is secure. Woolley's digging strategy was to excavate residences as deep as Level IV[W]; the Levels VI–V[W] houses were dug only in order to clear the way to the Level VII[W] palace (ibid.: 172).

Woolley attributes fragments of two buildings, one found on top of the other, to this level (ibid.: 173, Fig. 61; herein Plan 24). The older one reuses some of the walls of the Level VII[W] palace, but only following a period in which the palace area was deserted. This house "was replaced by what was clearly a large building well constructed on very different lines, and that building did not outlast Level VI" (ibid.: 174).[5] The excavator cannot determine in which of the buildings the finds originated (ibid.). These two sub-levels of Level VI[W] are canceled by walls that Woolley attributes to Level V[W], and which are also canceled—this time by a Level IV[W] structure, the Level IV[W] house 39/C (ibid.).

Level VI[W] Fortress

Few additional wall fragments, which could possibly be part of Level VI[W], were found in the Level IVA[F] palace soundings (ibid.: 107–108). Here (Plan 28), again, one of the walls cancels an earlier large structure that is convincingly attributed by Woolley to Level VII[W], but Level VI[W] is represented by one building phase only. All the Level VI[W] wall fragments were gathered into one

---

[3] and in another place (Mazzoni 2002: 131): "Tell 'Atchana provides so far the only complete pottery seriation for the entire period."

[4] This matter was first raised by Woolley (1955: 132), and was examined in recent years by Tony Wilkinson (2000: 170–173), who found a Late Chalcolithic site buried under several meters of sediment close to the eastern-most slope of the mound. Casana and Gansell (2005: 157–158; see also Casana 2003: 252) tried to attack this question applying intensive ground collection (Plan 27), but to no avail. They reached the conclusion that it is more likely that there was no lower town at Tell Atchana. Nevertheless, they estimate that the alluvium accumulation around Tell Atchana is 3 m. (ibid.: 159). Therefore, no surface collection survey will be able to determine if a lower city is buried at Atchana. To the best of my knowledge, no clear positive results have emerged since this study. Placing the lower town north of the mound will explain the location of the Levels VII[W] and IV[W] city-gates, directly—or almost directly—into the palace (Woolley 1955: 145–151, 161–163), which then would have functioned as the upper city/palace gates, similar to LBA Megiddo (Ussishkin 1998) and Ugarit. Mara Horowitz reported in her presentation at the ASOR annual meeting in New Orleans (November 19th 2009) that the MKU expedition thinks that the lower town was located to the

southwest of the Tell, and that both the upper and the lower mound were almost encircled by one of the meanders of the Orontes River. If so, the entire northeast slope of the Tell was right on the river bank, and the Levels VII[W] and IV[W] city gates were in fact water gates, leading to the Orontes River. I believe that only systematic deep soundings in the fields around the site will determine if a lower town existed at Tell Atchana. Drilling in the lower town of Tell Ta'yinat, 800 m. north of Tell Atchana, in the same flood zone of the Orontes, shows accumulation of a meter of "sterile" sediments on top of the Iron Age city, and up to eight meters above Early Bronze Age pottery (Prof. Timothy Harrison in a tour at the site, July 2008 and personal communication, January 2009).

[5] In Chapter 3 I suggest that part of the later building of Level VI[W] is in fact the annexe to the Level IVA[F] temple.

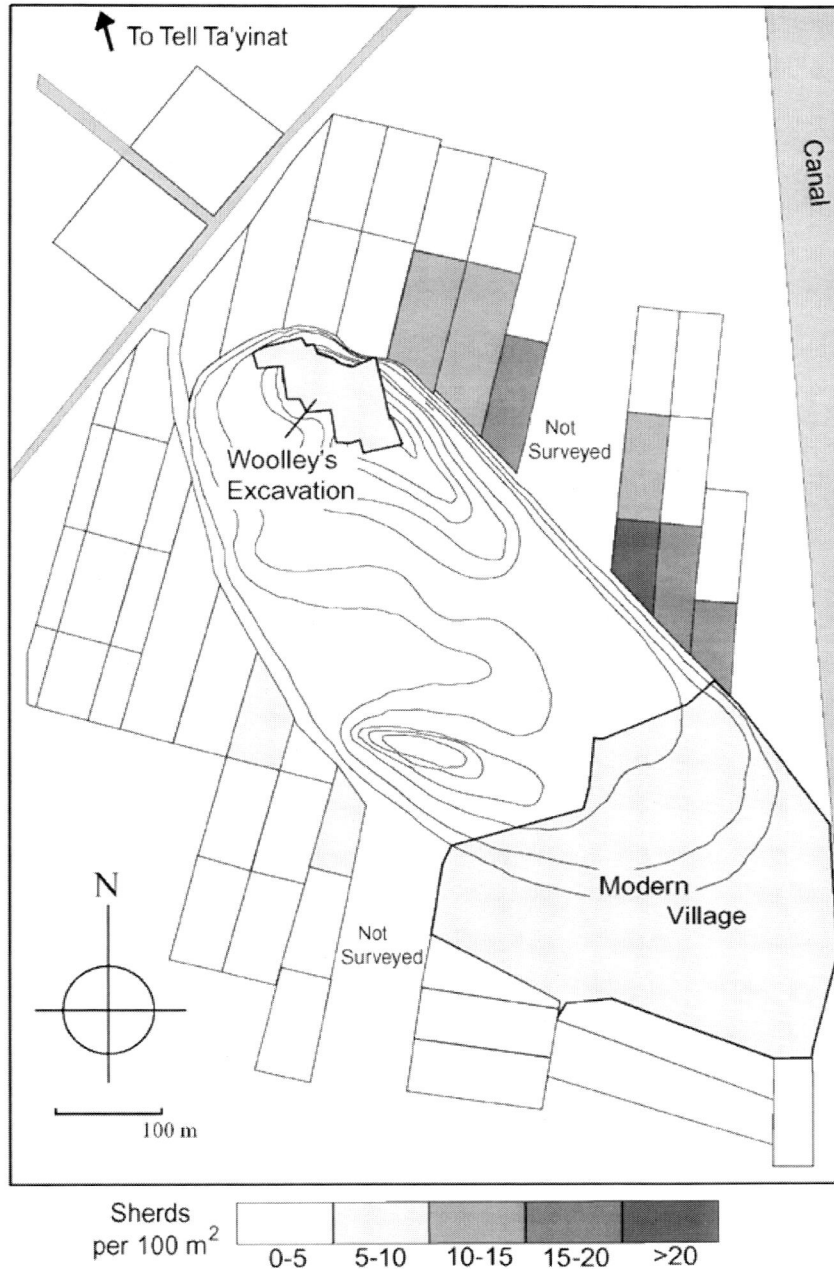

Plan 27. Sherd density map of fields surrounding Tell Atchana (after Casana & Gansell 2005: 165, Fig. 6.4)

plan, published by Yener (2005: 139, Fig. 4.28; herein Plan 29).

The subdivision of Level VI^W into VIA^W (early) and VIB^W (late) reflects the distinct sub-levels that Woolley found at the Level VI^W fortress (Plan 30), namely re-floorings and rearrangements of the earlier building (ibid.: 153–155; Gates 1987: 62).[6] This subdivision can be easily

harmonized with the two main residences, which were attributed by Woolley to Level VI^W.

4.3 Levels V–IV^W (–1420/1400)

Tables 7 and 8 summarize the views on the dates of Levels V^W and IV^W respectively. The plans of Levels VA^F, VB^F and IVA^F accompany this discussion.

Levels VB–IVA^F palaces

As in Level VI^W, the subdivision of Level V^W into VA^W

---

[6] Unlike the Levels IV^W and III–II^W fortresses, which were extensively excavated by Woolley (1955: 156–170), the excavation of the Levels VIAB^W and VAB^W fortresses is limited and fragmentary (ibid.: 133–134, 153–155). With the exception of the remains in squares Y–Z–8–9, Woolley did not remove the Level IV^W fortress, and therefore, only little can have been exposed of the earlier fortresses. The sub-levels of the Levels VIAB^W and VAB^W fortresses, described by Woolley, could even have been locally rebuilt or part of the still earlier level VII^W. Although

noticeably, there is no physical connection between the remains of the Levels VIAB^W fortress and the Level VII^W city gate, the only clear Level VII^W remains in the area, Woolley is convinced that his stratigraphic sequence is correct (ibid.: 133–134).

Table 6. Opinions on the date of Level VI[W]

	VIA[W] Beginning	VIA[W] End	VIB[W] End	Duration in years of VI–V[W]	
Smith 1940	Not before 1750		1595: capture of Aleppo by Muršili I	Not more than 267	
Landsberger 1954	1700: capture of Aleppo by Muršili I	1650	1500	200	
Woolley 1955: 390, 399	1750/1730		1595: capture of Aleppo by Muršili I	183/203 years	
Albright 1956; 1957	1550			100	
Kantor 1956: 158–160	1600: capture of Aleppo by Muršili I				
Goetze 1957a; 1957b	1650				
Tadmor 1966	Last quarter of 17th century				
Rowton 1970: 213	1645			95/100	
Tadmor 1970	1640				
Astour 1973	1570			110/120	
Collon 1975: 143	1650			150	
Williams 1975: 1160–1165; Williams and Hassert 1977–1978: 48, 53	1550/1540				
Na'aman 1976; 1979	1620/1615			100	
Gates 1976; 1981; 1987	1575: VIA[W]'s fortification should have lasted up to 25 years (count back from VIB[W])	1560/1550: due to Bichrome ware on the VIB[W] floor of the citadel	1525: capture of Aleppo by Muršili I	115/120	
Collon 1982: 3, 8	1650/1615: destruction by Ḫattušili I			115/150	
Kempinski 1983	1620/1615: destruction by Ḫattušili I			100	
Astour 1989	1575		1531	115	
Niemeier 1991	1650: destruction by Ḫattušili I				
Heinz 1992			1531: capture of Aleppo by Muršili I		
Dever 1992: 14	1550				
Stein 1997	1575			115/125	
van Soldt 2000	1535/1515		1500: capture of Aleppo by Muršili I	55/75	
Eder 2003; 2004	1660: 20 years after destruction of Level VII[W]	1600	1540	200	
Bergoffen 2003; 2005	1560	1540	1500	145	
Novak 2007	1540	-----	1499	90	
This study	1570/1510		1550/1480	70/130	

Archaeological Period of Level VI^W	Reasons	Closest Mesopotamian Chronology
		Middle
		Ultra High
	Smith 1940	Middle
LBA I	1) Level VII^W ends 1640/1630 (90/80 year gap between Levels VII^W and VI^W) 2) Bichrome ware at Levels VI^W and V^W is compared with Megiddo IX and Ajjul	Low
LBA I	1) Level VI^W and V^W's ceramics and glyptics are similar to Megiddo IX and Hama G 2) Egyptian Chronology as understood in 1950s	Middle
		Middle
		Middle
	Rowton believes that Level IV^W dates 1550–1473, after Swift 1958	Middle
		Middle
		Low
	Length of Level VII^W	Middle
Levels VI^W & V^W are confused, containing a variety of materials of various dates	Hittite and Egyptian synchronism require low chronology for Alalakh	Low
MBA IIB–C	1) Archaeologically, Level VII^W is MBA IIB, VI^W is MBA IIB–C, V^W is LBA I 2) Levels VI^W and V^W are significant timewise 3) Significant difference in prosopography between Levels VII^W & IV^W	Middle
MBA IIB/C – LBA I transition	1) Cypriote, especially Bichrome ware, and Southern Levantine ceramic synchronisms 2) Egyptian Chronology as understood in the 1970s	Low (but rejects fixed dates based on Ammiṣaduqa's Venus tablets)
		Middle
MBA IIB	1) Bichrome and Black Impressed wares in Levels VI^W and V^W 2) One can synchronize Alalakh, Megiddo and Tell el-Ajjul 3) Middle chronology must be used, as with low chronology the time span for Levels VI^W and V^W is about 50 years.	Middle
LBA I	Hittite history, synchronism with Egypt and archaeological analyses by others.	Low
	1) Date and style of Minoan frescoes 2) Late 17th century date for the eruption in Thera	
		Low
LBA IA	Presence of Cypriote Monochrome, Bichrome and Base Ring I	Low
MBA IIC	Ceramic parallels in Tell Hadidi and Mumbaqat	Low
	Aleppo was destroyed in 1500 only if Tuthmosis I attacked Syria afterwards	Ultra Low
VIA^W: MBA IIB VIB^W: MBA IIB–LBA I	1) Bichrome ware (1600-1460) dates Levels VIB–V^W in which it was found 2) Analysis of the scarabs agrees with this date	Ultra High (Muršili I's devastation of Babylon at 1665)
	Cypriote imports in Levels VI–V^W	Low
-----	End: *mašiktu* in Aleppo (Muršili I?)	Ultra Low
	Tell Atchana's stratigraphy	Low/Ultra Low

Table 7. Opinions on the date of Level V^W

	VA^W Beginning	VA–VB^W Transition	VB^W End	
Smith 1940	1594		1483	
Landsberger 1954				
Woolley 1955: 390, 399	1595: capture of Aleppo by Muršili I	1527: capture by Tuthmosis I	1447: Niqmepa is a Mittanian subject	
Albright 1956; 1957			1450	
Kantor 1956: 158–160			1500	
Goetze 1957a; 1957b			1500	
Swift 1958	1550			
Rowton 1970: 231			1550	
Collon 1975; 1982			1500	
Williams 1975				
Na'aman 1976; 1979			End of 16th century	
Gates 1976; 1981; 1987	1525	1490	1460	
Kempinski 1983			1520/1515	
Astour 1989	1531	1510?	1460	
Stein 1997		1470?	1460/1450	
Van Soldt 2000	1500. capture of Aleppo by Muršili I	1490	1460	
Eder 2003; 2004	1540	1500	1460	
Bergoffen 2003; 2005	1500	1450	1415	
Novak 2007	1499	-----	1450	
This study	Not before 1550 and no later than 1480	1490/1465	1465/1440	

(early) and VB^W (late) reflects the distinct sub-levels that Woolley found at the Level V^W fortress (Plan 30), namely re-floorings and rearrangements of the earlier building (Gates 1981: 6). Gates (ibid.: 7) identifies that starting with Level VA^W "…there are major modifications in the fortress plan. The outer wall was cut back; the rampart was raised and repaved… More of the interior rooms are preserved, and it is in them that one can see signs of the siege which marked the end of VA." Gates believes that the re-flooring of the Level VA^W fortress, resulting in the Level VB^W fortress, should be interpreted actually as a sub-phase within Level VA^W (ibid.).[7] If correct, this observation also implies that sub-levels VAB^W in site H both belong to Level VA^W (Woolley 1955: 139–144). Gates convincingly assigns the foundation of the Level IV^W fortress (Plan 31) to the beginning of Level VB^F. She suggests that Idrimi was installed in the Level IV^W fortress during the Level VB^F period in one place (1981: 36) and that he actually built it in others (ibid.: 7, n. 26, 8). By doing so, Gates may have mistakenly implied that she dates Idrimi to Level

VB^W, while what she actually does is to give a totally different definition to Level VB^W, making it, in fact, an early stage of Level IVA^F. Supporting this idea with some restrictions, I believe that Level VB^W, being reshaped by Gates and by me (see below), together with Level IVA^F are in fact one phase, divided to two or even three sub-phases. These sub-phases correspond to the building projects of the three kings of the VB–IVA^F phase: Idrimi, Niqmepa and Ilimilimma. I offer the following scenario: Idrimi is responsible for the siege that ended Level VA^W, rightly re-dated by Gates to the end of the first sub-phase of VA^F. After several years (the short duration of Level VB^W or of the second sub-phase of Gates' VA), Idrimi builds his palace, the Level IV^W fortress, or what I call the Level VB^F palace (Plan 31).[8]

---

[7] Gates (1981: 36) quotes Woolley's idea that Tuthmosis I was behind the siege, adding to it the possibility that instead it was Parattarna of Mittani. She believes that Idrimi was installed during the Level VB^F period, which she defines in a different way than Woolley.

[8] Gates dates her Level VB to start in 1525 and end in 1460 (1981: 36–37). Her end date is based on the presence of Cypriote Bichrome ware in Level V^W. The reliability of this date is harshly attacked by Muhly (1985: 25–26) and Manning (1999: 361), but nonetheless is maintained by Gates (2000: 88). Even if one accepts Gates' dating of the Bichrome ware, it should be pointed out that Gates pushed the reason for Woolley's division of Level V^W to two sub-levels (A and B) exclusively into her Level VA. These sub-levels were the two building stages of the Level V^W fortress— the original was A, later replaced/built on by B. At the same time, Gates (1981: 7–8) imported another feature into Level VB^W, which became the main structure of this sub-level: the Level IV^W fortress, which is not part

Archaeological Period	Reasons
	Smith (1940)
LBA I	Levels VI–V^W Bichrome ware is compared with Megiddo IX & Ajjul
LBA I	1) Level VI^W and V^W ceramics & glyptic similar to Megiddo IX and Hama G 2) Egyptian Chronology as understood in the 1950s
LBA I	Amuq sequence
	1) Alalakh IV^W must end before Tuthmosis III took over the area in 1473 2) Level IV^W should be long enough for three reigns 3) Swift 1958
LBA I	Parattarna & Sauštatar: end of 16th cenutry
MBA–LBA transition	Level V^W ends during the Syrian wars of Tuthmosis III. The Bichrome ware is dated with the assumption that Tuthmosis III destroyed Megiddo IX in 1468/1467
LBA I	
LBA I	
	1) Ilimilimma I was the king of Aleppo when Muršili I captured it. 2) Idrimi ruled in Alalakh 1490–1460
LBA I	1) Bichrome ware (1600–1460) dates Levels VIB–V^W in which it was found 2) Analysis of the scarabs agrees with this date.
LBA I	Cypriote pottery in Alalakh
-----	Cypriote Bichrome Ware and Local (Syrian) ware in Level VII^W tradition
LBA I	New definitions of VB^F and VA^F

Was Idrimi the king of Level VB^W or IVA^F? I propose that he was neither. Idrimi was the king of the rearranged Level VB^F (modification of the proposal of Gates 1981), which is earlier than the Level IVA^F Niqmepa and Ilimilimma palace (Plan 32), but includes mostly Level IV^W buildings, such as the Level IV^W fortress (now the Level VB^F palace), and all of the Level IV^W residences.[9] In fact, the only differences between Level VB^F and Level IVA^F are in the area of the

of the ceramic discussion since it was in use until the end of Level IVA^F. The outcome is that of Wooley's original Level VB^W, only the later (final) sub-phase of several Level V^W buildings is included by Gates in her Level VB, which by no stratigraphic archaeological reason should be divided into A and B. Gates (1987: 62), nevertheless, divides it into early and late, and since Bichrome ware is found in some of them, she dates Level VB^W to end circa 1460. I propose that being single-phased, each of the few Level V^W buildings should be treated as either Level VB^F or Level VA^F—where many of them are assigned by me. None of the Cypriote Bichrome sherds, catalogued by Gates (1976: 82–84), were found in locations that project their date on the buildings that I assign to Level VB^F. Therefore, the date of Level VB^F is detached from Gates' ceramic analysis of the date of Level V^W.

[9] Gates (1989: 68) writes that "Woolley was not particularly interested in excavating according to natural stratigraphy, but that he had a tendency to pursue sequences that were based on these monumental constructions; this is most definitely a problem in Level V and Level IV since there is no clear break between the two. In fact there are some buildings that were built in Level V and continue into Level IV without interruption, that is: the occupation is continuous; all the material from there is a mixed bag…"

temples and palaces. The Level V^W temple (possibly VB^F, since I date the Level V^W shrines to VA^F) was replaced by the Level IVA^F temple (see Chapter 3), and on the eastern part of the Level VB^F palace, two new wings were built, each on an area of less than one-fifth of the palace: the Niqmepa and the Ilimilimma palaces (Woolley 1955: 110–131; and see below). The Level VB^F palace continued to function together with the new wing (Plans 33 and 34); that is, the Niqmepa and Ilimilimma palaces are no more than two wings of new orientation (due to topographical restrictions), located within an existing palace.

Von Dassow in her important socio-historical analyses of Level IV^W (1997, 2002, 2005, and 2008) disputes the idea that the square monumental building (southwest wing in Plan 32), which Wooley called "the Niqmepa palace," was built by Niqmepa rather than by Idrimi. Von Dassow's (2008: 34–42) arguments are:

1) Idrimi-related tablets were found in both the Level IV^W fortress (Plan 31; since Gates 1981, argued to be Idrimi's Level VB^F palace) and the Level IV^W Niqmepa palace. If indeed the latter was built by Niqmepa son of Idrimi, why did Woolley find a tablet of the time of Idrimi (AlT 71) in a building which was built after

Table 8. Opinions on the date of Level IV[W]

	IVA[F] Beginning	IVA[F] End	IVB[F] End	
Smith 1940; 1949	1483		1370	
Schaeffer 1948	1450			
Landsberger 1954	1510	1440		
Woolley 1955: 399	1447		1370	
Albright 1950; 1956; 1957	1450	1400		
Goetze 1957b	1500			
Hrouda 1957	1500			
Swift 1958			Before 1400	
Rowton 1970: 231	1550	1473 (probably refers to the end of IVA[W])		
Astour 1972	1460/1450	1410/1400		
Collon 1975: 167; 1982: 3	1500	1400	1365	
Na'aman 1976; 1979	End of the 16th century			
Gates 1976; 1981; 1987	1460			
Oller 1977				
Kempinski 1983	1520/1515			
Stein 1989				
Astour 1989	1460	1430/1425		
Márquez Rowe 1997				
Stein 1997	1460/1450	Post 1425	1340	
Van Soldt 2000	1460			
Eder 2003; 2004	1460			
Zeeb 2004				
Bergoffen 2003; 2005	1415	1380/1375	1340	
Novak 2007	1450		1340	
Von Dassow 2008	1475	1400		
This study	1465/1440	1420/1400	1353/1341	

Idrimi's Level	Reasons
IV^W (1414–1385/1375 assuming Niqmepa is his father)	
Idrimi: 1510–1480; Niqmepa: 1480–1455, Ilimilimma: 1455–1440	Synchronism between Idrimi, Parattarna of Mittani, Nuzi's 1st generation, Pilliya of Kizzuwatna and Zidanta II of Hatti. Synchronism between Niqmepa, Sauštatar of Mittani, Itḫiya of Arrapḫa?, Nuzi's second generation, Ir-^{d}IM of Tunip, Ibirānu of Ugarit
IV^W (assuming Niqmepa is his father)	
V^W (Idrimi: 1480–1450/1440)	1) Idrimi could attack Hatti only when latter was weak 2) The death of Idrimi is not long after Tuthmosis III's campaign to the northern Levant (1457 at the latest)
	Level III^W ends at 1400
IV^W	1) Alalakh IV^W must have ended before Tuthmosis III took over the region in 1473 2) Level II^W pottery dates to the 14th century B.C.E. (Swift 1958)
V^W	
IV^W	1) Base ring II ware in Level IV^W palace not before 1425. 2) Mycenaean pottery at the Level IV^W palace dates to 1400 or later. 3) Niqmepa's reign: mid-late 15th century.
IV^W	Parattarna and Sauštatar are dated to the end of the 16th cenutry
VB (Gates')	Collon 1975
V^W	
IV^W	
V^W (Idrimi and Addu-Nīrārī)	Addu-Nīrārī succeeded Idrimi's rule over Alalakh Idrimi: 1510–1480 Addu-Nīrārī: 1480–1460 Niqmepa: 1460–1440 Ilimilimma: 1440–1425
V^W	
VB^W	Absence of Bichrome ware and presence of Base Ring II and LH IIIA wares
Overlaps with VA^W and VB^W	
VB^W	Idrimi reign begins on 1490
	The accession year of Tuthmosis III is 1479
VB^W	
Overlaps with VA^W and VB^W	Cypriote White Slip ware, Nuzi ware
IV^W	
Mid-VA^F and VB^F	

69

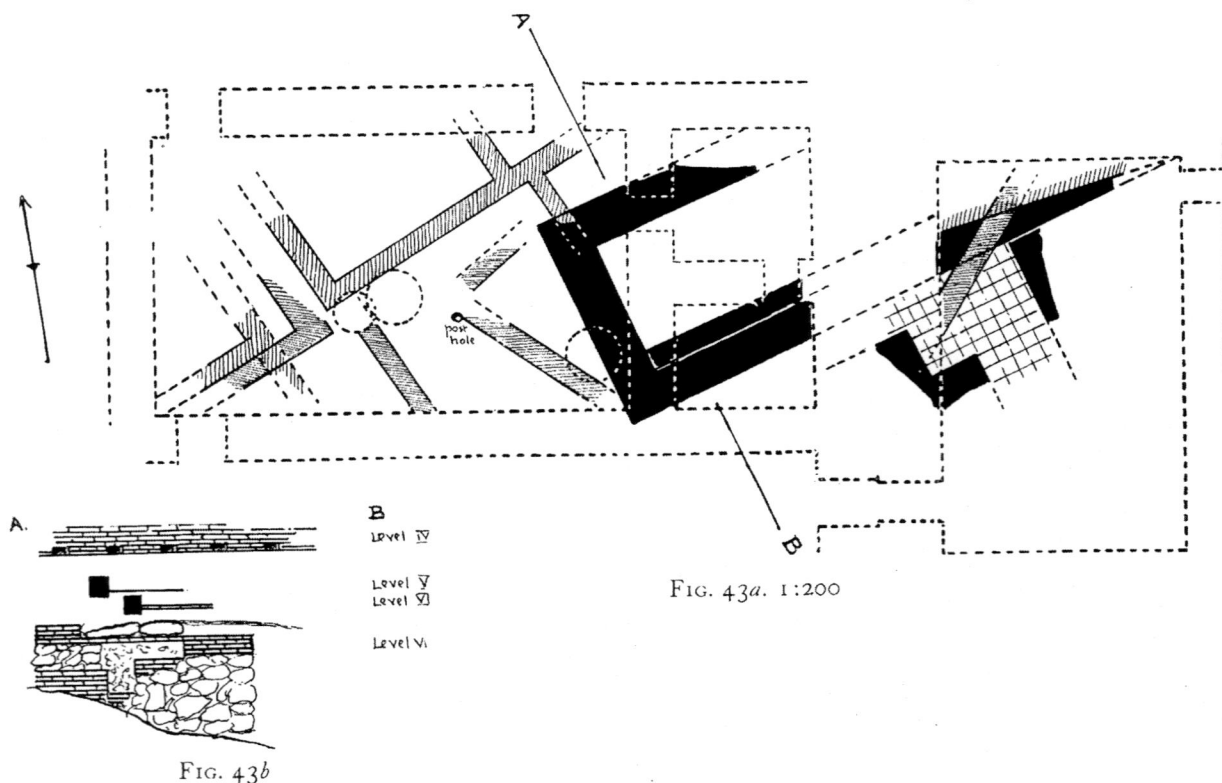

FIG. 43a. 1:200

FIG. 43b

Plan 28. Levels VI–V^W buildings found in the sounding in the Level IV^W palace (after Woolley 1955: 107, Fig. 43a–b)

his death? Why would a record of slave sale from Idrimi's time have been removed into a new palace? It is better to assume that this tablet was abandoned in its original archive and later neglected by Niqmepa and Ilimilimma.

2) The Idrimi statue's inscription states that he built a house and that his throne is like kingly thrones. The Level IV^W Niqmepa palace could neatly correspond to this description.

3) The reason Woolley attributes the Level IV^W palace to Niqmepa is his assumption at the time that Niqmepa was the founder of the dynasty, Ilimilimma was his son and Idrimi was Niqmepa's grandson. Woolley thought that the Niqmepa palace was the palace of the dynasty founder; had he known that Niqmepa was not he, he would have attributed the palace to Idrimi. Therefore, we should not be misled by the building's name.

Von Dassow's arguments are substantial, and should be considered seriously when analyzing the archaeology of Idrimi. Yet, I think that basing her argument on the find spot of AlT 71 is relatively weak. As von Dassow herself demonstrates (2008: 36, n. 87), the Level IV^W palace and fortress function at the time of Niqmepa and Ilimilimma as one palace, in which tablets of all three kings of the dynasty are found. The pattern in which these tablets are archived at the time of Ilimilimma is indeed noteworthy. However, tablets, as all objects, are meaningful moveable heirlooms and their location could inform us as to their

significance or insignificance to Ilimilimma, and to the way he organized his palace, rather than as to the identity of the builder of the palace. von Dassow's view that at one point, before or right after the destruction of the Level IVA^F palace, Ilimilimma moved his archive to another location (2008: 58–62), makes her argument even weaker. If all that was found of the Alalakh IV^W archives are the part that was considered "dead", while Ilimilimma left the site with the rest, it implies that these archives went through a large scale sorting, which could end up with many documents moving from one place to another.

I agree with von Dassow that the Idrimi inscription is trustworthy when it comes to the description of building a new palace. However, it is very likely that this new house was the Level IV^W fortress, now the Level VB^F palace (Plan 31). In the same way that von Dassow claims that Woolley's terminology is misleading when he uses the name "Niqmepa's palace," it is misleading when he consistently names palaces as fortresses. He actually does so twice: with the Levels III–II^W fort (Plan 35; now the Level IVB^F palace) and with the Level IV^W fortress (Plan 31; now the Level VB^F palace). Moreover, Woolley made two incorrect assumptions that in a way cancel each other; first, he places Niqmepa as the first king in the dynasty-line and second, he assumes that the construction of the Level IV^W fortress is contemporary with the construction of the Level IV^W Niqmepa palace. Once these two are resolved Idrimi could be the king of Level VB^F, a phase which is now rearranged to consist almost entirely of Level IV^W buildings.

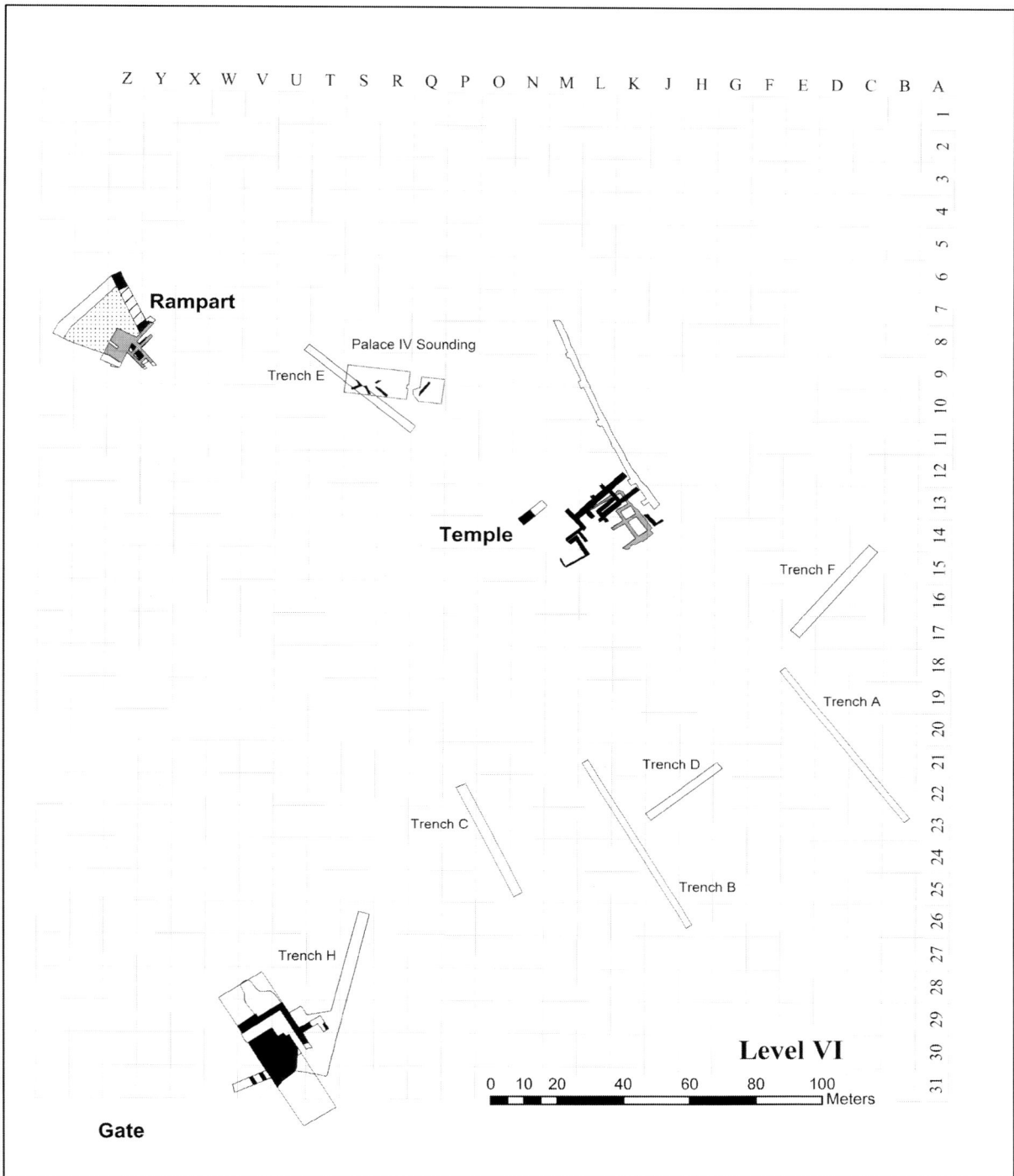

Plan 29. Plan of Level VI^W (after Yener 2005: 139, Fig. 4.28)

SECTION OF NE FRONT OF FORT
LEVELS I–VII

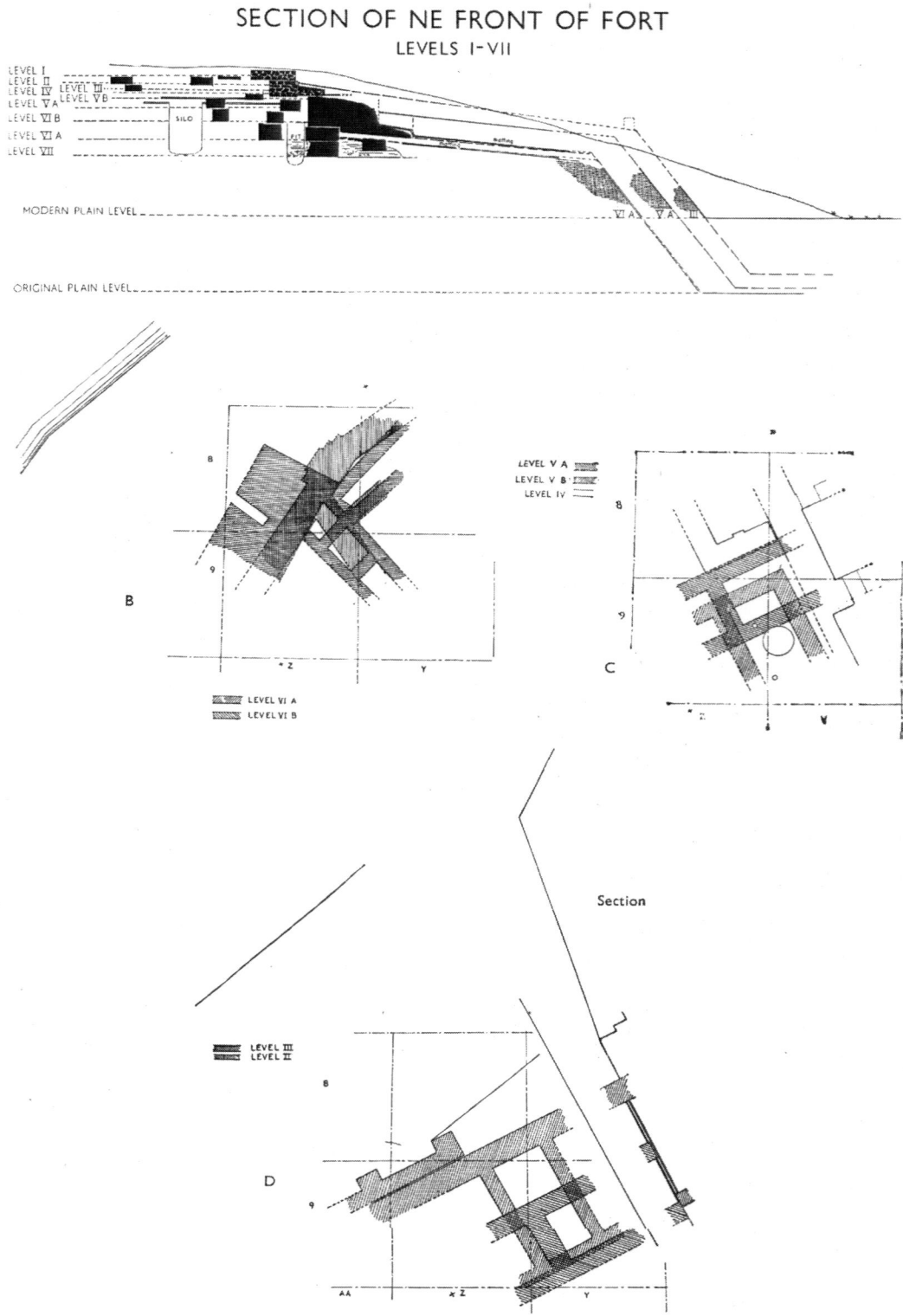

FIG. 58

Plan 30. Levels VII–I^W fortresses and fortifications in the northeast (after Woolley 1955: 154, Fig. 58)

THE NORTHWEST GATE OF THE TOWN AND PART OF THE CASTLE

LEVEL IV

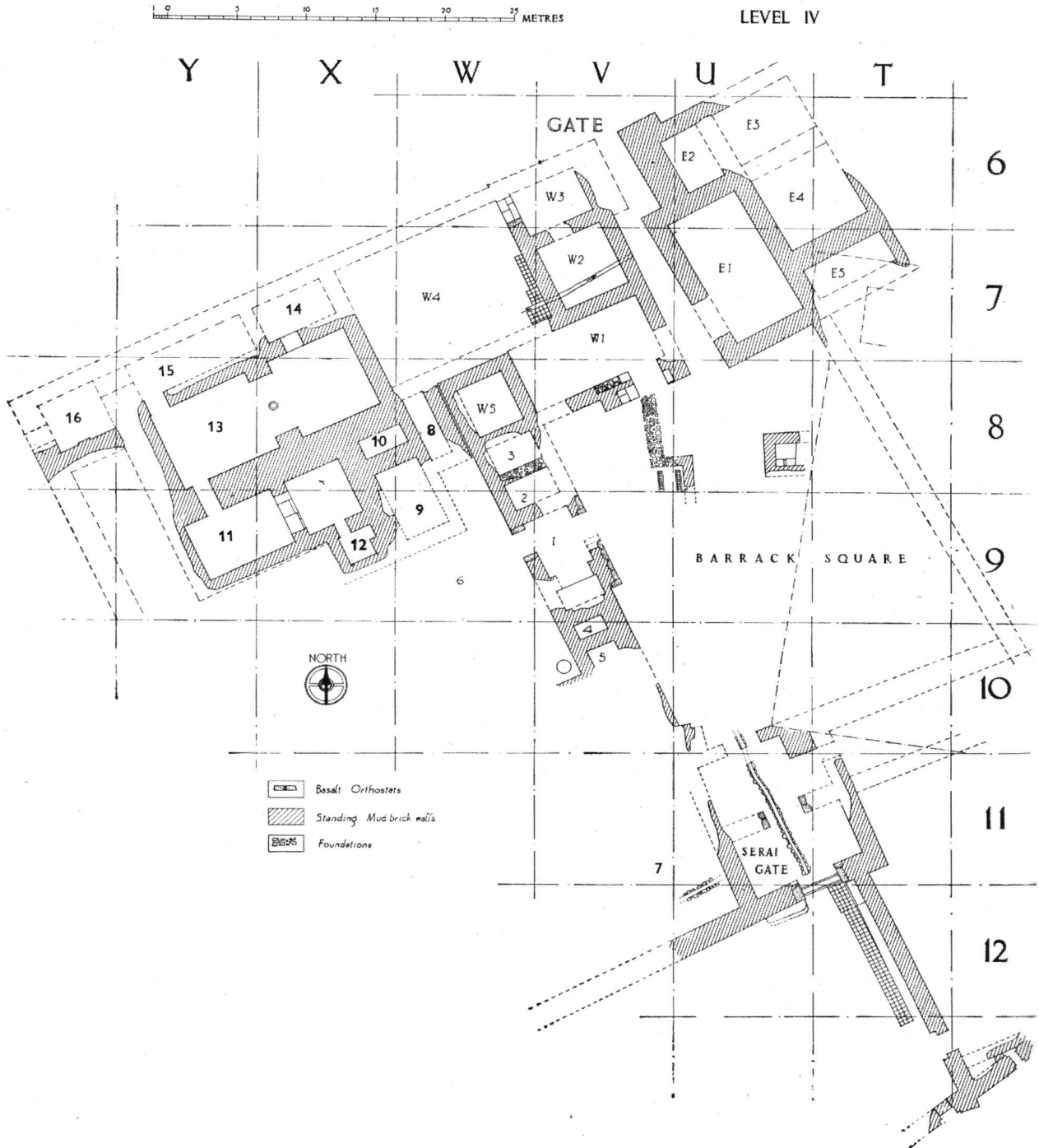

FIG. 57

Plan 31. Level IV^W fortress/Level VB^F palace (after Woolley 1955: 152, Fig. 57)

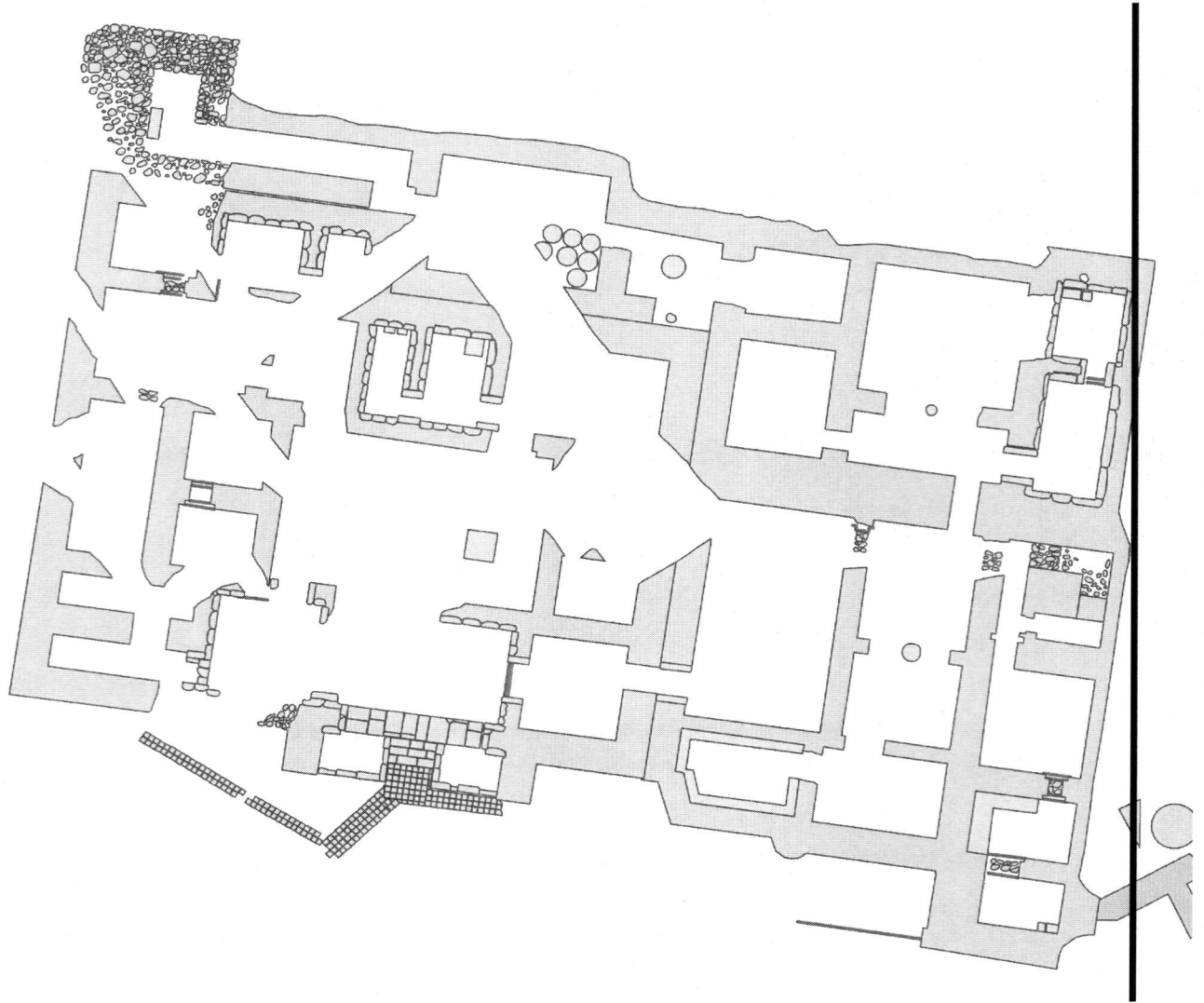

Plan 32. Level IV^W Niqmepa and Ilimilimma palace (image by Eudora Struble)

THE LEVEL IV PALACE

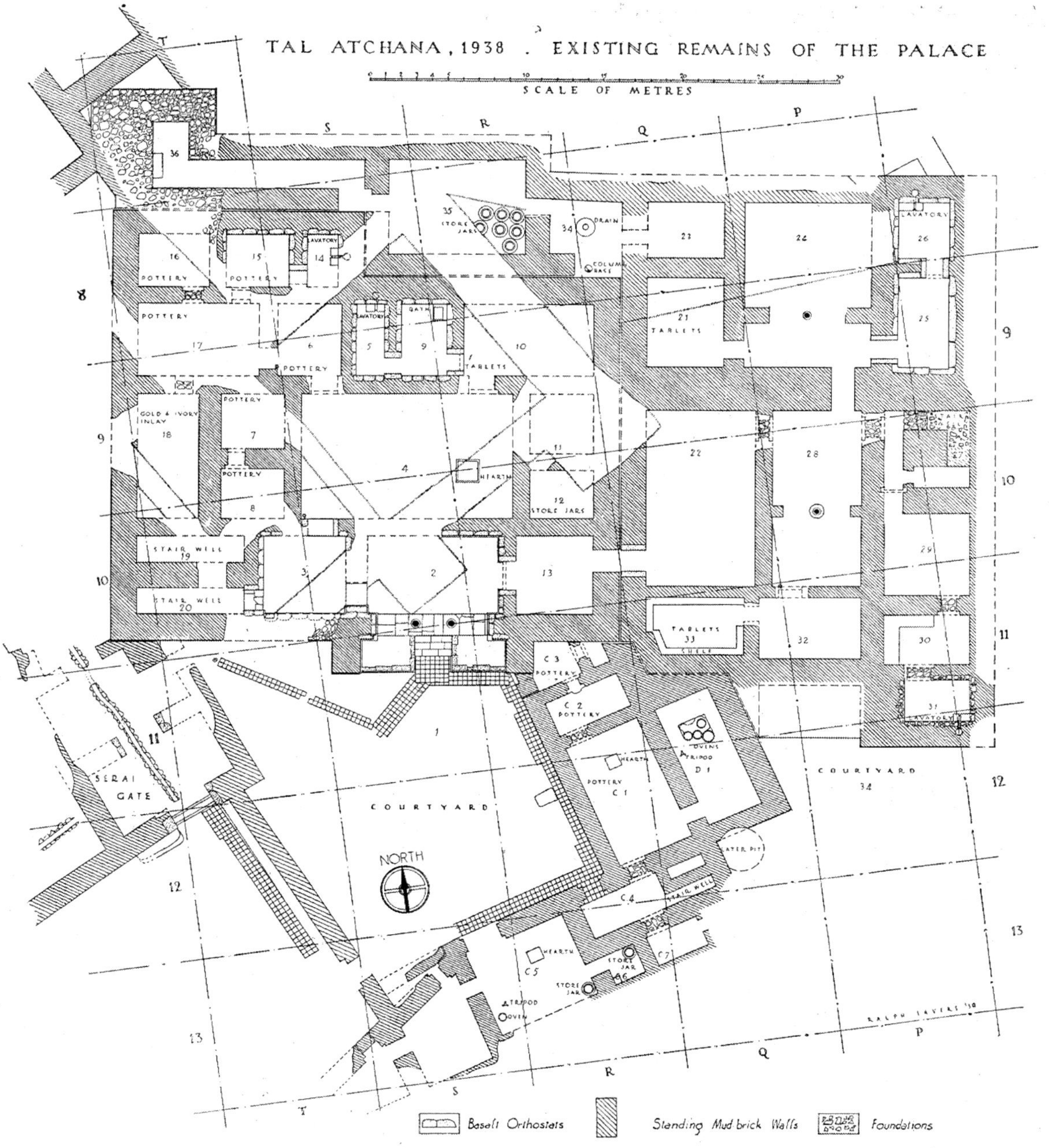

FIG. 44

B 2501

I

Plan 33. Level IV^W/IVA^F palace (after Woolley 1955: 113, Fig. 44)

THE LEVEL IV PALACE

115

TEL ATCHANA 1938. RESTORED PLAN OF THE PALACE.

Fig. 45

Plan 34. Level IV^W/IVA^F palace. Reconstruction (after Woolley 1955: 115, Fig. 45)

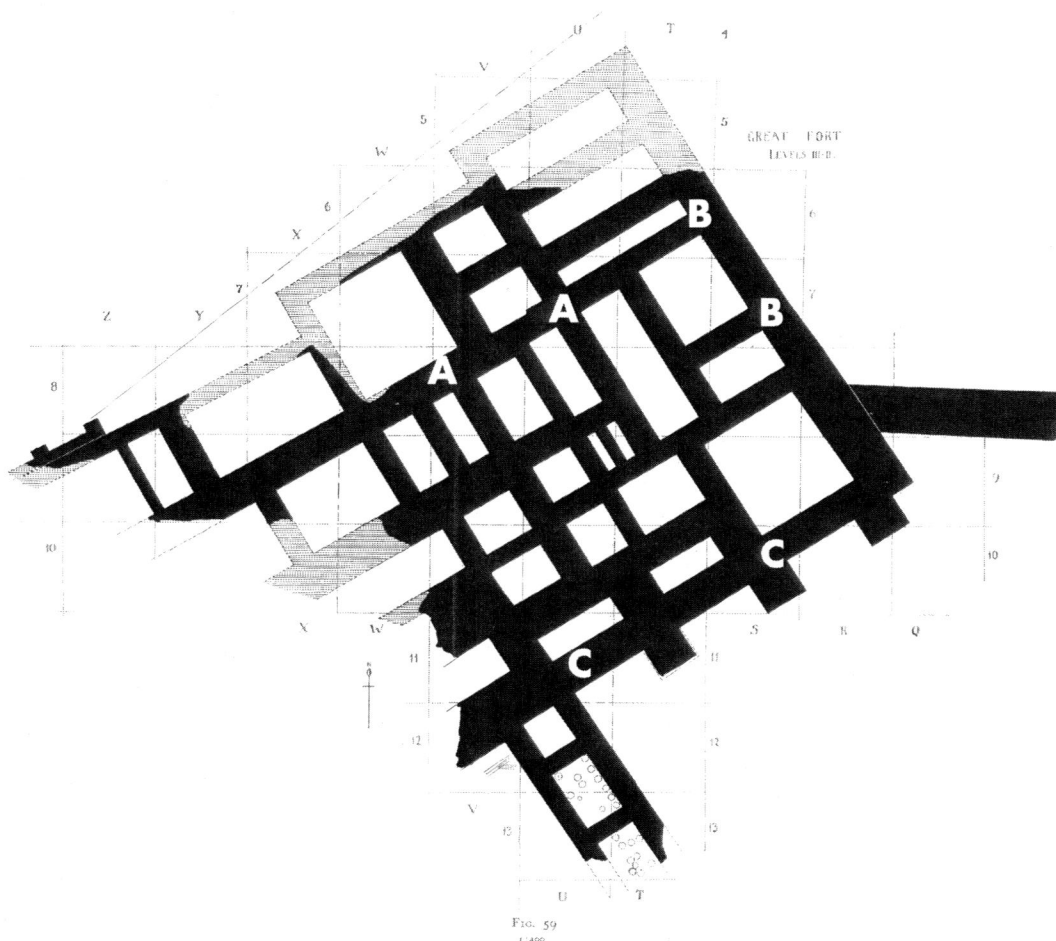

Plan 35. Levels III–II^W fort/Level IVB^F palace (after Woolley 1955: Fig. 59)

Undeniably, von Dassow's proposal that Idrimi actually built the "Niqmepa palace," and Niqmepa constructed the "Ilimilimma palace," is at this stage an irrefutable option, especially if one assumes that Ilimilimma's reign was too short for him to be able to build the northeastern wing of the Level IVA^F palace (Plan 32), as possibly derived from the chronological distribution of the tablets within the Level IV^W archives (von Dassow 2005: 45–46, 49–51; 2008: 45). Nonetheless, I believe that my reconstruction is more likely for the following reasons:

1) It allows each of the three kings (Idrimi, Niqmepa, Ilimilimma) to build his own wing of the palace, while continuing to use the palace of his predecessor. This is a typical dynastic behavior that places the symbolic dimension of the palace and its power in the right context: consisting of both continuity and innovation.

2) The Level IV^W fortress (Plan 31) is the earliest palace of this level. Misnamed by Woolley, some of its glory was temporarily taken from it. Nevertheless, more than half of it (the southeastern wing) was never excavated, and it is still covered by the unexcavated parts of the Level IVB^F palace (Plan 35, Levels III–II^W fort). Moreover, the Level VB^F palace (Plan 31) is five or six times bigger than each of the new wings of the Level IVA^F palace, Niqmepa's and Ilimilimma's,

both of similar size (Plan 32). In fact, the Niqmepa and Ilimilimma palaces are not palaces at all, but two impressive new wings in a drastically larger existing palace, in which they are both integrated. If Idrimi was the first king of the Level IV^W dynasty, the larger Level VB^F palace belongs to him. It is not likely that he decided to build into his palace an additional wing of completely different orientation, as the Niqmepa palace.

3) It is well harmonized in the macro-stratigraphy of Alalakh, which I have examined by analyzing sub-phases and phases, rather than by relying solely on the function of the palace.

4) It shows that in fact very little is at stake, since most scholars agree that Idrimi belongs to Level IV^W. Some scholars simply name Level IV^W buildings as Level VB^F, but the essence of these buildings (finds, date, historical figures, etc.) does not change. Unless we find a clear reliable dedication of a building to an historical figure, discovering who, Idrimi or Niqmepa, built the first wing of the Level IV^W palace, is beyond the scope of archaeology. If one accepts that historical facts are embedded in the Idrimi inscription, then one probably agrees that Idrimi ruled for about 30 years, and that during this period he built a new palace. This observation reduces the dispute over the identity of

the builder of southwestern wing of the Level IVA[F] palace to a dispute over 15–20 years, sometime in the mid-fifteenth century.

5) It allows Idrimi to be the one who besieged and conquered Level VA[W] Alalakh, now the first sub-phase of Level VA[F] (Summary Tables 1 and 2; see also above and Gates 1981: 7, n. 26), and who a few years later built the next feature in the stratigraphy: the Level IV[W] fortress, also known as the Level VB[F] palace. Von Dassow also attributes to Idrimi the siege of Level VA[W] Alalakh (2008: 43, n. 99), but at the same time believes that he built the Level IV[W] palace. If this was true, then Idrimi, in addition to these two significant activities, also rebuilt the Level VA[W] fortress, creating the Level VB[W] fortress (second stage of VA, according to Gates), and built the Level IV[W] fortress. These are too many rebuilding activities for the reign of a single king, since they include three demolitions and three building projects in the same spot!

An approach closer to mine (although ignoring the complexity of the Level IV[W] palace complex) is presented by some supporters of the ultra-low Mesopotamian chronology like van Soldt (2000: 112), who would like to see Idrimi as "overlap[ping] with VA", and Novak (2007: 396), who follows him. According to my stratigraphy of Tell Atchana, this approach works well as long as the end of Level VI[W] is not attributed to Idrimi, but to some other reason—Muršili I is certainly the favorite candidate for this destruction among the supporters of the ultra low chronology, but it is only one possible explanation for this devastation. Clearly, placing Idrimi very early in the fifteenth century will be also in favor of Freu's new chronology of Mittani (2008), where on the basis of the recently published tablets from Umm el-Marra and Tall Bazi he adds Sauštatar II to the Mittanian king list and accepts Wilhelm's suggestion (1976) to include in it another king: Parattarna II. These additions require him (due to later synchronism of Mittanian and Egyptian kings) to push Parattarna I (contemporary with Idrimi) to 1500–1480 and Sauštatar I (contemporary with Niqmepa) to 1480–1460. On the strength of synchronism between Parattarna I and Sauštatar I with Hittite and Kizzuwatnean kings, and owing to the Hittite king list, Freu (2008) and others believe that only a middle-like chronology or higher is plausible. There were eight (!) Hittite kings that represent five or six generations (Beckman 2000: 26) between Muršili I and Zidanta II, the contemporary of Idrimi and Parattarna I. It is hard to believe that this number of generations can represent less than one hundred years. Therefore, if indeed Freu (2008) is correct he is supplying serious ammunition to the supporters of a middle-like Mesopotamian chronology (but see Beckman 2000; Wilhelm 2004; Novak 2007: 396, n. 41).

As for the end of Level IVA[W], I accept von Dassow's explanations and conclusion that the Level IVA[W] palace was destroyed around 1400 (2008: 39–42). Placing Idrimi in the first quarter of the fifteenth century (Freu 2008)

requires ending Level IVA[F] circa 1420 B.C.E., which is archaeologically possible. It also annuls the reasoning of Stein (1989: 60), which allows the Level IVA[F] palace to end as late as 1375 B.C.E. It leaves Bergoffen (2005: 65) alone in her fourteenth century date (1380/1375 B.C.E.) for the destruction of the Level IVA[F] palace, although even she has accepted 1400 B.C.E. as a valid date for this destruction, based on her evaluation of Cypriote imports (ibid.: 72). I am not confident that the study of various Cypriote wares has developed to such an extent that their presence or absence should dictate so precise a date (within a range of five years). Therefore, I can not see how Bergoffen's study stands in the way of dating the end of Level IVA[F] within the range of 1420 to 1400 B.C.E.

Level VA[F] Shrines

Woolley (1955: 174–175; Gates 1981: 11; Yener 2005: 107) reports the discovery of a Level V[W] shrine underneath the southeast wall of the Level IV[W] house 39/B and southeast of it (Plan 36). Gates (1981: 11) summarizes Woolley's description as follows: "the shrine was built as a single, narrow room oriented northeast southwest in the usual Alalakh fashion. A paved doorway was set near the corner of the northwest wall... The entire shrine was built on a raised platform made of rubble, revetted with mudbrick and lined with matting and a layer of red clay." An additional parallel wall a few meters northwest of the northwestern wall of the platform causes Yener (2005: 107) to state, following Woolley's reconstruction (1955: 175), that "another shrine to the west is indicated... the overall impression of a parallel suite of sanctuaries devoted to indigenous deities is given material expression by relief-decorated, triangular stela depicting a deity wearing horned, conical headgear found there in the second shrine" (Plan 37). Other than the stela (AT/39/119), Woolley (ibid.) connects to the shrines only one additional object, a small gold crescent pendant (AT/39/103). Woolley (ibid.: 174) thought that the preserved shrine (in the southeast) lasted into Level IV[W], because he believes that rooms 1 and 2 in the Level IV[W] house 39/B (Plan 36) were built later than the other rooms, and thus allow the rest of this Level IV[W] house to coexist with the shrine.

According to his reports and plans, Woolley did not remove the shrines. However, during the 1950s a farmhouse was built on this part of the excavation, and damaged these buildings immensely (Plans 38 and 39).[10] We know nothing about the pottery that was found in the shrines. Stratigraphically, they could have been built as early as

---

[10] The farmhouse is represented by the large shape in the bottom right side of Plan 38. A superposition of the northwest walls of the Level IV[W] house 39/B and the Levels III–II[W] house 38/A can be observed in this plan on the northwest edge of the farmhouse. Since the shrines are southwest of the observed walls of the Level IV[W] house 39/B, it is clear that it was demolished when the farmhouse was built. Plan 39 is the current land registry of Tell Atchana. Only the parcel marked with the letter "C" in the northwest side of the mound was declared a site of cultural heritage (under the authority of the Hatay Museum). This is an area of about 10,000 m² (10 dunam or 1 ha.), less than five percent of a site of 210 dunam (21 ha.).

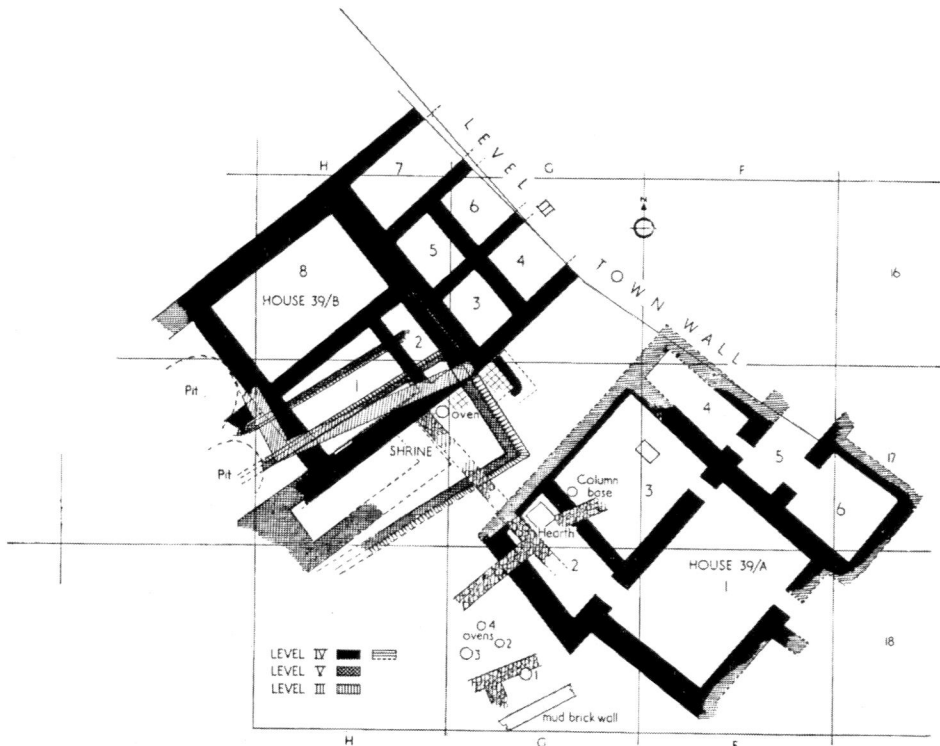

FIG. 63. Houses 39/A and 39/B, Level IV

Plan 36. Level IV^W houses 39/A–B and Level V^W shrines (after Woolley 1955: 179, Fig. 63)

Level VI^W,[11] but I find it very attractive to locate them in Level VA^W. The short coexistence between the shrines and the Level IV^W houses 39/A and 39/B prevents me from lowering the shrines to Level VA^F, without lowering also the Level IV^W houses 39/A and 39/B to VB^F, as I do below. Level VA^F, or more probably, VB^F building fragments (Plan 28), which could be part of the Level VB^F palace, were also excavated in the Level IV^W Niqmepa palace sounding (Woolley 1955: 106–108). No other Level VA^F residences were excavated.

Levels VB–IVA^F Residences

Discussing the Levels V–IV^W house 39/C Woolley declares that "in this area, as elsewhere over the whole site, Level IV follows closely on Level V with what is clearly a gradual and peaceful transition" (1955: 174). In what follows I will claim that most of the Level IVA^F residences have their origins in Level VB^F and that they went through a steady but slow process of change, as one would expect to happen in residences during a relatively calm period of two to three generations (from Idrimi to Niqmepa). I will also claim that these residences were destroyed or went out of function together with the Level IVA^F palace during the time of Ilimilimma. New houses were built on them in the beginning of Level IVB^F/Levels III–II^W, the time between the overthrow of Ilimilimma (circa 1420–1400) and the

defeat of Itūr-Addu by Šuppiluliuma I (1353/1341).[12] Woolley believes that the Level IV^W houses 37, 39/A, 39/B and 39/C functioned all through Level IV^W until they were destroyed by Šuppiluliuma I. His different date is based on his interpretation of the Levels III–II^W remains as built under Hittite rule. My reasons for an earlier date of the remains of Levels III–II^W that includes them in Level IVB^F are discussed separately below.

Level IV^W houses 37 and 39/A (Plans 36, 40)

Nothing in Woolley's description of the Level IV^W house 37 (1955: 175–178) suggests any stratigraphic complexity about this building. The underlying area was not excavated by Woolley, and thus, we do not know its stratigraphic relationships with features of earlier periods. It is described as a well preserved fourteen-room residence in which many artifacts were found; most or all of these probably date to the end of Level IVA^F, by simple comparison between the finds in the house and the finds in the Level IV^W palace and fortress (Yazıcıoğlu 2004: tables 2, 3, 10, 14–17).[13]

When Batiuk and Burke (2005) reassembled all the separately published plans of Level IV^W they found out that the Level IV^W house 37 overlaps with the Level IV^W house 39/A in square F18 (Plan 26 includes their compilation of Plans 36 and 40). Yener (2005: 109) explains that "if the plan of House 37 is correctly placed in the grid square

---

[11] Woolley reports that he found some remnants of a Level VI^W temple on top of the Level VII^W palace and underneath the Level IV^W temple (1955: 65–66, 67, Fig. 29b; herein Plan 23).

[12] See discussion on the dating of this event in Section 3.3, note 41.
[13] I would like to thank Bike Yazıcıoğlu for providing me a copy of her unpublished MA thesis.

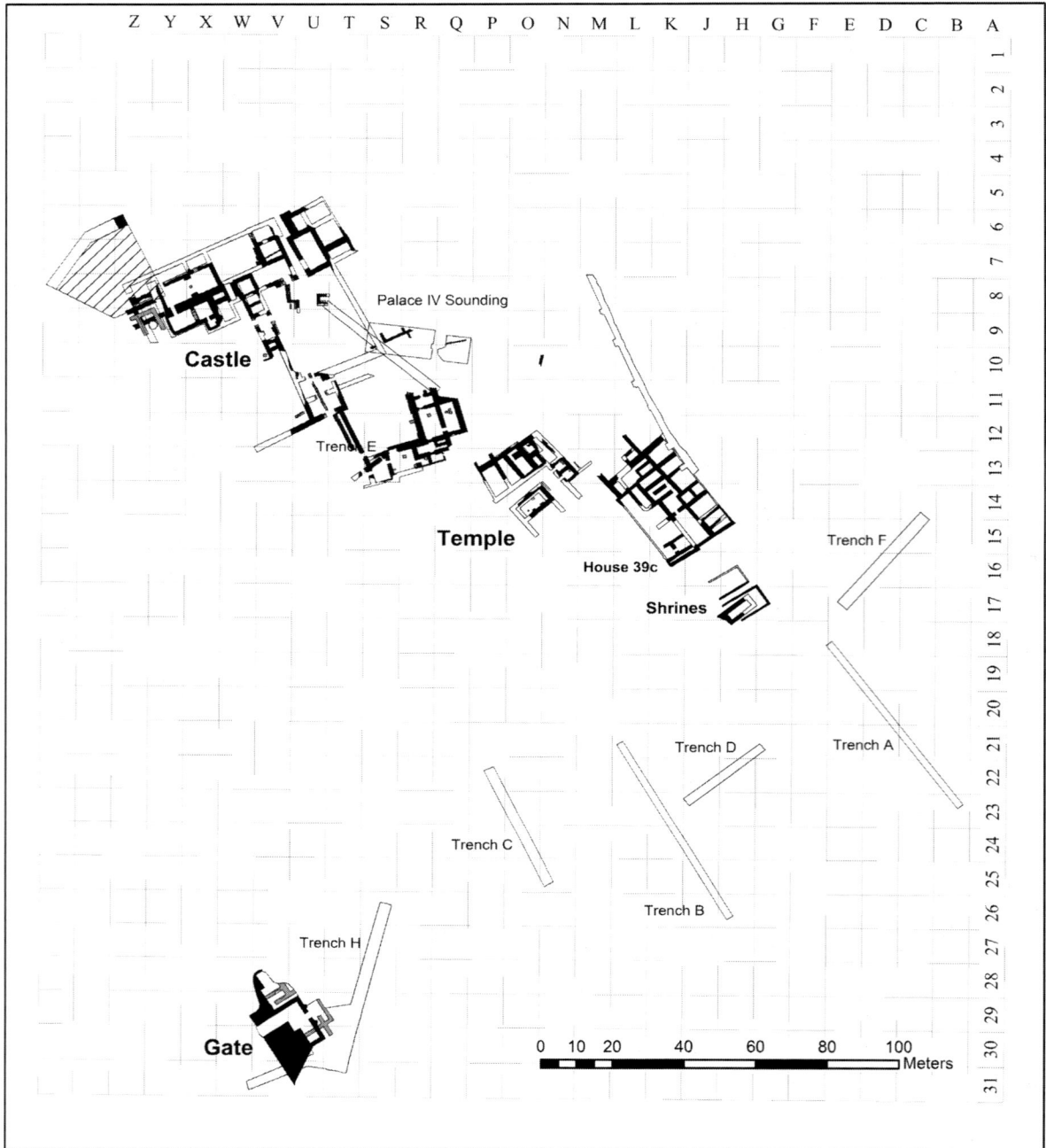

Z Y X W V U T S R Q P O N M L K J H G F E D C B A

Palace IV Sounding

Castle

Trench E

Temple

House 39c

Shrines

Trench F

Trench D

Trench A

Trench C

Trench B

Trench H

Gate

0 10 20 40 60 80 100 Meters

N

Level V

Plan 37. Plan of Level V^W (after Yener 2005: 140, Fig. 4.29)

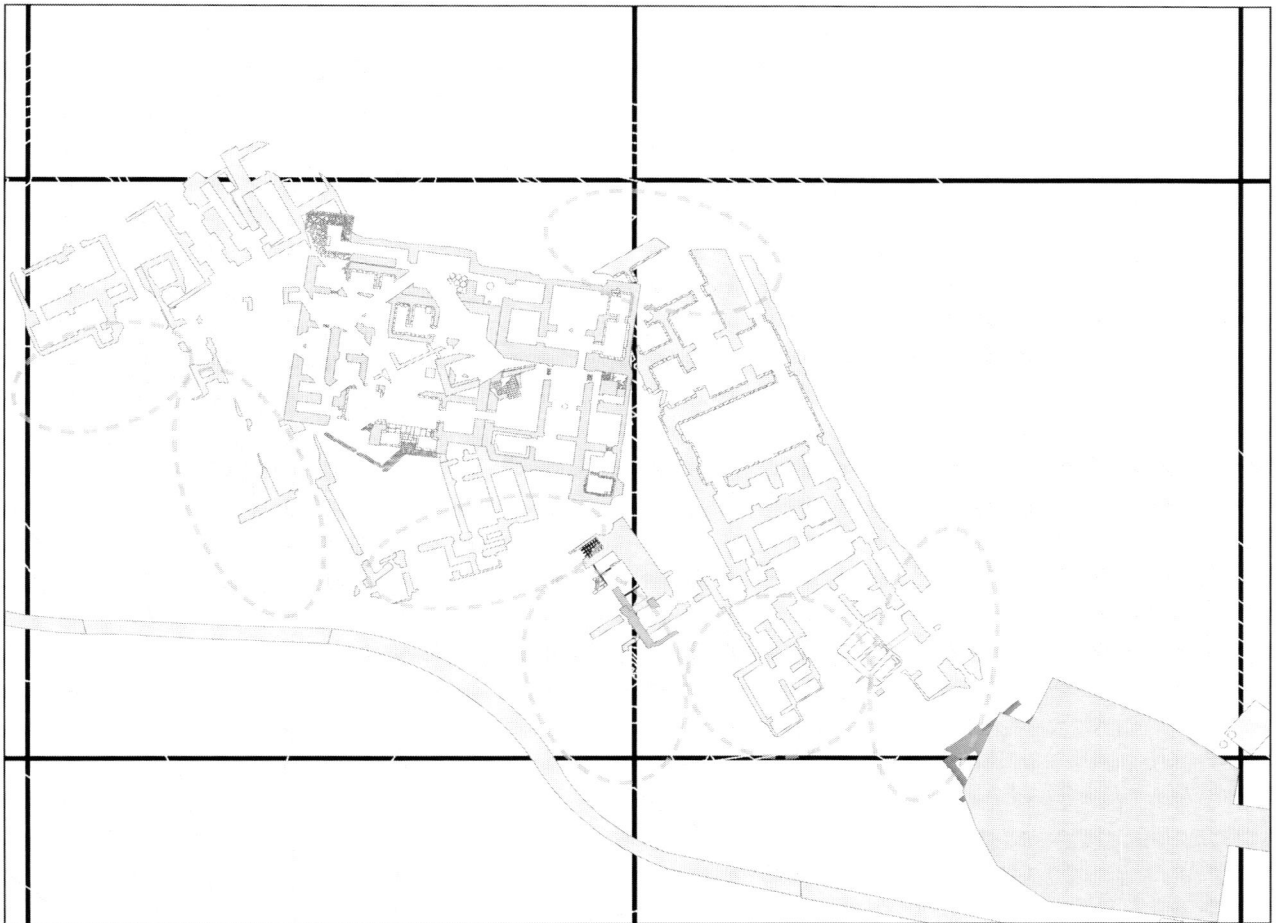

Plan 38. Superposition of Levels VII^W and IV^W palaces, the Level IV^W fortress, the buildings around them and a modern farmhouse (image by Eudora Struble)

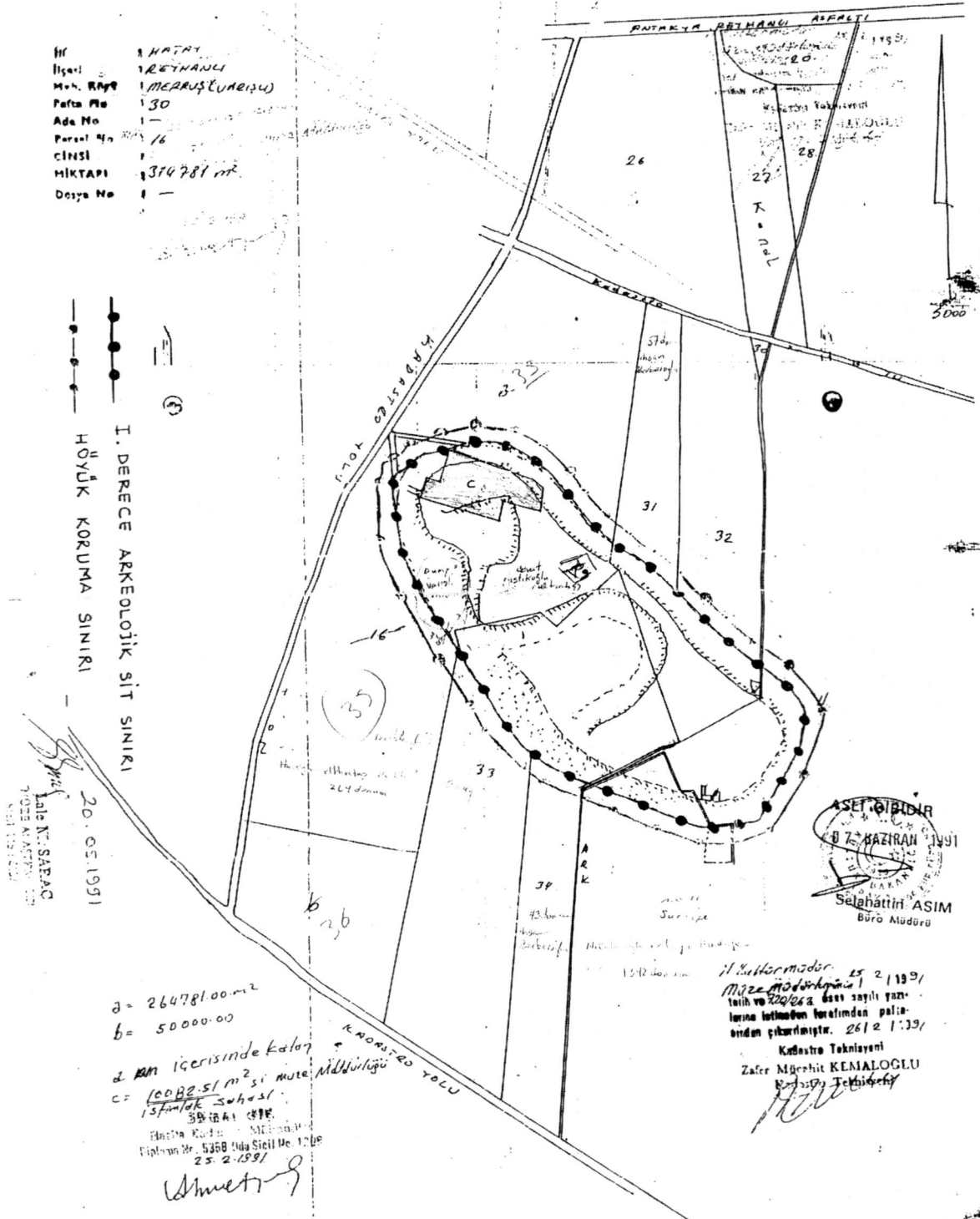

Plan 39. The Turkish government land registry of Tell Atchana, 1991.

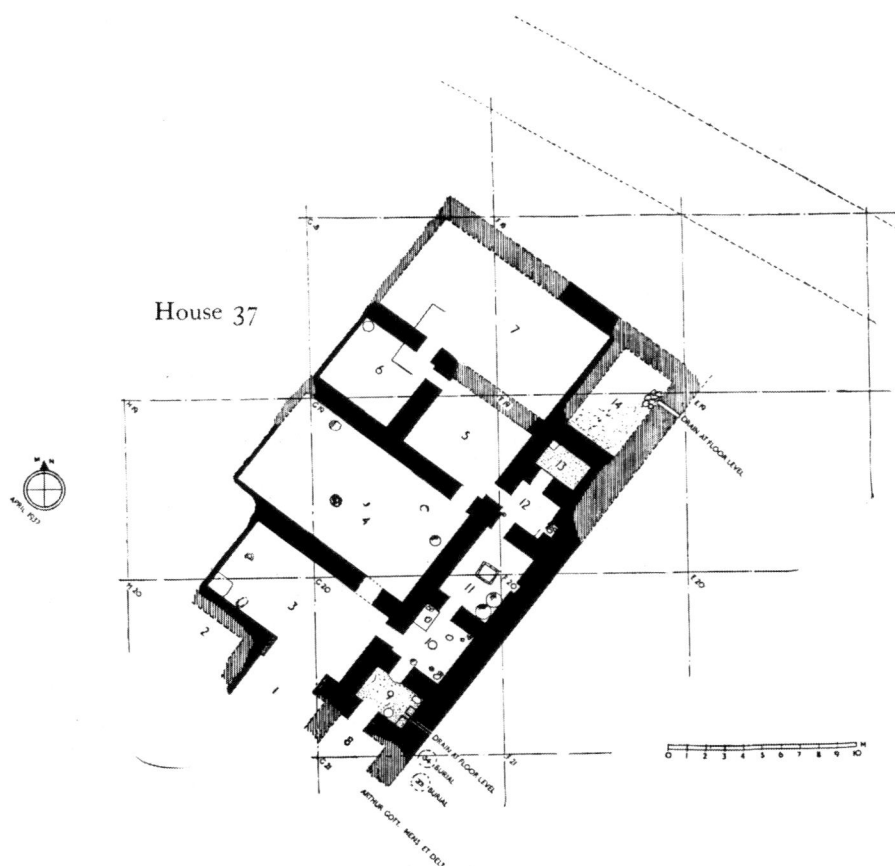

FIG. 62

Plan 40. Level IV^W house 37 (after Woolley 1955: 176, Fig. 62)

and does date to Level IV, then the two buildings overlap in Square F18, suggesting a phase displacement here." Unlike the rest of the levels under discussion in this paper, Woolley did publish a level plan for Level IV^W (Plan 41). In Woolley's plan the Level IV^W house 37 does not overlap with the Level IV^W house 39/A, but shares its northwest wall. If Woolley indeed made a mistake here, then the Level IV^W house 37 was built later than the Level IV^W house 39/C for the simple reason that it was excavated in 1937, two years before, and obviously above, the Level IV^W house 39/C. In this case, at least part of the Level IV^W house 39/C, if not the whole feature, is earlier in date than the Level IV^W house 37.[14]

---

[14] Bergoffen (2005: 31, n. 176) solves this problem by moving the Level IV^W house 37 ten meters (one square) to the east: "the grid on the plan Fig. 62 (here Plan 40—A.S.F.) was erroneously shown one square west of the position recorded on Pl. XXII (here Plan 41—A.S.F.). If the reconstructed northeast wall of the building were in square F18, it would run over the middle room 1 of house 39/A." Bergoffen feels that something is wrong, but does not put her finger on the heart of the problem. Woolley on both Plans (40 and 41) actually placed the northeast wall of the Level IV^W house 37 in square E18, as becomes evident upon careful consideration of his recording system. In Plan 40, as (inconsistently) elsewhere, squares are designated by letter-number combinations in the top left corner of the square to the right, as I explained in Chapter 2. Moreover, on Plan 41 he shows that the northwest wall of the Level IV^W house 37 is one and same as the southeast wall of the Level IV^W house 39/A, but as Batiuk and Burke (2005) deduced, this is not in harmony with Plan 36 of Level IV^W house 39/A.

There are two more options, which I believe are more likely to be correct:

1) In the previous chapters I described in length the weaknesses of Woolley's recording system. One of the main flaws is Woolley's grid, which was oriented to more than one "north." This surveying error caused Woolley to use, in fact, more than one grid, while naming these grids with one system of labels, as if they were one grid. One of these grids is oriented to the magnetic north. Three of the plans that were drawn in April 1937 were oriented to the magnetic north of that month and not to the grid-north as they should have been. These were the plans of the Level IV^W house 37 (Plan 40), the Levels III–II^W houses 37/A–D and 38/A (Woolley 1955: 187, Fig. 65; herein Plan 42) and the Level I^W houses 37/A–B (Woolley 1955: 194, Fig. 68; herein Plan 43). Unlike the Level IV^W house 37 (Plan 40), the Level IV^W house 39/A (Plan 36) is oriented to grid-north. When Woolley published the complete Level IV^W plan (Plan 41), he corrected the plan of Level IV^W house 37, tilting it several degrees to the east.

2) In his description of the Level IV^W house 39/A Woolley (1955: 178) writes: "It had been founded early in the Level IV period, so much so that the destruction of its southeast quarter had been effected to make room

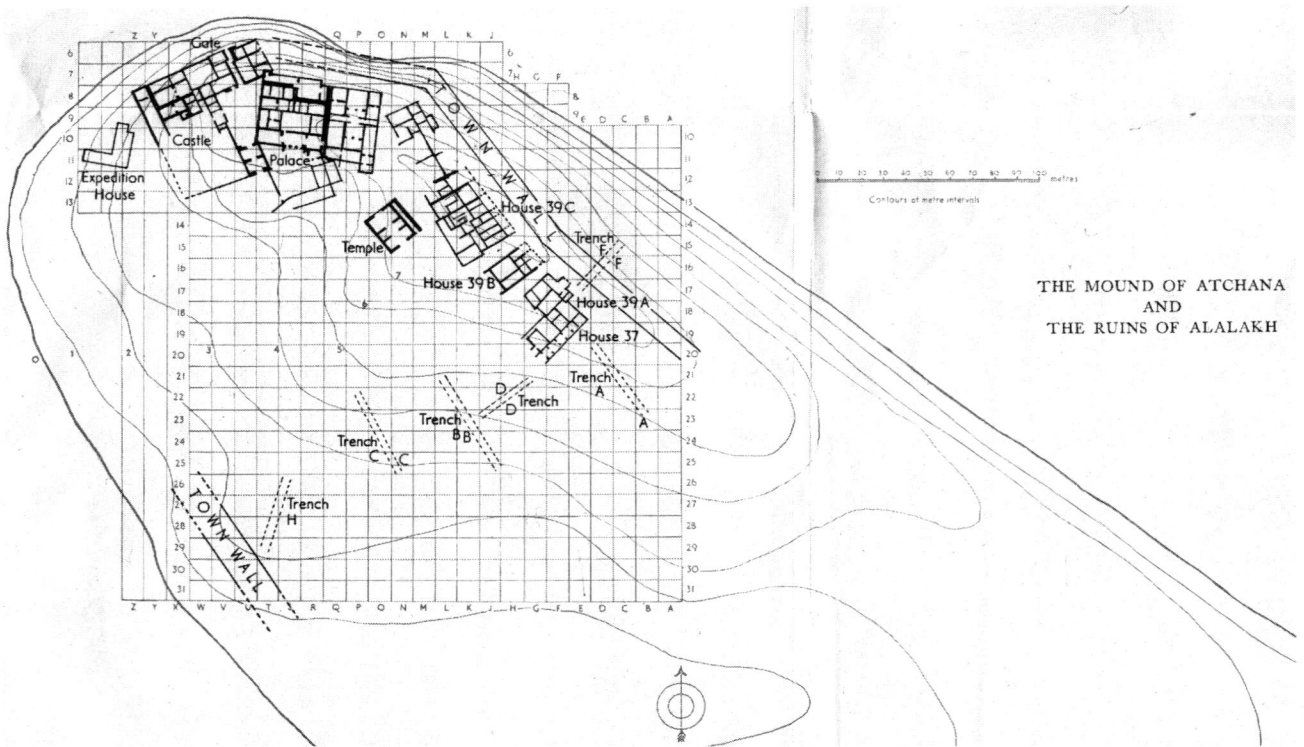

Above: **Plan 41. Plan of Level IV^W (after Woolley 1955: Pl. XXII)**

Below: **Plan 42. Levels III–II^W houses 37/A–D and 38/A (after Woolley 1955: 187, Fig. 65)**

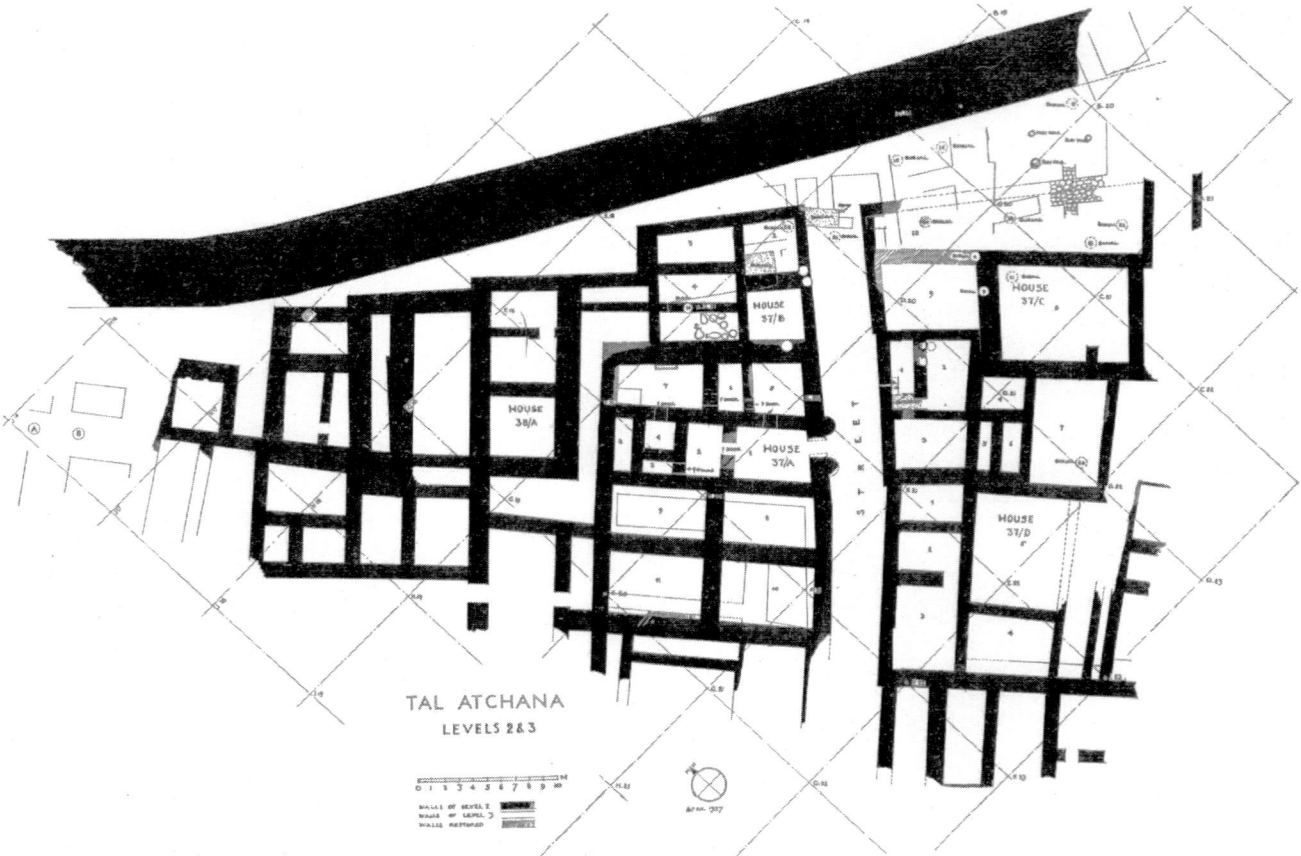

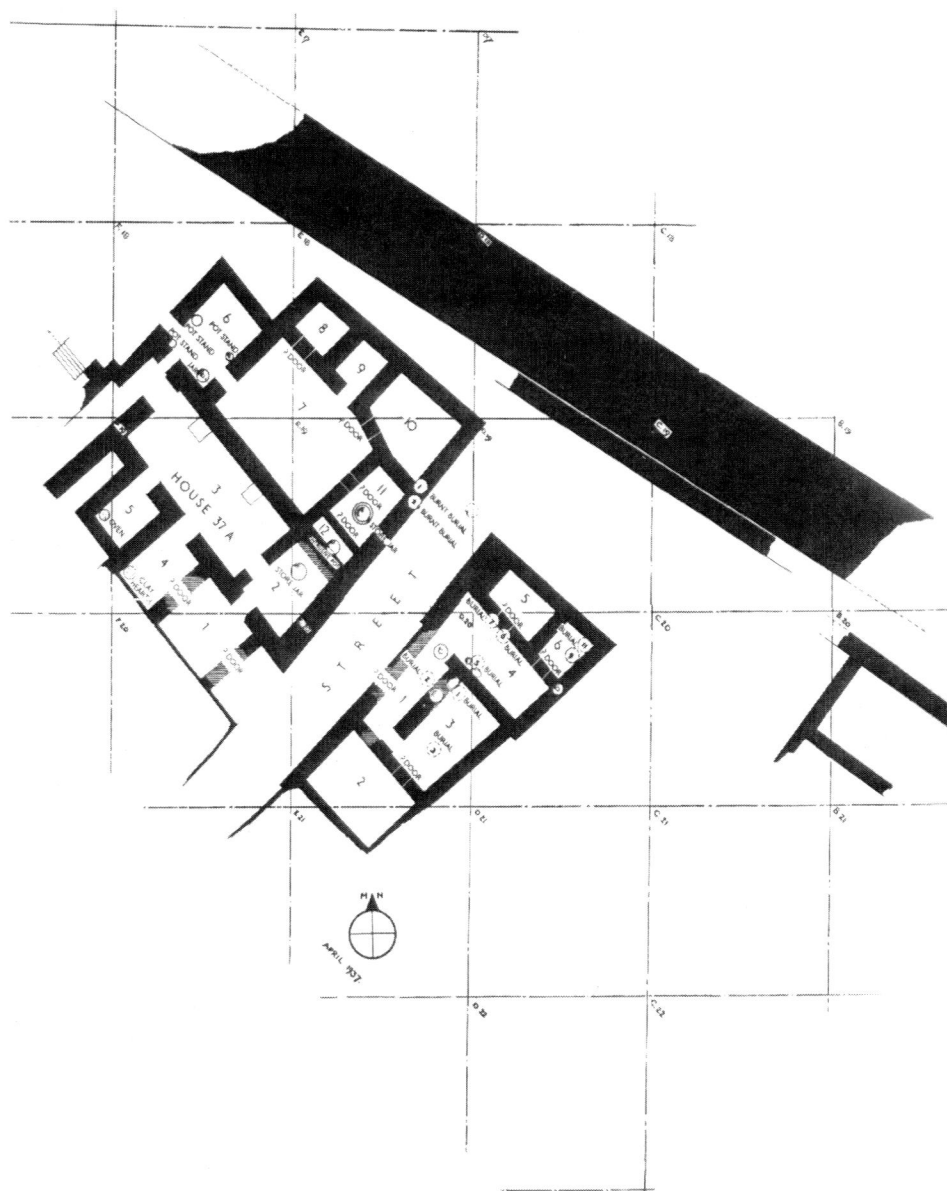

FIG. 68. Houses 37/A and 37/B, Level I

Plan 43. Level I^W houses 37/A–B (after Woolley 1955: 194, Fig. 68)

for its neighbor, house 38; but the rest of it had been rebuilt and was in contemporary use with that neighbor through the reminder of the period." This description is problematic mostly because Woolley never named a structure "house 38"—there are houses 38/A and 38/B of several periods, but no house 38. Even if he were referring to one of these, the Level II^W house 38/A is located southeast of the Level IV^W house 39/A, but is definitely not contemporaneous with it. The only contemporary structure, located southeast of the Level IV^W house 39/A, is Level IV^W house 37. This brings me to the conclusion that Woolley made a typing mistake in his description, writing "house 38" instead of "house 37." Reading his description once the typo is corrected, we learn that Level IV^W house 39/A was reshaped in order to allow the space for the Level IV^W house 37 to be built next to it. The Level IV^W house

39/A in Plan 36 represents its first building phase (early, could be its blueprint during Level VB^F), while the Level IV^W house 39/A in Plan 42 represents its final building phase (late, could be its blueprint during Level IVA^F).

The area underneath the Level IV^W house 39/A was not excavated by Woolley, and thus, we do not know its stratigraphic relationships with earlier period features. It is described as a soundly built, well-preserved structure with mud brick walls over rubble foundations, standing to an average height of one meter (Woolley 1955: 178–179). It is possible that the northeast rooms of the building (4, 5 and 6) are actually part of a separate building, the other remains of which were removed when the Levels III–II^W (IVB^F) city wall was built (ibid.). I date most of the structures of Levels III–II^W to Level IVB^F (see below).

Consequently, both Level IV[W] houses 37 and 39/A were destroyed either in the same event as the destruction of the Level IVA[F] palace, or as a result of a large scale construction project during the early days of Level IVB[F]. This project included the building of the most massive fortifications in the archaeological records of the city: the Levels III–II[W]/IVB[F] city wall.

In summary, it is more likely that the Level IV[W] house 37 was built in Level IVA[F] than in VB[F], but the two options are viable. The Level IV[W] house 39/A was built in Level VB[F] and ceased to exist, together with the Level IV[W] house 37, at the end of Level IVA[F].

My stratigraphic observation is that the two residences went out of function together with the Level IVA[F] palace. One way of examining this conclusion is to compare to what extent the artifacts unearthed in the residences and the palace are contemporaneous. This comparison can be easily made due to Bike Yazıcıoğlu's meticulous work, which summarizes the finds in the Level IV[W] residences and in the palace (2004: tables 2, 3, 10, 14–17). All the major imported or elaborate wares present in the final stage of the Level IV[W] house 37 are also present in the final stage of Level IV[W] palace and fortress. These include the following wares: Nuzi, White Slip, Base Ring and Red Lustrous Wheel-made.[15] None of these wares are reported found in Level IV[W] house 39/A.

Level IV[W] house 39/B (Plan 36)

Of this house (Woolley 1955: 179–180) only the central group of rooms was preserved (eight rooms in total). To the northeast, all rooms are cut by the Levels III–II[W]/IVB[F] city wall. To the southwest the area is disturbed by later level rubbish pits, a fact that caused Woolley not to excavate this house any further in that direction. There are several indications that the Level IV[W] house 39/B in fact consisted of two adjacent buildings: the (probably earlier) northeast Level IV[W] house 39/B (rooms 3–7), and the (probably later) southwest Level IV[W] house 39/B (rooms 1, 2 and 8). The full extent of both of these buildings is unknown. The indications that brought me to this conclusion are:

1) The double wall between the southwest rooms 2 and 8 and the northeast rooms 3, 5 and 7 was clearly built in two stages (ibid.). This is a typical phenomenon when one building is free standing, and the other one is built against an outer wall of the first built.
2) Woolley (ibid.: 180) admits that "in no case was it possible to trace features such as doorways", and therefore his reconstruction of the structure as one building is an hypothesis that opens the door for alternative reconstructions.
3) The width of the walls of each of the two houses, northeast and southwest, is almost identical within each unit, but very dissimilar from the other unit as if they were built in accordance to a different blueprint.

4) Woolley believes that at least part of the southwest house (rooms 1–2) was built later than the rest of the building because the preserved Level V[W] shrine (the southeastern) was contemporary with the northeast part of Level IV[W] house 39/B. If there were two shrines, which were simultaneously active, this would require not only rooms 1 and 2, but also room 8, to be later than the rest. These three rooms are more likely the northeastern segment of an independent building, than the southwest component of Level IV[W] house 39/B.

My next consideration is to date the two buildings, the Level IV[W] house 39/B northeast and southwest. Woolley (1955: 179) writes that "the building was remodeled at least once and probably twice… In the northwest half of it some of the walls may go back to Level V or are founded on Level V walls; the south part, however, is later and runs over the top of the Level V shrine…" He also reports (ibid.: 180) that "the ground-level in and round the house rose 0.50 m. to 0.60 m. during its occupation and at some time when this rise was in progress the shrine was abandoned and buried…" and that in room 1 of the later southwest segment "two floor-levels were noted, one 0.15–0.20 m. above the other, both of beaten clay mixed with rubbish. At a later period the shape of the room was altered, a new exterior wall being built askew, and new stone foundations were laid over the surviving brickwork of the northeast wall of the room." Woolley attributes this final remodeling to the Level III[W] period. Based on Woolley's observations I propose the following relative chronological scheme:

1) The shrines were built first during Level VA[F], or possibly even during Level VI[W]. They function as late as Level VB[F], when the Level V[W] temple becomes the worship center of the royal precinct.
2) The northeast segment was built alongside the shrines early in Level VB[F], and went out of use by the end of Level IVA[F], or early in Level IVB[F]. They clearly had gone out of use by the time the Levels III–II[W] city wall was constructed. Two floor levels were observed in rooms 3 and 6 (ibid.).
3) The southwest segment was built either late in Level VB[F] or early during Level IVA[F] after the shrines went out of function. It was replaced by a Level III[W]/IVB[F] building early in Level IVB[F], the walls of which are observable in Plan 36, mainly in square H17. Woolley suggests that room 8 "was certainly part of a Level V house incorporated in that of Level IV, for its walls went down, and connected with them there was a clay floor nearly 0.80 m. below the normal level of the Level IV floors." Nevertheless, he found in room 8 the same number of floors that he found in room 1 (two), and these floors correspond to a shred wall. If room 1 did not begin in Level V[W] (since it cancels the southeast shrine), there is no reason to believe that room 8 did. I interpret room 8 in its early Level IVB[F] stage as the cellar of a two-story building.

[15] See Bergoffen 2005 for details on the sub-groups of each ware, and more on specific vessels.

Fig. 64

Plan 44. Level IV^W house 39/C (after Woolley 1955: 181, Fig. 64)

The finds under the floor of room 1 include White Slip ware I and II, which is no surprise considering the mid-fifteenth century B.C.E. date of construction posited here.

Level IV^W house 39/C (Plan 44)

One of the largest residences at Tell Atchana, and certainly the largest in Level IV^W, is house 39/C, in which a clear indication for the existence of a second floor—a staircase in room 14—was found (Woolley 1955: 180–182, Fig. 64; herein Plan 44). Woolley reports that it is dated in its earliest phase to Level V^W (ibid.: 174–175), "but it was terribly ruined, the walls being so destroyed that the emplacement of the doorways could seldom be determined, and the stratification was so complicated that it was seldom possible to assign objects to a definite level" (ibid.: 181). Nevertheless, Woolley identifies several walls that are either reused Level V^W walls or Level V^W walls found under the Level IV^W floors (Plan 44). These are the walls between rooms 4, 5 and 7 and the original walls of rooms 1 and 2. Some of the walls of Level IV^W house 39/C were also reused as Levels III–II^W walls, "though for a building of entirely different character" (ibid.) All the northeast rooms of this building (4, 5, 7, 11, 15, 17 and 21) are more or less disturbed by the Levels III–II^W/IVB^F town wall (nicely represented in the Level VII^W palace section drawing, herein Plan 12). Remains of additional Level IV^W buildings were found northwest of the Level IV^W

house 39/C (ibid.: 137–139). Woolley barely describes them and in general terms only (ibid.), but he included them in his Fig. 53 (Plan 13), correctly inserted into Yener's Level IV^W outline (Plan 26). The growth and expansion of the Level IV^W house 39/C through time is similar to that of most of the other Level IV^W buildings. It was built during Level VB^F, when the city enjoyed a construction-boom under king Idrimi. It was in use uninterruptedly throughout the course of Level IVA^F until its replacement by a Levels III–II^W/IVB^F structure. Woolley attributes no dateable material to this building: the only way to place it on the chronological scheme is by applying stratigraphy. Two important stratigraphic phenomena are attested here: the ongoing rebuilding process from Levels VB^F to IVA^F and the termination of the building by the Levels III–II^W city wall (IVB^F). These two observable facts are common to three buildings (Level IV^W houses 39/A, 39/B-northwest and 39/C), and therefore, the date of the Levels III–II^W city wall (IVB^F) is crucial to any attempt in dating the time they went out of function. While Woolley dated this city wall to the Hittite occupation of Alalakh and hence assumed these buildings to have been destroyed when Šuppiluliuma I took over Alalakh (1353/1341), I believe that this city wall was built early in the Level IVB^F period, sometime between 1400 and 1380 (see below). The renovations that these buildings underwent suit a gradual development of residences

87

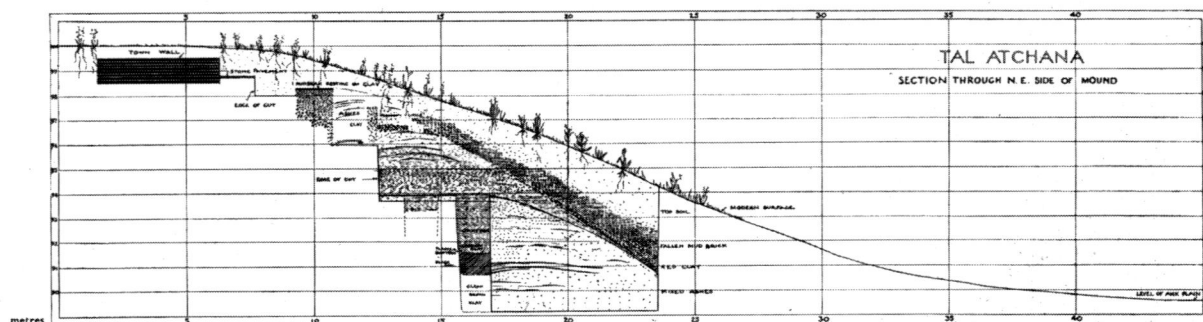

FIG. 52*a*

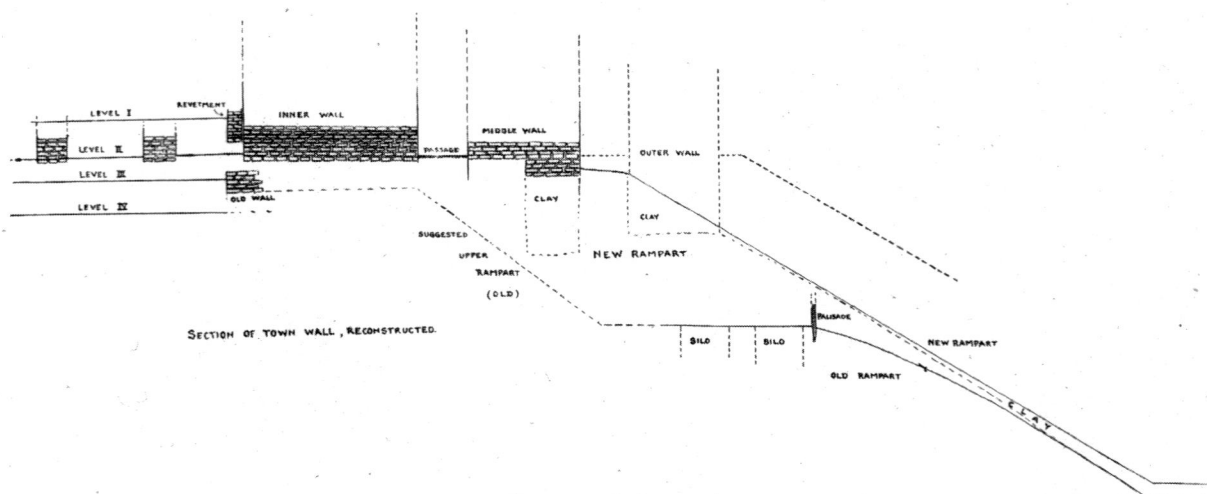

FIG. 52*b*. Scale 1:250

Plan 45. Trench F (after Woolley 1955: 136, Fig. 52)

as one would expect over a relatively calm period of 60 years or so, the time of Idrimi, Niqmepa and Ilimilimma, Levels VB–IVA[F].

Level IV[W] city wall and rampart

Woolley's interpretation of Trench F (Plan 45/a) presents remains of one city wall phase[16] (Level II[W]—"the embankments can be dated by their pottery content") and two layers of ramparts (1955: 135–137).[17] He dates the ramparts by comparing the pottery found in them to the pottery he knows from his excavated levels. His reasonable assumption is that the soil of which each rampart is constructed contains pottery of all previous levels to the

level in which it was constructed. Therefore, the latest type represented in the soil comes from one level before the level in which it was constructed. Woolley dates the lower one to Level VII[W], based on the presence in the soil of his pottery types 21, 23 and 100.[18] He dates the upper one to Level VB[W] or IV[W] based on the presence of White Slip ware, and the lack of the local painted banded ware. Woolley is aware of the limitation of this dating method of the features in Trench F (ibid.: 134)—it is little better than an educated guess. In chorus with Woolley's methodology, which is the best one can offer unless another section of the fortifications is excavated, I suggest that Level VB[F] is the one period in which a construction project of this scale could have taken place. It is probable that when Idrimi built his large palace, he also fortified the city as a whole. This date is also a compromise between Woolley's two optional dates.

The ramparts were clearly attested only in the northeast and northwest slopes of the site, and not in the excavations on the southwest slopes of the mound (Site H). Woolley makes a very reasonable assumption that the fortifications in the southwest were meek since the Orontes River

---

[16] named in this paper the Levels III–II[W]/IVB[F] city wall.

[17] Woolley added to his reconstructed section of Trench F (Plan 45/b) several stubs of city walls of Levels IV–I[W] (left part of the reconstructed section), though ruins of only two of the parallel walls of the Levels III–II[W]/IVB[F] city wall were in fact found intact. Woolley also reconstructs in Plan 47/b a stub of a city wall that according to the plan could belong either to Level IV[W] or III[W]. Since no independent Level III[W] was found, this must be a Level IV[W] city wall. The location of this wall in Trench F underneath the Levels III–II[W]/IVB[F] city wall, as well as below the Level I[W]/III[F] city wall revetment, places the wall in the middle of square E17. In Woolley's plan of Level IV[W] (Plan 41) the city wall is located only in the northeast corner of this square. In Yener's plan of Level IV[W] (Plan 26) the line of the city wall is properly corrected and it traverses square E17 in the middle.

[18] The suggested outlines of this rampart are marked in Woolley's plan of Level VII[W] (1955: Pl. XIV; herein Plan 46).

Photo 13. Tell Atchana, Tell Ta'yinat and Küçuk Ta'yinat in between in a CORONA 1970 satellite image. (after Casana 2003)

created a natural fortification along the southwest slope (ibid.: 139–142). The course of the river at the present time passes a few hundred meters west of the site as can be seen in the 1970 Corona satellite image (Photo 13). East of the river's meander passing closest to the site, we can observe the shadow of one ancient course of the river. The remains of this ancient river meander are located between the current meander and the site. It is likely that the ancients built the site as close as possible to the river, and that this proximity caused the accelerated erosion in the central-southwest part of the site, the area that is directly south of Woolley's grid (Plan 46).[19] This could also be the location of the important Orontes River gate of the site.

Dating city walls can be sometimes as devastating as dating their related ramparts. If the city was not significantly enlarged or contracted, the planners of its outer walls would normally have tended to follow and locate them on the same favored strategic outline, where remnants of their predecessors' walls were still observable. Therefore, many city walls are built on top of older city walls, and dividing one phase of walls from another can sometimes be hard to achieve. Woolley explains the deficiency of the Levels VI–V^W city walls by suggesting that the defenders of these levels reused

[19] While the Orontes south of Atchana must have been used as a major means of north–south transportation, the 85 km. of east–west transportation between Aleppo and Alalakh must have been traveled by land. The journey between Tell Atchana and the Mediterranean (40 km.) could be taken by land or by water, but land was also the only means of accessing the Belen pass (Syrian gates/pillars), 35 km. to the north. The size of the lake of Antioch at the time is doubtful (Casana 2003), but it is nonetheless likely that the road did not cross the plain through its lowest parts. Very close to Tell Atchana and Tell Ta'yinat the Orontes River's direction of flow shifts from north–south to east–west. For the past several hundred years one of the main bridges over the Orontes has been located two kilometers west of Tell Ta'yinat in the village of Demir Köprü (Arabic name, Jiser al Hadid), which translates to "The Iron Bridge." The word "iron" refers to a significant source of income

related to this bridge: an iron gate, placed on the stone bridge, allowed the opening and closing of the pass in accordance with the reception of fees and taxes from those crossing over. It is no great leap to assume that long before the Ottoman bridge was constructed, the rulers of both Alalakh and Patina benefited from tax collection at this strategic point. A small site between Atchana and Ta'yinat (Photo 13), known as Küçuk Ta'yinat (Ta'yinat al-Saghir—Small Ta'yinat, Amuq Survey site number 127), which was partially excavated by the Syrio-Hittite Expedition of the Oriental Institute in summer 1937 (Haines 1971: 64; Casana and Wilkinson 2005b: 227) may confirm this suspicion: No ceramic report is available for this excavation, and the site is now covered by a farmhouse, but its location and shape make it a possible candidate for a bridge-related structure. This will seem even more likely if it can be confirmed that the Orontes river course during the Late Bronze and Iron Age was, unlike nowadays, east and north of Tell Atchana, between Atchana and Ta'yinat (Casana and Gansell 2005: 159, 168).

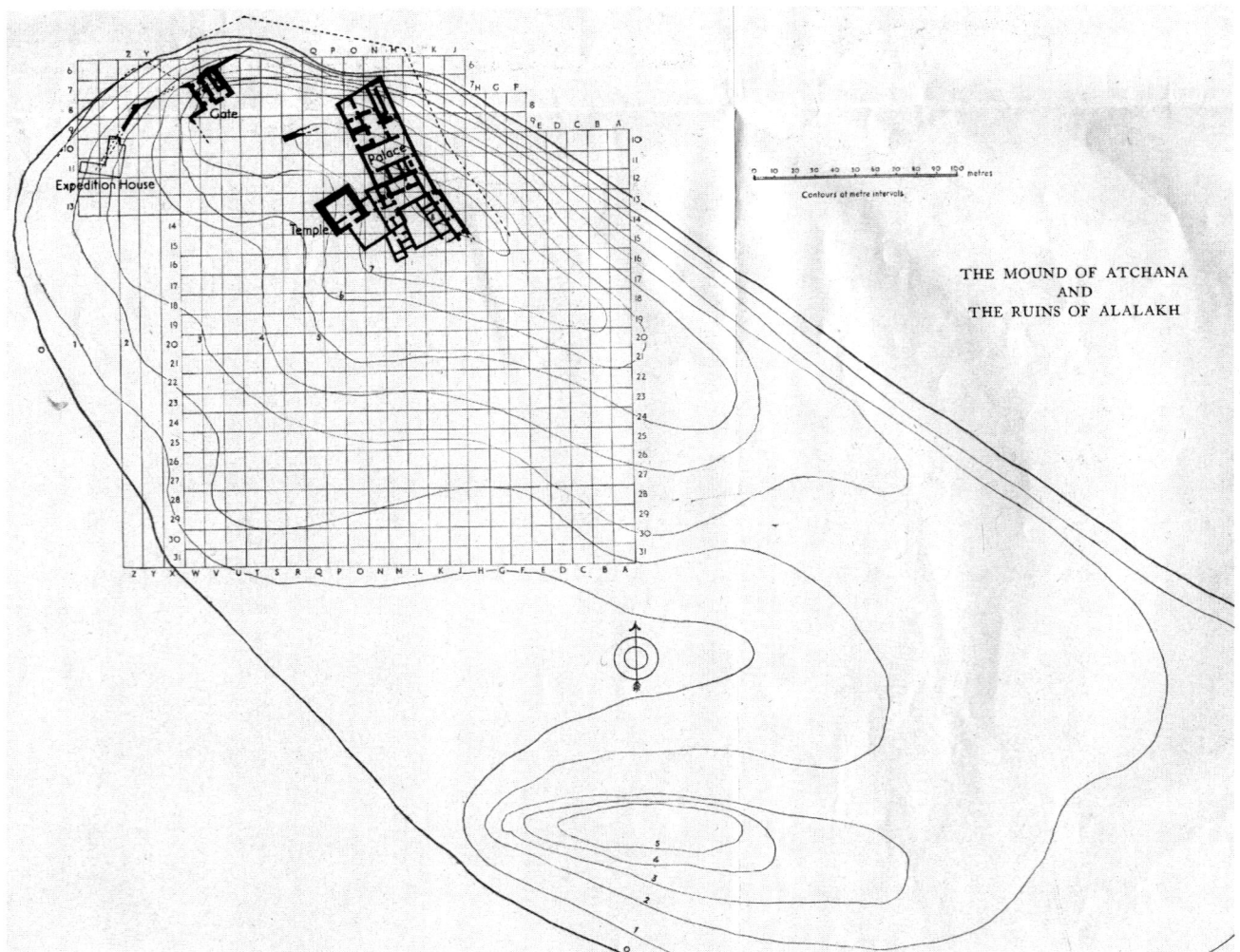

Plan 46. Plan of Level VII^W (after Woolley 1955: Pl. XIV)

the Level VII^W walls (ibid.: 137). This statement is followed by another assertion that is clearly incorrect: "in square K12 it was found that the town wall of Level IV rested immediately on the brickwork of Level VII, the inner faces of the two coinciding…" Woolley refers to Plan 12 to demonstrate his point. But as can be observed, subsequent to my addition of the square numbers and the identifications of walls of Levels VII–I^W to Section A–A of the Level VII^W palace sounding, square K12 is not represented in this section at all. The outer wall of the Level VII^W palace (Plan 46), which is also the Level VII^W city wall, is located in square J14. On top of this wall there are insignificant remains of what could be the Levels VI–V^W city wall.[20] Next in line is the outer wall of the Level IV^W house 39/C, which is also observable, although barely, in Plan 44, but this is by no means the Level IV^W city wall. The Levels III–II^W city wall (see also Plan 44) is located on top of the Level IV^W house 39/C wall. Is the picture in square K12 any different? The Level VII^W palace outer wall is located in square K12 (Plan 46). Records of Level IV–II^W walls in square K12 are found in Plans 10, 13, 41 and 44. In three of the Plans (13, 41, 44) the outer wall of room 21

of the Level IV^W house 39/C would have been located in this square, had it survived. The Levels III–II^W city wall does indeed follow the Level VII^W palace outer wall in this square as can be seen in Plans 10, 13 and 44.

Woolley maintains elsewhere (ibid.: 139) that the Level IV^W city wall follows the contours of the Level VII^W fortification, but none of his published plans confirms this assertion; on the contrary, a comparison between his level plans of Level VII^W (Plan 46, where the city wall is the outer wall of the palace and of the gate) and IV^W (Plan 41, where it is labeled "Town Wall") shows that the city walls followed different routes.

4.4 The Dating of Levels VI–IV^W

Level VII^W in Alalakh is connected to the historical analysis of Mesopotamian (Babylonian) Chronology in two different ways:

1) the recorded synchronism between the Yamḫad dynasty and the dynasties of Mari and Babylon (Oliva 1999–2000), and

2) the very high probability that Ḫattušili I destroyed the

---

[20] Could it be that Woolley intended to write in the above quote VI instead of IV?

Level VII^W palace some years before his grandson Muršili I destroyed Babylon and Aleppo (van Soldt 2000: 108).

The dating of these historical figures, who are mentioned in the Level VII^W archives, and attested in the texts as contemporary with familiar figures from Aleppo, Mari and Babylon, is dictated by the different views on the absolute date of the relative Mesopotamian chronology (Pruzsinszky 2005). The latter is constructed from king lists, eponyms, chronicles, royal inscriptions, dated administrative or religious documents and calendars (Pruzsinszky 2005). Scholars with different views on the absolute chronology base their approaches on astronomical observations (Gurzadyan 2000 vs. Huber 2000; with detailed bibliography in Pruzsinszky 2005: 188), stratigraphic and ceramic sequences in relation to radiocarbon/AMS dates of other ceramic assemblages and their stratigraphic contexts (Gasche et al 1998a: 10–42; with detailed bibliography in Pruzsinszky 2005: 188), synchronism between Mesopotamian relative chronology and foreign chronologies (Ben-Tor 2004; bibliography in Pruzsinszky 2005: 184–189), dendrochronological studies (Manning et al. 2001; Kuniholm et al. 2005; with detailed bibliography in Pruzsinszky 2005: 188), generation counting of king-lists' sequences, both Mesopotamian and foreign (Beckman 2000; Wilhelm 2004), the absolute dates of foreign artifacts/documents found in Mesopotamia and the absolute dates of the contexts in which Mesopotamian artifacts/documents were found out of the region (Pruzsinszky 2005: 184–189; for example, the Šamši-Adad I bullae, found in the Sarıkaya palace at Acemhöyük: Manning 1999: 351; Manning et al. 2001).

A synchronism between Hatti and Alalakh Level VII^W was established by Landsberger (1954) who pointed out that Zukraši, a high officer mentioned in several Level VII^W texts, appears also in a Hittite text as holding the same position in Aleppo (Na'aman 1974: 273–274; but see Bunnens 1994). This synchronism was fine-tuned in 1957 when, in the course of excavation at Boğazköy, the German expedition found the bilingual annals of Ḫattušili I. This document claims that during his second campaign, Ḫattušili I sacked and destroyed Alalakh (Muhly 1975: 78–80; Manning 1999: 356–358). This synchronism did not, however, give an absolute date to the event. To do so, we must establish the date of the destruction of the Level VII^W palace by Ḫattušili I, and even more so, the date of the fall of Babylon (and Aleppo, possibly Alalakh) at the hands of his grandson Muršili I. Not only will this determine which of the Mesopotamian chronologies is correct, it could also have an enormous impact on our understanding of the ancient Near East in the second millennium.[21]

Numerous scholars have expressed their views on the dates of Levels VII^W, VI^W, V^W and IV^W in Alalakh, yet not all of them are in agreement on the correlation between Alalakh levels and international events. Therefore, even when scholars are in agreement about the Mesopotamian chronology (highest, ultra-ultra-high, ultra-high, high, middle, low, low-ultra-low or ultra-low—following Pruzsinszky 2005: 183—or even ultra-ultra-low and lowest, see Wilhelm 2004: 77) they do not necessarily agree on the dating of certain levels at Alalakh. Nor do many scholars agree any more on the validity of the Venus tablet chronological system and its outcome: accurate middle (1595), low (1531) or lowest (1467) dates for the devastation of Babylon by Muršili I (Manning 1999:363–364; Ben-Tor 2004: 45; Pruzsinszky 2005). This disagreement results with views that fall between ultra-low and low, low and middle and so on. I have attempted to pigeonhole them below to their nearest chronology. All views merge between the historical sources (from Alalakh and elsewhere) and the archaeological evidence (stratigraphy and pottery analyses), and plausibly align with either the ultra-high chronology (Eder 2003), the middle (Smith 1940; Landsberger 1954; Kantor 1956: 159–160; Goetze 1957a; Rowton 1958 and 1970: 211–215; Muhly 1975; Collon 1975: 143–144, 166–169; Na'aman 1976 ; Collon 1977; Na'aman 1979; Collon 1982: 3, 6–16; Kempinski 1983: 80–90, 216–221; Manning 1999: 341–366 with the revision of Manning et al. 2001 and 2003; Nigro 2003: 99; Freu 2008), the low (Albright 1956 and 1957; Williams 1975 :1161–1165; Gates 1976, 1981 and 1987; Dever 1992: 14; Heinz 1992; Bergoffen 2005), or the ultra-low (van Soldt 2000; Zeeb 2004; Novak 2007).

It is evident, then, that the available historical records make more than one chronology possible; many have therefore made efforts to determine the absolute dates of Levels VII^W, VI^W, V^W and IV^W on the basis of internal evidence from Alalakh.[22] This inside information is of course simply a dependence on another chronology—mostly analyses of the dates of the manufacture and export of Aegean and Cypriote wares found at the site. This method then introduces to the debate over Mesopotamian chronology the view of other chronologies, first and foremost, Aegean (Cypriote included), and indirectly, mostly through southern Levantine middlemen, Egyptian. This method may end in a tautology (McClellan 1989: 186).

The internal considerations from Alalakh are dependent first and foremost on the reliability of Woolley's excavations and analyses. They are based on the dates of imported pottery (Gates 1976, 1981 and 1987; Bergoffen 2005); on ceramic seriation (McClellan 1989 vs. Heinz 1993); on the assumed minimum duration for two specific archaeological levels (VI^W and V^W), each divided into two sub-levels (Na'aman 1976: 141–142 vs. McClellan 1989: 190); on the dating of Level IV^W, which is founded on both internal and external considerations (McClellan 1989: 188–189); on the profound differences in the prosopography between the Levels VII^W and IV^W archives (Na'aman 1976: 142–143)[23] and on whether one associates

---

[21] The question of whether "historically recorded" destructions indeed reflect archaeological destruction, such as the campaigns of Ḫattušili I and Muršili I, concerns all who believe archaeology is a tool in historical reconstruction (Manning 1999: 356).

[22] Good summaries of these efforts are by McClellan (1989) and Manning (1999).

[23] Na'aman (1974; 1976: 142–143) does not consider the difference in

the reign of Idrimi with Level V[W], V[F] or IVA[F]. Although this chronological discussion is not the center of my work, I have prepared chronological tables, already discussed earlier in this chapter, which summarize the different opinions on the date of Levels VI[W] (Table 6), V[W] (Table 7) and IV[W] (Table 8).

My own observation concerning the dates of Levels VI[W] and V[W] is not based on a step by step ceramic analysis of Levels VII[W]–V[W] or IV[W] as offered by Gates (1976, 1981, 1987), Heinz (1992, 1993) and Bergoffen (2003, 2005). It is, however, based on the analysis of the stratigraphy of Tell Atchana, which should precede any ceramic study. The stratigraphy must always come first and dictate its order over the ceramic typology and seriation of a site. It is true that on the odd occasion pottery reading can help us in pointing out mistakes that we make in the process of analyzing the stratigraphy, but even then, it is necessary to find out what went wrong with the stratigraphic inquiry.

In comparison to the rich architecture and finds of the Level VII[W] palace and temple and of Levels IV–I[W], very little was unearthed in Levels VI[W] and V[W]. There could be several explanations for this fact:

1) Underneath Level IV[W], Woolley was looking for monumental buildings only. The only significant buildings that he found were the Level VII[W] palace and gate.
2) Luckily, Woolley was not allowed to remove the Level IV[W] palace and fortress. Wherever he could probe under the Level IV[W] palace and fortress he found remains of Levels V[W] and VI[W], but these were far less noteworthy than the Level VII[W] and IV[W] palaces. The Level VII[W] palace that was excavated east of the Level IV[W] palace is most probably the eastern wing of a larger structure, mostly still buried under the Level VB–IVA[F] palaces, as implied by the level IV[W] palace probe.
3) The possibility of a habitation gap (hiatus) between Levels VII[W] and VI[W] or substantial reuse of the Level VII[W] palace during Level VI[W] was unanimously rejected.

Following my analysis of Level V[W], and the attribution of the second part of Level VA[F] and all of VB[F] to the reign of Idrimi, even fewer structures are left not linked with known historical figures from Alalakh, either of the milieux of the Level VII[W] archives or of that of the Level IV[W] archives. The Levels VI[W] and V[W] structures clearly bridge between Levels VII[W] and IV[W] in three places only (hence, complete stratigraphic sequence is attested): the private houses (see above and in section in Plan 12), the Level IV[W] palace probe (see above and in Plan 28) and the temple sounding (Woolley 1955: 67, Fig. 29b; herein Plan 23). The Levels VI–V[W] remains in these locations

are just fragmentary walls, which could easily be considered two sub-phases of one phase lasting anywhere from several decades to a century.[24] Clearly, none of these remains represents as elaborate a city as those of Levels VII[W], IVA[F] and IVB[F]. Naturally, there is no connection between importance and length of existence. Nonetheless, what we securely know of Levels VI–V[W] left behind very little accumulation. There is almost no distinction between Levels VII[W] and VB[F], as is clearly illustrated in Plans 12 and 23.[25]

The remains of the Levels V[W] and VI[W] fortresses and Levels V[W] and VI[W] site H do not bridge between Level VII[W] and Level IV[W], since according to Woolley he did not reach Level VII[W] in these locations at all. Their attribution to these levels is based either on Woolley's ceramic interpretation or on counting levels from topsoil down. I would like to suggest that some of the structures that Woolley attributes there to Levels VI–V[W] could actually be part of Level VII[W] or even Level VIII[W].

One of the main problems in the history of research of Alalakh is the emphasis placed on ceramic analyses of archaeological levels. Serious consideration was lacking as to whether Woolley's stratigraphy is correct and whether the buildings and sub-phases were properly attributed to a level. This caused an even higher mistrust of the ceramic results from Alalakh. More than a few scholars agreed that "… the Alalakh pottery report is in many respects unsatisfactory and misleading" (Gates 1987: 66). Gates is even more blunt elsewhere: "with the imports from Alalakh, I would say that you should never date any imports from elsewhere or any pottery from elsewhere on the basis of Alalakh context. That is, the imports can serve to give a general sense of the ceramic horizon at Alalakh, but not the other way. In other words you cannot say: this type of Cypriote ware is found in Alalakh Level VI and therefore it must date as early as this. There were too many slips, misattributions, labels which are penciled in: on the sherd as from one find spot and in the inventory as from another find spot and in the final report as from yet another find spot" (1989: 68). Manning (1999: 349) shares Gates' doubts: "some would say that rather than consider the problem of Alalakh, one must simply accept that the excavations and publication of Woolley on Alalakh are a problem, and so nothing can be satisfactorily resolved." He does not share Gates' confidence in the reported context and dating of the Cypriote Bichrome ware from Alalakh.

The fact that the ceramics from Levels VI–V[W] are so untrustworthy has brought some scholars to attack Alalakh's stratigraphy as a whole and declare it unusable: "It seems one cannot place too much reliance on the

---

[24] with the exception of the Level V[W] temple. Nevertheless the Level VI[W] temple is hardly a temple, if an independent building at all.
[25] Mazzoni (2002: 131) compares Alalakh with other northern Levantine sites and concludes: "Only at Tell 'Atchana do Levels VI and V give a picture of flourishing centre, with both fortifications and the temple rebuilt, which naturally continued into the rich Phase IV." One needs to consider the possibility that Tell Atchana is not an exception and that Levels VI–V[W] are far less significant than previously thought.

scribal tradition as proof of the time elapsed between Levels VII[W] and IV[W], but rather a result of Mittani "imposing upon Alalakh her own patterns and rule."

Table 9. Opinions on the dates of Levels III–0^W

	III^W Beginning	III^W End	II^W End	I^W End	0^W End	Reasons
Smith 1940: 46–47	1358	1285	1220	1190		Level II^W begins in 1275
Landsberger 1954	1440		1370: first half of Level II^W			
Woolley 1955: 399	1370	1350	1273	1194	1140	
Swift 1958		1400	Before 1300	1200		Amuq sequence
Rowton 1970: 230–231	1473	1400	Fourteenth century			Mycenaean pottery
Collon 1975: 169; 1982: 3, 15	1365		1300/1275	1200/1190		Based on Mycenaean pottery, Level IV^W palace must have been destroyed in 1400 or later
Stein 1997	1340					
Pruss 2002	1400			1180	1000/950	Amuq sequence
Bergoffen 2005	1340	1320	1253	1194		LH IIIB pottery
Novak 2007	1340					Nuzi Ware
This study	1420/1400		1353/1341	4 sub-phases (1210)	1190/1185	

stratigraphy of Alalakh for determining the finer points of chronology" (Eriksson 1992: 193), and "Woolley indeed seems to have mixed, confused, or been unable to resolve the stratigraphy in places, and scholarship has to accept the limitations of the data" (Manning 1999: 359).

I agree that when it comes to Levels VI–V^W the archaeological data is limited to such a degree that only further careful excavations may make it a truly key site in the quest for an archaeological solution to the problem of Mesopotamian chronology of the second millennium B.C.E. Gates' (1976; 1981; 1987) attempt to solve this problem archaeologically is a marvelous exercise that suffers from a starting point of insufficient data, a fact that invited amply of legitimate criticism. Alalakh as a whole is not a reproduction of Levels VI–V^W, and all later levels are sufficiently recorded to allow for a new interpretive approach to Woolley's stratigraphy. But as I suggested above, even Levels VI–V^W can give us some indication of their length of existence (from the end of Level VII^W to the take-over of Alalakh by Idrimi), which is most likely between several decades and a century. With Idrimi's conquest of the city in the first quarter of the fifteenth century (van Soldt 2000: 110–112; Novak 2007: 395–397) or during the second quarter of the fifteenth century (Wilhelm 1976: 160; von Dassow 2008: 42), both low-like and ultra-low Mesopotamian chronology would work for Alalakh. If Level VI^W and the first part of Level VA^F lasted a maximum of 100 years (possibly even fifty years or less), and the first part of Level VA^F ended in 1495/1470 (Idrimi's conquest of Alalakh), then Ḫattušili I did not destroy Level VII^W before 1595, but possibly long after this date, as late as 1520. The outcome of these dates, which should not be based primarily on data from Alalakh, is that Muršili

I, being the grandson of Ḫattušili I, conquered Babylon sometime between 1575 and 1500.

My Alalakhian view in support of the low-like or ultra-low Mesopotamian chronology is far from being conclusive. A large-scale field reexamination of the stratigraphy of Levels VII–IV^W is called for, as well as radiocarbon and ceramic analyses of each level, both individually and comparatively. Woolley excavated in Alalakh two "cities" (Levels IVA^F and IVB^F) and three palaces (Levels VII^W, IVA^F and IVB^F). It is obvious that the Level VII^W palace ruled over a well-built city. It is very tempting to follow the archaeological paradigm, attributing a "city" to a century, and therefore to place Level VII^W in the sixteenth century, the Level IVA^F "city" in the fifteenth century and the Level IVB^F "city" in the fourteenth century.

4.5 Level IVB^F (1420/1400–1353/1341)

The plan of Level IVB^F accompanies this discussion.

In the previous chapter I proposed that the Levels III–II^W fort was built as early as during Level IVB^F (first half of the fourteenth century B.C.E.), and that the Level III^W temple was in fact the Level IVB^F temple. Here below I am extending my proposal to include the missing buildings and structures of Level IVB^F: the Levels III^W and II^W private houses and the Levels III–II^W city wall.[26] The latter unavoidably succeeded the Level IVA^F private houses, which ceased to exist when the Level IVA^F palace was destroyed circa 1420–1400 B.C.E. Woolley (1955: 183–191) attributed to Level III^W the earlier building phase

---

[26] For different opinions on the dates of Levels III–0^W see Table 9.

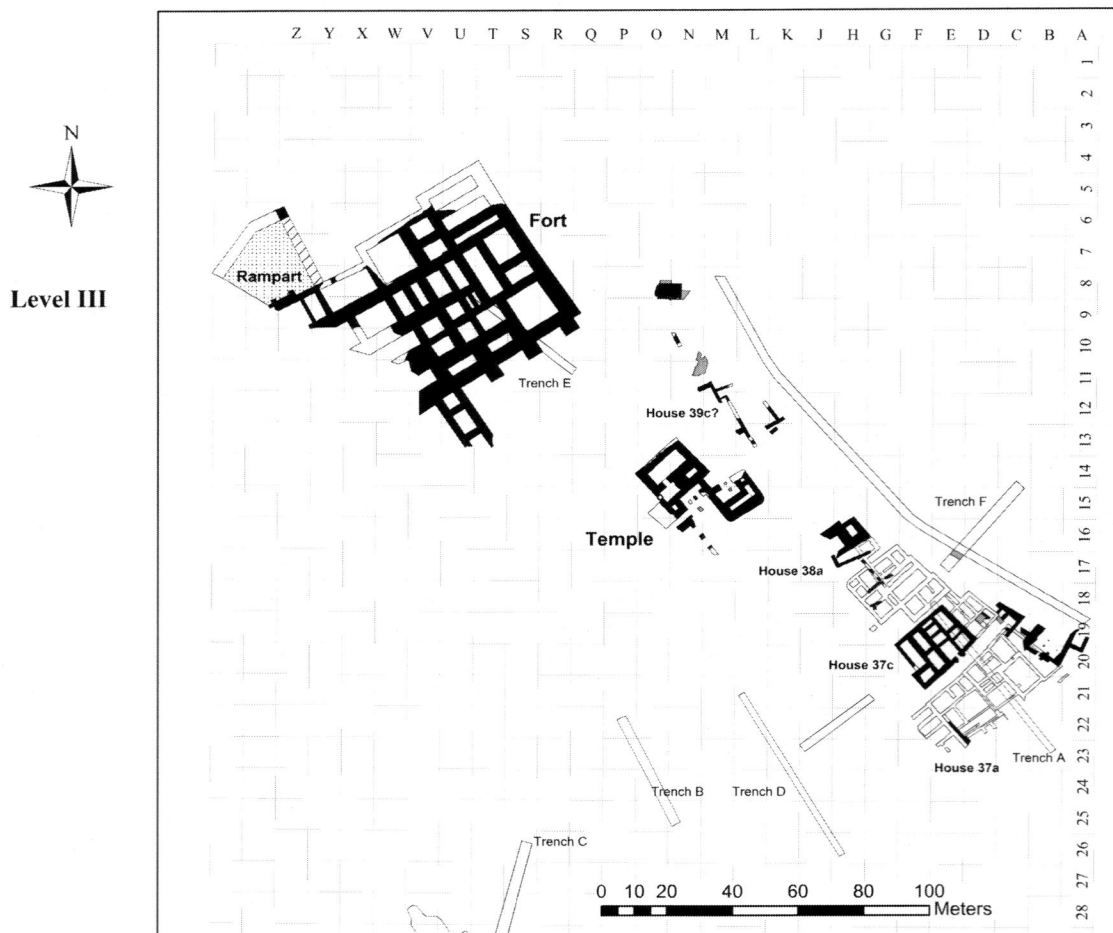

Plan 47. Plan of Level III^W (after Yener 2005: 142, Fig. 4.31)

of a similar-or-identical-to-Level II^W blueprint of houses 37/A–D (Plan 42), the one-phase building east of house 37/B and northeast of house 37/C, and the one-phase building remains under and southeast of house 39/C (Plan 10). Not only do the Level III^W private houses have no clear association with the Levels III–II^W city wall and fort (Plan 47), but the Levels III–II^W city wall in fact cancels the one phase building east of house 37/B and northeast of house 37/C. Woolley attributed to Level II^W houses 37/A, 37/B, 37/C, 37/D, 38/A and 39/C, which, in contrast, have clear connections to the Levels III–II^W city wall and fort (Plan 48). Therefore, the Level II^W private houses are contemporary with the Levels III^W–II^W city wall and fort, which I believe belong to Level IVB^F. The Level III^W private houses must belong to a short-living stage or sub-phase of rebuilding, right after the destruction of the Level IVA^F city. Hence, many of the Level III^W private houses are the earlier phase of the Level II^W private houses.[27] Level II^W stands for the reshaping of the Level IVB^F city into a more defensible structure with a fortified palace and city wall. The IVB^F city flourished for fifty-eighty years, a similar or longer duration than the Level IVA^F city, until its destruction by Šuppiluliuma I in 1353/1341. This destruction is well attested in the private houses. As

Woolley describes it (ibid.: 185): "Many of the walls of this group of Level II houses showed signs of fire, and it was noted that some of the room floors were littered with ashes. Over the whole area... there were quantities of bronze arrowheads and some clay sling-bolts... ...The evidence therefore is strongly in favour of the quarter's having been destroyed as the result of a struggle after which the houses were sacked and burned."

Historical aspects of Level IVB^F

The enthronement inscription of Addu-Nīrārī, king of Alalakh

None of the historical documents found in Alalakh originate from Level IVB^F, or are related to this period, with one possible exception: the inscription on the statue of king Idrimi. In the previous chapter I proposed that the true find spot of the statue of Idrimi was a pit dug from the floor of the annexe to the Level III^W temple, now dated to Level IVB^F. It is of course possible that the statue and its inscription survived from Level IVA^F or even VB^F in the temple compound of Alalakh, and as such was a precious heirloom. It is also possible that the inscription, or both the statue and the inscription, were created at the time of Level IVB^F, as I newly offered, and as was strongly accepted by Eva von Dassow in her recent book (2008: 32–38).

---

[27] "On the archaeological evidence I have always felt that Level III was a rather ephemeral period" (Woolley 1955: 396).

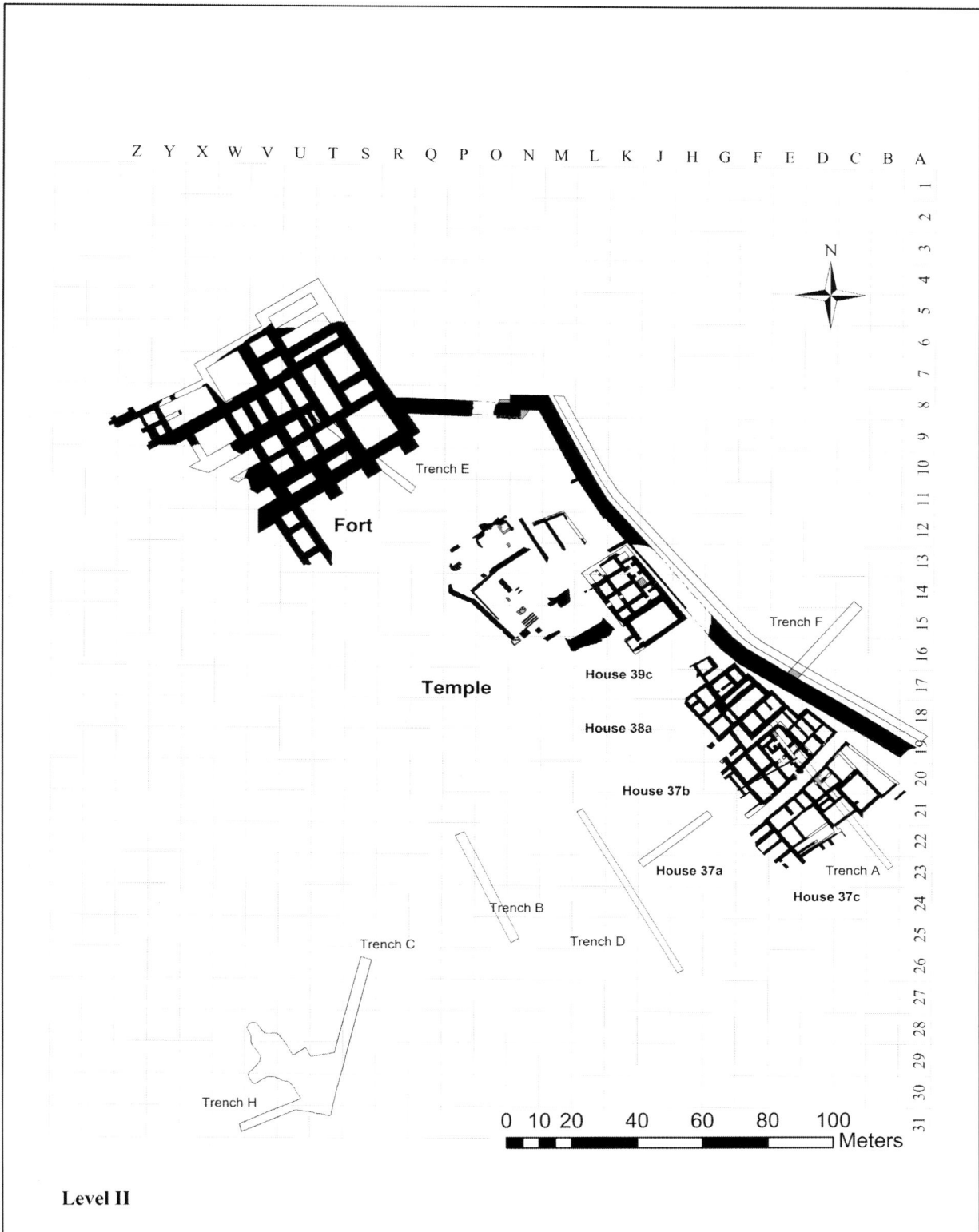

Plan 48. Plan of Level II^W (after Yener 2005: 143, Fig. 4.32)

The story of Idrimi son of Ilimilimma begins in Aleppo, his ancestral home. At a young age, however, a disastrous event forced him to flee with his brothers to Emar. Unlike his older brothers, Idrimi later decided to reclaim his hereditary power. He headed for Canaan, where he lived among the Hapiru for seven years, gathering warriors and building ships; eventually he succeeded in taking over Mukiš from the sea. He then established himself in Alalakh, becoming a vassal of Parrattarna, king of Mittani. Later, he fought against Hatti, destroyed several cities, and returned to Alalakh with booty and captives. The inscription claims that Idrimi reigned in Alalakh for thirty years, during which he built a palace and rebuilt the rest of the kingdom.

As I noted in Chapter 2 of this work, at the time of the statue's discovery, this biographical inscription represented an innovation in the region, causing some scholars to doubt its historicity and/or authenticity.[28] The genre seemingly went on to become very popular in the Levant during the Iron Age; indeed, many scholars have found parallels between the narrative of Idrimi and biblical accounts such as those of Joseph (Albright 1950: 20), David (Buccellati 1962) and Joash (Liverani 2004: 147–159), as well as with several other autobiographical inscriptions associated with Iron Age monuments (Sasson 1981: 310).

Philologically, however, other issues soon presented themselves. Na'aman and Kempinski (1973: 217–218) were the first to point out the problem with the unusual colophon of Šarruwa the scribe in lines 98–101 of the inscription. The difficulty is in the fact that "...there is no parallel case in the Akkadian and West Semitic corpus of royal inscriptions for the kind of long blessing dedicated to the scribe who composed the text. This becomes even more curious since the blessing for the ruler in whose name the inscription was written is oddly missing." (Na'aman 1980: 107).

Na'aman and Kempinski (1973: 218; Na'aman 1980: 107) suggest that Šarruwa inserted his name to replace that of the king, trusting his fellow-scribes not to release this fact. This suggestion was not well received, and it was pointed out that Šarruwa would have taken an unreasonable risk by doing so (Sasson 1981: 311; Oller 1989: 413; Márquez Rowe 1997: 200, n. 16). One should be careful not to trust the ancients to be reasonable all the time. Yet, since I believe that there is a more viable explanation to Šarruwa's action, I join the critics.

Dietrich and Loretz (1981: 244–250; Oller 1989: 413–414) deconstruct the statue and inscription to several hypothetical sources:

1) the statue;
2) the cheek lines (102–104);
3) a tablet, which is summarized in the main narrative of the inscription (lines 1–91); and

4) the curses and the blessings for Šarruwa (lines 92–101).

They claim that the statue first stood un-inscribed, then the cheek-lines were inscribed, probably post Idrimi's death.[29] In the second line on the cheek (line 103) they read the eighth sign as DUB(ṭuppī),[30] and assume that this is a reference to a tablet of the "Deeds of Idrimi" that only years later, during the reign of Niqmepa or Ilimilimma, would be summarized and inscribed on the statue by Šarruwa the scribe. Only then did Šarruwa supplement the inscription with the formulae of curses and blessings, inserting his name, trusting his fellow-scribes to keep this fact undisclosed. This DUBious explanation was rejected for the same reasons that Na'aman and Kempinski's explanation was (Oller 1989: 414; Márquez Rowe 1997: 200, n. 16). Oller points out that DUB is not a definitive reading for the problematic sign, that the cheek inscription by itself does not identify the king, and "that we are still left with the question of why Šarruwa did what he did" (Oller 1989: 414). Critics aside, Dietrich and Loretz bring to the fore an interesting concept, which deserves further discussion: the statue and the inscription were not necessarily created at the same time; the deeds of Idrimi as described in the statue's inscription could be a quote or a summary of another composition, most probably in the form of a tablet.[31]

Sasson (1981), followed by Longman III (1991: 60–77), raises the possibility that this inscription is a "simulated" or "fictional" autobiography, and that several hundred years stand between Idrimi, the historical figure, and the manufacture of his statue and inscription. Sasson's arguments, neatly summarized by Oller (1989: 414–415), are:

1) The name of one of the correspondents in a Hittite letter found in Level I[w] begins with the sign ŠAR, possibly followed by RU, and therefore, this must be the Šarruwa, who inscribed the Idrimi inscription.
2) The most similar first person narrative inscriptions in Anatolia, Cilicia and the Levant are dated to the late LBA II and early Iron Age II, and not to the fifteenth century B.C.E.
3) The style of the sculpture and the throne base are late LBA and not MBA–LBA transition or LBA I.

---

[28] See the discussion on the subject in 2.1.

[29] Na'aman (1980: 108) shows that all the attestations of Šarruwa the scribe are from the time of Niqmepa (5) and Ilimilimma (1) and none from the time of Idrimi. "It is obvious, therefore," he writes, "that Šarruwa belonged to a later generation than Idrimi and could not have been an eye-witness to most of the adventures described so vividly by him."

[30] Rather than ALAM (ṣalmī) (Greenstein and Marcus 1976: 66). See also Na'aman (1980: 116).

[31] Na'aman (1980: 109–110) emphasizes some of the striking differences in language and style between the Idrimi inscription and other texts composed by Šarruwa. He explains these differences by suggesting that in the Idrimi inscription Šarruwa follows strict genre formula. Márquez Rowe (1997: 179, 202, n. 32) is pointing out that Šarruwa claims twice, in lines 98–99, that the text is his own composition, and that there are similarities in spelling between the Idrimi inscription and some of the tablets composed by him. See also the arguments of Sasson (1981: 311).

4) The archaeological level in which the statue was found is dated to the end of the thirteenth century B.C.E.

5) Woolley's perception that the Mukišians were actively and symbolically resisting the Hittite occupation is archaeologically proven.

The last three arguments are archaeological in nature. I discuss and reject Woolley's notion of "archaeology of resistance" in Alalakh in the section that deals with Atchana/Nuzi ware below. I already studied at length the question of where the statue of Idrimi was actually found (Chapter 3; Fink 2008b), and reached the conclusion that it was found in a significantly earlier phase than Woolley believed. The idea that the sculpture's style is late LBA is not accepted by most art historians and archaeologists (Mayer-Opificius 1981; 1983; Merhav 1985; Oller 1989: 416; Bonatz 2000: 196–198; Matthiae 2000: 393–394; Akermans and Schwartz 2003: 334, 336, 347). Sasson's critics discussed the first two arguments thoroughly and convincingly rebutted them on philological and historical grounds (Márquez Rowe 1989: 179–181; Oller 1989: 416–417; Mayer 1995: 334–335; von Dassow 1997: 21–22).

Post Sasson's sensation there were other suggestions. Oller (1989: 413) wrote that "if Šarruwa was responsible for the actual composition of the text, Idrimi may have been so pleased with the work that he afforded him the honor of 'signing' the inscription and receiving a bit of immortality along with his sovereign." Oller earnestly and justly coins his own explanation as "not very convincing."
Other scholars entertained the idea that the statue, or just the inscription, was posthumous. The idea was raised already by Orthmann (1964: 225–226). Márquez Rowe (1997: 179–181) took it one step further; examining the inscription carefully he asserted that:

1) The inscription is dated to the reign of one of Idrimi's heirs, thus, it is posthumous.

2) Addu-Nīrārī is the chosen successor of Idrimi according to the inscription formula. Therefore, the text was composed during Addu-Nīrārī's reign over Alalakh.

3) The reign of Addu-Nīrārī followed Idrimi's reign, and it was succeeded by the reign of Niqmepa.

4) The statue and the inscription are an *ex voto* dedicated by Šarruwa (the blessing for Šarruwa "corresponds properly to the classical Mesopotamian phrase in votive texts") to the deceased and worshipped king Idrimi.

While I find it hard to believe that this monumental inscribed statue is just an *ex voto* dedicated by Šarruwa in one of the temples of Alalakh (Márquez Rowe 1997: 180), I support the idea that the inscription was fashioned during the reign of one of Idrimi's heirs. Unlike Márquez Rowe, I would like to raise the possibility that Addu-Nīrārī did not succeed his father, but rather his nephew Ilimilimma. Consequently, Šarruwa, the experienced scribe, who served under Niqmepa and Ilimilimma (Na'aman 1980: 108), was

the kingmaker who enthroned Addu-Nīrārī. I believe that the statue was inscribed during a period of turmoil in the history of Alalakh, following the traumatic destruction of Level IVA^F, probably by the Hittites. At this moment of havoc and mayhem (Level III^W = early IVB^F) there was an immediate need to reestablish the Idrimi dynasty. Thus, the Idrimi inscription constitutes, in fact, the enthronement inscription of Addu-Nīrārī, king of Alalakh, and the re-establishment of the Idrimi (Aleppan) dynasty that conceivably ruled over Alalakh, almost uninterruptedly, from the days of Yamhad onward (van Soldt 2000: 113). I trust that this explanation is at least as good as other past-proposed solutions to this problem.

What are the circumstances in which Šarruwa could earn his eternity blessing himself on this inscription? Who is Addu-Nīrārī, and why we don't find his name in any of the tablets of the archives of Level IV^W palace? And who smashed the statue of Idrimi? Who buried it and why? Here are my arguments:

In the first wave of reactions to the publication of the statue and inscription of Idrimi (Smith 1949) many of the scholars who analyzed the inscription offered an historical reconstruction in which Addu-Nīrārī son of Idrimi was the king of Alalakh (Albright 1950: 19; Goetze 1950: 231; Legrain 1951: 105; to name just a few).[32] The Idrimi dynasty, as reflected in the Idrimi inscription, was:

Ilimilimma (from Aleppo)
Idrimi son of Ilimilimma
Addu-Nīrārī son of Idrimi

This is in contrast to the dynasty as reflected in the Level IV^W archives (Wiseman 1953: 5–8):

Idrimi
Niqmepa son of Idrimi
Ilimilimma son of Niqmepa

The two presumably contradicting lists were followed by attempts at dynasties that merged the two (Smith 1949: 59; Woolley 1955: 392–395). The interpretation that the Level IV^W tablets endow us with a more reliable account of the dynasty, and that Addu-Nīrārī, whether the chosen heir or not, never reached the throne, is now widely accepted. This interpretation is supported mostly since Addu-Nīrārī's name is not attested in any of the Level IV^W tablets, neither as royalty nor as an ordinary man (Wiseman 1953: 5–9).

Addu-Nīrārī is not the only Level IV^W king not attested in any of the Alalakh texts. Indisputably, Itūr-Addu was the last king of Level IV^W/IVB^F. His name is known only due to the texts found at Ugarit (CTH 46; Beckman 1999: 34–36). Without this external source we would not have known Itūr-Addu existed at all. No Level IVB^F

---

[32] See also Kühne (1982: 220), who assumes that Addu-Nīrārī ascended to the throne after Idrimi died, and supported the Egyptians. Kühne believes that Addu-Nīrārī was replaced by his brother Niqmepa, who was loyal to Mittani.

archive was found, and given the state of preservation of the Level IVB[F] palace, the chances of finding one are slim at best. I believe that this is also the reason that Addu-Nīrārī's name has not been found so far— other than in the Idrimi inscription, it was only attested in the Level IVB[F] archive.

Addu-Nīrārī could have been the biological son of Idrimi, a blood relative of the admired king or even just an ordinary person, who claimed that Idrimi designated him as his heir, as suggested by von Dassow (2008: 32). Assuming he was the son of Idrimi, he could have been born shortly before his father's death, and thus he was in his late thirties-early forties by the time the Level IVA[F] palace was destroyed— ready to take over the kingdom. The scheme in which uncles succeeded their nephews is known in the ancient Near East—take the famous example of Ḫattušili III taking over the reign of his nephew Urḫi-Tešub in Hatti (Bryce 1998: 284–291). The king maker of somewhat unusual capture of the throne must be an honorable person, preferably old, who represents the Idrimi dynasty, and could be the voice of its legacy. No one could be better as a king-maker than the old scribe Šarruwa, who served under Niqmepa and Ilimilimma, and whose written documents for many years stood as the word of the king. Šarruwa must have signified the continuity of the Idrimi dynasty and the livelihood of the city and kingdom, desired by those people of Alalakh who survived the destruction.

Many of the passages of the Idrimi inscription would have served the political agenda of king Addu-Nīrārī:

1) Idrimi's story begins with the *mašiktu*, the "evil", a political crime that occurred in Aleppo, during which Idrimi's father Ilimilimma was probably murdered (lines 3–4; Márquez Rowe 1997: 183–184; van Soldt 2000: 110). Van Soldt proposed (ibid.: 110–112) that the one who carried out the *mašiktu* was none other than the Hittite king Muršili I, who wrought destruction in Aleppo and Babylon in the same year.[33] Therefore, Idrimi is the survivor of a Hittite raid, whose mission is to restore his father's kingship. So too is Addu-Nīrārī himself.[34]

2) If he is indeed a younger son of Idrimi, he was also the young brother, who took on his older brothers' birthright and reigned over Alalakh (as Idrimi is in lines 7–12 of the inscription).

3) It is likely that in order to survive the Level IVA[F] destruction Addu-Nīrārī had to leave his hometown and only upon the aggressor's retreat could return to Alalakh (compare to lines 13–42 of the Idrimi inscription).

4) Alalakh of Level IVB[F] must have been a Mittanian vassal, and Addu-Nīrārī had to renew the vassal agreement with Mittani once crowned (compare to lines 42–58 of the Idrimi inscription).

5) To the people of Alalakh of the first half of the fourteenth century it was clear that out of the north the evil should break forth upon all the inhabitants of the land of Mukiš, that is, from the stronghold of the Hittites. Addu-Nīrārī must present himself as the king who will protect his people from that danger. This propagandistic message was probably embedded into the inscription when fifteenth century Kizzuwatna was replaced with fourteenth century Hatti. In von Dassow's words (2008: 38), "an invasion of Kizzuwatna could reasonably be represented as a campaign 'against Hatti,' especially from the standpoint of the fourteenth century, which incidentally accords with the hypothesis that the statue inscription was composed then rather than in the fifteenth century" (compare to lines 59–63 of the Idrimi inscription).

6) Addu-Nīrārī was facing one of the greatest challenges in the history of Alalakh: rebuilding the palace, the temple(s), and the residences, and fortifying the city against the northern threat in an unprecedented and unparalleled formidable way, as described below (beginning in Section 4.5). He probably had to do the same in other towns and villages all over Mukiš (compare to lines 64–91 of the Idrimi inscription).

There are supplementary aspects that are in support of my suggestion: the crudeness of the inscription can be explained by the post-destruction hardship and temporary lack of professional stone dressers, or by Šarruwa's attempt "to make his inscription look even older than he was" (von Dassow 2008: 32–33).[35] The blessing for Šarruwa can be attributed to his special status as a king maker, which allows him some liberties in the inscription—as an old man he is praying to the gods to give him good health, protect him and be his guardians. What is more, the inscription does not mention the names of Niqmepa and his son Ilimilimma. The reason must be the author's wish to emphasize his direct lineage to Idrimi while detaching himself from Ilimilimma who lost and brought disaster over Alalakh.

Who removed the statue of Idrimi from its throne, chipped its nose and broke its feet? Who buried it face down, and why? The likely occurrence is the conquest of Alalakh by Šuppiluliuma I as I previously demonstrated (Chapter 3; Fink 2008b). I tend now to believe that the damage to the statue and its burial practice are more likely to be an act of humiliation than an expression of honor.

Bringing Addu-Nīrārī back into the royal dynasty of Alalakh takes us one meaningful step closer towards a complete historical reconstruction of the Alalakh dynasty of Levels VB–IVB[F]. Currently, we do not know if additional king(s) ruled over Alalakh between Addu-Nīrārī and Itūr-Addu. Similarly, there is no way to know if Itūr-Addu is a kin of

---

[33] For the unfeasibility of the *mašiktu*'s being caused by Tudḫaliya I see Wilhelm 2004: 71, n. 2.

[34] For the likelihood that Level IVA[F] palace was destroyed by the Hittites, see von Dassow 2008: 61.

[35] "The scribe who carved the inscription had neither the requisite knowledge of the diplomatic medium of that age – Akkadian – nor of the pertinent cuneiform script. His style is barbarous and his signs show little consistency; some signs have as many as twenty variants or more" (Speiser 1951: 151).

Addu-Nīrārī. I propose that the following is the dynasty that governed Mukiš over the 150-year span from the early fifteenth to the mid-fourteenth centuries B.C.E.:

Idrimi son of Ilimilimma (from Aleppo)
Niqmepa son of Idrimi
Ilimilimma son of Niqmepa
Addu-Nīrārī son of Idrimi
King X?
Itūr-Addu

Allaiturahhi of Mukiš and Giziya of Alalakh

There are also some indirect testimonies to the importance of Levels IVA^F and IVB^F in Alalakh far beyond the borders of Mukiš. It is now well established that Hurrian and Akkadian texts of many genres reached Kizzuwatna and Hatti from the northern Levant (Görke 2007). There are several specific attestations that mark Alalakh as the source of these works. Among them are the ritual texts of Allaiturahhi of Mukiš and Giziya of Alalakh (Haas and Wegner 1988: 48–207; Miller 2004: 506–511; Görke 2007: 245; Haas 2007). Miller (2004: 506) believes that these texts "presumably came to Hattusa with the incorporation of Kizzuwatna under Tuthaliya I (I/II) and Arnuwanda I," but having originated in Mukiš they must have been "exported" from Mittanian Mukiš to Kizzuwatna. The remaining questions are: when and how? Miller (ibid.: 507–511) offers several scenarios:

1) Tuthaliya I employed scribes during his northern Levantine raids to record the rites of the practitioners of oral ritual arts, and this was the occasion in which these rituals were written. Since it is likely that Level IVA^F in Alalakh was destroyed in one of these raids, I believe that it is possible that the collection of rites was not necessarily peaceful, and that Allaiturahhi of Mukiš and Giziya of Alalakh could have been captured in Alalakh and brought to Hattusa or Kizzuwatna by Tuthaliya I. If this is the case, Allaiturahhi of Mukiš and Giziya of Alalakh represent the civilization of Level IVA^F, not of Level IVB^F.

2) Allaiturahhi of Mukiš and Giziya of Alalakh were already residents of Kizzuwatna when Tuthaliya I annexed it to Hatti. The Hittite scribes interviewed them there. If that is the case, what are the circumstances that brought them there? The destruction of Level IVA^F? The popularity of Allaiturahhi and Giziya in Kizzuwatna or Hatti?

3) These are Hittite copies of texts found in Kizzuwatnean archives at the time of Tuthaliya I. The texts arrived there during Alalakh Level VB^F or IVA^F when Kizzuwatna, or parts of it, were ruled by Alalakh, a Mittanian vassal.

4) These rituals are in fact pseudo-Allaiturahhi of Mukiš and pseudo-Giziya of Alalakh. Hittite scribes, who composed them, attributed them to the famous figures of Alalakh. Alternatively, these rituals could be partly based on original core-texts of Allaiturahhi and Giziya. In this context, Miller (ibid.: 511) raises

the possibility that Allaiturahhi and Giziya are not historical figures at all.

5) Obviously, it is incorrect to construe the rites of Allaiturahhi of Mukiš and Giziya of Alalakh as more than they are: a remote testimony to the cultural and ritual importance of Mittanian Mukiš.

Alalakh in Kayalıpınar

In Section 3.3, I suggest that several administrative tablets, which make a unique group among the archives of Alalakh, may have originated in Level IVB^F (previously published in Fink 2008b: 187–188). Von Dassow (2008: 63) convincingly insists that they originated in one of the Hittite levels of Alalakh. Unlike this group, a tablet in Hurrian (Wilhelm 2006), which was found in 2005 in Kayalıpınar, a site in the district of modern Sivas, centrally located in the Hittite heartland, may still belong to Level IVB^F, and possibly even originated in Alalakh. The genre of the text, which we understand only in part, is unclear: it is either a detailed letter, or an historical text similar in genre to the Hittite annals (ibid.: 233). It is also unknown who the author of the text is and whether it was composed in Hatti, Mittani or the northern Levant. It describes a military campaign in which Mukiš and Kizzuwatna are involved—clearly some cities in Kizzuwatna and north of Alalakh (Tilmen Höyük?) are under attack (ibid.: 235). Wilhelm dates the text to the first half of the fourteenth century B.C.E. In his published paper he dates it to the time of Tuthaliya I, but in a recent public lecture he mentioned the time of Tuthaliya II as his preference.[36] This tablet could be the missing description of the events that brought an end to the Level IVA^F city at the time of Ilimilimma and his possible contemporary (and aggressor) Tuthaliya I (von Dassow 2008: 61–62). Even if it is not, it may yet add some flavor to the very dull historical reality of the archaeologically rich Level IVB^F: for example, this mysterious document could have originated in Alalakh, describing the campaigns of Mukiš on behalf of Mittani against the cities to the north.

The Hittite treaty with Mukiš

KBo 13.55 (CTH 136) is a fragment of a Hittite treaty, probably with Mukiš (Klengel 1995: 412; Devecchi 2007: 207). Devecchi in her recent edition of this fragment (ibid.: 211) claims convincingly that this must be a treaty with Mukiš based on the presence of "all the male deitie[s and the female deities] of Mukiš" as witnesses to the treaty. She also believes (ibid.) that the Hittite king behind this treaty is Šuppiluliuma I. Devecchi bases her point of view on the following grounds:

1) the male and female deities of Kizzuwatna, who are witnesses to this treaty, are mentioned only in Šuppiluliuma I's treaties;

2) The paleography of KBo 13.55 (CTH 136) corresponds to texts of the time of Šuppiluliuma I;

---

[36] A lecture in Tel Aviv University on December 29th, 2008 on the occasion of the retirement of Prof. Itamar Singer.

3) plausible historical reconstruction places it in the reign of Šuppiluliuma I.

I discussed this text and Devecchi's work with Boaz Stavi, who is currently writing his Ph.D. thesis on Šuppiluliuma I, and the following observations were raised in our communication:[37]

1) The attestation of the male and female deities of Kizzuwatna as witnesses in this treaty could be dated as early as the annexation of Kizzuwatna to Hatti (CTH 41—the Šunaššura treaty; Beckman 1999: 17–26) during the reign of Tudḫaliya I (Singer 1994: 94, and see additional literature there). Therefore, if Level IVA[F] was indeed destroyed by Tudḫaliya I (von Dassow 2008: 61–62), then a vassal treaty could have been forced on Alalakh at that occasion. If it existed, the treaty was clearly not kept by Alalakh for very long, as both CTH 46 and the archaeological data clearly point out that Alalakh was a Mittanian vassal during Level IVB[F], as I will show in this chapter. One possibility is that the short-term, irresolute Level III[W] stands for the time that Alalakh followed the word of this treaty before Mittani regained power in the region. Stavi (personal communication) suggests that treaty could have been kept even as late as the time of Arnuwanda I, the successor of Tudḫaliya I, if indeed Arnuwanda I's treaty with the Men of Išmerika (CTH 133; Beckman 1999: 13–17) reflects Hittite territorial control beyond Kizzuwatna. I believe that even if some of the cities mentioned in the Išmerika treaty are east of the Euphrates and Karkamiš, as claimed by Goetze (1940: 47–48), or west of the Euphrates and north of Karkamiš, as claimed by Freu (2001: 26), yet Alalakh was not necessarily under Hittite influence, whether direct or indirect. Devecchi (2007: 214) eliminates this option altogether, with no sufficient justification.

2) The most probable occasion for the signing of the treaty between Hatti and Mukiš is Tudḫaliya II's campaign to Mt. Nanni (Güterbock 1956: 61–62; Singer 1999: 623), which either reached the borders of Mukiš or, more likely, required crossing Mukiš from north to south (see below). Šuppiluliuma I attended this campaign as a high ranking officer in his father's army. In his MA thesis Stavi (2006: VI–IX) suggested that this campaign dates to the final years of the reign of Tudḫaliya II, and not as reconstructed previously. If so, one would expect Mukiš to become a Hittite vassal during the campaign, and to be punished by Šuppiluliuma I, when ten years or so later it breached the treaty and headed a regional coalition against the Hittites

(Klengel 1992: 109).[38] Devecchi (2007) ignores this option.

3) The treaty was signed between Šuppiluliuma I and the defeated Mukiš during the first Syrian war (Devecchi 2007). Thus far I assume that Mukiš was annexed to Hatti during the first Syrian war. However, it is possible that the process was more gradual, and that only after breaking the treaty with the Hittites, later in the reign of Šuppiluliuma I or even during the reign of Muršili II, was Mukiš annexed to the empire. Subsequently, the city was punished, and the majority of its residents were exiled. The first affirmative sign of the existence of a Hittite governor in Alalakh is the orthostat of Tudḫaliya DUMU.LUGAL dated to no later than Level IIA[F], which is the first phase of the Hittite stronghold (see Summary Table 1). Evidently, already at one point during the reign of Muršili II, there was no local king in Alalakh: the people of the land of Mukiš[39] are the ones who write a direct petition to Muršili II (CTH 64; Beckman 1999: 173–175).

Tudḫaliya II's campaign to Mt. Nanni

Another possible attestation of Alalakh during Level IVB[F] is the Tudḫaliya II and Šuppiluliuma I campaign to Mt. Nanni. Fragment 8 of the Deeds of Šuppiluliuma I (Güterbock 1956: 61–62; Hoffner 1997) describes a Hittite military campaign, led by the father of Šuppiluliuma I, Tudḫaliya II, to Mt. Nanni.[40] By geographical proximity any campaign from the north to Mt. Nanni could have concluded with the occupation of Alalakh or parts of Mukiš. The "Deeds of Šuppiluliuma" were composed at the time of Muršili II, the son of Šuppiluliuma I, and are written as if narrated by Muršili himself: whenever Muršili refers to "my father" and "my grandfather" he describes events in which Šuppiluliuma I and Tudḫaliya II are respectively involved (Güterbock 1983: 32–33).

To this day, most scholars embrace Güterbock's collation (1956), reconstruction, translation and the numbering system of the many fragments of the "Deeds." Güterbock (ibid.) places the description of the campaign to Mt. Nanni into the first reconstructed tablet of the "Deeds." In his MA thesis Stavi (2006: VI–IX) suggests that fragment 8 is part of a later tablet, and therefore, that this campaign dates to the final years of the reign of Tudḫaliya II, and not as reconstructed before. This fragment (from line 3 on) was translated by Güterbock as follows:

> (3) [And] my grandfather from [....................
> tu]rned, and he [went] into [.........................].
> And when he [came] to Mount [Nanni], on Mount
> Na[nni............]. But my father [..................…..]
> forth, and the troops of the tribes {EREN.MEŠ ZU-

---

[37] Email correspondence 12/08–02/09. I thank Boaz Stavi for sharing with me some of his ideas. I am looking forward to the completion of his dissertation, where some of these topics are revisited and developed further and beyond. Stavi's Tel Aviv University dissertation is supervised by Profs. Nadav Na'aman and Jared Miller.

[38] If we follow Güterbock's (1956) arrangement of the tablets, the time that passed between the campaign to Nanni and Šuppiluliuma's first Syrian war is more likely to be 20–25 years. This time frame does not weaken my argument.

[39] DUMU[meš] KUR *Mu-kiš* (RS 17.237)

[40] Kempinski (1993: 83) suggests that both fragments 7 and 8 describe this campaign; 7 is mostly illegible however.

TE-E} to […And] who [went (?) to] atta[ck……..,
he att]acked [him], and the population [……..] on
Mount Nanni agai[nst ……]. (12) But when my
grandfather undertook to reestablish [the country
of …., PN], the son of Zittara, [told him in] (the
town of) Ḫa[-…]: "Ḫalpamuwa, who was [……]
in the country, [.….].

Astour (1981: 18) believes that this fragment, "relating to
Šuppiluliuma's earlier life, tells how he, while still only
a prince, participated in a campaign under the leadership
of his father, and was sent by him to dislodge Sutu-troops
(ERIN.MEŠ *Sú-te-e*) from Mt. Nanni." Astour suggests
that "the presence of Sutians—i.e., soldiers recruited
from among Syrian tribesmen—as adversaries of the
Hittites, points to Syria as the theater of the campaign."
Kempinski (1993: 84) proposes that Šuppiluliuma I's "first
assignment was in the south, on the Syrian border, where
hopeless attempts were made to hold the areas regained
by Tudḫaliya II and Ḫattušili II during the latter part of
the 15th century B.C. These attempts also led to the first
clashes with Mitanni…"

Although fragmentary, there is a consensus that the
passage represents a campaign of Tudḫaliya II to the
northern Levant, led by Šuppiluliuma I, then a prince.
The campaign reaches Mt. Nanni where some Sutians are
approached. The exact year of this campaign is an enigma,
since we do not know when Tudḫaliya II's reign began or
how long he ruled over Hatti.

Where is Mt. Nanni? Hittite sources refer to the twin
peaks Ḫazzi and Nanni, which are identified by most
scholars with Strabon's Mt. Casius/Kasion and Mt. Anti
Casius/Kasion respectively (Singer 1999: 623; Healey
2007 and see detailed bibliography there). In line with
this identification, Bordreuil (1989a: 274; 1989b) suggests
that Nanni is one of the southern summits of the mountain
range known as Kel Dağ in Turkish and as Jabel al Aqraᶜ
in Arabic.[41] Other suggestions are by Kempinski (1993:
83–84) and Popko (1998: 124), who identify Nanni with
the Amanus range, and by Dijkstra (1991), who locates it
east of Kel Dağ along the Ugarit-Mukiš border, among the
northern summits of Jabel Nusairiye. The most accepted
identification of Nanni with one of the summits of Kel
Dağ, or even Dijkstra's identification, requires that the
Hittite troops cross through Mukiš on their way to Nanni.

Šuppiluliuma I's first Syrian war

The first Syrian campaign of Šuppiluliuma I brought with
it great changes to the northern Levant and symbolizes to
many a turning point in the history of the ancient Near
East. This campaign marks the decline of Mittani as the
northern superpower and indicates the Hittites as the old-
new superpower, which moves from being on the fringe to

sharing control of the eastern Mediterranean with Egypt.
Mukiš, the cultural stronghold of Mittani in the west, is
the obvious victim of such a transformation of power.
Furthermore, being the leader of the coalition against the
marching Hittite troops made Mukiš even more vulnerable
in this war. Many have tried to reconstruct Šuppiluliuma
I's Syrian wars, and currently, the subject is under research
and significant revisions are in the making (i.e. Stavi's
dissertation). For that reason, I limit my discussion to
a short survey of the literature. The first Syrian war is
attested in CTH 46, 49, 51 and 53. The reaction to the
Hittite expansion southward is echoed in many of the el
Amarna texts. Among the major works on Šuppiluliuma
I's Syrian wars in the last twenty years one can include
Bryce (1989 and 1998: 174–193), Klengel (1992: 106–
111), Giles (1995), Beckman (1999: 17–58), Singer (1999:
629–636), Lackenbacher (2002: 71–76) Altman (2002 and
2004), Freu (2006: 43–49) and Miller 2007.

The case of Atchana/Nuzi ware

Atchana/Nuzi ware is one of the Nuzi Ware subtypes and
is clearly Mittanian in origin and nature. One of the most
encouraging details of my new stratigraphic arrangement
is that this ware can now be dated in Tell Atchana to the
first half of the fourteenth century, when Alalakh is still
a vassal of Mittani.[42] Woolley (1955: 347–350) argues
that Atchana/Nuzi ware lasts in Alalakh until 1273, but I
am able to show that, perhaps more logically, it does not
continue to appear at the site as a significant ware type
once the Hittites take over the region.

Atchana/Nuzi ware can be found at Tell Atchana in
Levels V–II^W (ibid.). Because it was mostly attested in
Level II^W (now more often than not reassigned to Level
IVB^F) together with Nuzi ware, Woolley considered it to
have been manufactured during the second half of the
fourteenth and first half of the thirteenth centuries, during
the Hittite suzerainty of Mukiš. Woolley's interpretation
(1953: 139) of the incongruous presence of Mittanian ware
in what he otherwise saw as an historically proven Hittite
context was creative, to say the least, and yet has gone
largely unchallenged. This may simply be because of the
relative scarcity of Nuzi ware sherds at sites other than
Tell Atchana, one of the places where this type of pottery
was first identified; in Alalakh it is found in large numbers
and *in situ*. "This pottery," Woolley writes (ibid.) on the
subject, "as we have seen, was by origin Mitanni and was
introduced to Alalakh in the time of the Mitanni suzerainty;
it was indeed a symbol of suzerain power. It was now
being manufactured locally by the Alalakh potters, but one
cannot believe that its origin was forgotten; its astonishing
popularity during the Hittite period looks very much like
an act of bravado, flaunting in the face of the conqueror the
emblem of the real sentiments of the people." Rearranging
the stratigraphy of Tell Atchana disentangles the
convoluted tale that Woolley created, of local Mukišians

---

[41] Bordreuil (1989a: 274) believes it is the summit on the sea shore,
located between Kassab and Ras al Bassit *"dont le nom turc est Kara
Douran."* The elevation of the summit, referred by Bordreuil as Mt.
Nanni (ibid.: 270) is 1129 m., exactly 600 m. short of the summit of Kel
Dağ, the unambiguous Mt. Ḫazzi.

[42] I thank Virginia Rimmer Herrmann for allowing me to quote her
University of Chicago seminar paper "A New Look at Nuzi Ware and its
Implications for Alalakh," dated March 17th, 2005.

Table 10. Atchana/Nuzi and Nuzi wares at Tell Atchana (after Herrmann 2005)

Level	Quantity	Locations	Notes
VI[W]	4 sherds		Intrusive?
V[W]	1–3 sherds (?)	Level V[W] temple; private houses?	
IV[W]	Parts of at least 13 vessels	1 Level IV[W] grave; Level IV[W] house 37; Level IV[W] Palace	Nuzi ware is more red
III[W]	Few sherds	Level III[W] houses; Level II[W] temple filling; Level III–II[W] fort courtyard fill	
II[W]	Lots	2 Level II[W] graves; Level II[W] houses and street; Level III–II[W] fort cellar floor	Atchana/Nuzi Ware is more black
I[W]		(houses)	All seeming Level I[W] are attributed to Level II[W]

who resisted Hittite occupation by producing fine resistance ware, painted with profuse shapes of flowers, birds and geometric forms that according to Evans (1936) and Woolley (1955: 397) they somehow adopted from none other than the Minoans (!)[43]—if only the Hittites had understood how profound the ceramic resistance against them was! This rearrangement places Atchana/Nuzi ware, possibly an import,[44] in its true context as the popular fine banquet ware used by the elite Mukišians in the kingdom of Itūr-Addu and his level IVB[F] predecessors.[45]

Nuzi ware has been a popular subject of study since its first attestations at Nuzi (Hrouda 1957; Cecchini 1965; Stein 1984; Pfälzner 1995 and 2007, to name a few. Recent studies are by Novak (2007) and Soldi (2006; 2008), as well as many excavation reports). None, however, has treated the subject of Tell Atchana's Atchana/Nuzi ware as attentively as does Virginia Rimmer Herrmann, in her 2005 unpublished seminar paper. Herrmann surveys the different attestations of Atchana/Nuzi ware in Woolley's excavations at Tell Atchana, finally showing that all reliable attestations are in Levels V–II[W], with a clear concentration in Level II[W] (Table 10):

Woolley found that there were two or three pieces of Nuzi ware in Level V, and that "otherwise it only occurs towards the end of Level IV, is common in Level III, most abundant in Level II, and is completely absent from Level I" (1955: 347). Specifically he counted 25 fragments of Nuzi ware from Level IV and 40 from Level II (1955: 348). Of those attributed to Level V, the one secure find spot given is a rubbish-pit in the temple area (Woolley 1955: 347, n. 5). Level IV examples were found in various rooms of the palace (pieces of at least 13 vessels) (1955: 118–130), in the foundation trench for Ilimilimma's addition to the palace (1955: 348, n. 5), in house 37 (several sherds) (1955: 177), and in grave ATG/39/86 (1955: 210, Pl. CIV, center left). Though Woolley states that the ware is "common" in Level III, exact find spots are rarely forthcoming. Examples seem to have been found, however, in the Level III houses (1955: 184), in the temple area in the filling for the Level II temple (1955: 81, n. 1), and in the fort courtyard under the Level II floor (1955: 168). In Level II, Nuzi ware was abundant in the houses and in the street between houses 37/A–B and 37/C–D (1955: 184ff.). Pieces were also found above the Level II floor of the fort cellar (1955: 168), in the foundation trench for the Level I fortification wall (1955: 169), and in two graves, ATG/38/7 in the fortress courtyard (1955: 169), and ATG/38/38, dug into the ruins of the Level III wall (1955: 207). Woolley found that all of the fragments of Nuzi ware which might on first glance appear to belong to Level I could actually be attributed to Level II instead (1955: 192–198). Once again, therefore, in keeping with its designation as a luxury ware, Nuzi ware was associated with the palace and with elite housing at Alalakh, but interestingly hardly any examples were found in the temple area.

---

[43] Woolley (1955: 397) states that "the Cretan inspiration of the 'Atchana' ware is unmistakable…" Surprisingly, the idea that Nuzi ware is a very late imitation of Kamares ware is still quite popular (Pfälzner 2008: 199). For criticism of this idea and alternative suggestions see Mallowan (1939: 892), Kantor (1945: 571–596), Frankfurt (1956: 142–143), and Crowley (1989: 214–215), who relates the Atchana/Nuzi ware to LH II and LH III pottery.

[44] To the best of my knowledge, no scientific examination of the origin of the ware has yet been published, neither petrography, nor NAA. I was told by Nathaniel Erb-Satullo, a graduate student from Harvard University, that he is currently working on chemical and mineralogical analysis of ceramics from Nuzi.

[45] Woolley's explanation may be read as a narrative of his own time in the Amuq in the late 1930s, when Arabs (Sunni and Alawite of Syrian identity) and Turks fought over the suzerainty of modern-day Mukiš. Woolley, who spent two years of his life in the Kastamonu camp of war prisoners in northern Anatolia (Woolley 1921) treated the Amuq, from the very beginning of his work there, as Syrian by its past and present. He expressed his deep concern over the annexation of the Sanjak of Alexandretta to Turkey, as recorded in several of his letters from the time, now in the archive of the British Museum: for example, one he wrote to Charles Baxter of the British foreign office dated June 30th, 1938. Did Woolley draw a parallel from Syria to Mittani and from Turks to Hittites, as the Turks themselves strongly did at the time? It is very tempting to identify these events with Woolley's analysis of the cause for the manufacture of the Atchana ware.

In his study, Sebastiano Soldi writes (2006: 93) that the only way to fully understand Nuzi ware in the northern Levant would be to reconsider the stratigraphy of Alalakh and the dig records. My stratigraphic analysis places the Level II^W private houses in Level IVB^F, or, in absolute chronological terms, in the first half of the fourteenth century. Beyond the stratigraphy, there are several strong arguments for placing Atchana/Nuzi ware in the first half of the fourteenth century rather than in 1350-1273 B.C.E., Woolley's date range:

1) *Atchana ware motifs are not unique.* For many years, Atchana/Nuzi ware of Level II^W was considered to be a later type of Nuzi Ware (i.e., Cecchini 1965: 37; Pfälzner 2007: 248–249). There are two main justifications for this opinion:
   a) Woolley's stratigraphy that dates it to 1350–1273, and
   b) Atchana/Nuzi ware's unique set of motifs (Photos 14–16) as compared to the familiar Nuzi ware types up to the 1990s.

I have already disputed the first reason at length. As for the second, Herrman uses finds from more than thirty sites with attestations of Nuzi ware[46] to show that this organic style of decoration, heretofore considered a unique, local development at Tell Atchana, can in fact be found and is published at the following sites: Tell Beydar (Bretschneider 1997: Tf. II.2; herein Photo 17) in its Mittanian stratum, Tell al-Rimah (Postgate et al. 1997: 55 and Pl. 71; herein Photo 18) and Tell Hamida (Zimansky 1995: 81, figure 6a).

Several facets of the connection between Tell Atchana and Nuzi ware caused the Atchana/Nuzi ware to look like a unique phenomenon:
   a) The wide variety of types and decoration types found at the site;
   b) The establishment of Tell Atchana as a central site for Nuzi ware early in the history of Nuzi ware scholarship; and
   c) The fact that one of the decoration types of Nuzi ware, found at Atchana, resembles the Kamares ware more than any other Nuzi ware decoration style.

Atchana, of all Nuzi ware sites, was closest to the Mediterranean and Aegean worlds, in terms of geography as well as of material culture. Unlike most of the sites where Nuzi ware is present, Tell Atchana received a large number of Aegean imports during the Late Bronze Age. Therefore, it was assumed that Atchana was the cultural meeting point, the very locus where east met west.[47]

2) *Similar quantative patterns, overlapping dates.* Nuzi ware is securely attested at Tell Atchana from Level V^W/V^F to the private houses of Level II^W/IVB^F. In accordance with my analysis of Level V^F, the first appearance of Nuzi ware at Tell Atchana is securely dated to the first half of the fifteenth century, but the ware could feasibly have reached Tell Atchana (or been manufactured there) for the first time in the last quarter of the sixteenth century. Nuzi ware had reached its peak at the time of Šuppiluliuma I's destruction of the site in 1353/1341. It may have remained in use though not as broadly as before, during Alalakh's final phase as a city, in some of the private houses of Level I^W—now classified as Level III^F and dated to the second half of the fourteenth century. Woolley also found Atchana ware in Level I^W, which he consistently reassigns to Level II^W (1955: 192–198). During the 2003 season of the University of Chicago dig at Tell Atchana one vessel of Khabur ware was found *in situ* on the floor of the last occupation phase of the city (that is: local phase 1 in Areas 2–3 = Level I^W private houses = Level III^F).[48] This shouldered beaker (Photo 19) is very similar to Khabur ware of both of Pfälzner's Middle Jazirah IA and IB pottery.[49] Another Atchana ware beaker (Photos 20 and 21) was found *in situ* on a floor of the last Mittanian phase of the site (local phase 2 in Areas 2–3 = Level II^W private houses = Level IVB^F). Both local phases 1 and 2 in Areas 2–3 had carried significant number of *ex situ* Nuzi post sherds (Photos 22 and 23). Therefore, the maximum range of the ware, which Woolley defined as Nuzi and Atchana/Nuzi wares at Tell Atchana, is 1520–1340 B.C.E., but 1470–1350 B.C.E. is a range of higher probability. It is possible that some Nuzi ware vessels were inherited or manufactured by the local population and were in use through the final destruction of the city, sometime in the last quarter of the fourteenth century B.C.E. The date of Nuzi ware in its native soil, the Jazirah, is quite problematic. As Pfälzner (2007: 244) describes it, "Nuzi ware is abundant both in Middle Jazirah I A and I B context", which are the periods in which Early and Late Mittani pottery traditions are respectively represented. Pfälzner's dates (ibid.: 232–234) of Middle Jazirah I A and I B[50] are 1550–1400/1350 and 1400/1350–1270 respectively.[51] Clearly, the dates of Middle Jazirah I A and I B are far from being final and firm. Moreover, "there is no formal or decorative development of Nuzi ware during its existence" (ibid.:

---

[46] Herrmann surveys the finds from the following sites: 1) Cilicia: Kinet Höyük. 2) Northern Levant: Tell Atchana/Alalakh, Çatal Höyük, Tell Ta'yinat, Umm el-Marra, Qatna, Hama. 3) Upper Euphrates/Balih Rivers: Tell Aushariye, Tell Munbaqa/Ekalte, Meskene/Emar, Tell Jidle, Hammam Ibn esh-Shehab, Hammam et-Turkman. 4) Upper Habur River: Tell Fakhariyah, Tell Chagar Bazar, Tell Qabr el-Kebir, Tell Tuneinir, Tell Abu Hafur (Ost), Tell Hamida, Tell Beydar, Tell Barri, Tell al-Hamidiya, Tell Bderi, Tell Brak, Tell al-Rimah. 5) Tigris River and beyond: Tell al-Hawa, Tell Gigan, Kar Tukulti Ninurta, Tell Dhahab, Ninveh, Assur, Nuzi, Aqar Quf/Dur Kurigalzu.

[47] This idea is in line with the reason that brought Woolley to dig Tell Atchana at the outset (1953: 13–16).

[48] It was examined in the area and identified as Mittanian in nature by Prof. Peter Pfälzner.

[49] Such as vessels number 81, 83 , 85 and 89 of the Middle Jazirah I A (Pfalzner 2007: 266–267) or 215, 216, 219 of the Middle Jazirah I B (ibid.: 278).

[50] Equal to Late Bronze Age IA and IB in a scale of LBA I–III.

[51] Pfälzner's date (ibid.: 232) of Middle Jazirah IA appears by mistake as 1550/1400–1350 in his two summary tables. 1550 represents an average date for Muršili I's ride on Babylon and the beginning of the Late Bronze Age in the region. One should move this date in accordance with one's approach to the Mesopotamian chronology. Therefore, if indeed Muršili I caused the end of Level VI^W in Alalakh, a date within Level VA^F could represent the introduction of Nuzi ware to the site when, or closely after, Idrimi took over Alalakh, and a decade or two after it appears for the fist time in the Mittanian heartland.

Above: **Photo 14. Atchana/Nuzi ware ATP/37/2 (after Woolley 1955: Pl. CIIa)**

Below: **Photo 15. Atchana/Nuzi ware ATP/37/240 (after Woolley 1955: Pl. CIIIa)**

Photo 16. Atchana/Nuzi ware from Amuq phase O in Tell Ta'yinat (on display at the museum of the Oriental Institute, University of Chicago)

Above: **Photo 17. Nuzi ware from Tell Beydar (after Bretschneider 1997: Tf. II.2)**

Below: **Photo 18. Nuzi ware from Tell al-Rimah (Postgate et al. 1997: Pl. 71)**

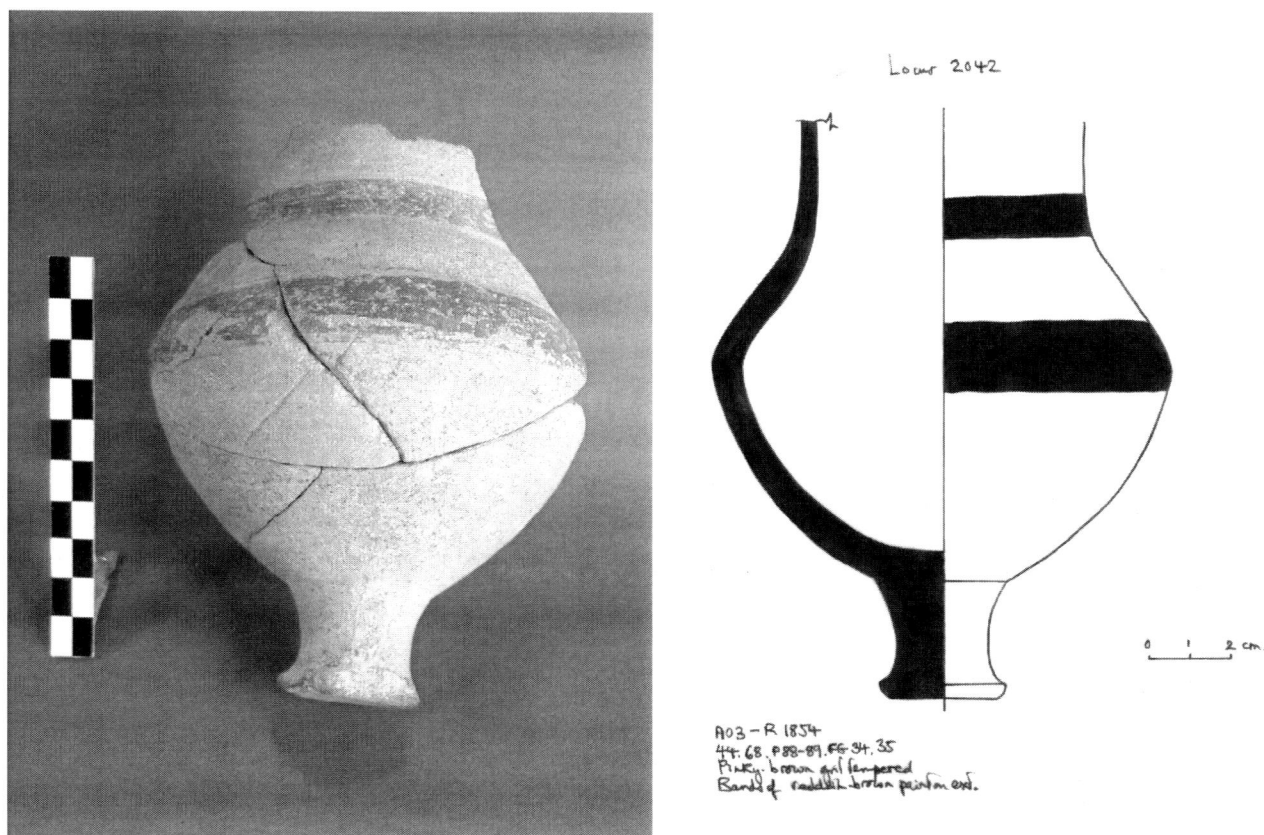

Photo 19. Khabur ware excavated by the University of Chicago expedition at Tell Atchana, Area 2, Square 44.68, Locus 03-2042, object number A03-R1854c (Photo: Nita Lee Roberts. Drawing: Dominique Collon)

244), and consequently, it is almost impossible to date it within Middle Jazirah I A or I B context. Pfälzner (ibid.) believes that "there are some hints at a possible development of motives," from Middle Jazirah I A to I B, as well as motifs that are more common in one of the periods, although no real quantative multi-site study of this subject is available so far. Pfälzner's (ibid.: 248) observation is that Nuzi ware is "definitely better known from Middle Jazirah I B contexts, but it remains to be seen if this reflects an actual quantitative development or if this picture depends on the current state of research." In his comparison to Tell Atchana, he makes Alalakh Levels V–III^W contemporary with Middle Jazirah I A, and Level II^W with Middle Jazirah I B. Most of the Nuzi ware vessels found in Alalakh were in Level II^W, and the pattern of increase in number of Nuzi ware vessels in the fourteenth century that Pfälzner observes during Middle Jazirah I B is clearly parallelled at Tell Atchana. Nevertheless, the comparison to Alalakh will be accurate for our purposes only if the beginning of Middle Jazirah I B is circa 1400 B.C.E., which is Pfälzner's highest date for this transition. Level II^W/IVB^F in Alalakh starts circa 1400 and ends no later than 1353/1341.

Pfälzner further points out that Atchana/Nuzi ware is in fact "a special sub-type of Nuzi ware, which occurs in association with normal Nuzi ware…" (ibid.), and that its shapes correspond to the Nuzi ware typology. Therefore, it should be considered contemporary with

Nuzi ware; it certainly does not post-date it.[52] We must also remember that due to lack of excavations, we know very little of Nuzi ware in the western part of the Mittanian Empire. It is most likely that Atchana/ Nuzi ware is simply a Western Mittani decoration style of Nuzi ware. In the studies of Nuzi ware to date too much emphasis is given to decoration and too little to form and technology. Typology should treat all three equally.

3) *Other than in Assyria, only in Mittanian layers.* As clearly demonstrated by Pfälzner (ibid.: 232, 238) Nuzi ware was found only in Mittani related strata and ceased with the end of Mittanian suzerainty (end of Middle Jazirah I B). There is one notable exception: in the heartland of Middle Assyria, the new master of the Mittanian centers (Pfälzner 1995: 106–160). The date of the termination of Nuzi ware in the Jazirah is simply the date of the destruction of the final Middle Jazirah I B phase in each site. This date is not one and the same for all sites and it follows the complicated political history of Mittani in the fourteenth and thirteenth centuries.[53] In Alalakh, the end of level II^W/ IVB^F stands for the end of the period in which Mukiš was a vassal of Mittani—the time Šuppiluliuma I

---

[52] Pfälzner (2007: 249) is mentioning the Tell Baydar vessel (Photo 17) as a proof for the synchronization between Middle Jazirah IB and Atchana/ Nuzi ware.

[53] The term "Mittani" for a layer does not imply an ethnic assignment of the pottery concerned. It has purely political-geographical significance (Pfalzner 2007: 231).

Above: **Photo 20. Nuzi beaker, excavated by the University of Chicago expedition at Tell Atchana. Area 2, Square 44.45, Locus 03-2077**

Below: **Photo 21. Nuzi beaker, excavated by the University of Chicago expedition at Tell Atchana. Area 2, Square 44.45, Locus 03-2077**

Above: **Photo 22. Nuzi ware excavated by the University of Chicago expedition at Tell Atchana, Area 2.**

Below: **Photo 23. Nuzi ware excavated by the University of Chicago expedition at Tell Atchana, Area 2.**

conquered the kingdom (1353/1341). As Herrmann puts it in her paper:

> At almost all of the newly excavated sites, Nuzi ware went out of use during the period of Middle Assyrian domination, and a Middle Assyrian official ceramic assemblage replaced the old Mittanian one… Perhaps its use was then restricted to the extreme upper echelons of Assyrian society at the capitals of Assur and Kar Tukulti-Ninurta, accounting for the late attestations there. If the use of Nuzi ware was indeed so characteristic and even symbolic of the political elite of Mittani and its vassals, then, it is still strange that the peak of its use in Alalakh occurred, according to Woolley, after the Hittite conquest of the site. I find Woolley's explanation of this unconvincing. Perhaps a reevaluation of the site's stratigraphy and chronology in the upcoming excavations will help to clarify this issue.

Herrmann is right: the term "Mittani pottery" is employed for the homogenous groups of ceramics from the core region of Mittani during the time of the Mittani-state (Pfälzner 2007: 232). This is also the case of Atchana/Nuzi ware, the most popular decorated ware during the time Mukiš was a vassal of Mittani.

4) *If local, why disappeared?* Woolley (1955: 397) describes the end of Atchana/Nuzi ware as a sudden event—Nuzi ware ends with Level II^W and the dominant fine ware is from then on (Level I^W) Mycenaean pottery.[54] As I stated above, I find it unlikely that Atchana/Nuzi ware as well as other Mittanian related wares disappeared so suddenly in Alalakh. Rather, it must have become scarcer and scarcer as supply routes were blocked and heirlooms were broken.

There is no proof that Nuzi ware at Atchana was imported (no petrography and NAA studies to date). Nonetheless, the circumstances in Level I^W in which

a) there is no known change of population in Alalakh between Levels II^W and I^W,
b) the Hittites annexed the region,
c) the Mittanian influence ended and
d) (another?) imported fine ware at Tell Atchana, LH IIIA:2, became suddenly dominant,

bring me to believe that most of the Nuzi and Atchana ware vessels were imported to Alalakh. Ostensibly, this is the extraordinary event in which the end of one imported ware (Nuzi) marks the beginning of another; the relative prevalence of each ought to reflect the dominant geo-political framework and governing superpower in Mukiš in their time.

5) *Replaced by mid-late fourteenth century ware.* Stratigraphically, Atchana/Nuzi ware of Level II^W is sealed by Level I^W, in which a large amount of LH IIIA:2 pottery (see detailed discussion in Section 5.1) was found. LH IIIA:2 dates from 1390/1370–1320/1300 B.C.E.,[55] and therefore post-dates the Atchana/Nuzi ware; 1353/1341 then is a very reasonable end date for the presence *en masse* of Atchana and Nuzi wares at Alalakh.

6) *Atchana/Nuzi ware does not exist in other Amuq sites.* In his unpublished dissertation on the University of Chicago Amuq ceramic sequence (K to O), Gustavus Swift (1958: 26–36, 58) dated Phase M to 1550–1400, equating it with Levels V–III^W in Alalakh (see the adopted Tables Swift 1958 Table 5 vs. Pruss 2002 Table 1). Phase M was excavated in both Çatal Höyük (Amuq) and Tell Judaidah (see Swift Table 1), but little Nuzi ware was attested in it. Swift (ibid.: 23) reports on several Nuzi ware vessels that were unearthed in phase M of Çatal Höyük (Amuq) in the 1930s and still have not yet been published.[56] In particular one should note a beaker (Photo 24), which is best parallelled with a beaker from Tell Brak, Pfälzner's type number 222 (2007: 278). He dates the style to Middle Jazirah I B. This period begins no earlier than 1400 B.C.E. (ibid.: 232), thus possibly contradicting Swift's (1958: 58) and Pruss' (2002: 162) tendency to end Amuq M at 1400. Although Atchana/Nuzi ware is not attested at Çatal Höyük (Amuq), its contemporary ware, the later Nuzi ware, is.

Swift's second argument for ending Amuq M at 1400 is the absence of Mycenaean pottery from the Phase M assemblage (1958: 28–29). Remarkably (see Section 5.1), Mycenaean pottery becomes a main component of the assemblage only in Level I^W, so it is not surprising that it did not vastly reach secondary Amuq sites. It now seems likely then that Phase M at the Amuq ended somewhat later than 1400, during the fourteenth century, and that the same event which caused the disappearance of Nuzi ware from Tell Atchana also caused the destruction of Amuq phase M: namely, Šuppiluliuma's take over of Mukiš in 1353/1341. Alternatively, Phase M could have ended in 1320/1313, when the city of Alalakh ceased to exist (see Section 5.1 below).

7) *Imports and heirlooms.* Nuzi ware in its different types (including Atchana ware) is a charming fine ware, and as such may have been a popular choice for imports and heirlooms. The vessels found in the Royal Tomb in Qatna and in Hama must be imports (Pfälzner 2008: 199). The attestation of Nuzi ware at Emar is another clear case of an heirloom vessel, found in a burial (Margueron 1975: 66, 68, Fig. 6). The Atchana/Nuzi ware beaker (Photo 16), found at Tell Ta'yinat is certainly an heirloom (Swift 1958: 29–30). According to Herrmann, the vessel, now on display at the Museum of the Oriental Institute in Chicago, was found in Amuq phase O, dated to Iron Age II. The distance between Ta'yinat and Atchana

---

[54] See, for example, his (Woolley 1955: 195, n. 1) note that even when published in preliminary reports that Nuzi ware types were found in Level I^W, it was in fact found under the Level I^W floor.

[55] http://projectsx.dartmouth.edu/classics/history/bronze_age/lessons/les/24.html

[56] Marina Pucci, Lynn Swartz Dodd and Heather Snow are respectively in the process of publishing the University of Chicago excavations at the Amuq sites of Çatal Höyük, Tell al Judaidah and Tell Ta'yinat.

COMPARATIVE CHRONOLOGY: THE SYRIAN EXPEDITION AND WOOLLEY'S EXCAVATIONS, LATER PERIODS

Syrian Expedition					Woolley's Excavations		
Phase	Proposed Date	Palestine-Syria: Period	Palestine-Syria: Site	Mesopotamian Connections	Site	Level	Woolley's Date
O	950- 550		Hama E Meg. V-III TBM B_3, A	Late Assyrian	Tab. al-Akrad	Surface	
N	1150- 950		Hama F Tarsus "Transit."		Tell Atchana	O	ca. 1140
					Tell Atchana Tell Atchana	I II	1273-1194 1350-1273
M	1550-1400	L.B. I	Hama G	Mitannian	Tell Atchana Tell Atchana Tell Atchana	III IV V	1370-1350 1447-1370 1595-1447
					Tell Atchana Tell Atchana	VI VII	1750-1595 1780-1750
L	1900-1780	M.B. II A	Hama H Tarsus M.B. Mersin XI-IX		Tell Atchana	VIII-XIV	3100-1780
K	2000-1900	M.B. II A			Tell Atchana	XV-XVII?	3400-3100

Above: **Swift Table 5. Amuq phases K–O and Alalakh: a comparative chart (After Swift 1958: 58)**

Below: **Pruss Table 1. Amuq phases and Alalakh: a comparative chart (After Pruss 2002: 162)**

Periode	ungefähre Datierung	Amuq	Chatal Hüyük I	Chatal Hüyük II	Tell Judaidah	Alalach
SBZ I	1550–1400	M		12–13	12–15	V IV
SBZ II	1400–1180					III II–I
EZ I	1180–1000/950	N	7–10	9–11	9–11	"0"
EZ IIA	1000/950–900	Oa	6–5	8–7	8	
EZ IIB	900–720	Ob	4–3	6–2	7	
EZ III	720–540	Oc			6	

Abb. 1 Schichtenabfolge im Amuq-Gebiet in der Späten Bronze- und Eisenzeit

EXCAVATED AREAS OF PHASES K TO O, BY SITE

Phase	Chatal Hüyük	Tell al-Judaidah	Tell Ta'yinat
O	Entire Areas I to VI	D7,8,E7–9,F7–10; J14–15,K14,L14; J9,G12,F15; TT20	Late: Entire Excavated Area Early: Traces
N	Area I: V13,W15 Area II: N13,N14 Area IV: E4,J9 Area V: P4 Area VI: T8	F7,F8,F9; G7,H7,J7; TT20,D8/1	Traces
M	Area II: N13,N14 Area V: P4	TT20,K6 D8/1,F7 D14	Traces
L	Traces	TT20,K6 D8/1,F7	
K	Traces	TT20	

Swift Table 1. Excavated areas of Amuq phases K–O by site (After Swift 1958: 10)

is less than one kilometer. A very reasonable state of affairs could be that one of the Iron Age II inhabitants of Ta'yinat dug this special pot out at then deserted Tell Atchana.

In Woolley's description of the violent destruction of Level II^W (now IVB^F) he also discusses the vanishing Atchana/Nuzi and Nuzi wares (1955: 186): "…the ware disappears abruptly and completely with that destruction; it is never found in the Level I houses which immediately succeeded those of Level II. This requires an historical explanation." Based on all that I have demonstrated above, the historical explanation must be the Hittite conquest during Šuppiluliuma I's first Syrian war.

Level IVB^F palace (Plans 30, 35)[57]

As suggested in my discussion of the temples, I believe that the Levels III–II^W fort was built during the Level IVB^F period. This was part of a vast rebuilding of the city, which was partly destroyed (and severely harmed) in the attack that caused the destruction of the Level IV^W/IVA^F palace.[58]

The Level IV^W fortress archive ceased to exist at the same time that the Level IV^W palace archives did. Woolley admits that the stratigraphy of this area was very complicated, episodic and inconsistent (1955: 130–131). This drew him to his erroneous conclusion regarding the date of the destruction of the Level IV^W fortress, now established as the Level VB^F palace, and which functioned as such to the end of Level IVA^F. As I show in Chapters 3 and 4, there are no archaeological, historical or philological reasons that stand in the way of dating the fortress, which was attributed by Woolley to Levels III^W and II^W, to the beginning of Level IVB^F, shortly after the destruction of the Level IVA^F palace and fortress. The building, named by Woolley "the Level III–II^W fort", could, in fact, be the stronger, larger and higher palace of Itūr-Addu, king of the land of Mukiš, or even of Ilimilimma, if he indeed survived the destruction of his palace. This building could have lasted for many years and served as the palace of the Hittite governor of Alalakh.

The Level III^W temple, a significant building project in itself, was most likely built at the same time as the Levels III–II^W fort; nonetheless, both building projects occurred

---

[57] Photos: 1) general: Woolley 1955: Pl. XXXIVa–b. 2) tablets: A photo of tablet 447 (ATT/47/25) is found in Woolley/Box 15 at the UCL special collection. See also Wiseman (1953) 113, Pl. XLVII–L. 3) Pottery: Woolley 1955: Pl. CIIa.

[58] Woolley (1953: 134) is far from being certain of his dating of the Levels III–II^W fort: "although the evidence was rather intangible I felt

justified in asserting that it had been erected in the Level III period and continued in use throughout the period of Level II."

Photo 24. Nuzi ware beaker from phase M of Çatal Höyük (Amuq)

during the Level IVB[F] period, several decades before Šuppiluliuma I conquered Alalakh.

This important building is the largest structure excavated in Alalakh. It is oriented NE–SW, very similarly to the Level IV[W] fortress (probably Idrimi's Level VB[F] palace). It is possible that whoever built it tried to follow in the footsteps of Idrimi, and distance himself from Niqmepa and Ilimilimma, at least in terms of orientation.[59] Throughout the occupational history of Alalakh most buildings are oriented based on their individual positions in relation to the city walls. Clearly, the city plan in Alalakh, at least from Level VII[W] on, was formed from the city wall inwards, and most of the walls run either perpendicular or parallel to the city wall. The course of the city wall has barely changed throughout its recorded manifestations. Following this observation I would like to suggest that the three rooms excavated in squares U12, U13 and T13 in the southern end of the fort (Plan 35) are the only rooms excavated so far of considerable additional wing of this palace. The largest section of the Level IVB[F] palace excavated until now consists mostly of the palace's northern wing, between walls *A*, *B* and *C* of Plan 35, as well as the southwestern projections of walls *A* and *C*. The built area between wall *A* and the city wall is also part of the northern wing, whose shape in the northwest is dictated by the course of the city wall. Unlike the northern wing, the three rooms in squares U12, U13 and T13 are oriented to the southwest city wall. We do not know the course of the city wall on the southwest slope of the tell. Nevertheless, if these three rooms do represent another unexcavated wing,[60] it is plausible that the Level IVB[F] palace occupied the whole northwest summit of the mound (Woolley 1953: 134) and therefore was absolutely exceptional in its enormous size of up to 8,000–9,000 m² (compare with 6,000 m², which is the maximum possible area of the of the Level IVA[F] palace in its last days, assuming it included all of the Level VB[F] palace). Woolley reports in one place (ibid.) that he excavated no less than 260 by 260 feet of this structure, elsewhere that he worked an 80 by 80 m. (6,400 m²) square (1955: 167). Based on Woolley's plan and scale I calculate that he cannot have excavated more than 4,500 m² of this building, but more likely he excavated roughly 3,800 m², courtyards excluded. Even so, this is the largest building discovered at Atchana.

The northern wing of the Level IVB[F] palace was built on the most elevated part of the site; the southern wing, of which only three rooms were excavated, was built on a lower terrace, and was better preserved (ibid.: 167–169). Of the north wing only the podium/foundation walls are preserved. They are 2.6–5.8 m. thick, and form a V shape: the width of the brickwork decreases with the depth of the foundations–each course of bricks of the wall foundation is placed on the course below it and on the soil to the two sides of this course (ibid.). The lowest course of bricks in this V shape foundation is built of stone (boulders, heavy limestone rubble and basalt slabs, and even orthostats in secondary use). All together the V shape foundation is preserved to a maximum height of 4 m., and in some spots it goes below the floors of the Level IVA[W] palace.[61] The foundations of the palace's outer walls are 4–5 m. thick, and they were 3–3.5 m. deep (ibid.: 167). The boxes between the foundations were filled in solidly with bricks to a depth of at least 1.6 m. as reported in one place (Woolley 1953: 133) or at least 3 m. as reported in another (Woolley 1955: 167). The top of this fill could be the floor surface of the lowest story of this structure, but Woolley reports that most of the floors in the northern wing have disappeared (ibid.). No thresholds were found, and therefore the top of this fill is not the floor, unless the boxes between the foundations (they look like rooms on Plan 35) were used as cellars and approached from the floor above. Woolley (ibid.: 168) claims that he identified a staircase (located in squares V10 and V11), where "the brick filling rose higher than elsewhere, above what appeared to be floor-level, and so may well have been the packing for a flight of steps."[62]

The southern wing is on a lower terrace, and two of the three rooms excavated there (in squares U12, U13 and T13) were clearly used as storage (ibid.: 168 and Pl. XXXIIIb; Woolley 1953: Pl. 15b). They were entirely taken up by jars sunk 0.3 m. in the ground. The northernmost of the three (in square U12) is "completely ruined, and the one point of interest about it was that it has been served by an exterior drain of which the open channel beyond the intake survived against the SW wall" (Woolley 1955: 168).

The central room was better preserved than the others; its northwest wall stands up to 1.8 m., and its southeast to 0.3 m. Its floor was of clay, and "scattered about in the soil beneath the clay floor" the so-called "Boğazköy type" tablet (ATT/47/25 = AT447) was found (ibid.). Woolley writes that the tablet certainly belongs to Level III[W] (IVB[F]), which he believes is Hittite. In fact, this tablet, which he considered to be Hitite, was Woolley's main justification for dating the Levels III–II[W] fort to the time of Šuppiluliuma I. Yet the text is not Hittite, but rather a Sumerian lexical list (Lauinger 2005: 54; Wiseman 1953: 113, Pl. XLVII–L); this could date to significantly earlier than the Hittite takeover of Alalakh, and therefore so too could the Level IVB[F] palace. In the same room, above the floor, an almost whole 'Atchana' ware beaker (ATP/37/2) was also found (Woolley 1955: 168, Pl. CIIa).

Of the southern room only about half remained, due to its location near the terrace edge. Woolley explains that the three rooms are storage cellars. He believes that their layout, as well as the storage jars, originated in Level III[W], and was used until the end of Level II[W] (1953: 135).

---

[59] I do not understand how Woolley (1955: 168) connects the building's orientation with the Niqmepa palace/wing.

[60] Woolley's dig house is located on top of the projecting extension of the northern wing.

[61] There is good reason to believe that some of the Level IVA[W] palace material, as recorded by Woolley, could have possibly originated in the Level IVB[F] palace or vice versa.

[62] This room or installation is marked on Plan 35 as if it is a thick wall. Notably, the double narrow room dug in squares U8, U9, T8 and T9 looks like a better candidate for a staircase.

The southeast wall of the northern wing of the Levels III–II^W (IVB^F) fort, which faces toward the city, is fortified with square buttresses set at regular intervals. Woolley (1955: 168) suggests that the main entrance to this complex was originally located in square S11, between the second and the third buttresses; still, he has no evidence to prove this. South of the buttresses, Woolley (ibid.: 167) attributes to Level III^W a large open space (piazza), which is leveled and discontinuously brick-paved, but not raised to the height of the inside of the fort. This piazza is bounded by the northern Level III–II^W city wall and the buttressed wall. The piazza is re-floored with clay, which remains only in patches, accumulating 0.8 m. above the original pavement (ibid.: 168). The layer between the two floors (brick and clay) is described by Woolley (ibid.: 168, n. 1) as stratigraphically unreliable; however, several finds originate from this piazza. First, quite a few Atchana ware sherds were found all through the deposit between the two floors (ibid.); more remarkable, though, were the cremation burial of an infant (ATG/38/7), found "in a fine amphora of painted Nuzi ware" (ATP/38/17), buried from the Level II^W floor, through the Level III brick floor and "almost down to the Level IV palace rubbish" in squares R14 and S13 (ibid.: 169, 206, Pl. CIIc);[63] and the ivory statuette (AT/38/38) found high up in the court, and dated by Woolley to Level II^W (ibid.: 168, Pl. LXXVIc).[64]

The only Hittite finds in the courtyard come from unsealed, and therefore, uncertain, contexts. One is a seal inscribed with Luwian hieroglyphs, AT/38/135 (no. 156 in Barnet's catalogue in Woolley 1955: 266–267): it was found in square S12, below the level of the brick-floor (Level III^W floor), but not underneath it, that is—not explicitly sealed by it. Woolley pigeonholes it to Level III^W (ibid.: Pl. LXVII₁₅₆).[65] Another Luwian seal, AT/38/153 (no. 159 in Barnet's catalogue; ibid.: 267), was discovered "quite high up in the filling and therefore out of its true horizon" (ibid.: 169, Pl. LXVII₁₅₉).[66]

Only scant remains of the Levels III–II^W fort superstructure were preserved, making it hard to track its building sub-phases. Nevertheless, at one point, at the northwestern edge of the site, Woolley records two building phases in the foundations of this structure (Plan 30; 1955: 155, Fig. 58d, 169–170). I attribute the earlier of these (Level III^W) to Level IVB^F (the first half of the fourteenth century), and the later one (Level II^W) to Levels III-IIB^F, when the fort/palace functioned as the residence of the Hittite governor.

Similar, certainly not less significant, evidence for the existence of two sub-phases is poorly reported by Woolley (ibid.: 170).[67] Woolley writes that in Level II^W "the interior of the castle was remodeled…" and especially that "the floor level is raised 0.5 m. and the rooms are differently planned, old walls being buried and new walls not resting on but cutting through them." Woolley adds (ibid.) that "the new walls are of the same white-spotted material as the walls of Level III, but unlike Level III, the Level II walls have no stone foundations." This indicates yet again the long duration of this building.

Levels III–II^W/IVB^F City Wall

As was previously emphasized, the differences between Levels III^W and II^W are minor. In many ways, one should treat these levels as one phenomenon or possibly as two sub-phases of one larger phase. These sub-phases can be traced only in some parts of the site (certain private houses); in the rest of the excavated site they are not observable. Woolley probably only divided the material into two levels because he observed the long duration in which some of these features functioned—a duration that I tend to extend even further, by implying some modification to these layers. As I wrote above, my main claim is that Levels III–II^W are in fact Level IVB^F and date to the first half of the fourteenth century B.C.E., not to the second half of the same century and the first quarter of the thirteenth century, as claimed by Woolley and the scholarship to follow. Nonetheless, some of the features that Woolley identifies with these levels continue to be in use after Šuppiluliuma I takes over the site in 1353/1341. These include the Levels III–II^W/IVB^F fort, the Levels II^W/III^F temple (which was probably built only after the Hittite conquest) and the Levels III–II^W city wall, which was reinforced with a revetment during Level I^W/Level III^F.

Woolley's descriptions of the city wall/s of Level III^W and Level II^W are inconsistently tagged and therefore, contradictory. Analyzing all his references to these walls, I conclude that they all actually concern only one city wall, that of Levels III–II^W, which is drawn in its complete form in Yener's (2005) plan of Level II^W (Plan 48). No convincing references to a city wall built earlier than Level II^W or later than Level IV^W exist in Woolley's records.[68]

[63] Woolley mistakenly refers to it as Pl. CIId. In the pottery card of the amphora Woolley claims that it was found in square R13. The card is currently in Woolley's archive at the UCL Special Collection.

[64] despite the fact that in the object card, now at the UCL Special Collection, it is described as a top soil find (ibid.: 168, Pl. LXXVIc).

[65] In personal communication, Shay Gordin writes: "AT/8/135 is a biconvex seal which has the same name on both sides (made out of green steatite). The photo is bad but I could perhaps find a parallel in a seal impression from Nisantepe of a certain *Lamu* (see number 201–202 at Herbordt 2005 and Hawkins 2005). The top sign is likely *la* (LINGUA), as it could not be anything else, and the bottom sign seems to be a bad *mu*. But I will have to check this with the original to be sure. As for the title on the right of the name it could be REX.FILIUS "prince" or AURIGA (again I need the original to be sure)."

[66] Shay Gordin in personal communication as above: "AT/8/153 is a biconvex seal. The original photos are as usual upside down, likely because they could not identify the signs very well. Side A for me is the photo on the left: it contains the signs (from top to bottom): BOS-FRATER2 or the good name *Muwanani*. The titles which appear to the left of the name and on the bottom register are: BONUS2 VIR2 and AURIGA. Since in cuneiform the name *Muwanani* is a woman's name, I still hesitate whether VIR2 is actually FEMINA, but for this we do need a better photo or the original at hand. Side B has the name *nu-nu* (both nu₂) and the title AURIGA. *Nunu* is a very common name in cuneiform (Laroche 1966: no. 897). In conclusion, it is a double name biconvex seal, either belonging to two male AURIGA, or less likely to a man and

his wife AURIGA (?). For such seals see Mora 1988."

[67] Woolley did not publish a separate Level II^W plan of the fort, and this written description is the only record of this sub-phase of the fort/palace.

[68] Yener's reconstruction of a Level III^W city wall (Plan 47) is groundless. What is really depicted in white outline in Yener's plan for Level III^W (Plan 47) is a wall that Woolley reconstructs as part of the Levels III–

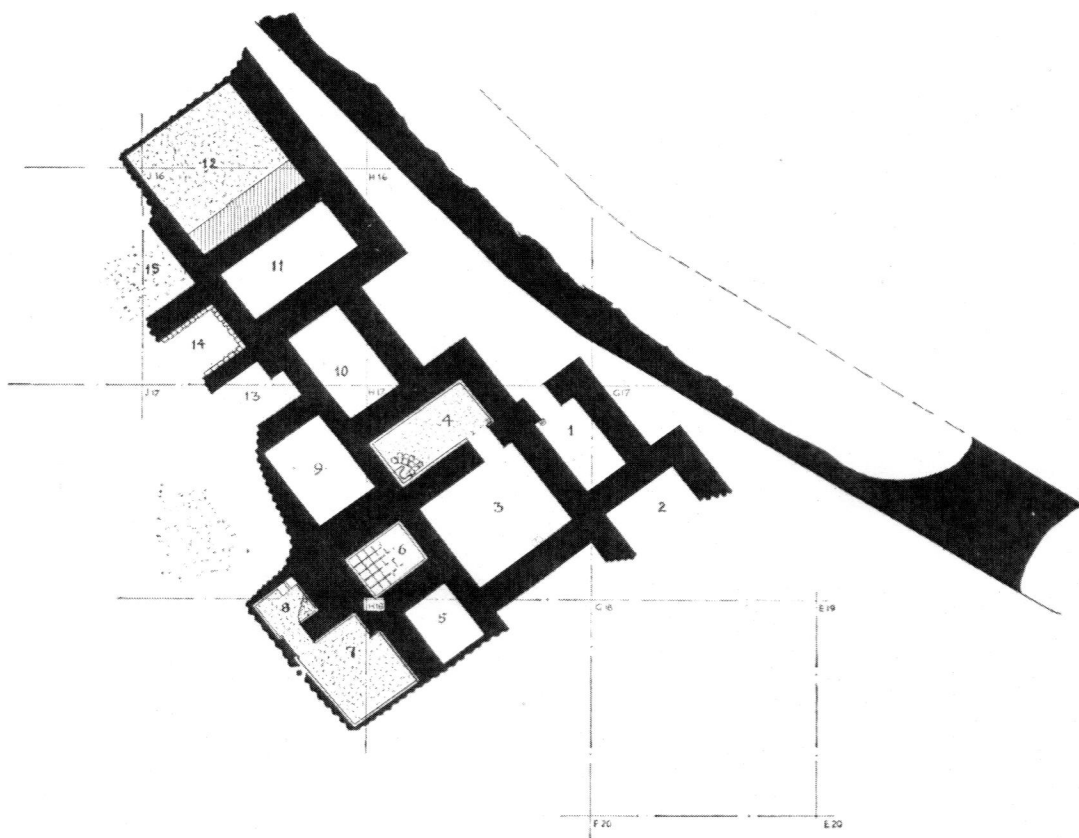

FIG. 67. House 38/A, Level I

Plan 49. Level I^W houses 38/A (after Woolley 1955: 192, Fig. 67)

Woolley refers to the Levels III^W and II^W city wall(s) in the following descriptions and plans, which I trace from northwest to southeast:

a) The main description of the Levels II^W and III^W city walls in his town defenses chapter (Woolley 1955: 144–145).
b) The city wall in Plan 35 (ibid.: Fig. 59).
c) The Level III^W city wall in Plan 36 (ibid.: Fig. 63).
d) The city wall in Plan 40 (ibid.: Fig. 62).
e) The Level II^W city wall in Plan 42 (ibid.: Fig. 65).
f) The Level II^W city wall in Plan 43 (ibid.: Fig. 68).
g) The Level II^W city wall in Plan 13 (ibid.: Fig. 53).
h) The Levels II^W and III^W city walls in Plan 45 (ibid.: Fig. 52a–b).
i) The Level III^W city wall in Plan 44 (ibid.: Fig. 64).
j) The Level II^W city wall in Plan 12 (ibid.: Fig. 2).
k) The Level II^W city wall in Plan 10 (ibid.: Fig. 66).

l) The Level II^W city wall in Plan 49 (ibid.: Fig. 67).[69] According to Woolley's description (1955: 144) "the town wall was rebuilt in the Level III period, presumably by the Hittites after their capture of the city and destruction of its monuments." The builders of this wall did not follow the old line of the Level IV^W city wall, instead locating it parallel to the Level IV^W city wall to the southwest. In doing so they removed or severely damaged the northeast parts of the Level IV^W private houses, as well as the corridor between these houses and the Level IV^W city wall (ibid.). Therefore, at least in the excavated area, the Level III–II^W city wall circumscribed a somewhat smaller site than the Level IV^W city wall. Woolley (ibid.) assumes that the builders of the city wall chose to reduce the city size because they planned to build a double wall (like the outer lower town city wall in Zincirli of the Iron Age II), though this feature was not actually found by the excavators.[70]

II^W city fortifications in one of his figures (1955: 138, Fig. 53; herein Plan 13). This wall is described by Woolley in one place as the outer wall of a Level II^W Zincirli-like double-city wall (1955:144) and in his presentation of Trench F (ibid.: 144–145, 136, Fig. 52a–b; herein Plan 45) as the middle wall of the Level II^W triple-city wall system. Yener (ibid.: 110) writes the following: "the circuit wall of Level III is conjectured from Woolley 1955: figures 63–64, and the Trench F section in Figure 52 (and thus depicted in white outline in fig 4.31)." However, the city wall marked in the three plans, cited by her, is in fact part of the city wall that she included in her plan of Level II^W. She repeats this erroneous claim elsewhere (ibid.: 109).

[69] Three of the squares on this plan are mislabeled by Woolley: E19 is in fact F18, E20 is F19, and F20 should be G19. The logic behind the corrections of the square numbers is as following: 1) only the three corrected numbers are in harmony with the rest of the square numbers in this plan, and 2) The Levels III–II^W/IVB^F city wall crosses these squares, and by comparison to other plans of the same city wall only the corrected square numbers are possible. See also Chapter 4, note 14.
[70] Nonetheless there are several supporting pieces of evidence: Woolley excavated paved and cemented floors along the inner and outer face of the city wall, as observable in Plan 13 (1955: Fig. 53). The inner face paved area is in squares O8, O9, N8 and N9. The outer face pavement is attested in squares O8 and N8 (ibid.: 144). I agree with Woolley that the

Woolley claims that the inner face of what he calls the Level III^W city wall is attested in squares L10, L11, L12, and M12,[71] while the wall in its full width (3.90 m.) was found in N8 and O8. Nothing is left of the *glacis*.

Following the description of what he calls the Level III^W city wall, Woolley (ibid.: 145) writes the following: "the Level II wall system has been described above, in so far as it is preserved, but the remains are not complete." From here on he adds more information on what he calls the Level II^W city wall, recording data for the same city wall under two names used interchangeably—the Level III^W city wall and the Level II^W city wall. This is a consistent problem throughout Woolley's records. Clearly, all twelve records of the Level III^W or II^W city walls above are the descriptions of one and only one city wall, which existed over an impressively long period of time.

The first record is seemingly based on Woolley's excavations in squares L10, L11, L12, N8 and O8, where he attributes the city wall to Level III^W. The second record of the same city wall (now called Level II^W) seems to be based on the excavation of Trench F (squares E16, E17 and D16). There, Woolley interpreted the northward-looking section as showing inner and middle city walls, in addition to which he reconstructs an outer city wall, which was not preserved. The width of the middle city wall is 3.25 m.[72]

What about the rest of the attestations (listed above as b–l) of the Level III^W or Level II^W wall? Together they form a long, formidable, coherent, firmly constructed, well-planned fortification, meticulously described in Yener's (2005) plan of Level II^W (Plan 48). This city wall is connected to and was built together with the Levels III–II^W fort, which I interpret as the Level IVB^F palace, and which was later (post 1353/1341) used to house the Hittite governor of Mukiš.

Let's follow the wall from northwest to southeast as it is attested in the different plans (listed above as b–l): The

city wall is attached to the Levels III–II^W/IVB^F fort (Plan 35) and passes through the following 10 by 10 m. squares: R8, Q8, P8 (Plan 35); O8, N8 (Plan 13; Woolley 1955: 144); M8, M9, L9, M10 (Plan 13); L10, L11 (Plans 10, 13; Woolley 1955: 144); K11 (Plan 13); L12 (Plan 13; Woolley 1955: 144); K12 (Plans 10, 13, 44); J12 (Plan 13); K13, J13 (Plans 10, 44); J14 (Plans 10, 12, 44); H14 (Plans 10, 44); H15, G15, G16, F16 (Plans 36, 42, 49); F17 (Plans 36, 40, 42, 49); E16 (Plans 40, 42, 49); E17 (Plans 40, 42, 43, 45, 49); D17, D18, C18 (Plans 40, 42, 43); C19, B18, B19, A19, A20 (Plans 42, 43).

Woolley (1955: 145) describes the Levels III–II^W (here IVB^F) city wall as "the most elaborate and the most imposing that Alalakh ever had." He is right. This wall marks one of the under-evaluated high points in the history of Alalakh: the gigantic building project of Level IVB^F, sometime in the beginning of the fourteenth century B.C.E. This project began 10–15 years after the destruction of Level IVA^F, which allowed some temporary residences (Level III^W) time to grow. Once the Idrimi dynasty rallied, however, it gathered its forces to initiate a large-scale building project, of which we have glamorous archaeological records and virtually no written documentation.

Level IVB^F residences

Levels III–II^W house 37/A (Plans 42, 47, 48; Photo 14)[73]

Woolley excavated four houses on what he calls (1955: 183) "the 1937 site." These were named the Levels III^W and/or II^W houses 37/A–D (Plan 42). Woolley reports (ibid.) that "the Level III houses had been largely obliterated by the builders of the succeeding period. For the most part those builders reproduced exactly or nearly exactly the old houses; they leveled the walls and on the trimmed stumps of them laid their new brickwork, only occasionally departing from the original plan to the extent of enlarging one room at the expense of another or turning two rooms into one by the omission of a cross-wall." Levels III–II^W house 37/A follows these two observations. Its Level II^W northeast half follows the Level III^W blueprint, unlike the southwest part, where there are considerable changes from Level III^W to Level II^W.[74]

The area where Level II^W houses were not built on top of the Level III^W houses is in squares B19, B20, C18 and C19 (Woolley 1955: 183). There, several Level III^W buildings were either covered/replaced by the new Levels III–II^W/IVB^W city wall or removed in order to allow access to the wall or to a gangway along it (ibid.). We do not know much about the Level III^W buildings since Woolley (ibid.) decided that "nothing is to be gained by publishing the disconnected fragments of walls and floors which alone represent the Level III houses." Regardless of the lack of published plans, Woolley reports that all Level III^W walls represent one short phase only, and whenever rebuilding is

---

only logic for having pavement out of the city wall is if another outer wall circumscribed the city wall that we know.

Woolley's interpretation of the section (looking northwest) of the fortification Step Trench F (Plan 45) includes a triple city wall for Level II^W, of which the inner wall, the middle wall and the paved corridor between them are observable in both the section drawing (upper part of Plan 45 or ibid.: Fig. 52a), and its interpretation (lower part of Plan 45 or ibid.: Fig. 52b). This corridor resembles the pavement outside of the city wall, which appears in Plan 13. All other walls in Woolley's interpretation (Plan 45b) are not observable at all in the section drawing (Plan 45a), including what he calls there "the old wall", which he appears to attribute in this interpretive drawing to both Levels IV^W and III^W.

In the on-line report (alalakh.org/report_2008.asp) of the current excavator of the site, Mustafa Kemal University of Antakya, it is claimed on behalf of Christian Hübner, who conducted magnetometry and resistivity survey on the site in 2008, that "the city fortification system appears to be a double, possible casemate wall visible in the SW." The available image in the website is far too small to judge.

[71] Woolley (1955: 144) lists square M12 as one of the squares the Level III^W city wall goes through. This is impossible: no city wall of any level went that deep into the city. In accordance with the order of appearance in Woolley's list he must have meant square K12.

[72] On Plan 45, however, the middle city wall is reconstructed as circa 4.4 m. wide, and the inner city wall as 7 m. wide.

[73] The house numbers in two of Yener's 2005 plans (herein Plans 47 and 48) are consistently incorrect. For the correct house numbers see Plan 42.

[74] The Level II^W walls are marked in solid black on Plan 42, while the Level III^W walls are drawn in their outline only.

attested, it is undoubtedly attributed to Level II[W]. Nowhere in Level III[W] was more than one floor-level detected, and if the walls were not reused in Level II[W], they were shaved down to the Level II[W] floor-level (ibid.). Furthermore, Level III[W] was not violently destroyed, but peacefully and gradually replaced by Level II[W] (ibid.: 183–184)—that is, Level III[W] is an early short sub-phase of Level II[W].

Likewise, the preservation of the Level II[W] houses is rather unimpressive, although they do provide coherent blueprints (ibid.: 185). The buildings are mostly known from the preserved one-course stone foundations with some or no mud brick superstructure; only a few of the thresholds are clearly identifiable. The floors were of beaten earth and occasionally of "white cement," especially in the toilets and bathrooms (see Fink 2008a).

The entrance to house 37/A is impressive: half columns are attached to it on both sides of the outer wall (Woolley 1955: 186). The only reason Woolley (ibid.) chose to include and exclude rooms in this house is the coherent solid rectangle that rooms 1–11 create together (there are hardly any thresholds preserved). He admits that one could easily exclude rooms 10 and 11 and add them to the barely known structure to the southwest, or merge Level II[W] house 37/B (where again no thresholds are found) with the Levels III–II[W] house 37/A to form one unit.

In room 1 one of the most famous examples of Atchana/Nuzi ware was found (Photo 14; ibid.: 186, Pl. CIIa). Woolley (ibid.) suggests that room 3 may have held a staircase to the second floor, of which no trace was found, and that room 2 was a light well. In Room 7 he proposes that a rectangular brick base was a hearth. This room, together with room 6, was also remodeled during its lifespan. In room 10 plain ware vessels of two types were unearthed; in room 11, a bronze arrowhead.

Level II[W] house 37/B (Plans 42, 47, 48)

This house was poorly preserved. A Mycenaean pot and some Cypriote Milk Bowls were found in the street southeast of the building.[75] An Atchana/Nuzi krater was found in room 5 (ibid.: Pl. CIIIf), as well as store jars and a fragment of Mycenaean stirrup jar.

Levels III–II[W] house 37/C (Plans 42, 47, 48)

This house, like the other Level II[W] houses, was violently destroyed. A breach was made from the street into room 1 at the northwest external wall of the house by the aggressors (ibid.: 188). Room 1 was a toilet (Fink 2008a: 170–173, 190). Room 2 yielded several Nuzi ware vessels. Room 5 was a staircase (Woolley 1955: 185) or a storeroom (ibid.: 188). It was full of baked clay sling-bolts and ballista-balls (ibid.: 185, 188). In room 8 Woolley found evidence that the house was

remodeled, a possible indication of the transition from Level III[W] to Level II[W].

The bulk of Atchana/Nuzi and Nuzi ware found in this level at the site came from the street between the Levels III–II[W] houses 37/A–B and 37/C–D, and "most of the rest" from Room 1 of Level III–II[W] house 37/C (ibid.: 185).

Shallow remains of the Level III[W] sub-phase are attested between Levels III–II[W] house 37/C and the Levels III–II[W] city wall.

Level II[W] house 37/D (Plans 42, 47, 48)

This house is also ill-preserved, its doorways largely untraceable (ibid.: 189). Woolley believes that room 5 was a central courtyard. He found fragments of Atchana/Nuzi ware in room 1 and half of a White Slip II milk-bowl in room 5. Woolley notes (ibid.) that Level II[W] is rather late for White Slip II; in my analysis, this is no longer the case, since its context is now Level IVB[F].

Levels III–II[W] house 38/A (Plans 42, 47, 48)

House 38/A represents the remains of one very large building or perhaps several smaller buildings (ibid.). Again, no floors were preserved and only one threshold was found (in square G17). Most of the walls were either built during the Level III[W] sub-phase or are an accurate re-built of the Level III[W] walls.

Levels III–II[W] house 39/C (Plans 10, 12, 47, 48)

Level II[W] house 39/C is an exception, since it does not follow the wall lines of its Level III[W] predecessors. Woolley reports that Level III[W] private houses were unearthed beneath Level II[W] house 39/C in Squares J–M-14–16 (ibid.: 184), "but little sense could be made of the plan." Either in the Level III[W] remains, or at the Level II[W] foundations, in square L13, Woolley unearthed fragments of White Slip II milk bowls and Base Ring II zoomorphic vessels (ATP/38/14; ibid.: Pl. CXXVf). In square M14 he found parts of wheel-made Red Lustrous ware, Nuzi ware, Mycenaean vessels described by Woolley as "L.M. IIIb" with no additional specifications, and in square K14 an alabaster stand (AT/39/264; ibid.: Pl. LXXXII[29]). Local ware vessels were found in all squares. These finds are high quality and of unusual quantity; the poor context in which they were dug calls into question the location of the finds. Parts of the later temples of Alalakh were located in squares M14 and L14 (Plan 8), among them the annexe to the Level III[W]/IVB[F] temple and the Paluwa shrine. Is it possible that at least some of these finds originated in one or more of these temples? Moreover, the proximity of house 39/C of his different Mittanian phases (from Levels VB[F] to IVB[F]) to the contemporaneous temples may imply a connection between its inhabitants and the temple activity.[76]

---

[75] The "L.M. III vase with the design of a snake spotted in white" cannot be found in the nonexistent Pl. CXXXIV (Woolley 1955: 186). Could this possibly be vessel *l* in Pl. CXXVIII?

[76] This suggestion was first raised by Bike Yazıcıoğlu during the University of Chicago seminar on Alalakh, winter 2005, which I attended.

The Level II^W house 39/C is relatively well preserved and its complete blueprint has been recovered (ibid.: 189). Its walls were thicker than the norm but had no stone foundations. Woolley (ibid.) deduces in accordance with the blueprint that two of the rooms were unroofed: room 11 functioned as a light well, and room 1 was a walled courtyard. He also assumes that room 12 was the main or the only entrance to the house, and that the house carried two floors—though no staircase was found. The house is equipped with two almost identical bathroom-suites: rooms 6–7 and 9–10 (Fink 2008a: 170–173, 191–193). During the lifetime of one of the bathrooms, room 7, a new cement floor was laid down 0.25 m. above the original. In the filling between the floors, sealed by Level II^W from above and below, Woolley (1955: 191) turned up a fragment of White Slip II Milk Bowl and numerous sherds of Atchana/Nuzi ware. We can now quite safely treat the luxurious Tell Atchana style of furnishing a toilet or two in almost every known residence as a Mittanian phenomenon. Re-dating Levels III–II^W to IVB^F attributes almost all of the toilets at Tell Atchana to the period when Mukiš was a Mittanian vassal. The great similarity to Nuzi (Fink 2008b: 169) does not start and end with Nuzi ware: Atchana and Nuzi also share the same style of toilets, which is now contemporaneous in both sites.

Many of the rooms contained local pottery. Room 14 contained fragments of wheel-made Red Lustrous ware, a bronze arrow head and the horns of a large bull (Woolley 1955: 191). Room 15 had three cylinder seals (AT/39/166–168),[77] a Mycenaean piriform vase (ATP/39/168), beads and some plain ware (ibid.). In room 16 Woolley found more Atchana/Nuzi ware goblet sherds, one of which was found to fit a sherd excavated in the rubbish pit just northeast of this room. This rubbish pit is rich in finds and is very close to the annexe to the Level III^W temple, thus it could actually be a favissa of the Level III^W temple. Among the objects excavated at the pit were Atchana/Nuzi ware sherds, several vessels of local ware and a red marble lamp (AT/39/280; ibid.: Pl. LXXIX). Woolley believes that the lamp is Cretan in origin and style (ibid.: 294–295). This is confirmed by Warren (1969: 55–56), who writes that it is impossible "to date the lamp firmly to LMI or LMII–IIIAI" (ibid.); at any rate, it should not be dated to later than the second half of the fifteenth century B.C.E., making it a recent heirloom. Bevan (2007: 125) agrees that the lamp could be dated into the broad LMI–IIIA range, and suggests likewise that it may be a post-Neopalatial product.

---

[77] Woolley (1955: 191) mentions three cylinder seals, but refers specifically only to two: AT/39/166–167. According to the object cards (now at the UCL Special Collections) AT/39/166–168 were found in room 15. Of the three cylinder seals, AT/39/166 and AT/39/168 were discarded. This is confirmed by Collon 1982: 24, who dates the remaining seal (ibid.: 61–62) to the fifteenth–fourteenth century.

Chapter Five

Levels III–IB^F: Hittite Alalakh

5.1 Level III^F (1353/1341–1320/1313)

This chapter is a discussion of Alalakh's decline, when it passes from its status as a wealthy capital into thousands of years of obscurity. The archaeological remains of the later levels at Tell Atchana are largely patchy and difficult to interpret; nevertheless I sum up the relevant finds here. Along with the evidence of regional ground surveys and pottery analysis, I believe I conjure up a reasonable picture of the last days of the once-great city and kingdom.

The plan of Level III^F accompanies this discussion.

Level III^F is the final phase of Alalakh as a city, before it dwindles into a Hittite stronghold. It is a period of transition in Alalakh: the swan song before the final destruction. We can date Level III^F to the second half of the 14th century or the later part of the Amarna period. The fortifications of Tell Atchana were damaged when Šuppiluliuma I conquered the city; here they are repaired, and a revetment built against the inner face of the Levels III–II^W/IVB^F city wall. The excavated area at Tell Atchana clearly reveals that the rebuilding of the private houses is spread out; the houses are not packed together as they were in the earlier phases.[1] This is probably due to Šuppiluliuma I's Syrian wars, the political instability of the region during the Amarna period (Freu 2006: 43–49), and the LBA decline of many Levantine cities, of which Alalakh was no exception. Plan 50 is Yener's (2005: 152) plan of Level I^W. This is an uncritical composition of Woolley's different building plans of Level I^W, following Yener's assumption that Woolley's stratigraphy is correct. Level III^F, on the other hand, is only partly a mirror image of Level I^W. It includes some of the Level I^W private houses (37/A, 37/B, 37/C and 38/A), the Level II^W temple (see discussion in Chapter 3), and the Levels III–II^W/IVB^F fort in its second building phase during Levels III-IIB^F, of which we know very little (see Section 4.5).

Discussing the fort, Woolley writes (1955: 133): "actually we found that there were more re-buildings of the fortress than there were building-levels in the domestic quarter, but in spite of this the changes fitted in with the scheme quite unexceptionally." This is the right observation, but the wrong explanation! There are more re-buildings of the fort because the fort lasted for longer than Woolley thought. The Level IVB^F palace/Levels III–II^W fort was probably refurnished and used as a governor's palace by central figures in the Hittite administration. Later on it would be used by at least three Hittite princes: Tudḫaliya DUMU. LUGAL, Šukur-Tešub DUMU.LUGAL and Paluwa DUMU.LUGAL.

The deportation of the people of Mukiš

In this work I assume that Alalakh and Mukiš were conquered during Šuppululiuma I's first Syrian war and that this war occurred early in his reign (Singer 1999: 629–634). The two dates that I quote for the first Syrian war (1353 and 1341) are derived from the current competing synchronizations of Hittite and Egyptian chronologies of the reign of Šuppululiuma I. One of the dates that I cite for the first Syrian war of Šuppululiuma I is in line with 1344/1343 B.C.E. as the king's year of accession (Wilhelm and Boese 1987: 105–109; Bryce 1998: 168; Wilhelm 2004: 72–74). Na'aman (1996) and Parker (2002) insist on an earlier date for his enthronement. Recently, Miller (2007: 282–284) dated the reign of Šuppululiuma I to 1356–1330. Therefore, the other possible date for the first Syrian war is 1353 B.C.E.

The Level III^F Mukiš is smaller than the Level IVB^F kingdom, since Šuppululiuma I granted Ugarit parts of Mukiš's southern districts. This is clearly the reason for some discontent in Mukiš, presented in a complaint letter to Muršili II, asking him to order the annexed area to be returned to Mukiš (van Soldt 2005: 51–64). In fact, according to CTH 64, it was Niqmepa, king of Ugarit, who appealed to Muršili II to investigate the case, in which he was sued by the people of Mukiš, probably at the court of Šarre-Kušuḫ, king of Karkamiš and the brother of Muršili

---

[1] Compare the eastern part of the excavated area (most of the private houses) of Plan 50 with Plan 48 (Level IVB^F).

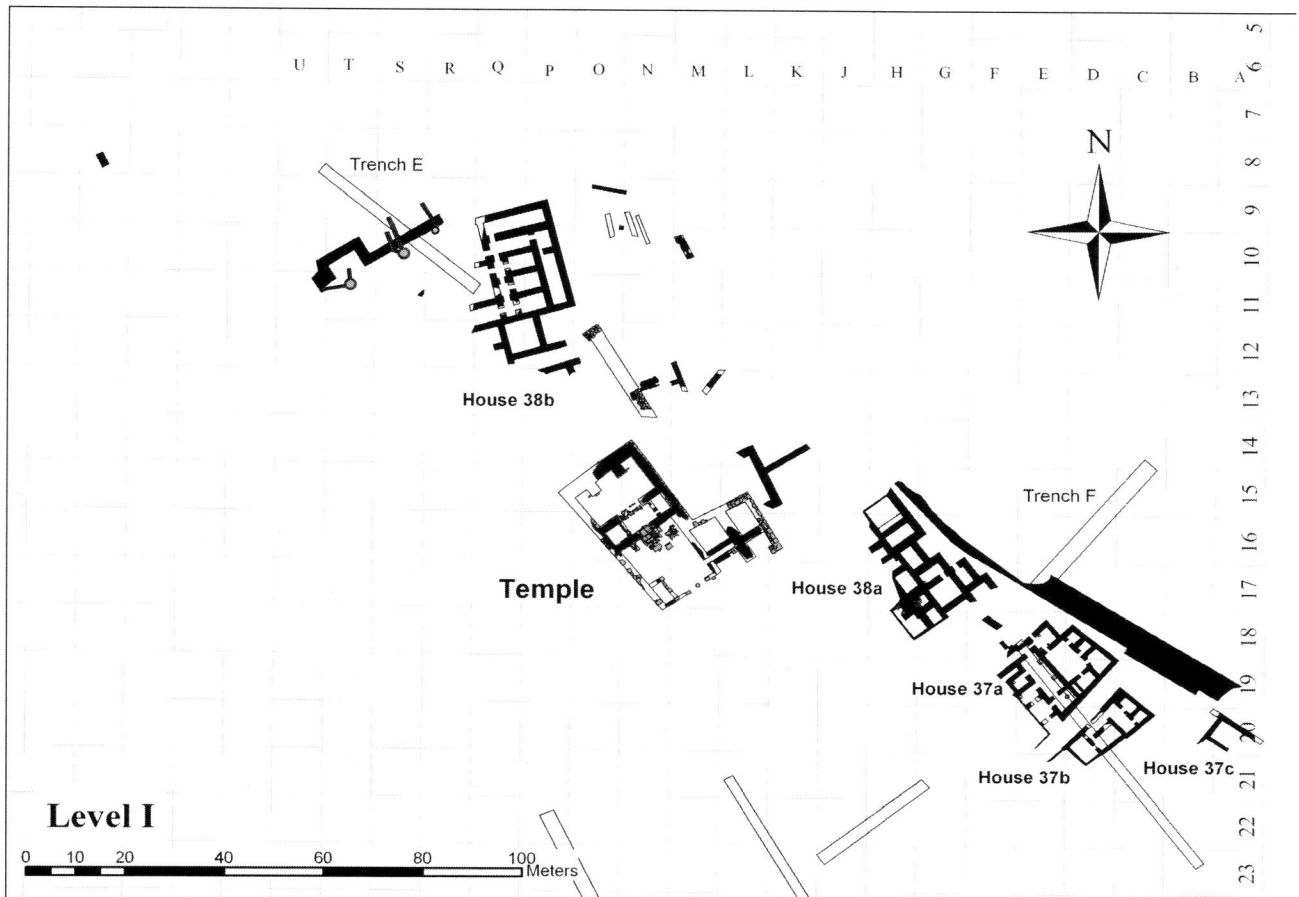

Plan 50. Plan of Level I^W (after Yener 2005: 152, Fig. 4.33)

II. The latter refused to transfer the land back to Mukiš. We do not know what the outcome of this refusal was, but it is clear that the "people of the land of Mukiš" appealed no earlier than year 9 of Muršili II (1320/1313), during or after the later stage of Nuḫašše's uprising against Muršili II, when Niqmepa had already succeeded Ar-Ḫalba as the king of Ugarit (Brice 1998: 216–223). The partially preserved "ten year annals of Muršili II" together with the restoration of the lacunas, which are based on the "comprehensive annals of Muršili II" (Beal 2000; Mineck 2006), narrate a fairly coherent report on the fate of Tette, king of Nuḫašše and his repeating regional upheavals against the Hittites. None of the records ties Mukiš to the events, but clearly CTH 64 (van Soldt 2005: 51–64) is an echo of the attempt by the people of the land of Mukiš to regain their southern frontier, probably in return for their loyalty to Muršili II during the unrest. Even more so, they tried to profit from what seems to be the refusal of Ar-Ḫalba, king of Ugarit, to help the Hittites in their fight against Tette (Beckman 1999: 173; Singer 1999: 637–638), hoping that this was the right occasion to seize their territory back. Their application came too late, since by the time it was discussed by Muršili II, Ar-Ḫalba had already been replaced by his brother Niqmepa, either forcefully or peacefully, during the ninth year of Muršili II (ibid.: 638). Seemingly, once refused, the unsatisfied People of Mukiš made a fatal mistake by expressing their dissatisfaction in a way that encouraged Muršili II to put an end to Alalakh

as a city and exile its population, possibly together with many other Mukišians. There are no historical records of this event, but the archaeological records are clear and well established both by the re-analysis of Woolley's excavations (below) and by the University of Chicago project at the site (Yener, Schloen and Fink 2005: 47). It is also confirmed by the current Mustafa Kemal University project in the site (www.alalakh.org), the 2008 report, which I discuss below. The exact date of this event is of course unknown, but archaeologically, it is well-attributed to the end of the thirteenth century B.C.E. I argue that it is very likely that most of the people of Mukiš were expelled to the Anatolian heartland; others may have moved to other locations, or run away as fugitives. Some stayed, continuing their work in the fertile fields of the Amuq; Alalakh as a city, however, was deserted. Some of the additional supporting evidence of my views is:

1) Hatti needed people, either because of the long and severe plague (Brice 1998: 223–225),[2] or because of its expansion and its military campaigns. According to his annals, Muršili II deported tens of thousands of people into the Anatolian heartland, mainly from western Anatolia (Brice 1998: 209–216; Beal 2000; Mineck 2006). As revealed by Hoffner (2002: 61), the

---

[2] which according to Muršili II's prayer was brought into Hatti by displaced captives from Syria at the time of Šuppiluliuma I (Hoffner 2002: 65).

THE FIELD CAMPAIGNS, SITES AND FIELD-REGISTER
SERIES RELEVANT TO PHASES K TO O

Campaigns	Sites		
	Chatal Huyuk	Tell al-Judaidah	Tell Ta yinat
1. Jan. to June 1933	CP 1–363 (pottery) C 1–401 (other objects)		
2. Oct. 1933 to Apr. 1934	A 1–2848	Z 1 – 1178	
3. Oct. 1934 to Apr. 1935	B 1–2915	Y 1 – 1050	T 1–222
4. Sept. 1935 to June 1936	E 1–438	X 1 – 5164[a]	T 223–1264
5. July to Nov. 1937			T 2000–3277
6. Apr. to Aug. 1938			T 3278–3850[a]

[a]Objects from phases earlier than K make up a large proportion of these groups.

Above: Swift Table 2. The field campaigns relevant to Amuq phases K–O (after Swift 1958: 11)

Below: Swift Table 11. Chronology of Amuq phases N and O (after Swift 1958: 198)

CHRONOLOGY OF PHASES N AND O

Phase and Stage	Date	Red-slipped Burnished Ware	Cypriote Wares
Od	550 ⋯ 725	Almost entirely wheel-burnished Elaborate rims increase	Cypro-Geometric III Cypro-Archaic I, rarely II
Oc	⋯ 800	Wheel-burnished increases Elaborate rims appear Hand-burnished diminishes	Cypro-Geometric III
Ob	⋯ 900	Wheel-burnished begins Hand-burnished continues	Cypro-Geometric II and III
Oa	⋯ 950	Hand-burnished only	Cypro-Geometric I and II (sherds)
N	⋯ 1150	None	Cypro-Geometric I (rare)

122

available records show that Muršili II captured more civilian non-combatants (*arnuwala* or NAM.RA) than any other Hittite king, and the recorded numbers of people he transferred are on a different scale altogether: 89,500.[3] Although most of the transferred captives on record are not from the northern Levant, the annals of Muršili II include records of Nuḫaššean captives (ibid.: 64). This record supports the possibility that this was the destiny of the inhabitants of Alalakh. Captives occupied a higher position in the Hittite society than ordinary slaves and they are mentioned in military annals, letters, laws, treaties, depositions, cult inventories, royal prayers, rituals, and festival descriptions (ibid.: 62; Watkins 1994: 644–662; Haase 2003: 633–634). Usually, the destination of the captives, if given, is Ḫattuša, and sometimes it is more specific: the king's estate or the private estates of Hittite soldiers (Hoffner 2002: 63). There is even a record, dating to the reign of Muršili II, that displaced captives (NAM.RA) were forced to settle a site (Tiliura) that had been abandoned for centuries (ibid.: 64). The Hittites were occupied with chasing fugitives in general, and displaced captives in particular (ibid.: 65; Beckman 2003: 762). Mineck (2006: 253; see also Beal 2000: 83) describes how this obsession is reflected in the Muršili II annals: "Muršili's usual argument and justification for initiating the campaigns was that his opponents refused to provide him with troops or they had in their possession certain displaced persons that he claimed… The civilian captives were an important issue for the Hittites, and typically, the Hittite treaties included provisions concerning their extradition." Maintaining a system of semi-free displaced captives required severe punishments for fugitives: some of them were blinded upon capture, a practice well known from biblical sources (ibid.: 68).[4] All in all, one should assume that the fact that we have on record more cases of displaced deportees from western Anatolia is mere chance. This phenomenon was equally as significant and as influential in some of the northern Levantine cities, and can be seen as a major reason for the decrease in population in the northern Levant during the LBA from the mid-fourteenth century B.C.E. on.

2) *Argumentum ex silentio*: Alalakh and Mukiš are barely mentioned among the thousands of documents found in neighboring kingdoms (mainly Ugarit) and in the archives of Ḫattuša. Whenever Alalakh and Mukiš are mentioned in a thirteenth century context it is either from a purely military perspective or as a source for agricultural produces. The few published documents among the small number of relevant documents are discussed in Section 5.2.

The Amuq Surveys: When does Amuq phase M end?

Several years before Woolley reached the Sanjak of Alexandretta (1936) to initiate his work at Al-Mina and Tell Atchana,[5] the University of Chicago, Oriental Institute, Syrio-Hittite expedition was already well established in the region. It conducted massive exposures, notably at Çatal Höyük (Amuq), Tell Judaidah and Ta'yinat, as well as the Amuq survey (Braidwood 1937; McEwan 1937; Braidwood and Braidwood 1960; Haines 1971; Swift Table 2 at left). As the region was surveyed, several key sites were chosen to be partially or intensively dug, and the ceramic sequence of the whole region was established in blocks of several centuries each: from A (early) to V (modern) (Haines 1971: 1–2; see also Haines Tables below). By the standards of the 1930s both the method and the execution of the survey were groundbreaking. Alas, 75 years later only a tiny portion of the Amuq pottery has yet been published. This is mostly in Swift's unpublished dissertation (1958), which includes some fine-tuning of phases K–O of the original rough sequence.[6] In this work I am mainly interested in the dating of phase M, the Late Bronze Age horizons of the Amuq sequence, and in the differing opinions of the phase M-N transition through the Iron Age I horizons.

Swift and Pruss on Amuq phase M

The original presentation of the dating of Phase M by the Syrio-Hittite expedition, to 1600-1200 B.C.E., is treated by Haines (1971: 2; and see his Tables below). Earlier, Swift (1958: 26-36, 58) had dated phase M to 1550-1400, equating it with Levels V–III^W in Alalakh (see Swift 1958 Table 5 in Section 4.5). Much more recently, Pruss (2002: 162) accepts this dating, but equates it with Alalakh Levels V–IV^W only. Both Swift and Pruss agree that the hiatus between Phases M and N lasted several hundred years. Swift begins phase N at 1150 (see Swift Tables 5 and 11) while Pruss starts it at 1180 (see Pruss Table 1 in Section 4.5). They both equate it with Level 0^W at Alalakh, but this comparison is groundless. There are no Iron Age I remains at Tell Atchana, and there are neither stratigraphic nor ceramic justifications for this comparison. My stratigraphic analysis takes the only coherent feature of Level 0^W, the temple, and offers it a context: Level IB^F (Table 5 and Summary Tables 1 and 2). Notably, even this feature, the Level 0^W temple, is known only from two photos and a brief description (Woolley 1955: 89–90). No ground plan is known and no pottery is associated with it.[7]

---

[3] Compare to 7,000 by Ḫattušili III and 3,330 by Šuppiluliuma I (Hoffner 2002: 61).

[4] Another group of captives, who were drafted for general service like maintenance of buildings and roads, was the ^{LÚ.MEŠ}*hippares* (Hasse 2003: 633). Hasse (ibid.) is doubtful if this group is connected with the NAM.RA.

[5] Woolley also received a permit to conduct excavations in two other important Amuq sites, Tell Salihiyyah and Bozhöyük, as is revealed in a 1935 letter, sent to Woolley by the Secretary General of the French Department of Antiquities. The letter is at the archives of the British Museum and I am thankful to Dr. Alexandra Fletcher and archivist Christopher Denvir for making it available to me. More on the importance of Tell Salihiyyah and Bozhöyük can be found in Casana 2009.

[6] The architecture was published in Haines 1971; the Iron age stamp seals recently in Meyer 2008. Unfortunately, Pruss' dissertation (1996) is still unpublished and not widely distributed. See also Pruss 2002 for a summary of his work.

[7] The only object associated with this temple is a basalt offering table (Woolley 1955: 89, Pl. XIIIb).

SEQUENCE OF CULTURAL PHASES IN THE PLAIN OF ANTIOCH, WITH APPROXIMATE DATES*

Phase	Description	Approximate Date	Tell al-Judaidah	Chatal Hüyük	Tell Tayinat
V	Modern Arab		?	x	x
U	Medieval Arab			I	
T	Byzantine			I	
S	Early Christian		I	?	
R	Roman		II	II	
Q	Hellenistic	300–64 B.C.	III	II	?
P	Syro-Hellenic	500–300 B.C.	III	II	?

* In this table x = "present"; the Roman numbers denote those which had been originally assigned to Periods at the individual sites.

Above: **Haines Table 1. Amuq phases P–V (after Haines 1971: 1)**

Below: **Haines Table 2. Amuq phases A–O (after Haines 1971: 2)**

SEQUENCE OF CULTURAL PHASES IN THE PLAIN OF ANTIOCH, WITH APPROXIMATE DATES (*cont.*)

Phase	Description	Approximate Date	Tell al-Judaidah	Chatal Hüyük	Tell Tayinat
O	Syro-Hittite	1000–500 B.C.	IV	III	I
N	Levanto-Helladic IV (Sub-Mycenaean)	1200–1000 B.C.	V	IV	II
M	Levanto-Mycenaean	1600–1200 B.C.	VI	V	
L	Qatna affinities (*ca.* 17th–18th B.C.)	1800–1600 B.C.	VII	x	
K	Hama, etc., affinities (*ca.* 18th–20th B.C.)	2000–1800 B.C.	VIII	x	
J	Chalciform pot series	2400–2000 B.C.	IX	x	x
I	Smeared-wash pot series	2600–2400 B.C.	X	x	x
H	Red-black burnished pots (Early Dynastic affinities)	3100–2400 B.C.	XI	x	x
G	Jemdet Nasr affinities	3500–3100 B.C.	XII		x
F	Uruk affinities	4000–3500 B.C.	XIII	x	
E	Obeid affinities	4500–4000 B.C.	?		
D	Derived Halaf and earliest Obeid affinities, etc.	±4500 B.C.	?		
C	Developed primitive and true Halaf affinities	5000–4500 B.C.	XIV		
B	Developed primitive and first painted wares, etc.	± pre-5000 B.C.	XIV		
A	Primitive burnished ware	?	XIV		

Phase M is attested mainly at Çatal Höyük (Amuq) and Tell Judaidah (see Swift Table 1 in Section 4.5 and Meyer Tables 2 and 3), located twenty kilometers northeast and east of Tell Atchana respectively (Plan 51). Nonetheless, the 1930s survey shows 13 confirmed phase M sites and another 19 sites that were probably inhabited during phase M, for a total of 32 sites (Braidwood 1937: 50; herein Plan 52; Pruss 2002: 163, and 164, Pl. 2). Pruss (ibid; Braidwood 1937: 49; herein Plan 53) compares it to phase N, the Iron Age I phase, which is rich with LH IIIC pottery, where there are 33 confirmed sites and 16 probable ones (a total of 59 sites). Only half of the phase M sites are re-inhabited during phase N. Pruss finds it astonishing that in the Iron Age I, a period considered by many to be a "Dark Age," the Amuq is more inhabited than during the Late Bronze Age, and that clearly, there is no significant continuity in the settlement pattern. Indisputably, phase N of the Amuq sequence calls for new study. I hope that the detailed forthcoming publications of this phase in Çatal Höyük (Amuq), Tell Judaidah and Ta'yinat,[8] as well as the new excavations in Tell Ta'yinat (Harrison 2007 and 2008), will shed new light on this important subject.

Nevertheless, there are serious faults in Pruss' methodology, and consequently also in his conclusions. First, he does not present any data on the settlement size in either phase M or N. There are possibly more phase N sites than M sites, but they could amount to merely a fraction of the inhabited area of fewer in number, but larger phase M sites. Second, the pottery collected in the different sites was never published or exposed to public observation. Moreover, the local Amuq ceramic sequence of the Late Bronze and Iron Ages is basically unknown—no typology has so far been made, and all the interpretations are based either on imported ware, Woolley's Tell Atchana final report (1955; I previously discussed its limitations in detail), or the inadequately argued conclusions of Swift's dissertation, where very few pot sherds are drawn. Unfortunately, McClellan's quantative study (1989), which is based on Woolley's exceedingly discriminatory collection and poor data, is not helpful either.

Pruss' conclusions on Amuq phase M may be partly right, yet they are based on uncertain ground: he believes that there is a clear decline in the Amuq during the Late Bronze Age phase M (2002: 163, 172–173), due to the smaller number of settlements in the LBA in comparison to Iron Age I. The obstacle is that the survey data that he is using shows a complete hiatus from 1400 B.C.E. on. However, the relatively small number of pre-1400 B.C.E. phase M settlements in the Amuq in fact corresponds to the reigns of the three kings of the Idrimi dynasty,[9] one of the most intensively recorded periods of growth and prosperity in Mukiš in general and in Alalakh in particular (von Dassow 2008). It is impossible to accept any claim for decline in the Amuq during Alalakh Levels VB–IVA^F.

Furthermore, in his effort to prove his long LBA hiatus in the Amuq, Pruss looks for ways to demonstrate that Alalakh post 1400 B.C.E. was a small cow town. While he (ibid.: 162) correctly suggests that Level IV^W does not end with Šuppiluliuma's campaign and that the connection between the end of Level III^W and the riots following the accession of Muršili II is no longer valid, Pruss speciously downgrades the Levels III–II^W fort/Level IVB^F palace to "a modest structure" and makes an unfounded statement that the city of Levels II^W/IVB^F and I^W/III^F has neither defensive wall nor palace (ibid.). Obviously, Pruss did not study the stratigraphy of Tell Atchana in great detail, nor did he work the finer points of the Amuq phase M pottery.

From an historical perspective, Pruss' reconstruction is impossible as well. In his first Syrian war (1353/1341), Šuppiluliuma I faced a sturdy coalition, led by Itūr-Addu, king of the land of Mukiš (CTH 46; Beckman 1999: 34–36). Is it possible that Itūr-Addu was the king of one run-down town? Once defeated, Mukiš is punished and forced to give away its southern territory of many villages to Ugarit, ally to the Hittites, and from this event on, a Hittite vassal (Singer 1999: 634–636). A few decades later Muršili II was facing the appeal (CTH 64; Beckman 1999: 174–175; van Soldt 2005: 51–64) of the people of the land of Mukiš to return these lands and villages to Mukiš, that is, to reverse his father's edict. Muršili II refused (Singer 1999: 639–640). These two historical documents prove that Mukiš was inhabited at least until the ninth year of Muršili II (see above). Of course, Mukiš and the Amuq plain are not synonyms (von Dassow 2008: 66): the Amuq plain is the heartland of a geographically larger kingdom, mostly hilly and mountainous. Nevertheless, it is unsafe to assume that Alalakh stood by itself in the midst of the Amuq while the surrounding smaller towns and villages of Mukiš were abandoned and destroyed, leaving only those villages on the Ugarit border, which were taken from Mukiš.

A better way to bridge between Tell Atchana data and the survey data is to follow my new analysis of the stratigraphy of Tell Atchana and, as already suggested above in my discussion of Nuzi ware, to accept an end date for phase M that is later than 1400 B.C.E. I propose that the hiatus between Amuq phases M and N begins towards the end of the fourteenth century (1320/1313).[10] The destruction, or at least the severe decline, of phase M is one and the same as the destruction of Level III^F, the final level of the city of Alalakh (to be succeeded by the stronghold of Alalakh). I propose that this destruction was the result of intentional deportation of the people of Mukiš by Muršili II.

Casana on Amuq phase M

The Oriental Institute renewed its activity in the Amuq in 1995 by resurveying the region (Amuq Valley Regional Project or AVRP) and conducting excavations of various scales at Tell Judaidah, Tell Kurdu and Tell Atchana (Yener et al. 2000; Yener, Schloen and Fink 2004a; 2004b;

---

[8] Marina Pucci, Lynn Swartz Dodd and Heather Snow are respectively in the process of publishing the Chicago excavations at these Amuq sites.
[9] Idrimi, Niqmepa and Ilimilimma.

[10] but see Pucci's analysis below.

I	II	III	IV	V	VI	Periode
1						S
2					1	P-R
	1	1				
	2	2				
3	3		1			S P Ä T — Oc
		3				
	4					
	5	4				
		5	2		2	M I T T E L — Ob
4	6	6			3	
		7	3		4	
				1	5	
5	7					F R Ü H — Oa
		8	4		6	
6	8				7	
7	9	10	5	2		
8	10			3	8	N
9	11	11	6	4		
	12			5		M
10	13			6		

Abb. 2: Korrelation der Bauphasen in den einzelnen Grabungsbereichen von Çatal Hüyük.

Meyer Table 2. The correlation between Amuq phases and trenches at Çatal Höyük (after Meyer 2008: 12)

DEF (GHJ-7)	J-9	G-12	J14-16 K-L-14	F-15	K-6	TT-20
1						S
2		1		1		R
3	1	2				Q
4		3		2		P
5	2	4	1	3		Oc
6	3	5	2			Ob
7	4	6				
8						On
9						
10						N
11						
12						M
13					1	
14						
15						
16					2	L
					3	
17					4	
					5	
						K

Abb. 3: Korrelation der Bauphasen in den einzelnen Grabungsbereichen von Tell el-Ğudeideh.

Meyer Table 3. The correlation between Amuq phases and trenches at Tell el-Judaidah (after Meyer 2008: 14)

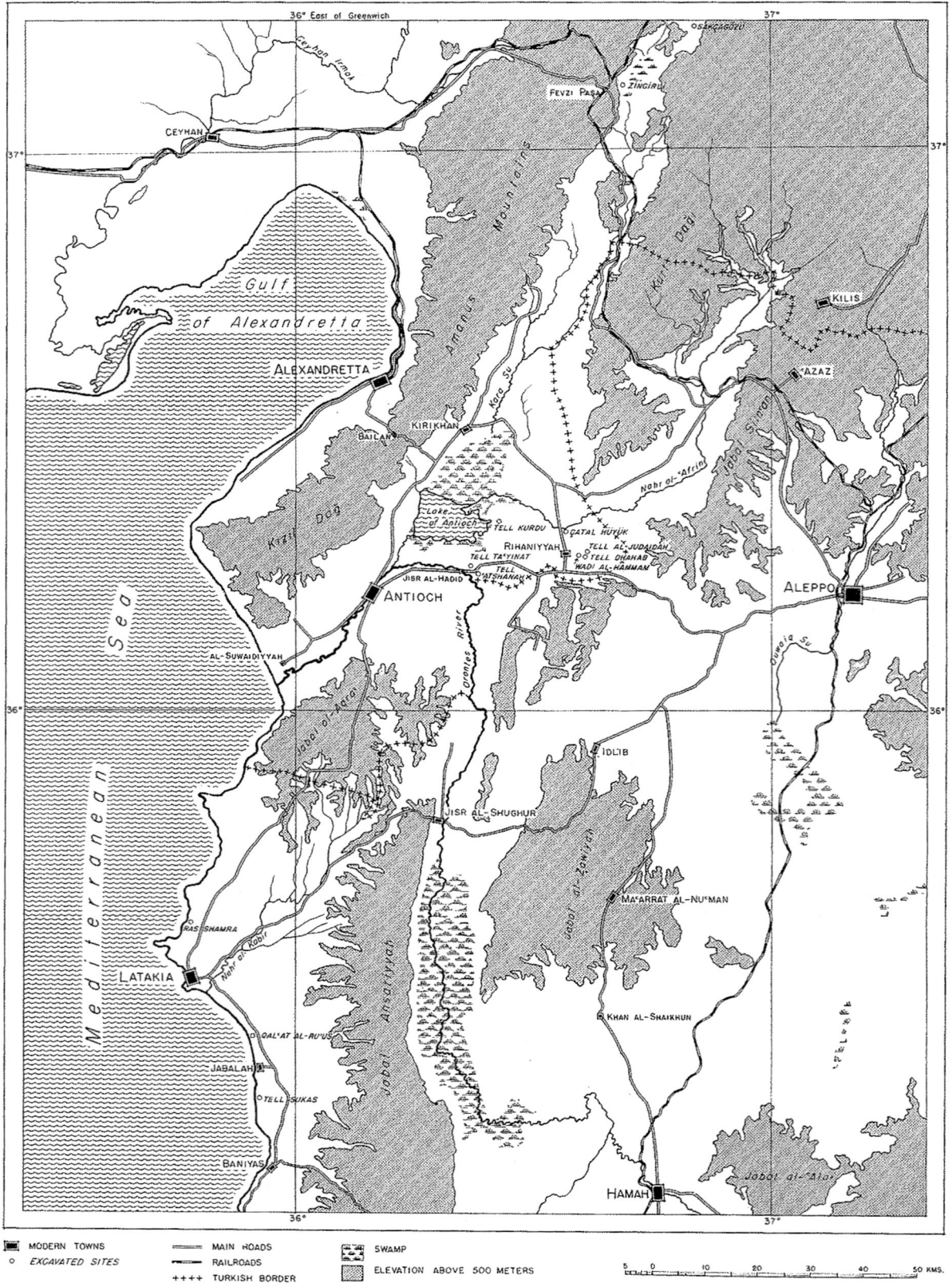

MAP OF NORTHWEST SYRIA AND HATAY

Plan 51. The Northern Levant in the 1930s (Amuq sites are marked) (after Haines 1971: Pl. 1)

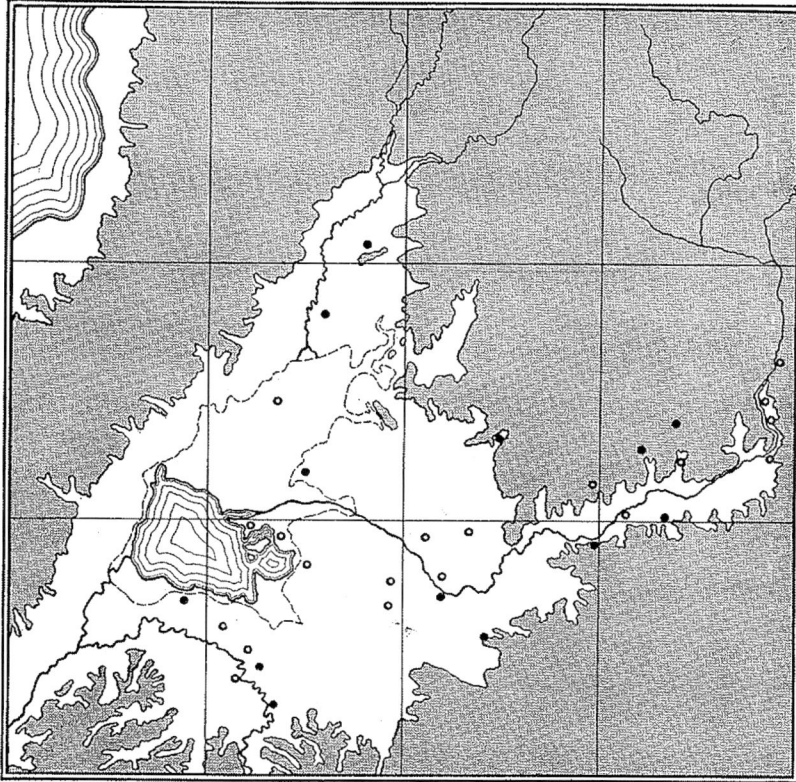

MAP XVII.—DISTRIBUTION OF JUDAIDAH VI WARES

Above: **Plan 52. The Amuq settlement pattern during phase M based on the University of Chicago 1930s survey (after Braidwood 1937: 50)**

Below: **Plan 53. The Amuq settlement pattern during phase N based on the University of Chicago 1930s survey (after Braidwood 1937: 49)**

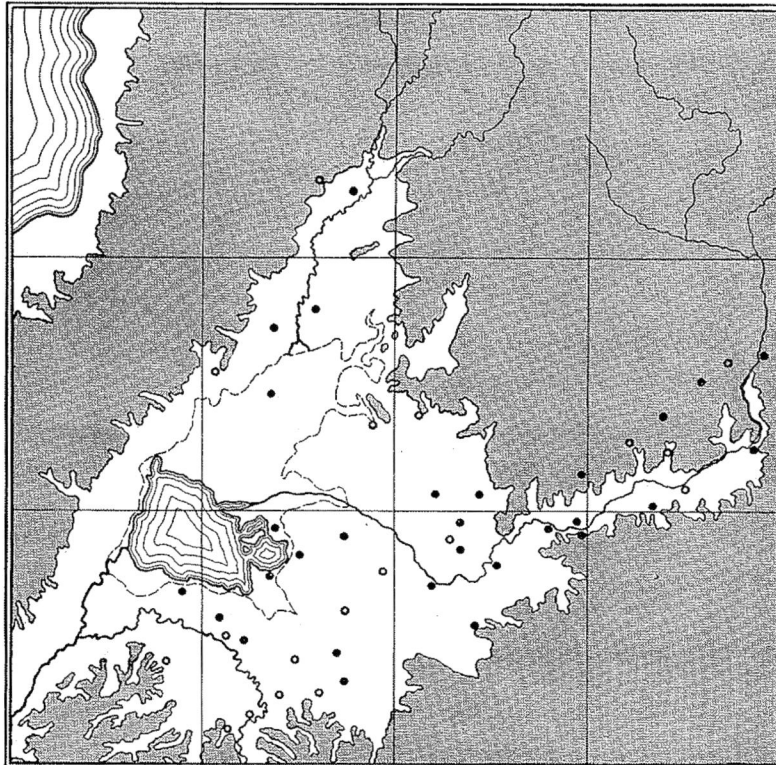

MAP XVI.—DISTRIBUTION OF JUDAIDAH V WARES

2005; Yener 2005; Casana 2003; 2007; 2009; Gerritsen et al. 2008). No doubt, the AVRP was aimed to refine the knowledge of settlement history in the Amuq, and so far, it has been only partially successful in doing so. In a brief preliminary report on the AVRP surface collection, Verstraete and Wilkinson (2000: 187–189) propose that Amuq M continued through 1200 B.C.E., with Amuq N to follow immediately after.[11] They claim (ibid.: 188) that Aegean ceramics were found on 5 of the phase M sites in the AVRP survey.[12] Mycenaean pottery at Tell Atchana, Tell Judaidah and Çatal Höyük (Amuq) and Cypriote White Slip II were found in two additional Amuq sites. Thus far, the pottery is not published. Based on Verstraete and Wilkinson's collection data, Amuq phase M could equally end at 1400, 1300 or 1200 B.C.E.

Another AVRP survey discussion of the LBA at the Amuq is found in the studies of Casana (2003; 2007; 2009). While Casana's work on the settlement patterns is very impressive and in some aspects innovative, it is missing the study of the actual pottery collected in the different surveyed sights. The ceramic distinctions between Late Bronze Age and Iron Age are very vague, and almost no pottery is published to date. Amuq phase N is hardly mentioned at all by any of these studies. The lack of a good secure published ceramic sequence in the Amuq later than Amuq phase J thus poses a major problem for Casana's (and any other such) study—when the Tell Atchana report (Woolley 1955) and Swift's dissertation (1958) are the only references for local Amuq pottery, one is in trouble. Thoughtlessly, the AVRP was initiated before the correct groundwork was done: the ceramic sequence must be carefully excavated and recreated based on different Amuq sites, and published (as Braidwood and Braidwood 1960), before conclusions of great magnitude can be drawn based solely on surface collection. The AVRP results so far can be judged only on a very *longue durée* scale—they tell us nothing of the transition between Amuq phases M and N (see for example Casana and Wilkinson 2005a: 37–40).

Casana (2009: 12–17) is aware of this problem and makes some important observations on the limitations of surface collections when trying to track the Late Bronze Age in the Amuq:

1) The second millennium ceramic sequence of the northern Levant is still rather poorly understood, and the available evidence suggests that most standard wares have a very long chronological range, from MBA to LBA and sometimes into the Iron Age. Currently, according to Casana, the only reliable way to distinguish the Late Bronze Age (Amuq M) from earlier phases of the second millennium in an unstratified ceramic collection is through the presence of extremely rare imported or imitation Mycenaean, Cypriote or Nuzi wares. Casana believes that when

imports are not found the whole assemblage is marked by most surveys as MBA instead of MBA–LBA.

2) All MBA–LBA Amuq sites but two (Tell Atchana and Tel Bahlila) are covered, literally sealed, by intensive Iron Age (phase O) occupation. Therefore only very few MBA–LBA sherds are found in surface collection in most Amuq tell-sites.

3) 80%–90% of the LBA ceramic assemblage is dominated by plain, sand tempered, pink to orange buff wares, which are hard to identify securely as LBA.

4) As in many other surveys, some sites are occupied by modern activity (from buildings to fields, military posts to private land) and therefore are not available for systematic survey.

Casana divides the MBA–LBA sites into four ranks:

1) excavated sites;
2) large surface collection of MBA and/or LBA diagnostics;
3) some surface collection of MBA and/or LBA diagnostics; and
4) few second millennium B.C.E. sherds.

Then, he compares and merges (see Casana Table 1) his data with Braidwood's (1937). Out of eighty-six sites in the list, only nineteen AVRP sites fall within categories 1 and 2. Six additional sites are assigned to category 2, based on Braidwood's survey (ibid.). The rest of the sites are almost equally divided between categories 3 and 4. A summary of the MBA–LBA settlement pattern shows that most of the Amuq tell sites were occupied during at least some part of the second millennium B.C.E. (Casana 2009: 14; herein Plan 54).

Casana's next step is to plot in one figure all the MBA–LBA sites on record according to their area and height[13] (Casana 2009: 17; herein Plan 55). As one can see, Tell Atchana, even without considering the possibility of the existence of a lower town, is by far the largest site in the region. At the same time, it is lower than most sites. The reason, after intensive excavations in both Tell Atchana and Tell Ta'yinat, is obvious: the two proximate sites are in fact one site that shifts its location back and forth from one period to another. It may have done so between what was at the time the two banks of the river (Casana and Gansell 2005: 159, 168): Atchana in the chalcolithic period (Wilkinson 2000: 171), Ta'yinat during the Early Bronze Age (Braidwood & Braidwood 1960: 13–14),[14] Atchana during the second millennium until the end of the LBA (Mellink 1957), and Ta'yinat again during Iron Age I–II (Harrison 2009). All other sites are divided between

---

[11] See also Venturi (2007: 85–86).

[12] Aegean pottery and local imitations were additionally found by the AVRP survey in 18 Amuq phase N sites (Verstraete and Wilkinson 2000: 187–188).

[13] Casana (2009: 16) explains that the relative height of tell sites "may be understood as a proxy measure for the density of settlement, the duration of occupation, and the presence of monumental buildings and fortification walls at any individual site."

[14] Astour (1992: 8) reports that Alalaḫu is attested in the third millennium archive of Ebla. If this is correct, Middle Bronze and Late Bronze Age Tell Atchana inherited the name Alalakh from Tell Ta'yinat of the Early Bronze Age.

TABLE 1. All sites in the Amuq Valley where evidence of MBA-LBA occupation has been recorded. Sites are ranked on a scale of 1 to 4 according to quality of the evidence for occupation (see main text). Braidwood's (1937) assessments of certainty and phasing are indicated parenthetically where they differ from the AVRP.

Site	Name	Quality	Date	Site	Name	Quality	Date
136	Tell Atchana	1	MBA-LBA	174	Tell Abdal	3	MBA
167	Chatal Höyük	1	MBA-LBA	187	Hısırlık Tepesi (Hösürlük)	3	MBA
176	Tell al-Judaidah	1	MBA-LBA	195	Atçı Tepe	3	MBA
9	Dana Höyük	2	MBA-LBA	208	Temel Kizilkaya	3	MBA
11	Paşakoy	2	MBA-LBA	215	Sekizevler (Asgundur)	3	MBA
40	Baytarlı (Toprakh)	2	MBA-LBA	73	Çamurlu (Tell Jabur)	3 (2)	(MBA)
84	Bözhöyük	2	MBA-LBA	75	Tell Keçebey	3 (2)	(LBA)
86	Karatepe	2	MBA-LBA	41	Kiremitlı	(3)	MBA
89	Böztepe	2	MBA-LBA	7	Yusuflu	4	MBA
133	Tell Bahlilah	2	MBA-LBA	10	Baglama (ain al-Samah)	4	MBA
134	Halak Tepe	2	MBA-LBA	12	Acarköy (Halilağa Höyük)	4	MBA
173	Ermeneia (Sha'ir 'Askar; Şabi)	2	MBA-LBA	15	Köyüncu (Tell Mahmutlu)	4	MBA
180	Tell Hijar	2	MBA-LBA	26	Ada Tepe (Tell Abu Sha'ir)	4	MBA
186	Kemalağa Çiftliği	2	MBA-LBA	27	Kırkhız Pinar (Baş Pınar)	4	MBA
214	Eskidegirmen Tepe	2	MBA-LBA	80	Tell el-Rasm	4	MBA
252	Tarla Höyük	2	MBA-LBA	103	Tabarat Maştepe	4	MBA
253	(no name)	2	MBA-LBA	105	Tutlu Höyük	4	MBA
283	Tomsa Höyük	2	MBA-LBA	116	Büyük Avara	4	MBA
286	Zengin Tepe	2	MBA-LBA	124	Tell Keleş	4	MBA
81	Yeşilova (Damalka al-Qibli)	(2)	MBA	132	Tabarat Jalil	4	MBA
147	Tell Salem	(2)	MBA	143	Besarslan (Tell Hamda)	4	MBA
150	Tell Saye (Tell Asir)	(2)	MBA	151	Kara Tash (Nejar Tepe)	4	MBA
162	Dağlağan	(2)	MBA	192	Abalakli (2)	4	MBA
164	Tell Davutpaşa	(2)	MBA	196	Golbası Höyük	4	MBA
172	Tell Qirmidah (Tell Kirmit)	(2)	MBA	209	Kizilkaya	4	MBA
3	Kirmitlı Höyük	3	MBA	216	Annephı Höyük	4	MBA
5	Guzelçe	3	MBA	227	Tell Habash (Sultan Merkezi)	4	MBA
6	Yassiyurt	3	LBA	231	Ahmet Sahbaz Cifligi	4	MBA
16	Çataltepe	3	(LBA)	246	Çakalı Karakol	4	MBA
17	Soğuksu Höyük	3	MBA	19	Tell Karadurmuslu	4 (2)	(MBA)
18	Guzel Höyük	3	(LBA)	52	Akpinar Höyük	4 (2)	(MBA)
28	Tell Maltah	3	MBA	55	Tell Kurcaoğlu	4 (2)	(MBA)
35	Balderan (Bokluca)	3	MBA	36	Tell Kizilkaya (Gavurköy)	4 (3)	(MBA)
46	Gökçeoğlu	3	MBA	2	Boklukaya	(4)	(MBA)
99	Yurt Höyük	3	MBA	20	Ali Bey Höyüğu	(4)	(MBA)
104	Tell al-Terzi	3	MBA	28	Tell Maltah (Matta)	(4)	(LBA)
107	Hurriyet (Tarābat Hurriyet)	3	MBA	29	Eşen Tepe (al-Kanisah)	(4)	(MBA)
123	Sicanlı	3	MBA	33	Firka (Tell Firgah)	(4)	(MBA)
129	Tell Salihiyyah	3	MBA	37	Yanik Tepe	(4)	(LBA)
138	Tell Saluq	3	MBA	45	Killik (Tarābat 'Arab Ahmad)	(4)	(MBA)
158	Yazi Höyük	3	MBA	135	Tulail al-Sharqi (Tell al-Sheikh)	(4)	(LBA)
166	Putoğlu	3	MBA	152	Ayrancı Doğu (Ayrancı Şarki)	(4)	(LBA)
120	Tell Mirmiran (Tell Anbar)	3	LBA	163	Tell Musharrafah (Müşrefe)	(4)	(LBA)

Casana Table 1. MBA–LBA Amuq sites according to different Amuq surveys (after Casana 2009: 15)

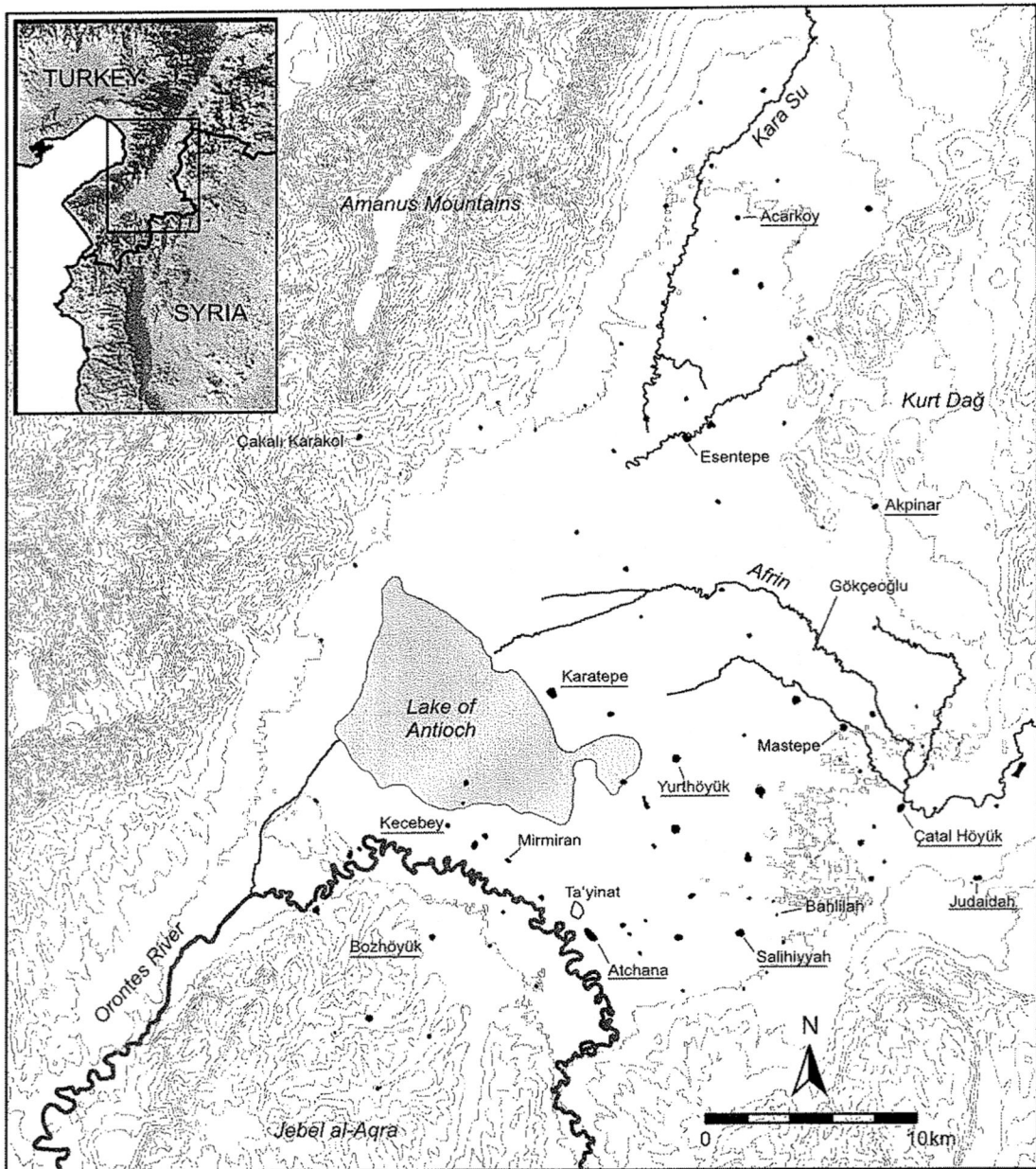

Figure 2. Archaeological sites in the Amuq Valley where evidence of Bronze Age occupation has been recorded by the AVRP or Braidwood (1937). Underlined sites are the largest Bronze and Iron Age tells in the region. For complete descriptions of sites, see Casana and Wilkinson (2005).

Plan 54. The Amuq settlement pattern during MBA and LBA based on University of Chicago AVRP (after Casana 2009: 14)

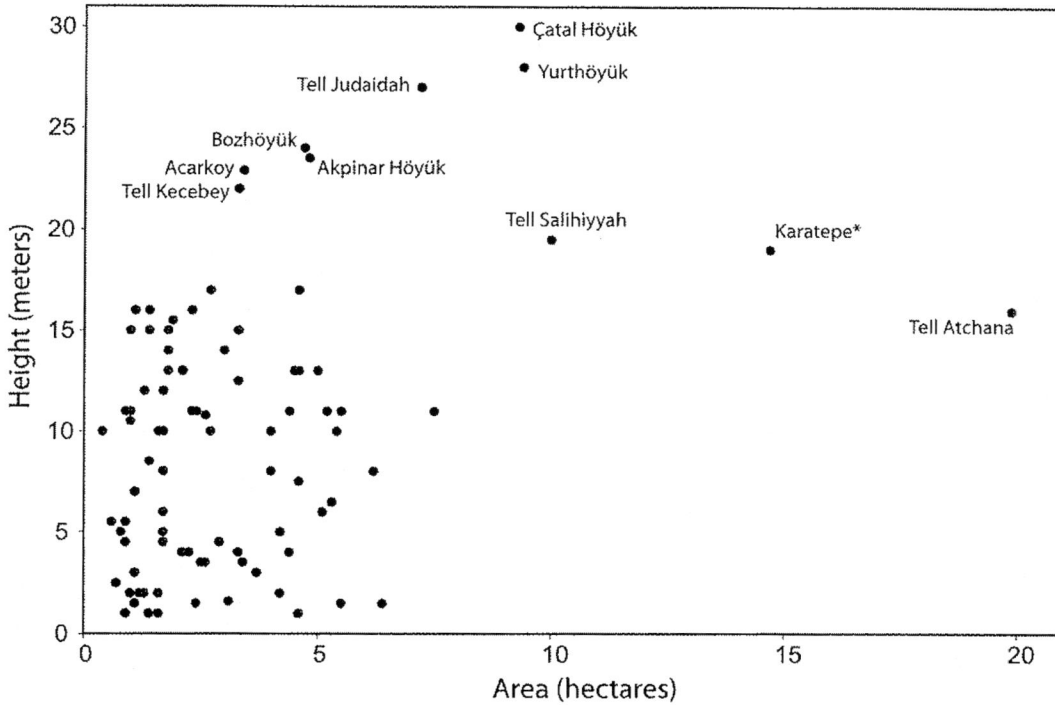

Figure 4. Area vs. height plot of Bronze Age sites recorded by the AVRP. Tell Atchana is by far the largest in terms of area, but nine other sites (labeled) are distinctly taller and generally larger than most other sites.
* Karatepe (AS 86) is a very large site, but its measured area is exaggerated by the presence of later settlement and recent agricultural earth moving.

Above: **Plan 55. Area vs. height plot of AVRP recorded tell sites in the Amuq (after Casana 2009: 17)**

Below: **Plan 56. AVRP survey site size vs. number of households in the Level IV^W census data (after Casana 2009: 29)**

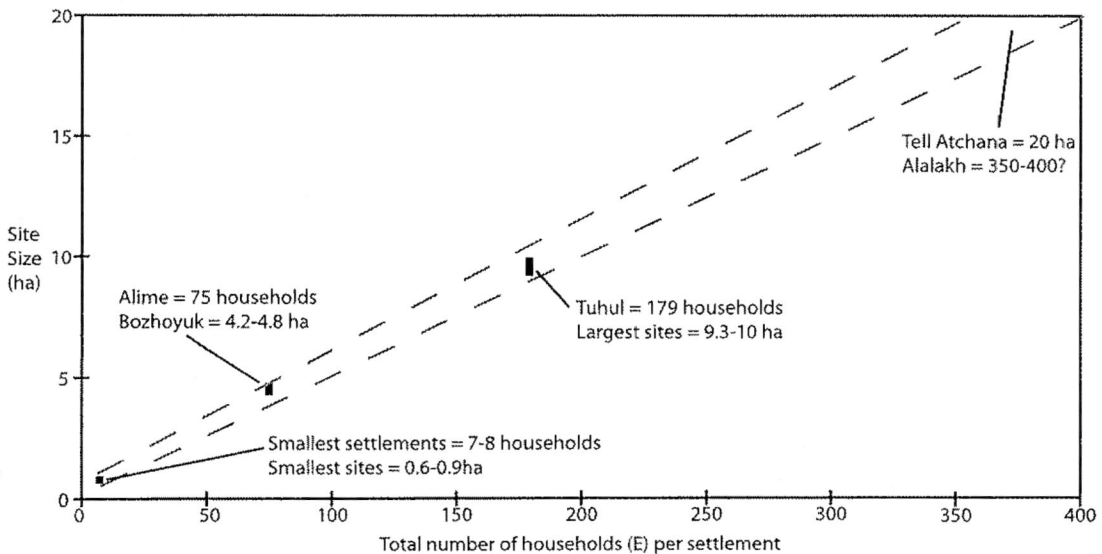

Figure 5. Comparison between site size and the number of households per settlement as recorded in the Alalakh census lists. Dashed lines represent the approximately linear relationship between these variables.

two additional tiers: secondary (4–10 ha. / 19–30 m. high) and tertiary (1–5 ha. / 1–15 m. high).

As I have already noted, Casana's weak point is that he has to base his study on the assumption that all or most the second millennium tell sites were extensively inhabited in the fifteenth century B.C.E., at the time that the Level IVA[F] archives were active. This educated guess will probably end up empirically proven by future ceramic study that will compare Atchana Level IVA[F] with the survey material. Nonetheless, Casana does not contribute anything to the discussion of whether Amuq M ends before the end of the LBA, and if so, when.

To support his assumption that he can locate the Level IV[W] sites, Casana claims that the majority of the cities and villages of Mukiš, which were mentioned in the "census" lists of the level IV[W] archives, are within the AVRP survey area. He compares the number of MBA–LBA AVRP sites (19 confirmed LBA, 72 with second millennium occupation, and 10–12 sites, where no second millennium pottery is found, but "where we might reasonably expect such occupation to have been present")[15] with the number of Mukiš settlements in the Level IV[W] lists: 168 (Serangeli 1978; Niedorf 1998, 1999; von Dassow 2008: 64–67, 362–370, 501–514).[16] Even after adding a maximum number of possible Mukiš settlements—some outside the perimeters of the AVRP survey—Casana's numbers do not even approach the number of census-recorded settlements. Casana suggests that the explanation is in the concept of the discontinuous border, where polities could be spatially fragmented; i.e., the king of Mukiš could own settlements and lands that located far away from Alalakh, without maintaining territorial continuity all the way from Alalakh to these distant locations. What is more, the king of Mukiš could buy, sell, receive as a present or inherit these lands and cities. While refuting several identifications of toponyms made by Astour (1963, 1969, 1989) as well as his claim for Mukiš's suzerainty over and territorial continuity all the way to Aleppo and beyond,[17] Casana accepts some of Astour's unpopular geographically-remote identifications, under the framework of polities that are spatially fragmented.[18]

I believe that most of these settlements survived the first stage of the Hittite takeover of the region. Only better ceramic study will confirm if indeed sometime towards the end of the thirteenth century most of these towns and villages were abandoned and why.

---

[15] These numbers are slightly different than the numbers appearing in Casana Table 1, which is reproduced below.

[16] Casana (2009: 23) assumes that the real number of settlements is considerably higher, since half of the names mentioned in the "censuses" list appear there only once, which makes it possible that missing tablets would have added a significant number of additional toponyms.

[17] For more observations on Astour's identifications see von Dassow 2008: 64–67.

[18] Casana ends up with a graph (2009: 29; herein Plan 56) describing the relations between settlement size (AVRP data) and number of households in the site (Alalakh IV[W] census data). Assuming there were 6–10 people in a household, he suggests that 100–200 people per hectare of site is the correct population estimate for Levantine LBA.

Pucci on Amuq phase M

A study that may shed new light on the end of LBA in the Amuq is being conducted these days by Marina Pucci, who carries the complicated mission of the publication of the Oriental Institute excavations at Çatal Höyük (Amuq), seventy years after their completion. Pucci finds in Çatal Höyük clear ceramic evidence that the site was inhabited during the thirteenth century B.C.E. She wrote the following to me in personal communication (January 2009):[19]

> As far as the stratigraphy of Çatal Höyük is concerned, the areas which show a clear sequence in the passage from Phase M to Phase N are two (II and V) and the excavated extent is quite limited. This said, however, the sequences show continuity in the occupation at the site without breaks. There is a functional rearrangement of the areas with a different architecture, however no traces of abandonment or heavy destruction. Consequently Phase M ends with the appearance of the LH IIIc middle pottery (first half of the 12th century) both imports and local production, with the disappearance of the local common ware with strong similarities to the so called drab ware and this phase includes the period of the Hittite occupation. In my opinion, this change in the continuity of occupation shows a clear phenomenon: the town lost its contacts to the Hittite empire and survived opening to the Mediterranean Sea. Because it was only a village and it was not located on the coast, there was no need to invade or destroy it.
>
> The presence of Nuzi ware in the layers dating to Phase M is very scattered and scarce so that it is possible to affirm that at Çatal Höyük only the latest Phase M was archaeologically investigated, and that the passage from Mittani to Hittite influence is not documented and that during the last phase of period M Nuzi ware was not a common type of ware.

Phase M at Çatal Höyük was excavated in limited, but adequate, area. For example, of phase M at Trench II only 200 m[2] are exposed (Pucci, personal communication; Meyer 2008: 12, Table 2, reproduced herein). The only other location in which it was found is Trench V. Although the excavators did not reach the internal floors of the phase M buildings, the destruction yielded several types that closely resemble the pottery found on the Oberstadt at Ḫattuša and in the Hittite thirteenth century layers at Kinet Höyük (Pucci, forthcoming and personal communication). The excavators also found several White Slip II vessels and a few Mycenaean sherds that are most probably LH

---

[19] I thank Marina Pucci for discussing this matter with me both in writing and over the phone, and for allowing me to quote both means of communications. I also receive from Pucci her kind permission to quote her forthcoming contribution to the proceedings of the 2008 ICAANE meeting in Rome.

IIIB. These ceramic observations clearly support the idea that Çatal Höyük was inhabited during the thirteenth century B.C.E., though assumptions are limited due to the size of the dig and its incomplete nature. In addition, the alignment of the walls of phase N "remains identical to the alignment of phase M buildings, indicating that probably some remains of other M structures were either only visible or still in use" when phase N was built (Pucci, forthcoming).

Under the limitations of the excavation extent, it is possible that not only at Tell Atchana, but also at Çatal Höyük, a small settlement survived to the end of the LBA. As we know from Atchana, the dramatic decline of the inhabited area in the site does not mean a total abandonment. An Afrin village such as Çatal Höyük may possibly have survived due to its location only 65 km. from Aleppo, which continues to be a major Hittite center well into the thirteenth century B.C.E. If indeed the new inhabitants of Amuq phase N were looking for the existing settlements (habitually, they were not founding new sites), and if indeed most of the existing settlements in the thirteenth century were located in the eastern Amuq, at the Afrin Valley, this could explain the clump of Amuq N sites in the east (Plan 54).

Mycenaean Pottery in Alalakh

Mycenaean ceramics from Alalakh were published by Woolley (1955: 369–376), Morris and Crouwel (1985) and Koehl (2005a). Koehl presented an additional study of Mycenaean pottery, unearthed in Alalakh by the University of Chicago expedition during the 2003–2004 seasons at the annual meeting of AIA in Boston, January 2005 (Koehl 2005b).[20]

It is clear that Woolley published only a small portion of the Aegean ceramics that he found: thirteen complete or restorable Mycenaean vessels and an additional eighteen sherds (Koehl 2005a: 415). Morris and Crouwel added eight sherds to the corpus (ibid.).[21] Koehl studied and published an additional 128 fragments, which had been stored at Woolley's dig house on Tell Atchana. Together with the older publications, Koehl's article (2005) brings the minimum number of published Mycenaean vessels at Atchana to eighty four (ibid.: 416). During the 2003–2004 seasons of the University of Chicago dig at Atchana yet another 38 Mycenaean sherds were excavated, all studied by Koehl. While the Chicago sherds represent a minimum of 24 vessels, the total number of LH IIIA:2 found up

to 2004 at Atchana is 108, which at present, "comprises the largest assemblage of Late Helladic IIIA:2 pottery in the Levant" (Koehl: AIA 2005). While there are more Mycenaean pots in Ugarit and in Tell Abu Hawam, northern and southern Levantine sites, the pottery there date later, to LH IIIB:1 (ibid.). The bulk of the Atchana Mycenaean pottery "belongs to the same chronological horizon as the Aegean pottery from Tell el Amarna, the Ulu Burun shipwreck and the Persian Garden tombs at Akko" (ibid). Koehl's ceramic comparison between Alalakh and Ugarit adds to the fact that Mukiš and Alalakh are hardly mentioned in texts from Ugarit—yet more proof that Alalakh was not a city any more at the apogee of the Ugarit archives, during the thirteenth century B.C.E. (see Section 5.2 below).

Woolley (1955: 376, 398) uses Mycenaean pottery as his main tool in dating Level I^W in Alalakh. His identification of all the Level I^W Mycenaean pottery as LH IIIB, together with the misidentification of the orthostat of Tudḫaliya DUMU.LUGAL as that of king Tudḫaliya IV while he was still a crown prince (Niedorf 2002), brought him to the conclusion that Level I^W was in existence during most of the thirteenth century B.C.E.[22] Clearly, the date of the orthostat of Tudḫaliya DUMU.LUGAL is significantly earlier than Woolley's estimated date (see Section 3.3). Stratigraphically, Level I^W does not hold as one phase any more, and its different buildings and structures are redistributed between Levels III–IB^F (see Summary Tables 1 and 2). The remaining question is whether Woolley's analysis of the Mycenaean pottery is accurate, and therefore requires dating all the Level I^W buildings in which he excavated Mycenaean pottery as LH IIIB or later. Since Woolley first analyzed the Mycenaean pottery at Atchana (1955: 369–376), views on the Aegean pottery of the site have changed tremendously. While the earliest Aegean pottery found at Atchana is LM IB/LH IIA and LH IIB, the latest and by far the largest group is, according to Koehl, LH IIIA:2, all of standard Mycenaean fabric (ibid.). Markedly, Koehl dates sherds of one or a few stirrup jars to LH IIIB:1 or even later (ibid.; 2005 AIA presentation).[23] Based on the pottery excavated in 2003 and 2004 Koehl limits the latest type to LH IIIA:2 late, which he dates to the latter half of the fourteenth century BCE.[24] To sum up Koehl's opinion in his publication (2005), presentation (AIA 2005) and Chicago excavations report, the majority

---

[20] I attended at Koehl's presentation. Moreover, I would like to thank him for sending me the full text of his talk, as well as a summary of his study, which was part of the 2003–2004 Oriental Institute project at Tell Atchana.

[21] Morris and Crouwel (1985: 86) note: "many of the pieces catalogued here have no recorded find-spot; in fact, several fragments seem never to have been registered and therefore have no excavation number. One or two have letters penciled on them which probably refer to trenches. The extremely disturbed nature of the site means that, even when the actual level of a find is known, it cannot be regarded as reliable indication of date." I do not share Morris and Crouwel's opinion on the stratigraphy of Tell Atchana, but clearly it is almost impossible to make a reliable claim over the origin of most of the unpublished pottery of the site.

[22] For the first reappraisal of Woolley's date of the Mycenaean pottery in Alalakh see Swift 1958: 34, 40–42. Swift, followed by Rowton (1970: 230–231), was the first to identify the bulk of the Mycenaean pottery of Level II^W as LH IIIA pottery.

[23] Jeremy Rutter (personal communication, December 2008) sees no reason not to group this stirrup jar with the large assemblage of LH IIIA:2. Koehl possibly changed his mind in his 2003–04 report to the Chicago expedition, writing that "I believe that none of the Mycenaean imports at Atchana need date later than LH IIIA:2 late." Koehl's identification of the LH IIIB may be in line with an erroneous date in his paper (2005: 415) where he suggests that the Hittites lost their control over Alalakh around 1275 B.C.E. This idea is unfounded and out of date (see Chapter 3 for my discussion of the orthostat of Tudḫaliya DUMU.LUGAL).

[24] On Rutter's website (http://projectsx.dartmouth.edu/classics/history/bronze_age/lessons/les/24.html) Late Helladic IIIA:2 is dated to ca. 1390/1370 – 1320/1300 B.C.E.

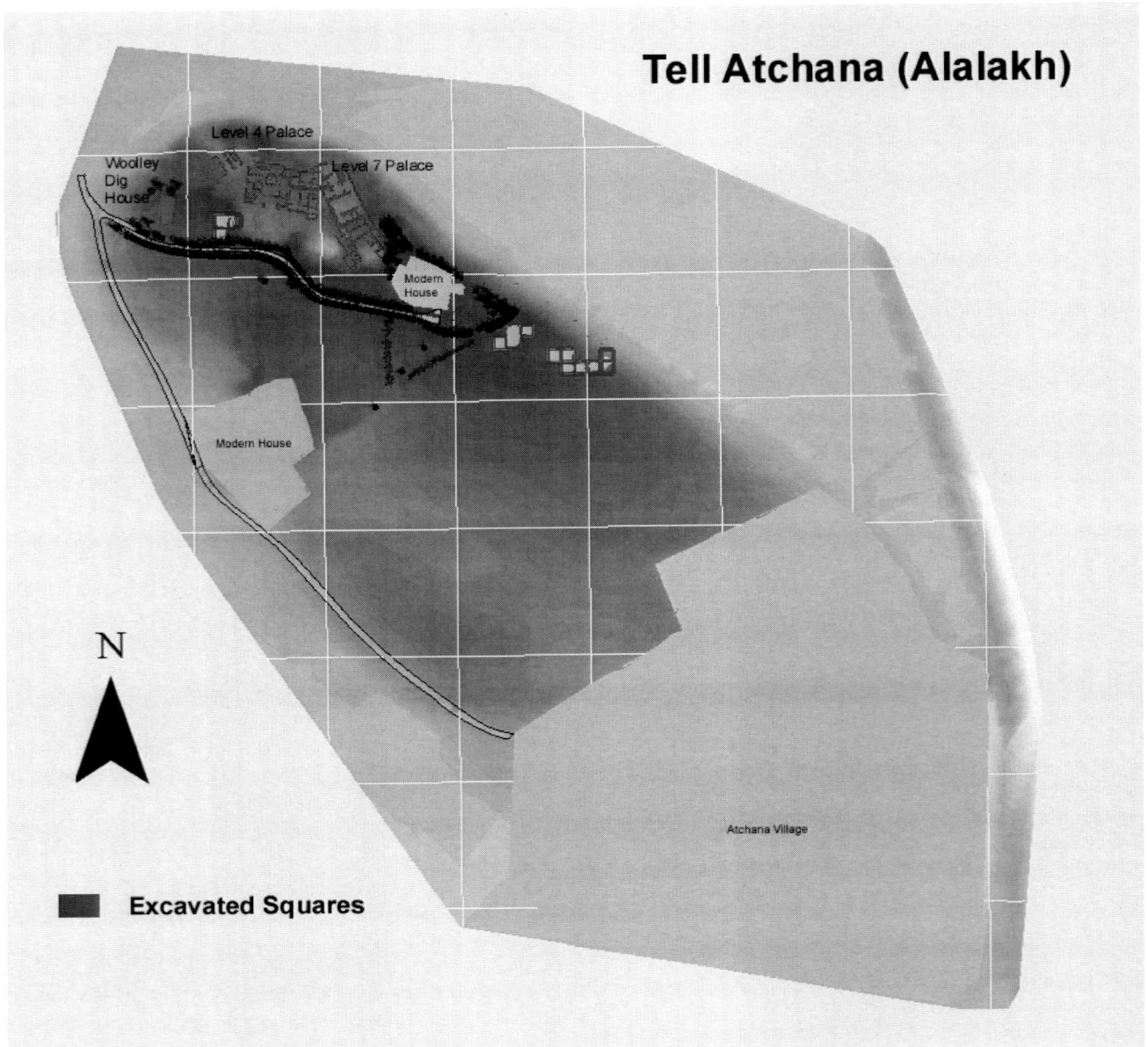

Plan 57. The squares excavated by the University of Chicago expedition to Tell Atchana, 2003–2004 (image: Eudora Struble)

of the Mycenaean pottery at Tell Atchana (and 100% of the Mycenaean sherds excavated in Area 2) are LH IIIA:2, and the small minority of the pottery is either earlier or even later than LH IIIA:2. It is possible that importation did cease all together, but if it continued into LH IIIB, it was done in very small quantities. It is very significant that all the Mycenaean pottery excavated during the Chicago campaign was LH IIIA:2 late, since they all originated in the two final sub phases of the site occupation in Area 2, east of the area in which Woolley excavated the Levels VI–I[W] private houses (Plan 57).[25]

This fact, together with several other considerations, allows me to suggest that most of Tell Atchana was not occupied at all beyond the last decades of the fourteenth century

B.C.E. Unlike most of the Mycenaean pottery examined by Koehl, those sherds that originated in the Chicago excavation were carefully excavated, and although most of the sherds were not found *in situ* on floors, but in secondary deposits, the way they were handled and marked by the excavators makes them at least as secure as those which originated from Woolley's most secure context. The great similarity between the Mycenaean assemblage of the Chicago excavation and the one at el Amarna, Egypt, as pointed out by Koehl, and the relatively large number of types, makes it almost certain that these are not heirlooms from earlier phases, but indeed represent quite accurately the assemblage of the mid–late fourteenth century B.C.E. One does not expect heirlooms to have so important a presence in a typical assemblage of imports at the era. It is also uncommon that such a large percentage of the imports in a given assemblage (one-sixth) will be of heirlooms. Therefore, even if Cline's idea (1991) of a Hittite embargo

---

[25] The author supervised the digging in Area 2 in both 2003 and 2004 over a total area of 800 m². Only two coherent final phases were dug in the area during the two seasons. See Yener, Schloen and Fink 2004a; 2004b; 2005; Fink 2008a.

over Mycenaean imports is correct[26]—and Alalakh seems to be a way to prove it, since Mycenaean imports to Alalakh ceased with LH IIIA:2, possibly not many years after Mukiš was annexed to the Hittite empire—the truth is that it is purely coincidental, since not only did the imports cease, but so did Alalakh as a city.

Indeed, late LH IIIA:2 is strongly represented in the final occupation of the site, in the area excavated by the University of Chicago. Woolley identifies Level I^W with most of the Mycenaean imports, now all analyzed as mid–late fourteenth century LH IIIA:2. Furthermore, of Woolley's three sub-phases of Level I^W, he mentions the latest ones, "the upper strata of that level" as a main find spot of (now known to be LH IIIA:2) Mycenaean pottery (1955: 374, 398). In contrast, Level II^W private houses have very few LH IIIA:2 imports; the dominant painted ware is Atchana ware, which pre-dates (and is basically sealed by) LH IIIA:2, giving it a likely date somewhere in the early fourteenth century. Moreover, there is one place where the Level II^W LH IIIA:2 pottery is represented at its zenith: the Level II^W temple, where a whole chariot-krater was found (Woolley 1955: 396, Pl. CXXVIIIa). Allegedly, fragments of the same type were also found in the Level III^W temple (ibid.). By shifting the Level II^W temple and most of the Level I^W private houses to Level III^F, and the Level III^W temple to Level IVB^F as I have suggested (see Chapter 3 and Summary Table 1), LH IIIA:2 is brought back to its well established date (Mountjoy 1986, 1993; Leonard 1994).[27] Conspicuously, in his publication of the Mycenaean sherds stored at Woolley's dig house (2005: 416), Koehl notes that two-thirds of the fragments were marked as originating from Levels IV^W and III^W, which for Woolley represent the last phase of Mittanian rule and the first phase of Hittite domination. Such high amounts of Mycenean sherds would be surprising for my stratigraphic analysis, since in it both levels fall under Mittanian supremacy. However, in his AIA 2005 presentation, Koehl himself admitted that the 'level'—if indeed these markings refer to levels—indicated on at least some of the pottery is far out of reasonable phase (too early by half a millennium), and therefore, unreliable. I have difficulty pursuing an argument that relies on pencil marks of roman numerals with no other related documentation.

The dates of Level 0^W (and hence, Level I^W) were also dictated by Woolley's (1955: 203–205, 373–374, 398–399) assumptions about the dates of the graves that were dug into the ruins of Level I^W. Most significant is the mis-identification of some of the vessels as LH IIIC imports, which required a twelfth century date or later. This misidentification joins another misidentification (ibid.: 203, 399, Pl. LXVI$_{131}$) of an object found in

one of the Level 0^W burials (ATG/37/2), and which was already discussed above: a scarab that Woolley attributed to Ramses VI, and that is now ascribed to the time of Amenhotep III (Kitchen 1982).

At this point it is hard to tell whether or not Mycenaean imports were brought to Alalakh's Hittite military stronghold of the thirteenth century B.C.E. According to my stratigraphic analysis the only buildings in Alalakh that survived into the thirteenth century B.C.E. were the Levels IA–0^W temples, including the Paluwa shrine, the later stage of the Levels III–II^W fort and the Level I^W house 38/B. Of this list, Woolley records LH IIIB Mycenean pottery only in the Level I^W house 38/B (1955: 196–197): he notes three globular flasks of vertical type found in a grave, dug into room 2 in square P10 (ATP/38/5, 6, 7), another globular flask of vertical type (ATP/38/8) in room 2, a piriform jar on the floor of room 1 (*bugelkanne* ATP/38/226), and un-numbered Mycenaean sherds in room 4 (in context with Atchana ware).[28] Mountjoy ends this vertical type of globular flask (probably *FS 189*) in LH IIIA:2 (1986: 81, 108; 1993: 77; Leonard 1994: no. 1279–1281, 1306). Could these four vertical globular flasks and one piriform jar date to late in the thirteenth century? Are these heirlooms, still in circulation or dug or exposed somewhere in the latest phase of the large abandoned site? Or is Woolley's interpretation of the stratigraphy of Level I^W house 38/B inaccurate?

Level III^F private houses

Level I^W house 37/A (Plans 43, 50)

This is a large and well-planned house, which was found in very bad condition (Woolley 1955: 193). Most of the walls were built on the stumps of the Level II^W walls, and did not have any stone foundations (ibid.). The building was destroyed in heavy fire, which burnt the floors and walls into red brick color, and reduced many of them to powder (ibid.). While many of the thresholds are not restorable, most of the blueprint is (ibid.). The house faces at least two streets: one is parallel to the city-wall, and the other is between Level I^W houses 37/A and 37/B, where the main entrance to house 37/A is located (ibid.). House 37/A is built of two dividable units (northeast and southwest), each enjoying access from the outside (ibid.: 195). In the area to the northwest of the house, between Level I^W houses 37/A and 38/A, no Level I^W building was found, but Woolley suggests that house 37/A was actually extended to the northwest. Level III^F, being the last level of the city of Alalakh, and therefore, the last inhabited phase of most of the site, suffered from intensive robbery of building materials, to be reused in nearby Tell Ta'yinat. While Tell Atchana is located just 800 m. away from Tell Ta'yinat, the nearest stone quarry was located at least 10 km. away. It is obvious that the inhabitants of Ta'yinat of Amuq phases N and M (Iron Age I and II) used Tell Atchana as a prime source for building materials.

---

[26] although Singer (2006: 252–258) shows textual evidence for reciprocal trade between Ahhiyawans and Hittites.

[27] Alalakh is clearly not central to van Wijngaarden's book (2002: 113) on the use and appreciation of Mycenaean pottery. However, in his discussion of Mycenaean pottery at the site, van Wijngaarden makes some basic mistakes in his description of Tell Atchana's stratigraphy, describing "the palace uncovered in Level V" as Niqmepa's palace, and dating the Level IV^W palace to the thirteenth century B.C.E.

[28] Woolley (1955: 197) finds it hard to believe that Atchana ware continued to be used so late. He writes: "it was noted that while they lay apparently above floor-level there was really no floor preserved and 'their appearance here might be accidental'—it would indeed be the only known occurrence of this ware in Level I."

The entrance to the southwest wing of the house is probably into room 1, "a clay-floored lobby" (Plan 43; ibid.: 193). Room 1 leads to room 2, where several vessels of local ware were found, and to room 4, where a clay hearth was unearthed in the west corner. Room 3 is an open court that leads to four different rooms: 2, 4, 5 and the unnumbered, partially excavated room at its northwest end. It is clay-floored, and against its northeast wall, two large and one small brick-built bases were excavated. In addition, Woolley found there a brick-edged hearth, a hinge stone, a base of a large jar sunk into the floor, two basalt tripod bowls, and a bronze chisel, axe and sickle (ibid.: 195). Room 5 contained a bread oven. In room 6, the lobby room of the northeast wing, several ring stands were found. The presence of a large number of ring stands in many of the later-level private houses in Tell Atchana shows that this was a common way to keep a jar standing, almost as popular as sinking them into the ground. Room 7 is the open court and the light well of the northeast wing— all the rooms of this wing are surrounding it (ibid.). All the walls of this room are a rebuilding of Level II^W walls except for the southeast wall and part of the northeast wall. In room 9 a fragment of a Mycenaean flask was found,[29] and a storage jar was excavated in room 11.

Several burials were dug into the walls of rooms 10 and 11. Woolley (ibid.) reports that the burials contained Mycenaean pottery, and therefore, must belong to the latest sub-phase of Level I^W. The implication of this idea would be that the house went out of function before the end of Level I^W. A better explanation is derived from my new stratigraphic scheme: house 37/A was burnt when the city of Alalakh ceased to exist (1320/1313), at the end of Level III^F. The inhabitants of the stronghold of Levels II–I^F probably buried their deceased nearby. The ruins of house 37/A were close enough to the stronghold and functioned, together with its vicinity (houses 37/B and 38/A) as the cemetery of Levels II–I^F (ibid.: 195–196).

Level I^W house 37/B (Plans 43, 50)

This house, located across the street from house 37/A, and likewise built on the stumps of Level II^W houses, was also heavily burnt and had mostly disappeared (ibid.: 196). Here, again "the area was honeycombed with the pits made for later burials… which had disturbed the levels as well as destroying the standing walls" (ibid.). For my explanation on the date of this cemetery see the above description of the Level I^W house 37/A. Several long gold bars, as well as two pairs of earrings (AT/37/29; ibid.: Pl. LXIXv), were found in room 5.

Level I^W house 37/C (Plans 43 (unlabelled), 50)

Of house 37/C only three walls are left, and no further information is disclosed about it.

Level I^W house 38/A (Plans 49, 50)

The walls of this large building are poorly preserved, mostly known at the foundation level only, and their top elevations are below the Level I^W floor levels (ibid.: 191). As in other Level I^W buildings, the walls were built on the stumps of Level II^W walls. It was impossible to track most of the doorways in this house (ibid.: 192). However, it seems that one of the entrances to the house was located in the narrow alley between the house and the city wall.

Just outside the door to room 1 a cylinder seal (AT/39/73) was found (ibid.), but it is doubtful whether it is dated to Level I^W (Collon 1982: 30).[30] In room 3 Woolley found a bronze arrowhead and a bronze pin. Room 4 had a cement floor and a dado of tiles covering the wall. At the south corner of this room "there was a three-sided tile and cement raised compartment," in front of which a tiled runnel was found (Woolley 1955: 192). Rooms 7 and 8 are a toilet unit. In room 12 Woolley finds possible evidence that the house was remodeled during Level I^W (ibid.: 193). Here, again, a grave containing unspecified Mycenaean pottery is dug into the latest phase of Level I^W—to be expected in view of my stratigraphic analysis. Woolley reports remains of floor in room 13 and floor remnants in the rest of square H17, where above the floor, the fragments of a Mycenaean chariot-krater were found. Woolley also relates one of the outstanding cylinder seals of Alalakh (AT/39/68; ibid.: 193; Collon 1982: 127–129) to this building, although it was found north of room 1 on the ruins of the Levels III–II^W/IVB^F city wall.

5.2 Level IIAB^F (1320/1313–1240)

The plans of Levels IIA^F and IIB^F accompany this discussion.

The city of Alalakh was probably destroyed ca. 1320/1313, and its inhabitants largely expelled. The royal compound of Level IVB^F, which was rebuilt during Level III^F, and included the Levels III–II^W fortress and the temple platform, was partially destroyed in 1320/1313, then immediately rebuilt. The remains of the Levels III–II^W fort/the Level IVB^F palace, as Woolley found them in the final phase of their occupation, represent the end of Level II^F. This is especially valid in the southern wing of the palace, where the floors of three of the rooms are preserved (Woolley 1955: 166–171). The two sub-phases of Level II^F (A-early and B-late) are based on the two building stages of the Level I^W temples, which are discussed in some detail above. Due to historical and archaeological reasons (Chapter 3) I dated Level IIA^F/the Level IA^W temple to 1320/1313–1280 and Level IIB^F/the Level IB^W temple to 1280–1240. The stronghold of Alalakh occupied a territory of 3 ha. at the most, while the area of the mound of Atchana (the city) is 21 ha., leaving aside the possibility

---

[29] Woolley (1955: 195) reports that this flask is similar to "ATP/38/37 on Pl. CXXXIII." Based on the pottery cards, ATP/38/37 is not a flask, but a jug, found in a different level and different location. Pl. CXXXIII does not exist in Woolley 1955 at all. I believe that Woolley meant to refer to ATP/38/7 in Pl. CXXVII.

[30] Collon (1982: 30): "The seal is attributed by Woolley to Level I on p. 192 and to Level III or later on p. 264 while a Level IV attribution has been entered in the field notes."

that there was a lower town. Although the final phases at Tell Atchana are the most intensively excavated, their state of preservation is poor: both the final phase of the city (Level III^F) and the stronghold levels must have been heavily looted by the builders of Iron Age Tell Ta'yinat in its different phases.

The recent excavations (2006–2009) of the site by Mustafa Kemal University, Antakya, offer confirmation for some of my arguments. In the web report of the 2008 season (Alalakh.org/report_2008.asp), the anonymous author writes that "tentatively the ceramics of phase 3 should be roughly contemporary with Woolley's Level IV palace." This testimony is based on the excavation in Area 4, which is located at the southwestern part of the site, far away from the palace and temple area of Woolley's old excavation. If indeed the local phase 3 in Area 4 is similar to the material excavated in the Level IVA^F/IV^W (= 1465/1440–1420/1400) palace, then local phase 2 is similar to Level IVB^F (1420/1400–1353/1341), and local phase 1 is similar to Level III^F (1353/1341–1320/1313). This is a fresh confirmation of my analysis that concludes that the city of Alalakh had ceased to exist by the end of Level III^F.

The same report (ibid.) offers a brief description and a low-resolution map of "geophysical remote sensing surveys over eight hectares of the site utilizing Geomagnetic Field Gradient measurements and resistivity measurements." One of the observations of Christian Hüber, who conducted the survey, is the possible existence of a "wall separating the Royal Precinct from the rest of the town in the southeast." This wall could have been built on top of the "wall separating the Royal Precinct from the rest of the town," but, if it exists, it must be in its final phase the wall surrounding the Hittite stronghold.

Alalakh in Ugarit

I already discussed one aspect of the historical background of this period in Alalakh (and the next one—Level I^F) in the chapter on the Alalakh temples. There, I brought to the fore three Hittite officials (Tudḫaliya, Paluwa and Šukur-Tešub), who were part of the northern Levantine Hittite administration (centered in Karkamiš), following their careers in the Alalakh stronghold and beyond. It is clear now that Alalakh had already lost its prime importance by the time of Muršili II. It probably became even less important following the Kadesh battle (1274) and the peace treaty between Ḫatušili III and Ramses II (1259), when the Egyptian and Assyrian threats over the northern Levant were removed from the Hittite agenda—at least for a while, until the time of Tudḫaliya "IV" and the battle of Niḫriya. This diminution in Alalakh's importance can be easily established by surveying the very few attestations of the city and the region of Mukiš in the abounding archives of the nearest neighbor Ugarit, and even further, by analyzing the context of these few citations. These attestations are in tablets of various dates. The earliest testimony (Bunnens

1987; Arnaud 1996: 47–54) is most probably from the time of Niqmepa son of Idrimi, dated to the fifteenth century Level IVA^F, and is beyond the time frame of this discussion. Another relatively well-dated testimony is the introduction letter of DUMU.LUGAL Šukur-Tešub, in all probability a governor of Alalakh (Lackenbacher 2002: 95–96), to Ammittamru III (1260–1235; Arnaud 1999; Singer 1999), king of Ugarit (see Section 3.3).

Mukiš is also mentioned in one of the Akkadian letters, found in Ugarit—RS 20.212 (Lackenbacher 2002: 103–104; Otten 1963: 8). This letter is very similar to several letters from Ugarit (Singer 1999: 716–717; Singer 2006: 248–249; Fink 2006: 684), among which figures the Ugaritic letter RS 18.038 of the time of ʿAmmurapiʾ II, king of Ugarit (1215–1190/1185). Singer suggests that RS 20.212 "may perhaps be inferred" from RS 18.038. In my recent article (Fink 2006: 686–687) I date the composition of RS 18.038 to early in the reign of ʿAmmurapiʾ II. Singer (1999: 716) describes RS 20.212:

> An Akkadian letter sent by the 'Sun' of Hatti to the king of Ugarit reprimands him for disobeying the orders of the King (of Carchemish) in the matter of a vital grain shipment... He reminds his vassal of the obligations he took upon himself in return for his exemption from corvée duties (*ilku*). He is supposed to provide one great ship with its crew for the transportation of 2,000 (*kor?*) of grain from Mukiš to Ura in one or two shipments. Two Hittite messengers, Ali-Ziti *reši šarri* (SAG.LUGAL) and Kunni, are sent to supervise the transaction. The letter concludes with the dramatic exclamation: '(It is a matter) of death or life!'

This letter makes it clear that the famine in the Hittite hinterland lasted for several decades before the empire came to its end (Singer 1999: 707; Lackenbacher and Malbran-Labat 2005: 238; Divon 2008). RS 20.212 is probably in line with the ongoing Hittite attempts to ship food from the Levant to the harbors close to Hatti, like that of Ura in Cilicia. Mukiš is either the place where the grain is grown or is the storage space for grain shipped down the Orontes, Afrin (*Aprê*) and Kara Su (*Saluara*) Rivers. It is not clear if the grain is stored in Alalakh or in another town: this could possibly be Sabuniye Höyüğü (Pamir and Brands 2005: 104), located five kilometers from the mouth of the river, and hence, more convenient for the ships of Ugarit to reach. Moreover, it is apparent that Mukiš cannot provide ships to transport the grain by itself. Nothing in this text contradicts my assumption that most of Alalakh's population was expelled during the last quarter of the fourteenth century B.C.E. On the contrary, collecting the grain of this fertile region is one of the expected activities of a Hittite (military?) stronghold. It is also understandable that the Hittites did not relinquish altogether the lush land of Mukiš, since it is well known in Hittite literature for its quality wine; even the Hittite queen Puduḫepa dreams about it, according to one text (Klengel

1975: 63–64), KUB 15.1, dated to the reign of Ḫattušili III (1267–1237). In it, the goddess ᵈHepat ᵁᴿᵁUda (Lebrun 2001: 330–332) is apparently revealing to Puduḫepa her passion for Mukišean wine (Klengel 1975: 63–64).

Another letter, most probably dated to the last days of Ugarit (and almost certainly, no earlier than the second half of the thirteenth century), is in Ugaritic—RS 16.402 (= KTU 2.33) (Albright 1958; Lipiński 1981; Pardee 1984; Dijkstra 1987: 42–46; Cunchillos 1989: 325–340; Pardee 2002). The letter is only partly preserved, but the three involved agents can be identified: the king of Ugarit, the queen (the recipient of the letter), and an important person called ʾIriritaruma, who is the sender. There is no doubt that this letter recorded dramatic events in Ugarit (Pardee 2002): the king is away waging war, and he is currently lodging by/on the Amanus (?) range; the enemy is in Mukiš, and ʾIriritaruma is assigned with the responsibility of furnishing the king with 2,000 horses, a mission he finds hard to fulfill.

It is now the consensus among scholars that the word *mgšḫ* in line 10 stands for "Mukiš" (del Olmo Lete and Sanmartín 2000: 265). Nonetheless, it is probably the only attestation of this word in Ugaritic so far, since the name does not appear in KTU 3.1 (Dietrich and Loretz 1963: 208, 213–214 vs. Knoppers 1993: 82–84 and Dalix 1998). Scholars disagree as to which events are the background of the composition of this letter: the extreme pressure of the Assyrian king Tukulti-Ninurta over the Hittites under Tudḫaliya "IV" (Lipiński 1981: 108–109; Klengel 1992: 140), or the final days of the kingdom of Ugarit (Astour 1965: 257–258; Singer 1999: 723–725; Pardee 2002: 106).[31] In both cases Mukiš is just the battlefield between Ugarit, possibly in the service of the Hittites, and the unknown enemy, either the Assyrians or the "Sea Peoples." In this text there is no evidence for any population in Mukiš, or reference to the role of Mukiš in this war or even to the Hittite stronghold at Alalakh. Indeed, we can probably date the destruction of that stronghold, shortly before the final days of Ugarit, based on this letter.

Singer (1999: 723–725) associates the Ugaritic letter RS 16.402 with RS 34.143 (Malbran-Labat 1991: 27–29; Zeeb 1992; Yamada 1992: 444–445), a letter in Akkadian, where a military operation in Mukiš is also mentioned. This well-preserved letter, written by the King (of Karkamiš) to an unnamed king of Ugarit, is not easy to interpret (Singer 1999: 723). Singer (ibid.) describes it as follows:

> First, the king of Ugarit is accused of misleading his master by claiming that his army is camped in Mukiš; according to the King's sources

Ugarit's army is in fact located in the town of Apsuna in the northern part of the kingdom of Ugarit. Second, the king of Ugarit is quoted as claiming that his chariotry is in poor shape and his horses are famished as a pretext for not sending his chariotry as demanded. Finally, the king of Ugarit is accused of keeping to himself the best *mariyannu*-troops while he sends to the viceroy only worthless soldiers.

Singer (1999: 725) suggests that the 2,000 horses mentioned in RS 16.402 are those demanded by the King of Karkamiš in RS 34.143. Pardee's translation (2002) of RS 16.402 makes Singer's assumption even more likely, since according to Pardee it is the king of Ugarit who orders ʾIriritaruma to bring him the horses, rather than ʾIriritaruma asking the queen of Ugarit for the horses, as was previously understood. Pardee's revised translation allows us to scrutinize the expected chain of command: the King of Karkamiš sends his directive to the king of Ugarit, and the king of Ugarit dictates it to one of his high officials, ʾIriritaruma. When the latter either cannot follow his king's order or does not want to fulfill it, the king of Ugarit replies to the King of Karkamiš in the same manner as ʾIriritaruma answers him, literally "recycling" ʾIriritaruma's explanations or excuses.

These letters, possibly along with others that remain unpublished (Malbran-Labat 1995: 107; 2008: 35), show that Mukiš is a battlefield—possibly even the place where an enemy vanguard or advance party is located. Since Mukiš is a crossroads between east and west, and north and south, the enemy needs to decide whether to advance along the westward road, towards Aleppo and Karkamiš, on the northeast road to Karkamiš, or southward, up the Orontes valley, approaching Ugarit. The King of Karkamiš expects Ugarit's troops to fight the enemy in Mukiš, where the enemy is, but he complains that the forces of Ugarit are in Apsuna (RS 34.143). Apsuna is located within the territory of Ugarit, northeast of the city of Ugarit (van Soldt 2005: 10, 104, 170). It is not located on the border of Ugarit and Mukiš, but probably in a strategic high position in the second line of towns and villages, northeast of the city of Ugarit. An enemy that approached Ugarit from Mukiš by land would have most probably marched along the Orontes River. Apsuna, therefore, would be the right place to stage an ambush. If the king of Ugarit indeed kept his troops in Apsuna, he was protecting Ugarit, possibly trying to "convince" the enemy to choose another direction: either the road to Aleppo or the one that leads to Karkamiš. I believe that RS 20.212, RS 16.402 and RS 34.143 all date to the reign of ʿAmmurapiʾ II, the last king of Ugarit. While RS 20.212 is probably from early in the reign of ʿAmmurapiʾ II, RS 16.402 and RS 34.143 are dated to its very end.

Two unpublished letters, excavated in 1994 in the House of Urtenu in Ugarit, may shed new light on the history of Mukiš in the thirteenth century. These are RS 94.2079, which is described by Malbran-Labat (2008: 26) as

---

[31] The third option, dating this Ugaritic letter to the time of hostility between Mukiš and Ugarit in the mid fourteenth century B.C.E., before Šuppiluliuma I's first Syrian war (for example, Dijkstra 1987: 46) seems to be out of date; most Ugaritic scholars accept Dalix' (1998: 5) claim that "no use of Ugaritic earlier than the thirteenth century B.C. may be proven." For additional literature on the date of RS 16.402 see Yamada 1992: 445, n. 70.

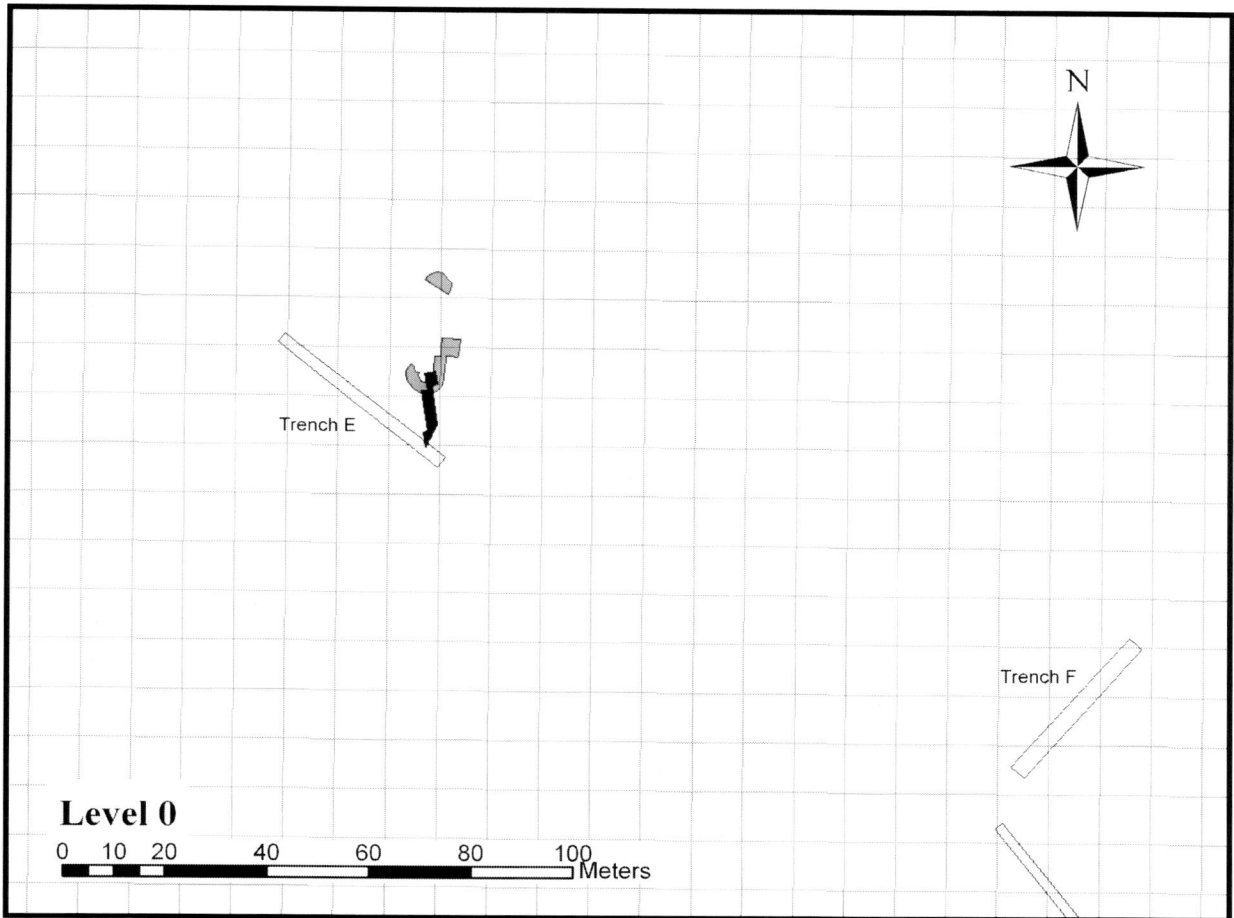

Plan 58. A proposed plan for Level 0^W (after Yener 2005: 144, Fig. 4.34)

composed "à propos de l'envoi de troupes à Alalaḫ" during the reign of one of the kings of Ugarit, who bore the name Niqmaddu; and RS 94.2389 (ibid.: 35), a fragment of a letter that describes the "situation à Alalaḫ." If RS 94.2079 is the letter Malbran-Labat previously hinted about (1995: 107), then she probably dates it to the reign of Niqmaddu IV (1225/1220–1215) (Arnaud 1999: 163; Lackenbacher 2002: 357); could it otherwise be dated to the reign of Niqmaddu III (1350–1315)? Malbran-Labat (1995: 107) writes that the turmoil originated neither from the Mediterranean nor from Anatolia, but rather from inland Syria, with roots to Mesopotamia. It is possible that once additional documents of the House of Urtenu archive are published, our understanding of Mukiš of the thirteenth century will be significantly different than it is today.

5.3 Level IAB^F (1240–1190/1185)

The plans of Levels IA^F and IB^F accompany this discussion.

It is now established that several letters from Ugarit bear out that the enemy was in Mukiš at least for a while, and that this enemy was strong enough to threaten Ugarit, and possibly Karkamiš as well. It is uncertain if all the letters describe one event, and if they do, whether it is dated to the final days of Ugarit, or earlier. If the enemy was in Mukiš, then this enemy's offensive may have been responsible for the destruction of Level IIB^F or of Level IA^F. Once the threat was removed, the Hittite stronghold could be rebuilt—explaining at least one of the Hittite-period reconstructions at Alalakh. As described above, the final phases of the Hittite stronghold are heavily robbed, probably by the builders of Iron Age Tell Ta'yinat.

The end of Level IIB^F marks also the end of the Levels III–II^W fort/IVB^W palace. A new building, Level I^W house 38/B, is built southwest of the fort, and clearly covers parts of it (Plan 7; Woolley 1955: 196–198). This building is probably more modest than the previous residence of the governor, but it is the best-planned "private house" in Alalakh, and must have functioned as an important administrative building. Only the west wing of the Level I^W house 38/B is preserved—its actual area could have been as much as three times what we currently know of this building. Nevertheless, Alalakh is now just a small military post. The small shrines and the Level I^W house 38/B replace larger temples and the fort/palace.

The Level I^W house 38/B is contemporary with the Paluwa shrine (in Level IA^F) and with the Level 0^W temple (in Level IB^F); both were discussed above. These three buildings are the only buildings of Level I[F]. All other remnants of walls that Woolley assigned to Levels I–0[W] (Plans 7, 58) are later than Level I[F], and are probably related to the considerable list of unstratified artifacts of post LBA periods found at Tell Atchana (Woolley 1955: 399, n. 4).

Level I[W] house 38/B

The Level I[W] house 38/B is a well-planned building, regularly laid out, with solid walls and no stone foundations (ibid.: 197). Woolley originally dated it to an early sub-phase of Level I[W] due to several later walls (squares R9 and R10) that cancel it (Plan 58; ibid.: 196), and which he assigned to Level I[W] or 0[W]. As I mentioned above, there is no necessity to date these walls to the LBA or to Iron Age I; therefore there is no reason why the Level I[W] house 38/B should date as early as Level IA[W]. Woolley's additional incentive to give it an early date is a grave (ATG/38/6; Woolley 1955: 205), dug into room 2 in square P10.[32] I have already discussed the finds in this grave, which include three intact Mycenaean globular flasks of vertical type (ATP/38/5, 6, 7; ibid.: Pl. CXXVIIc–e) and other Mycenaean pottery, actually found on the floors of the house. This pottery was recorded by Woolley as LH IIIB (1955: 196–197); it included another globular flask of vertical type (ATP/38/8) in room 2, a piriform jar on the

---

[32] This is ATG/38/6 and not ATG/38/5 (both described in Woolley 1955: 205) as claimed by Collon (1982: 73).

floor of room 1 (*bugelkanne* ATP/38/226), and unnumbered Mycenaean sherds in room 4. I note in Section 5.1 that Mountjoy ends the manufacture of this vertical type of globular flask (probably *FS 189*) in LH IIIA:2 (1986: 81, 108; 1993: 77; Leonard 1994: no. 1279–1281, 1306). I think we must consider the possibility that these items date to late in the thirteenth century, or that they are those heirlooms, still in circulation or dug or exposed somewhere in the latest phase of the large abandoned site. As we have seen, Woolley's interpretation of the stratigraphy of Level I[W] house 38/B may be inaccurate.

Other than the Mycenaean pottery, Woolley reports that he found local pottery and a rough basalt bowl in room 1, a piece of bronze scale armor (AT/38/137) in room 4, several local ware vessels in room 13 and a horseshoe-shaped ingot of copper in room 14, along with some local pottery.

Two additional graves were dug into the floors of Level I[W] house 38/B: ATG/38/5 in room 5, and ATG/38/10 in room 13 (Plan 7; Woolley 1955: 205). In ATG/38/5 two cylinder seals were found (AT/38/127a–b); both are identified by Collon (1982: 73, 114–115) as post-Mittanian seals of the late-fourteenth or even thirteenth century B.C.E. This date does not contradict my date of the Level I[W] house 38/B, especially since many cylinder seals are heirlooms. Noticeably, these seals are among the few latest cylinder seals found in Alalakh.

Chapter Six

Conclusions: Alalakh in the 15ᵗʰ–12ᵗʰ Centuries

In this study I rearranged the stratigraphy of LBA Tell Atchana following published and unpublished records. This rearrangement allowed me to reexamine the material culture and the historical records of LBA Alalakh. Although my work concentrates in Levels IV–0ᵂ it has important implications for the understanding of Tell Atchana from Level VIIᵂ on, and for any study of the excavations of Sir Leonard Woolley at the site. I consider and hopefully have contributed to various branches of learning with this study, including the Mesopotamian chronology of the second millennium B.C.E.; the statue and inscription of Idrimi and its historical background; Hittite policy and administration in the northern Levant; the history of the kingdom of Mukiš; the development of the city plan of Alalakh; the date of Nuzi ware; the contribution of the Amuq surveys to the study of Mukiš and its limitations; and the uniqueness of the Mycenaean pottery of Tell Atchana.

As we have seen, according to my new layout, many of the major buildings at Tell Atchana have been re-analyzed and re-dated, and are contemporaneous with different structures than they were before. As I see it, the main results and implications of my approach are as follows:

1) Levels VIᵂ and VAᶠ are thin layers that carry fewer structures than previously assumed.
2) The Level VBᶠ fortress is the palace of king Idrimi. This building functioned as the main palace during Levels VB-IVAᶠ, and was destroyed together with Level IVAᶠ in 1420–1400 B.C.E.
3) The Niqmepa and Ilimilimma palaces are in fact the later wings of the Levels VB-IVAᶠ palace.
4) All Level IVᵂ/IVAᶠ buildings were obliterated in one event.
5) Levels III-IIᵂ are in effect the city of Level IVBᶠ, when Alalakh was a Mittanian vassal, during the first half of the fourteenth century B.C.E. The city of Level IVBᶠ was conquered by Šuppiluliuma I in 1353/1341 B.C.E.

6) The Levels III-IIᵂ fort together with the Level IIᵂ temple and most of the Level Iᵂ private houses constitute Level IIIᶠ, which is the final stage of Alalakh as a city, and the only phase in which Alalakh functioned as a city under Hittite rule.
7) Alalakh ceased to exist as a city late in the fourteenth century B.C.E. (1320/1313). A Hittite stronghold replaced the city and occupied just a small part of the site.
8) The main structures of the Hittite stronghold were rebuilt several times: the temples thrice, the governor's palace at least once.

In view of recent comprehensive studies of the history, social structure and culture of Level IVᵂ/IVAᶠ (von Dassow 2008; Niedorf 2008), this substantial subject was only briefly discussed in my study. However, I examined thoroughly all the post-Level IVᵂ/IVAᶠ records relevant to Alalakh and Mukiš, originating in Tell Atchana and elsewhere. The following points are among the historical milestones, which are presented in this study:

1) The finds and the texts from Alalakh can be harmonized with the Mesopotamian ultra-low chronology. Nonetheless, they do not necessarily contradict the higher chronologies (at least up to the middle chronology).
2) I propose that the inscription on the statue of Idrimi dates to Level IVBᶠ. Addu-Nīrārī, son (?) of Idrimi, was the first king of Level IVBᶠ. Itūr-Addu was the last king of this level. Among the records of this period one may include a Hittite treaty with Mukiš (KBo 13.55 = CTH 136), Tudḫaliya II's campaign to Mt. Nanni, the Hurrian text from Kayalıpınar and the ritual texts of Allaituraḫḫi of Mukiš and Giziya of Alalakh. Considering these records in conjunction with the rich and significant Level IVBᶠ must drastically change our understanding of Alalakh of the fourteenth century B.C.E.
3) The importance of Level IVBᶠ Alalakh is also manifested in Šuppiluliuma I's well-recorded first

Syrian war. Mukiš led the coalition against the Hittites, and hence, was punished by being divided into two and annexed, partly to the Hittite empire (most likely to Karkamiš) and partly to Ugarit.

4) The chain of events (probably) related to Muršili II's campaigns in the northern Levant ends with the final destruction of Alalakh as a city, not earlier than year 9 of Muršili II (1320/1313). I suggest that the population of the city was deported to the Anatolian heartland as displaced captives (NAM.RA).

5) Alalakh of the thirteenth century B.C.E. is a Hittite stronghold where Hittite officials reside or which they frequent. Among them are Tudḫaliya, Šukur-Tešub and Paluwa, all titled "son of the king" (DUMU. LUGAL). I trace their careers and dates.

6) Alalakh and Mukiš are barely mentioned in the archives of Ugarit. When mentioned, the context is mostly military—the enemy is in Mukiš. Two unpublished letters from the House of Urtenu archive discuss the situation in Alalakh, most probably in the second half of the thirteenth century B.C.E. It is possible that once additional documents of the House of Urtenu archive are published, our understanding of Mukiš of the thirteenth century will be significantly different than it is today.

Excavations resumed at Tell Atchana in summer 2003 and are only minimally referred to in the present study. The final results of these excavations will no doubt affect in various ways the conclusions reached herein.

References

Akkermans, P. M. M. G. and Schwartz, G. M. 2003. *The Archaeology of Syria: From Complex Hunter-Gatherers to Early Urban Societies (ca. 16,000–300 BC)*. Cambridge: Cambridge University Press.

Albright, W. F. 1950. Some Important Recent Discoveries: Alphabetic Origins and the Idrimi Statue. *Bulletin of the American Schools of Oriental Research* 118: 11–20.

Albright, W. F. 1956. Stratigraphic Confirmation of the Low Mesopotamian Chronology. *Bulletin of the American School of Oriental Research* 144: 26–30.

Albright, W. F. 1957. Further Observations on the Chronology of Alalakh. *Bulletin of the American School of Oriental Research* 146: 26–34.

Albright, W. F. 1958. Specimens of Late Ugaritic Prose. *Bulletin of the American School of Oriental Research* 150: 36–38.

Altman, A. 2002. EA 59: 27–29 and the Efforts of Mukiš, Nuḫašše and Niya to Establish a Common Front against Šuppiluliuma I. *Ugarit-Forschungen* 33: 1–25.

Altman, A. 2004. *The Historical Prologue of the Hittite Vassal Treaties: An Inquiry into the Concepts of Hittite Interstate Law*. Ramat Gan: Bar-Ilan University.

Arnaud, D. 1996. Études sur Alalakh et Ougarit à l'âge du bronze récent. *Studi Micenei ed Egeo-Anatolici* 37(1): 47–65.

Arnaud, D. 1999. Prolégomènes à la rédaction d'une histoire d'Ougarit II: Les bordereaux de rois divinisés. *Studi Micenei ed Egeo-Anatolici* 41(2): 153–173.

Aro, J. 1954–1956. Remarks on the Language of the Alalakh Texts. *Archiv für Orientforschungen* 17: 361–365.

Astour, M. C. 1963. Place-Names from the Kingdom of Alalaḫ in the North Syrian List of Thutmose III: A Study in Historical Topography. *Journal of Near Eastern Studies* 22: 220–241.

Astour, M. C. 1965. New Evidence on the Last Days of Ugarit. *American Journal of Archaeology* 69: 255–258.

Astour, M. C. 1969. The Partition of the Confederacy of Mukiš-Nuḫašše-Nii by Šuppiluliuma: A Study in Political Geography of the Amarna Age. *Orientalia* 38: 381–414.

Astour, M. C. 1972. Ḫattušiliš, Ḫalab and Ḫanigalbat. *Journal of Near Eastern Studies* 31: 102–109.

Astour, M. C. 1981. Ugarit and the Great Powers. Pp. 3–29 in *Ugarit in Retrospect*, ed. G. D. Young. Winona Lake, IN: Eisenbrauns.

Astour, M. C. 1989. *Hittite History and Absolute Chronology of the Bronze Age*. Partille: Åström.

Astour, M. C. 1992. An Outline of the History of Ebla (Part 1). Pp. 3–82 in *Eblaitica: Essays on the Ebla Archives and Eblaite Language*, Vol. 3, ed. C. H. Gordon. Winona Lake, IN: Eisenbrauns.

Barnett, R. D. 1955. Bulla Seals with Hittite Hieroglyphic Inscriptions. Pp. 266–267 in *Alalakh: An Account of the Excavations at Tell Atchana in the Hatay, 1937–1949*, ed. L. Woolley. Oxford: The Society of Antiquaries.

145

Batiuk, S. and Burke, A. A. 2005. The Tell Atchana Mapping and GIS Project. Pp. 145–152 in *The Amuq Valley Regional Project*. Vol. 1. *Surveys in the Plain of Antioch and Orontes Delta, Turkey, 1995–2002*, ed. K. A. Yener. Chicago: Oriental Institute Publications.

Beal, R. H. 1992. *The Organization of the Hittite Military*. Heidelberg: Carl Winter.

Beal, R. H. 2000. The Ten Year Annals of Great King Muršili II of Hatti. Pp. 82–90 in *Context of Scripture*, vol. 2, ed. W. W. Hallo. Leiden: Brill.

Beckman, G. M. 1992. Hittite Administration in Syria in the Light of the Texts from Ḫattuša, Ugarit and Emar. Pp. 41–49 in *New Horizons in the Study of Ancient Syria*, eds. M. W. Chavalas and J. L. Hayes. Malibu: Undena.

Beckman, G. 1995. Hittite Provincial Administration in Anatolia and Syria: The View from Maşat and Emar. Pp. 19–37 in *Atti del II congresso internazionale di hittitologia*, eds. O. Carruba, M. Giorgieri and C. Mora. Pavia: Gianni Iuculano.

Beckman, G. 1999. *Hittite Diplomatic Texts*. Atlanta: Scholars.

Beckman, G. 2000. Hittite Chronology. *Akkadica* 119–120: 19–32.

Beckman, G. 2003. International Law in the Second Millennium: Late Bronze Age. Pp. 753–774 in *A History of Ancient Near Eastern Law*, vol. 1, ed. R. Westbrook. Leiden: Brill.

Beckman, G. 2007. Ugarit and Inner Syria during the Late Bronze Age. Pp. 163–174 in *Le royaume d'Ougarit de la Crète à l'Euphrate: Nouveaux axes de recherche*, ed. J.-M. Michaud. Sherbrooke: Éditions GGC.

Ben-Tor, A. 2004. Hazor and Chronology. *Ägypten und Levante* 14: 45–68.

Beran, T. 1957. Siegel und Siegelabdrücke. Pp. 42–58 in *Boğazköy III: Funde aus den Grabungen 1952–1955*, eds. R. Naumann, T. Beran, R. Hachmann and G. Kurth. Berlin: Mann.

Bergoffen, C. J. 2003. The Cypriot Pottery from Alalakh: Chronological Considerations. Pp. 395–410 in *The Synchronisation of Civilisations in the Eastern Mediterranean in the Second Millennium B.C.: vol. 2. Proceedings of the SCIEM 2000 — EuroConference, Haindorf, 2nd of May — 7th of May 2001*, ed. M. Bietak. Wien: Der Österreichischen Akademie der Wissenschaften.

Bergoffen, C. J. 2005. *The Cypriot Bronze Age Pottery from Sir Leonard Woolley's Excavations at Alalakh (Tell Atchana)*. Wien: Der Österreichischen Akademie der Wissenschaften.

Bevan, A. 2007. *Stone Vessels and Values in the Bronze Age Mediterranean*. Cambridge: Cambridge University Press.

Bienkowski, P. A. 1982. Some Remarks on the Practice of Cremation in the Levant. *Levant* 14: 80–89.

Bonatz, D. 2000. Syro-Hittite Funerary Monuments: A Phenomenon of Tradition or Innovation? Pp. 189–210 in *Essays on Syria in the Iron Age*, ed. G. Bunnens. Louvain: Peeters.

Bordreuil, P. 1989a. À propos de la topographie économique de l'Ougarit: jardins du midi et pâturages du nord. *Syria* 56: 263–274.

Bordreuil, P. 1989b. La citadelle sainte du Mont Nanou. *Syria* 56: 275–279.

Boutin, A. T. 2008. *Embodying Life and Death: Osteobiographical Narratives from Alalakh*. Unpublished Ph.D. Dissertation, University of Pennsylvania. Philadelphia.

Braidwood, R. J. 1937. *Mounds in the Plain of Antioch: An Archeological Survey*. Chicago: The University of Chicago.

Braidwood, R. J. and Braidwood, L. S. 1960. *Excavations in the Plain of Antioch I: the Earlier Assemblages, Phases A–J*. Chicago: The University of Chicago.

Bretschneider, J. 1997. "Nuzi-Keramik" aus der Unterstadt (Feld J). Pp. 231–243 in *Tell Beydar, Three Seasons of Excavations (1992–1994): A Preliminary Report, Subartu III*. Eds. M. Lebeau and A. Suleiman. Turnhout, Belgium: Brepols.

Bryce, T. 1989. Some Observations on the Chronology of Šuppiluliuma's Reign. *Anatolian Studies* 39: 19–30.

Bryce, T. 1998. *The Kingdom of the Hittites*. New York: Clarendon.

Buccellati, G. 1962. La "carriera" di David e quella di Idrimi, re di Alalac. *Bibbia e Oriente* 4: 95–99.

Buchanan, B. 1967. Five Hittite Hieroglyphic Seals. *Journal of Cuneiform Studies* 21: 18–23.

Bunnens, G. 1987. A Slave for Debt from Alalakh looked for in Ugarit (RS 4.449). *Abr-Nahrain* 25: 13–18.

Bunnens, G. 1994. Was There a Military Officer named *Zukraši* in the Alalakh Texts? *Abr-Nahrain* 32: 96–97.

Busink, T. A. 1970. *Der Tempel von Jerusalem: von Salomo bis Herodes*. Vol.1. Leiden: Brill.

Casana, J. 2003. *From Alalakh to Antioch: Settlement, Land use, and environmental Change in the Amuq Valley of Southern Turkey*. Unpublished Ph.D. Dissertation, University of Chicago. Chicago.

Casana, J. J. 2007. Structural Transformations in Settlement Systems of the Northern Levant. *American Journal of Archaeology* 112: 1–27.

Casana, J. J. 2009. Alalakh and the Archaeological Landscape of Mukish: the Political Geography and Population of a Late Bronze Age Kingdom. *Bulletin of the American School of Oriental Research* 353: 7-37.

Casana, J. J. and Gansell, A. R. 2005. Surface Ceramics, off-Site Survey, and Floodplain Development at Tell Atchana (Alalakh). Pp. 153–168 in *The Amuq Valley Regional Project: Vol. 1. Surveys in the Plain of Antioch and Orontes Delta, Turkey, 1995–2002*, ed. K. A. Yener. Chicago: Oriental Institute Publications.

Casana, J. J. and Wilkinson, T. J. 2005a. Settlement and Landscapes in the Amuq Region. Pp. 25–65 in *The Amuq Valley Regional Project: Vol. 1. Surveys in the Plain of Antioch and Orontes Delta, Turkey, 1995–2002*, ed. K. A. Yener. Chicago: Oriental Institute Publications.

Casana, J. J. and Wilkinson, T. J. 2005b. Appendix A: Gazetteer of Sites. Pp. 203–280 in *The Amuq Valley Regional Project: Vol. 1. Surveys in the Plain of Antioch and Orontes Delta, Turkey, 1995–2002*, ed. K. A. Yener. Chicago: Oriental Institute Publications.

Cecchini, S. M. 1965. *La Ceramica di Nuzi*. Rome: Centro di Studi Semitici.

Cline, E. 1991. A Possible Hittite Embargo against the Mycenaeans. *Historia* 40: 1–9.

Cohen, Y. and d'Alfonso, L. 2008. The Duration of the Emar Archives and the Relative and Absolute Chronology of the City. Pp. 3–25 in *The City of Emar among the Late Bronze Age Empires. History, Landscape, and Society: Proceedings of the Konstanz Emar Conference, 25.–26.04. 2006*, eds. L. d'Alfonso, Y. Cohen and D. Sürenhagen. Münster: Ugarit Verlag.

Collon, D. 1975. *The Seal Impressions from Tell Atchana/Alalakh*. Kevelaer: Butzon und Bercker; Neukirchen-Vluyn: Neukirchen Verlag.

Collon, D. 1977. A New Look at the Chronology of Alalakh Level VII: A Rejoinder. *Anatolian Studies* 27: 127–131.

Collon, D. 1982. *The Alalakh Cylinder Seals: A New Catalogue of the Actual Seals Excavated by Sir Leonard Woolley at Tell Atchana, and from Neighbouring Sites on the Syrian-Turkish Border*. Oxford: British Archaeological Reports.

Crowley, J. L. 1989. *The Aegean and the East: An Investigation into the Transference of Artistic Motifs between the Aegean, Egypt, and the Near East in the Bronze Age*. Jonsered: Paul Astroms.

Cunchillos, J. –L. 1989. *Correspondance: Introduction, traduction, commentaire*. Paris: Cerf.

Dalix, A. –S. 1998. Šuppiluliuma (II?) dans un texte alphabétique d'Ougarit et la date d'apparition de l'alphabet cunéiforme. *Semitica* 48: 5–15.

del Olmo Lete, G. and Sanmartín, J. 1996. *Diccinaro de la lengua Ugarítica*. Barcelona: Ausa.

Devecchi, E. 2007. A Fragment of a Treaty with Mukiš. *Studi Micenei ed Egeo-Anatolici* 49(1): 207–216.

Dever, W. G. 1992. The Chronology of Syria-Palestine in the Second Millennium B.C.E.: A Review of Current Issues. *Bulletin of the American School of Oriental Research* 288: 1–25.

Dietrich, M. and Loretz, O. 1965. Der Vertrag zwischen Šupiluliuma und Niqmandu: Eine philologische und kulturhistorische Studie. *Die Welt des Orients* 3: 206–245.

Dietrich, M. and Loretz, O. 1981. Die Inschrift der Statue des Königs Idrimi von Alalaḫ. *Ugarit-Forschungen* 13: 201–268.

Dijkstra, M. 1987. Marginalia to the Ugaritic Letters in KTU (I). *Ugarit-Forschungen* 19: 37–48.

Dijkstra, M. 1991. The Weather-God on Two Mountains. *Ugarit-Forschungen* 23: 127–140.

Divon, Sh. A. 2008. A Survey of the Textual Evidence for "Food Shortage" from the Late Hittite Empire. Pp. 101–109 in *The City of Emar among the Late Bronze Age Empires. History,*

Landscape, and Society: Proceedings of the Konstanz Emar Conference, 25.–26.04. 2006, eds. L. d'Alfonso, Y. Cohen and D. Sürenhagen. Münster: Ugarit Verlag.

Dussaud, R. 1950. Review of *The Statue of Idri-mi,* by Sidney Smith. *Syria* 27: 157–160.

Dussaud, R. 1951. L'autobiographie d'Idrimi. *Syria* 28: 350–351.

Eder, Ch. 2003. Die Datierung des Spätaltbabylonischen Alalaḫ. Pp. 227–289 in *Altertumswissenschaften im Dialog: Festschrift für Wolfram Nagel zur Vollendung seines 80. Lebensjahres,* eds. R. Dittmann, Ch. Eder and B. Jacobs. Münster: Ugarit-verlag.

Eder, Ch. 2004. Assyrische Distanzangaben und die absolute Chronologie Vorderasiens. *Altorientalische Forschungen* 31: 191–236.

Eriksson, K. O. 1992. Late Cypriot I and Thera: Relative Chronology in the Eastern Mediterranean. Pp. 152–221 in *Acta Cypria: Act of an International Congress on Cypriote Archaeology in Göteborg on 22–24 August 1991,* Part 3, ed. P. Åström. Jonsered: Åström.

Evans, A. 1936. Some Notes of the Tal Atchana Pottery. *The Journal of Hellenic Studies* 56: 133–134.

Fink, A. S. 2006. "The Historical Prologue in a Letter from Šuppululiuma II to ʿAmmurapi' king of Ugarit (RS 18.038)." Pp. 673-688 in *"I Will Speak the Riddles of Ancient Times:" Archaeological and Historical Studies in Honor of Amihai Mazar on the Occasion of his Sixtieth Birthday,* eds. Aren M. Maeir and Pierre de Miroschedji. Winona Lake, IN: Eisenbrauns.

Fink, A. S. 2008a. Levantine Standardized Luxury in the Late Bronze Age: Waste Management at Tell Atchana (Alalakh). Pp. 165–196 in *Bene Israel: Studies in the Archaeology of Israel and the Levant during the Bronze and Iron Ages in Honour of Israel Finkelstein,* eds. A. Fantalkin and A. Yasur-Landau. Leiden: Brill.

Fink, A. S. 2008b. Where was the Statue of Idrimi Actually Found? The Later Temples of Tell Atchana (Alalakh) Revisited, *Ugarit-Forschungen* 39: 162–245.

Frankfort, H. 1956. *The Art and Architecture of the Ancient Orient.* London: Penguin.

Freu, J. 2001. De l'indépendance à l'annexion: le Kizzuwatna et le Hatti aux XVIᵉ et XVᵉ siècle avant notre èra. Pp. 13–36 in *La Cilicie: Espaces et pouvoirs locaux. Actes de la Table ronde internationale d'Istanbul,* 2–5 novembre 1999, eds. É. Jean, A. M. Dinçol, and S. Durugönül. Istanbul: De Boccard.

Freu, J. 2006. *Histoire politique du royaume d'Ugarit.* Paris: L'Harmattan.

Freu, J. 2008. Note sur les sceaux des rois de Mitanni/Mittani. *N.A.B.U.* 2008/1 (Mars): 5–9.

Gasche, H., Armstrong, J. A., Cole, S. W. and V. G. Gurzadyan. 1998a. *Dating the Fall of Babylon: A Reappraisal of Second-Millennium Chronology.* Ghent and Chicago: University of Ghent and the Oriental Institute of the University of Chicago.

Gasche, H., Armstrong, J. A., Cole, S. W. and V. G. Gurzadyan. 1998b. A Correction to "Dating the Fall of Babylon: A Reappraisal of Second-Millennium Chronology (=MHEM 4), Ghent and Chicago, 1998." *Akkadica* 108: 1–4.

Gates, M. -H. C. 1976. *Alalakh—Tell Atchana, Levels VI and V: A Re-examination of a Mid-Second Millennium B.C. Syrian City.* Unpublished Ph.D. Dissertation, Yale University. New Haven.

Gates, M. -H. 1981. Alalakh Levels VI and V: A Chronological Reassessment. *Syro-Mesopotamian Studies* 4(2): 1–50.

Gates, M. -H. 1987. Alalakh and Chronology Again. Pp. 60–86 in *High, Middle or Low? Acts of an International Colloquium on Absolute Chronology Held at the University of Gothenburg 20th –22nd August 1987,* Part 2, ed. P. Åström. Gothenburg: Åström.

Gates, M. -H. 1989. Alalakh and Chronology Again: discussion. Pp. 67–73 in *High, Middle or Low? Acts of an International Colloquium on Absolute Chronology Held at the University of Gothenburg 20th –22nd August 1987,* Part 3, ed. P. Åström. Gothenburg: Åström.

Gates, M. -H. 2000. Kinet Höyük (Hatay, Turkey) and MB Levantine Chronology. *Akkadica* 119–120: 77–101.

Genz, H. 2006. Hethitische Präsenz im spätbronzezeitlichen Syrien: Die archäologische Evidenz. *Baghdader Mitteilungen* 37: 499–509.

Gerritsen, F., De Giorgi, A., Eger, A., Özbal, R. and T. Vorderstrasse. 2008. Settlement and Landscape Transformations in the Amuq Valley, Hatay. A Long-Term Perspective. *Anatolica* 34: 241–314.

Giles, F. J. 1995. The Relative Chronology of the Hittite Conquest of Syria and Aitakama of Qadesh. Pp.137–148 in *Trade, Contact, and the Movement of Peoples in the Eastern Mediterranean: Studies in Honour of J. Basil Hennessy*, eds. S. Bourke and J. –P. Descœdres. Sydney: Meditarch.

Goetze, A. 1940. *Kizzuwatna and the Problem of Hittite Geography*. New Haven: Yale University Press.

Goetze, A. 1950. Review of *The Statue of Idri-mi*, by Sidney Smith. *Journal of Cuneiform Studies* 4: 226–231.

Goetze, A. 1957a. Alalaḫ and Hittite Chronology. *Bulletin of the American School of Oriental Research* 146: 20–26.

Goetze, A. 1957b. On the Chronology of the Second Millennium B.C. *Journal of Cuneiform Studies* 11: 53–73.

Goetze, A. 1959. Remarks on the Lists from Alalakh IV. *Journal of Cuneiform Studies* 13: 63–64.

Görke, S. 2007. Religious Interaction between Ḫattuša and northern Syria. Pp. 239–248 in *Moving Across Borders: Foreign Relations, Religion and Cultural Interactions in the Ancient Mediterranean*, eds. P. Kousoulis and K. Magliveras. Leuven: Peeters

Greenstein, E. L. 1995. Autobiographies in Ancient Western Asia. Pp. 2421–2432 in *Civilizations of the Ancient Near East*. Vol. 4, ed. J. M. Sasson. New York: Scribner.

Greenstein, E. L. and Marcus, D. 1976. The Akkadian Inscription of Idrimi. *The Journal of the Ancient Near Eastern Society of Columbia University* 8: 59–96.

Gurney, O. R. 1953. Hittite Incantation. Pp. 116–118 in *The Alalakh Tablets*, ed. D. J. Wiseman. London: The British Institute of Archaeology at Ankara.

Gurzadyan, V. G. 2000. On the Astronomical Records and Babylonian Chronology. *Akkadica* 119–120: 177–186.

Güterbock, H. G. 1954. Carchemish. *Journal of Near Eastern Studies* 13(2): 102–114.

Güterbock, H. G. 1956. The Deeds of Supiluliuma as Told by his Son, Mursili II. *Journal of Cuneiform Studies* 10: 41–68, 75–98, 107–130.

Güterbock, H. G. 1986. Hittite Historiography: A Survey. Pp. 21–35 in *History, Historiography and Interpretation: Studies in Biblical and Cuneiform Literatures*, eds. H. Tadmor and M. Weinfeld. Jerusalem: Magnes.

Haas, V. 2007. Nitizen zu den Ritualen der Frau Allaituraḫi aus Mukiš. *Altorientalische Forschungen* 34: 9–36.

Haas, V. and Wegner, I. 1988. *Die Rituale der Beschwörerinnen* ^{SAL}*ŠU.GI*, vol. 1. Roma: Multigrafica.

Haase, R. 2003. The Hittite Kingdom. Pp. 619–656 in *A History of Ancient Near Eastern Law*, vol. 1, ed. R. Westbrook. Leiden: Brill.

Hagenbuchner, A. 1989. *Die Korrespondentz der Hethiter*. Vol. 2. Heidelberg: Carl Winter.

Haines, R. C. 1971. *Excavations in the Plain of Antioch*. Vol. 2. *The Structural Remains of the Later Phases: Chatal Hüyük, Tell al-Judaidah, and Tell Taʿyinat*. Chicago: Oriental Institute Publications.

Harrison, T. P. 2007. Neo-Hittites in the North Orontes Valley: Recent Investigations at Tell Tayinat. *Journal of the Canadian Society for Mesopotamian Studies* 2: 59–68.

Harrison, T. P. 2009. Lifting the Veil on a "Dark Age": Taʿyinat and the North Orontes Valley During the Early Iron Age. Pp. 171–184 in *Exploring the Longue Durée: Essays in Honor of Lawrence E. Stager*, ed. J. D. Schloen. Winona Lake, IN: Eisenbrauns.

Hawkins, D. 1995. "Great Kings" and "Country-Lords" at Malatya and Karkamiš. Pp. 73–85 in *Studio Historiae Ardens: Ancient Near Eastern Studies Presented to Philo H.J. Houwink ten Cate on the Occasion of His 65ᵗʰ Birthday*, eds. T.P.J. van den Hout and J. de Roos. Istanbul: Nederlands Historisch-Archeologisch Instituut te Istanbul.

Hawkins, D. 2005. Commentaries on the Readings. Part 3: Titles and Professions. Pp. 300–314 in *Die Prinzen- und Beamtensiegel der Hethitischen Grossreichszeit auf Tonbullen aus dem Nişantepe-Archivin Hattusa*, S. Herbordt. Mainz am Rhein: Philipp von Zabern.

Healey, J. 2007. From Ṣapānu/Ṣapunu to Kasion: The Sacred History of a Mountain. Pp. 141–151 in *"He unfurrowed his Brow and laughed": Essays in Honour of Professor Nicolas Wyatt*, ed.

W. G. E. Watson. Münster: Ugarit-Verlag.

Heinz, M. 1992. *Tell Atchana / Alalakh: Die Schichten VII–XVII*. Kevelaer: Butzon und Bercker; Neukirchen-Vluyn: Neukirchen Verlag.

Heinz, M. 1993. Anmerkung zu T. McClellan, "The Chronology of Ceramic Assemblages of Alalakh." *Akkadica* 83: 1–28.

Herbordt, S. 2005. *Die Prinzen- und Beamtensiegel der Hethitischen Grossreichszeit auf Tonbullen aus dem Nişantepe-Archivin Hattusa*. Mainz am Rhein: Philipp von Zabern.

Hoffner, H. A. 1997. Deeds of Šuppiluliuma. Pp. 185–192 in *Context of Scripture*, vol. 1, ed. W. W. Hallo. Leiden: Brill.

Hoffner, H. A. 2002. The Treatment and Long-Term Use of Persons Captured in Battle according to the Maşat Texts. Pp. 61–72 in *Recent Development in Hittite Archaeology and History: Papers in Memory of Hans G. Güterbock*, eds. K. A. Yener and H. A. Hoffner. Winona Lake, IN: Eisenbrauns.

Hrouda, B. 1957. *Die bemalte Keramik des zweiten Jahrtausends in Nordmesopotamien und Nordsyrien*. Berlin: Gebr. Mann

Huber, P. J. 2000. Astronomy and Ancient Chronology. *Akkadica* 119–120: 159–176.

Kantor, H. J. 1945. *Plant Ornament: Its Origin and Development in the Ancient Near East*. Unpublished Ph.D. Dissertation, University of Chicago. Chicago.

Kantor, H. J. 1955. Syro-Palestinian Ivories. *Journal of Near Eastern Studies* 15: 153–174.

Kempinski, A. 1983. *Syrien und Palästina (Kanaan) in der letzten Phase der Mittelbronze IIB-Zeit (1650–1570 V. Chr.)*. Wiesbaden: Otto Harrassowitz.

Kempinski, A. 1993. Supiluliuma I: The Early Years of his Career. Pp. 81–91 in *kinattūtu ša dārâti: Raphael Kutscher Memorial Volume*, ed. A. F. Rainey. Tel Aviv: Tel-Aviv University.

Kitchen, K. A. 1982. An Egyptian New Kingdom Scarab from Alalakh. *Levant* 14: 88.

Klengel, H. 1975. Neue Quellen zur Gescichte Nordsyriens im 2. Jahrtausend v. u. Z. *Altorientalische Forschungen* 2: 47–64.

Klengel, H. 1981. Historischer Kommentar zur Inschrift des Idrimi von Alalaḫ. *Ugarit-Forschungen* 13: 269–278.

Klengel, H. 1992. *Syria, 3000 to 300 B.C.: A Handbook of Political History*. Berlin: Akademie.

Klengel, H. 1995. Mukiš. *Reallexikon der Assyriologie* 8(5/6): 411–412.

Knoppers, G. N. 1993. Treaty, Tribute List, or Diplomatic Letter: KTU 3.1 Reexamined. *Bulletin of the American School of Oriental Research* 289: 81–94.

Koehl, R. B. 2005a. Preliminary Observations on the Unpublished Mycenaean Pottery from Woolley's Dig-House at Tell Atchana (Ancient Alalakh). *Aegaeum* 25(1): 415–421.

Koehl, R. B. 2005b. Observations on the Unpublished Mycenaean Pottery from Tell Atchana (Ancient Alalakh). A paper presented at the AIA meeting, Boston MA., January 2005.

Kühne, C. 1982. Politische Szenerie und internationale Beziehungen Vorderasiens um die Mitte des 2. Jahrtausends vor Chr. (zugleich ein Konzept der Kurzchronologie) mit einer Zeittafel. Pp. 203–264 in *Mesopotamien und seine Nachbarn: Politische und kulturelle Wechselbeziehungen im Alten Orient 4. bis 1. Jahrtausend v. Chr.*, ed. H. –J. Nissen. Berlin: Reimer.

Kuniholm, P. I., Newton, M. W., Griggs C. B., and P. J. Sullivan. 2005. Dendrochronological Dating in Anatolia: The Second Millennium B.C. *Der Anschnitt*, Anatolian Metal III, Supplement 18: 41–47.

Lackenbacher, S. 2002. *Textes akkadiens d'Ugarit: textes provenant des vingt-cinq premières campagnes*. Paris: Cerf.

Lackenbacher, S. and Malbran-Labat, F. 2005. Ugarite et les Hittites dans les archives de la "Maison d'Urtenu." *Studi Micenei ed Egeo-Anatolici* 47: 227–240.

Landsberger, B. 1954. Assyrische Königsliste und 'Dunkles Zeitalter': Mitanni. *Journal of Cuneiform Studies* 8: 47–61.

Laroche, E. 1960. *Les hiérolyphes Hittites I: L'écriture*. Paris: CNRS.

Laroche, E. 1966. *Les noms des Hittites*. Paris: Klincksieck.

Lauinger, J. 2005. Epigraphic Finds from the Oriental Institute's 2003 Excavations at Alalakh. *Journal of Near Eastern Studies* 64(1): 53–58.

Lauinger, J. 2008. The Temple of Ištar at Old Babylonian Alalakh. *Journal of Ancient Near Eastern Religions* 8(2):181–217.

Lebrun, R. 2001. Propos concernant Urikina, Ussa et Uda. Pp. 326-332 in *Akten des IV. Internationalen Kongresses für Hethitologie, Würzburg, 4.–8. Oktober 1999*, ed. G. Wilhelm. Wiesbaden: Harrassowitz.

Legrain, L. 1951. Review of *The Statue of Idri-Mi*, by Sidney Smith. *American Journal of Archaeology* 55(1): 105–106.

Leonard, A. 1994. *An Index to the Late Bronze Age Aegean Pottery from Syria-Palestine*. Åström: Jonsered.

Lipiński, E. 1981. Aḫat-Milki, reine d'Ugarit, et la guerre du Mukiš. *Orientalia Lovaniensia Periodica* 12: 79–115.

Liverani, M. 2004. *Myth and Politics in Ancient Near Eastern Historiography*. Ithaca: Cornell University Press.

Longman, T. III. 1991. *Fictional Akkadian Autobiography: A Generic and Comparative Study*. Winona Lake: Eisenbrauns.

Malbran-Labat, F. 1991. Letters. Pp. 27–64 in *Une bibliothèque au sud de la ville (Ras Shamra-Ougarit VII)*, ed. P. Bordreuil. Paris: Éditions Recherche sur les Civilisations.

Malbran-Labat, F. 1995. La découverte épigraphique de 1994 à Ougarit (les textes Akkadiens). *Studi Micenei ed Egeo-Anatolici* 36: 103–111.

Malbran-Labat, F. 2008. Catalogue raisonné des textes akkadiens de la "Maison d'Urtēnu." Pp. 21-38 in *D'Ougarit à Jérusalem: Recueil d'études épigraphiques et archéologiques offert à Pierre Bordreuil*, ed. C. Roche. Paris: De Boccard.

Mallowan, M. E. L. 1939. White-Painted Subartu Pottery. Pp. 887–894 in *Mélanges Syriens offerts à Monsieur René Dussaud*. Paris: Paul Geuthner.

Manning, S.W. 1999. *A Test of Time: The Volcano of Thera and the Chronology and History of the Aegean and East Mediterranean in the Mid Second Millennium BC*. Oxford and Oakville: Oxbow Books.

Manning, S.W., Kromer, B., Kuniholm, P.I. and M.W. Newton. 2001. Anatolian Tree Rings and a New Chronology for the East Mediterranean Bronze-Iron Ages. *Science* 294, no. 5551: 2532.

Manning, S.W., Kromer, B., Kuniholm, P.I. and M.W. Newton. 2003. Confirmation of Near-Absolute Dating of East Mediterranean Bronze-Iron Dendrochronology. *Antiquity* 77, no. 295: Project Gallery (http://antiquity.ac.il).

Marchetti, N. and Nigro, L. 1993. Una ricostruzione alternative del dispositivo di ingresso nel Palazzo di Niqmepa ad Alalakh. *Orient Express* 1993/2: 25–26.

Margueron, J. -C. 1975. Quatre campagnes de fouilles à Emar (1972–1974). Un bilan provisoire. *Syria* 52:53–85.

Márquez Rowe, I. 1997. Ḥalab in the XVIth and XVth Centuries B.C.: A New Look at the Alalah Material. *Wiener Zeitschrift für die Kunde des Morgenlandes* 87: 179–205.

Masson, E. 1975, Quelques sceaux Hittites hiéroglyphiques. *Syria* 52: 213–237.

Matthiae, P. 1975. Unité et développement du temple dans la Syrie du Bronze Moyen. Pp. 43–72 in *Le temple et le culte: compte rendu de la vingtième rencontre assyriologique internationale organisée à Leiden du 3 au 7 juillet 1972 sous les auspices du Nederlands Instituut voor het Nabije Oosten*. Istambul: Nederlands Historisch-Archeologisch Instituut te Istambul.

Matthiae, P. 2000. A Statue Base from the Western Palace of Ebla and the Continuity of the Old Syrian Artistic Tradition. Pp. 385–402 in *Variatio Delectat: Iran und der Westen. Gedenkschrift für Peter Calmeyer*, eds. R. Dittmann, U. Löw, R. Mayer-Opificius, B. Hrouda, P. Matthiae and S. Thürwächter. Münster: Ugarit-Verlag.

Mattingly, H. 1939. A Byzantine Hoard from Tel Atchana, North Syria. *The Numismatic Chronicle and Journal of the Royal Numismatic Society* 5th series 19: 179–180.

Mayer, W. 1995. Die historische Einordnung der 'Autobiographie' des Idrimi von Alalaḫ. *Ugarit-Forschungen* 27: 333–350.

Mayer-Opificius, R. 1981. Archäologischer Kommentar zur Statue des Idrimi von Alalakh. *Ugarit-Forschungen* 13: 279–290.

Mayer-Opificius, R. 1983. Rekonstruktion des Thrones des Fürsten Idrimi von Alalakh. *Ugarit-*

Forschungen 15: 119–126.

Mazzoni, S. 2000. Crisis and Change: The Beginning of the Iron Age in Syria. Pp. 1043–1055 in *Proceedings of the First International Congress on the Archaeology of the Ancient Near East. Rome, May 18th–23rd 1998*, Vol. 2, eds. P. Matthiae, A. Enea, L. Peyronel and F. Pinnock. Rome: La Sapienza.

Mazzoni, S. 2002. Late Bronze Age Pottery Production in Northwestern Central Syria. Pp. 129–151 in *Céramique de l'Âge du Bronze en Syrie*, Volume 1, eds. M. al-Maqdissi, V. Matoïan and Ch. Nicolle. Beyrouth: Institut Français d'Archéologie du Proche-Orient.

McClellan, Th. L. 1989. The Chronology of Ceramic Assemblages of Alalakh. Pp. 181–212 in *Essays in Ancient Civilization Presented to Helene J. Kantor*, eds. A. Leonards and B. B. Williams. Chicago, IL: The Oriental Institute of the University of Chicago.

McClellan, Th. L. 1997. Houses and Households in North Syria. Pp. 30–59 in *Les maisons dans la Syrie antique du IIIe millénaire aux débuts de l'Islam: pratique et représentations de l'espace domestique: actes du Colloque International, Damas 27–30 juin 1992*, eds. C. Castel, M. al-Maqdissi and F. Villeneuve. Beyrouth: Institut Français d'Archéologie du Proche-Orient.

McEwan, C. W. 1937. The Syrian Expedition of the Oriental Institute of the University of Chicago. *American Journal of Archaeology* 41: 8–16.

Mellink, M. J. 1957. Review of *Alalakh: An Account of the Excavations at Tell Atchana in the Hatay, 1937–1949*, by Leonard Woolley. *American Journal of Archaeology* 61(4): 395–400.

Merhav, R. 1985. The Stele of the "Serpent Goddess" from Tell Beit Mirsim and the Plaque from Shechem Reconsidered. *The Israel Museum Journal* 4: 27–42.

Meriggi, P. 1975. *Manuale di Eteo geroglifico: parte II: test 2ª e 3ª serie*. Roma: dell'Ateneo.

Meyer, J. -W. 2008. *Die eisenzeitlichen Stempelsiegel aus dem 'Amuq-Gebiet: Ein Beitrag zur Ikonographie altorientalischer Siegelbilder*. Friburg: Academic Press.

Miller, J. L. 2004. *Studies in the Origins, Development and Interpretation of the Kizzuwatna Rituals*. Wiesbaden: Harrassowitz.

Miller, J. L. 2007a. Muršili II's Dictate to Tuppi-Teššub's Syrian Antagonists. *KASKAL* 4: 121–152.

Miller, J. L. 2007b. Amarna Age Chronology and the Identity of Nibḫururiya in the Light of a Newly Reconstructed Hittite Text. *Altorientalische Forschungen* 34(2): 252–293.

Mineck, K. R. 2006. The Ten Year Annals of Muršili II: Excerpts. Pp. 253–259 in *The Ancient Near East: Historical Sources in Translation*, ed. M. W. Chavalas. Malden, MA: Blackwell.

Mora, C. 1987. *La glittica anatolica del II millennio A.C.: classificazione tipologica*. Pavia: Luculano.

Mora, C. 1988. Halpaziti e Kukulana: indagine sui sigilli ittiti a doppia intestazione. Pp. 159–167 in *Studu di storia e di filologia anatolica dedicate a Giovanni Pugliese Carratelli*, ed. F. Imparati. Firenze: Elite.

Mora, C. 1998. Osservazioni sull'uso del "geroglifico anatolico" in Siria nel II millennio a.C. Pp. 195–218 in *Il Geroglifico Anatolico*, ed. M. Marazzi. Napoli: Istituto Universitario Orientale.

Mora, C. 2004. "Overseers" and "Lords" of the Land in the Hittite Administration. Pp. 477–486 in *Šarnikzel: Hethitologische Studien zum Gedenken an Emil Orgentorix Forrer*, eds. D. Groddek and S. Röble. Dresden: Technische Universität.

Morris, C. E. and Crouwel, J. H. 1985. Mycenaean Pictorial Pottery from Tell Atchana (Alalakh). Annual of the British School in Athens 80: 85–98.

Mountjoy, P. A. 1986. *Mycenaean Decorated Pottery: A Guide to Identification*. Göteborg: Åström.

Mountjoy, P. A. 1993. *Mycenaean Pottery: An Introduction*. Oxford: Oxford.

Muhly, J. D. 1975. Near Eastern Chronology and the Date of the Late Cypriot I Period. Pp. 76–89 in *The Archaeology of Cyprus*, ed. N. Robertson. Park Ridge, NJ: Noyes Press.

Na'aman, N. 1974. Syria at the Transition from the Old Babylonian Period to the Middle Babylonian Period. *Ugarit-Forschungen* 6: 265–272.

Na'aman, N. 1976. A New Look at the Chronology of Alalakh Level VII. *Anatolian Studies* 26: 129–143.

Na'aman, N. 1979. The Chronology of Alalakh Level VII Once Again. *Anatolian Studies* 29: 103–113.

Na'aman, N. 1980. A Royal Scribe and His Scribal Products in the Alalakh IV Court. *Oriens*

Antiquus 19: 107–116.

Na'aman, N. 1996. Ammishtamru's Letter to Akhenaten (EA 45) and Hittite Chronology. *Aula Orientalis* 14: 251–257.

Na'aman, N. and Kempinski, A. 1973. The Idrimi Inscription Reconsidered. Pp. 211–220 in *Excavations and Studies: Essays in Honour of Professor Shemuel Yeivin*, ed. Y. Aharoni. Tel Aviv: Carta (Hebrew).

Naumann, R. 1971. *Architektur Kleinasiens von ihren Anfängen bis zum Ende der hethitischen Zeit*. Tübingen: Wasmuth.

Niedorf, C. F. 1998. Die Toponyme der Texte aus Alalaḫ IV. *Ugarit-Forschungen* 30: 515–568.

Niedorf, C. F. 1999. Noch einmal zu den Toponyme der Texte aus Alalaḫ IV. *Ugarit-Forschungen* 31: 889–893.

Niedorf, C. F. 2002. Ein hethitisches Brieffragment aus Alalaḫ. Pp. 517–526 in *Ex Mesopotamia et Syria Lux: Festschrift für Manfried Dietrich zu seinem 65. Geburstag*, eds. O. Loretz, K. A. Metzler and H. Schaudig. Münster: Ugarit-Verlag.

Niedorf, C. F. 2008. *Die mittelbabylonischen Rechtsurkunden aus Alalaḫ (Schnit IV)*. Münster: Ugarit-Verlag.

Niemeier, W. –D. 1991. Minoan Artisans Traveling Overseas: The Alalakh Frescoes and the Painted Plaster Floor at Tel Kabri (Western Galilee). *Aegaeum* 7: 189–201.

Nigro, L. 2002. The Middle Bronze Age Pottery Horizon of Northern Inner Syria on the Basis of the Stratified Assemblages of Tell Mardikh and Hama. Pp. 97–128 in *Céramique de l'Âge du Bronze en Syrie*, Volume 1, eds. M. al-Maqdissi, V. Matoïan and Ch. Nicolle. Beyrouth: Institut Français d'Archéologie du Proche-Orient.

Nougayrol, J. 1951. Review of The Statue of Idri-mi, by Sidney Smith. *Revue d'Assyriologie et d'archéologie orientale* 45(2): 151–154.

Nougayrol, J. 1956. *Le palais royal d'Ugarit, v. IV*. Paris: Imprimerie Nationale.

Novak, M. 2007. Mittani Empire and the Question of Absolute Chronology: Some Archaeological Considerations. Pp. 389–401 in *The Synchronisation of Civilisations in the Eastern Mediterranean in the Second Millenium B.C.*, Volume III, eds. M. Bietak and E. Czerny. Wien: Der Österreichischen Akademie der Wissenschaften.

Oates, D., Oates, J., and H. McDonald. 1997. *Excavations at Tell Brak, vol. 1: The Mitanni and Old Babylonian Periods*. London: British School of Archaeology in Iraq.

Oesch, J. 1996. Die Religion Alalachs. Pp. 49–64 in *Religionsgeschichte Syriens: Von der Frühzeit bis zur Gegenwart*, eds. P. W. Haider, M. Hutter and S. Kreuzer. Stuttgart, Berlin, Köln: Kohlhammer.

Oliva, J. C. 1999–2000. Alalakh VII Chronographica: Una Revisión del Archivo Sobre la Base de los Textos de Yarim-Lim. *Aula Orientalis* 17–18: 229–239.

Oller, G. H. 1977. *The Autobiography of Idrimi: A New Text Edition with Philological and Historical Commentary*. Unpublished Ph.D. Dissertation, University of Pennsylvania.

Oller, G. H. 1989. The Inscription of Idrimi: A Pseudo-Autobiography? Pp. 411–417 in *DUMU-E$_2$-DUB-BA-A: Studies in Honor of Ake W. Sjöberg*, eds. H. Behrens, D. Loding and M. T. Roth. Philadelphia: Occasional Publications of the Samuel Noah Kramer Fund.

Oppenheim, A. L. 1955. Review of *The Statue of Idri-mi*, by Sidney Smith. *Journal of Near Eastern Studies* 14: 199–200.

Oren, E. D. 1992. Palaces and Patrician Houses in the Middle and Late Bronze Ages. Pp. 105–120 in *The Architecture of Ancient Israel: From the Prehistoric to the Persian Periods: in Memory of Immanuel (Munya) Dunayevsky*. eds. A. Kempinski and R. Reich. Jerusalem: Israel Exploration Society.

Orthmann, W. 1964. Hethitische Götterbilder. Pp. 221–229 in *Vorderasiatische Archäologie: Studien und Aufsätze Anton Moortgat zum fünfundsechzigsten Geburstag gewidmet von Kollegen, Freunden und Schülern*, eds. K. Bittel, E. Heinrich, B. Hrouda and W. Nagel. Berlin: Gebr. Mann.

Otten, H. 1963. Neue Quellen zum Ausklang des Hethitischen Reiches. *Mitteilungen der Deutschen Orient-Gesellschaft zu Berlin* 94: 1–23.

Ottosson, M. 1980. *Temples and Cult Places in Palestine*. Uppsala: Acta Universitatis Upsaliensis.

Pamir, H. and Brands, G. 2005. The Asi Delta and the Asi Valley Archaeological Project in 2004 Samandağ and Antakya Surveys. *Anmed* 3: 103–108.

Pardee, D. 1984. PRU II 12 = RS 16.402 = KTU 2.33. *Archiv für Orientforschungen* 31: 215–219.

Pardee, D. 2002. Message of ʾIririṯaruma to the Queen (RS 16.402) (3.45X). Pp. 105–106 in *Context of Scripture*, vol. 3, ed. W. W. Hallo. Leiden: Brill.

Parker, V. 2002. Zur Chronologie des Šuppiluliumaš I. *Altorientalische Forschungen* 29(1): 31–62.

Pfälzner, P. 1995. *Mittanische und Mittelassyrische Keramik: Ein Chronologische, Funktionale und Produktionsökonomische Analyse*. Berlin: Reimer.

Pfälzner, P. 2007. The Late Bronze Age Ceramic Traditions of the Syrian Jazirah. Pp. 231–291 in *Céramique de l'âge du Bronze en Syrie*, Volume 2, eds. M. al-Maqdissi, V. Matoïan and Ch. Nicolle. Beyrouth: Institut Français d'Archéologie du Proche-Orient.

Pfälzner, P. 2008. Nuzi Ware Vessels. P. 199 in *Beyond Babylon: Art, Trade, and Diplomacy in the Second Millennium B.C.*, eds. J. Aruz, K. Benzel and J. M. Evans. New Haven: Yale University Press.

Popko, M. 1998. Zum Wettergot von Ḫalab. *Altorientalische Forschungen* 25: 119–125.

Postgate, C., Oates, D., and J. Oates. 1997. *The Excavations at Tell al-Rimah: The Pottery*. Wiltshire: British School of Archaeology in Iraq.

Pruss, A. 1996. *Die Amuq-Terrakotten: Untersuchungen zu den Terrakotten-Figuren des 2. und 1. Jahrtausends v. Chr. aus den Grabungen des Oriental Institute Chicago in der Amuq-Ebene*. Unpublished Ph.D. Dissertation, Martin-Luther University. Halle-Wittemberg.

Pruss, A. 2002. Ein Licht in der Nacht? Die Amuq-Ebene während der *Dark Ages*. Pp. 161–176 in *Die nahöstlichen Kulturen und Griechenland an der Wende vom 2. zum 1. Jahrtausend v. Chr.: Kontinuität und Wandel von Strukturen und Mechanismen kultureller Interaktion (Kolloquium der Sonderforschungsbereiches 295 "Kulturelle und sprachliche Kontakte" der Johannes Gutenberg-Universität Mainz, 11.–12. Dezember 1998)*, eds. E. A. Braun-Holzinger and H. Matthäus. Möhnesee: Bibliopolis.

Pruzsinszky, R. 2005. Ein Bibliographischer Wegweiser zur Absoluten Mesopotamischen Chronologie des 2. Jts. V. Chr. *Ägypten und Levante* 15: 181–201.

Pucci, M. forthcoming. The Chatal Höyük Publication Project: A Work in Progress. *Proceedings of 6th International Congress on the Archaeology of the Ancient Near East, Rome, 5th – 10th May 2008.*

Rowton, M. B. 1958. The Date of Hammurabi. *Journal of Near Eastern Studies* 17: 97–111.

Rowton, M. B. 1970. Ancient Western Asia. Pp. 193–239 in *The Cambridge Ancient History³*, eds. I. E. S. Edwards, C. J. Gadd and N. G. L. Hammond. Cambridge: Cambridge University Press.

Salvini, M. and Trémouille, M. –C. 2003. Les texts hittites de Meskéné/Emar. *Studi Micenei ed Egeo-Anatolici* 45(2): 225–271.

Sasson, J. M. 1981. On Idrimi and Šarruwa, the Scribe. Pp. 309–324 in *Studies on the Civilization and Culture of Nuzi and the Hurrians, in Honor of Ernest R. Lacheman on His Seventy Fifth Birthday*, eds. M. A. Morrison and D. I. Owen. Winona Lake: Eisenbrauns.

Serangeli, F. 1978. Le liste di censo di Alalaḫ IV. *Vicino Oriente* 1: 99–131.

Simon, Z. 2009. Kann Armā mit Haremhab gleichgesetzt werden? *Altorientalische Forschungen* 36: 340–348.

Singer, I. 1994. "The Thousand Gods of Hatti"; The Limits of an Expanding Pantheon. *Israel Oriental Studies* 14: 81–102.

Singer, I. 1997. Review of *Der Ulmitesub-Vertag/eine prosopographische Untersuchung*, by van den Hout, T. *Bibliotheca Orientalis* 54(3/4): 416–423.

Singer, I. 1999. A Political History of Ugarit. Pp. 603–733 in *Handbook of Ugaritic Studies*, eds. W. G. E. Watson and N. Wyatt. Leiden: Brill.

Singer, I. 2000. A New Hittite Letter from Emar. Pp. 65–72 in *Landscapes, Territories, Frontiers and Horizons in the Ancient Near East: Papers Presented to the XLIV Rencontre Assyriologique Internationale Venezia, 7–11 July 1997, Part II*, eds. L. Milano, S. de Martino, F. M. Fales and G. B. Lanfranchi. Padova: Sargon srl.

Singer, I. 2001. The Treaties between Karkamiš and Hatti. Pp. 635–641 in *Akten des IV. Internationalen Kongresses für Hethitologie. Würzburg, 4.–8. Oktober 1999*, ed. G. Wilhelm.

Wiesbaden: Harrassowitz.

Singer, I. 2006. Ships Bound for Lukka: A New Interpretation of the Companion Letters RS 94.2530 and RS 94.2523. *Altorientalische Forschungen* 33: 242–262.

Skaist, A. 2005. When Did Ini-Tešub Succeed to the Throne of Carchemish? *Ugarit-Forschungen* 37: 609–619.

Smith, S. 1939. A Preliminary Account of the Tablets from Atchana. *The Antiquaries Journal* 19: 38–48.

Smith, S. 1940. *Alalakh and Chronology*. London: Luzac and Company.

Smith, S. 1949. *The Statue of Idri-mi*. London: The British Institute of Archaeology at Ankara.

Soldi, S. 2006. La ceramica dipinta nalla Siria e Mesopotamia settentrionali tra Bronzo Medio e Bronzo Tardo: considerazioni sull'origine e lo sviluppo della ceramica di Nuzi. *Agoge* 3: 81–97.

Soldi, S. 2008. Recent Considerations about the Origin of "Nuzi Ware" in the Light of its Archaeological Contexts. Pp. 245–258 in *Proceedings of the 4th International Congress of the Archaeology of the Near East (29 March–3 April 2004, Freie Universität Berlin)*, vol. 2, ed. H. Kühne, R. M. Czichon and F. J. Kreppner. Wiesbaden: Harrassowitz.

Speiser, E. A. 1951. Review of *The Statue of Idri-Mi,* by Sidney Smith. *Journal of the American Oriental Society* 71(2): 151–152.

Stavi, B. 2006. *Studies on the History of Arzawa and Mira in the 15th and 14th Centuries B.C.E.* Unpublished M.A. Thesis, Tel Aviv University. Tel Aviv.

Stein, D. L. 1984. Khabur Ware and Nuzi Ware: Their Origin, Relationship, and Significance. *Assur* 4/1: 1–64.

Stein, D. L. 1989. A Reappraisal of the "Sauštatar Letter" from Nuzi. *Zeitschrift für Assyriologie* 79: 36–60.

Stein, D. L. 1997. Alalakh. Pp. 55–59 in *The Oxford Encyclopedia of Archaeology in the Ancient Near East*. Vol. 1, ed. E. M. Meyers. New York and Oxford: Oxford University Press.

Swift, G. F. 1958. The Pottery of the ʿAmuq Phases K to O, and its Historical Relationships. Unpublished Ph.D. Dissertation, University of Chicago. Chicago.

Tadmor, H. 1970. The Chronology of the Ancient Near East in the Second Millennium B.C.E. Pp. 63–101 in *The World History of the Jewish People: Patriarchs*, Volume 2, ed. B. Mazar. Tel-Aviv: Massada.

Taracha, P. 2008. The End of Šuppiluliuma's Reign and the Solar Omen of Muršili II. *N.A.B.U* 2008(1) (Mars): 22–23.

Ussishkin, D. 1970. The Syro-Hittite Ritual Burial of Monuments. *Journal of Near Eastern Studies* 29: 124–128.

Ussishkin, D. 1998. The Destruction of Megiddo at the End of the Late Bronze Age and its Historical Significance. Pp. 197–219 in *Mediterranean Peoples in Transition: Thirteenth to Early Tenth Centuries BCE*, eds. S. Gitin, A. Mazar and E. Stern. Jerusalem: Israel Exploration Society.

van Soldt, W. 2000. Syrian Chronology in the Old and Early Middle Babylonian Periods. *Akkadica* 119–120: 103–116.

Van Soldt, W. H. 2005. *The Topography of the City-State of Ugarit*. Münster: Ugarit-verlag.

van Wijngaarden, G. J. 2002. *Use and Appreciation of Mycenaean Pottery in the Levant, Cyprus and Italy (1600–1200 BC)*. Amsterdam: Amsterdam University.

Venturi, F. 2007. *La Siria nell'eta della transformazioni (XIII – X sec. a.C.): Nuovi contribute dallo scavo di Tell Afis*. Bologna: Clueb.

Verstraete, J. and T. J. Wilkinson 2000. The Amuq Regional Archaeological Survey. Pp. 179–192 in K. A. Yener et al. The Amuq Valley Regional Project, 1995–1998. *American Journal of Archaeology* 104: 163–220.

von Dassow, E. 1997. *Social Stratification of Alalah under the Mittani Empire*. Unpublished Ph.D. Dissertation, New York University. New York.

von Dassow, E. 2002. Lists of People from Alalaḫ IV Administrative Archives. *Ugarit-Forschungen* 34: 835–911.

von Dassow, E. 2005. Archives of Alalaḫ IV in Archaeological context. *Bulletin of the American*

School of Oriental Research 308: 1–69.

von Dassow, E. 2008. *State and Society in the Late Bronze Age: Alalaḫ under the Mittani Empire.* Bethesda: CDL.

Warren, P. 1969. *Minoan Stone Vases.* Cambridge: Cambridge University Press.

Watkins, C. 1994. *Selected Writings*, vol. 2. Innsbruck: Innsbrucker Beiträge zur Sprachwissenschaft.

Wilhelm, G. 1976. Parrattarna, Sauštatar und die Absolute Datierung der Nuzi-Tafeln. *Acta Antiqua Academiae Scientiarum Hungaricae*: 24: 149–161.

Wilhelm, G. 2004. Generation Count in Hittite Chronology. Pp. 71–79 in *Mesopotamian Dark Age Revisited: Proceedings of an International Conference of SCIEM 2000 (Vienna 8th–9th November 2002)*, eds. H. Hunger and R. Pruzsinszky. Wien: Der Österreichischen Akademie der Wissenschaften.

Wilhelm, G. 2006, Die hurritischsprachige Tafel Kp 05/226. *Mitteilungen der Deutschen Orient-Gesellschaft zu Berlin* 138: 233–236.

Wilhelm, G. and Boese, J. 1987. Absolute Chronologie und die hethitische Geschichte des 15. und 14. Jahrhunderts V. Chr. Pp. 74–117 in *High, Middle or Low? Acts of an International Colloquium on Absolute Chronology Held at the University of Gothenburg 20th –22nd August 1987*, Part 1, ed. P. Åström. Gothenburg: Åström.

Wilkinson, T. J. 2000. Geoarchaeology of the Amuq Plain. Pp. 168–179 in K. A. Yener et al. The Amuq Valley Regional Project, 1995–1998. *American Journal of Archaeology* 104: 163–220.

Williams, B. 1975. *Archaeological and Historical Problems of the Second Intermediate Period.* Unpublished Ph.D. Dissertation, University of Chicago. Chicago.

Williams, B. and R. Hassert. 1977–1978. Some Aspects of the Excavation at Tell Atchana, Part I: a Critical Review of Pottery from Levels XVII–VII. *Serapis* 4: 41–56.

Winstone, H. V. F. 1990. *Woolley of Ur: The Life of Sir Leonard Woolley.* London: Secker and Warburg.

Wiseman, D. J. 1953. The Alalakh Tablets. London: British Institute of Archaeology at Ankara.

Wiseman, D. J. 1959. Ration Lists from Alalakh IV. *Journal of Cuneiform Studies* 13: 50–62.

Woolley, L. 1921. *From Kastamuni to Kedos: Being a Record of Experiences of Prisoners of War in Turkey, 1916–1918.* Oxford: Clarendon.

Woolley, L. 1936. Tal Atchana. *The Journal of Hellenic Studies* 56: 125–132.

Woolley, L. 1937. Excavations near Antioch in 1936. *The Antiquaries Journal* 17(1): 1–15.

Woolley, L. 1938. Excavations at Tal Atchana, 1937. *The Antiquaries Journal* 18(1): 1–28.

Woolley, L. 1939a (21 May). *Sir Leonard Woolley's Excavations at Atchana: Extracts from Letters.* London: University College, Special Collections.

Woolley, L. 1939b (3 August). Alalakh: The City and Its Sculpture. *The Times.* London: 13–14, 16.

Woolley, L. 1939c (9 December). A New Chapter of Hittite Sculpture Opens. *The Illustrated London News.* London: 867–869.

Woolley, L. 1939d. Excavations at Atchana-Alalakh, 1938. *The Antiquaries Journal* 19(1): 1–33.

Woolley, L. 1947. Atchana 1946. *Man* 47: 60–61.

Woolley, L. 1948. Excavations at Atchana-Alalakh, 1939. *The Antiquaries Journal* 28: 1–19.

Woolley, L. 1949. Introduction. Pp. 1–9 in *The Statue of Idri-Mi*, ed. S. Smith. London: Institute of Archaeology at Ankara.

Woolley, L. 1950. Excavations at Atchana-Alalakh, 1946. *The Antiquaries Journal* 30(1): 1–21.

Woolley, L. 1953. *A Forgotten Kingdom.* Baltimore: Penguin.

Woolley, L. 1955. *Alalakh: An Account of the Excavations at Tell Atchana in the Hatay, 1937–1949.* Oxford: The Society of Antiquaries.

Wotzka, H. –P. 1990. The Abuse of User: A Note of the Egyptian Statuette from Knossos. *The Annual of the British School at Athens* 85: 449–453.

Wright, G. R. H. 1971. Pre-Israelite Temples in the Land of Canaan. *Palestine Exploration Quarterly* 103: 17–32.

Yadin, Y. 1972. *Hazor: With a Chapter on Israelite Megiddo.* London, New York: Oxford University Press for the British Academy.

Yamada, M. 1992. Reconsidering the Letters from the "King" in the Ugarit Texts: Royal Correspondance of Carchemis? *Ugarit-Forschungen* 24: 431–446.

Yamada, M. 1998. The Family of Zū-Ba^cla the Diviner and the Hittites. *Israel Oriental Studies* 18: 323–334.

Yazıcıoğlu, G. B. 2004. *Political Changes and Sociocultural Continuity in the Late Bronze Age Kingdom of Mukish Based on an Activity Pattern Analysis of the Level IV Citadel at Tell Atchana (Alalakh)*. Unpublished M.A. Thesis, University of Chicago. Chicago.

Yener, K. A. 2005. Alalakh Spatial Organization: Augmenting the Architectural Layout of Levels VII–0. Pp. 99–144 in *The Amuq Valley Regional Project*. Vol. 1. *Surveys in the Plain of Antioch and Orontes Delta, Turkey, 1995–2002*, ed. K. A. Yener. Chicago: Oriental Institute Publications.

Yener, K. A., Edens, Ch., Harrison, T. P., Verstraete, J. and T. J. Wilkinson. 2000. The Amuq Valley Regional Project, 1995–1998. *American Journal of Archaeology* 101: 163–220.

Yener, K. A., Schloen, J. D. and A. S. Fink. 2004a. Reliving the Legend: the Expedition to Alalakh, 2003. *The Oriental Institute News & Notes* 181: 1–6.

Yener, K. A., Schloen, J. D., and Fink, A. S. 2004b. Amuq Valley Regional Projects. Pp. 25–34 in *The Oriental Institute 2003–2004 Annual Report*. Chicago: The Oriental Institute.

Yener, K. A., Schloen, J. D., and Fink, A. S. 2005. Expedition to Alalakh (Tell Atchana). Pp. 46–50 in *The Oriental Institute 2004–2005 Annual Report*. Chicago: The Oriental Institute.

Zeeb, F., 1992. "Die Truppen sind unfähif." *Ugarit-Forschungen* 24: 481–498.

Zeeb, F., 2004. The History of Alalaḫ as a Testcase for an Ultrashort Chronology of the Mid-2nd Millennium B.C.E. Pp. 81–95 in *Mesopotamian Dark Age Revisited: Proceedings of an International Conference of SCIEM 2000 (Vienna 8th–9th November 2002)*, eds. H. Hunger and R. Pruzsinszky. Wien: Der Österreichischen Akademie der Wissenschaften.

Zimansky, P. 1995. The Origin of Nuzi Ware: A Contribution From Tell Hamida. Pp. 75–83 in *Studies in the Culture and Civilization of Nuzi and the Hurrians*, vol. 5, ed. D.I. Owen. Winona Lake, IN: Eisenbrauns.